A Taste *of* Scotland 2001

**THE GUIDE TO THE BEST PLACES TO EAT
AND STAY IN SCOTLAND**

Tower Restaurant

welcome
to the guide

THERE HAS NEVER BEEN a more exciting time to be working in the Scottish hospitality industry. There is a clear understanding by the Scottish Executive and the Public Agencies of the importance of quality food in Scotland and the role that this plays in tourism, and this recognition is vital in taking the industry forward and encouraging excellence.

Taste of Scotland has always been committed to a quality experience and it is heartening to see that our Taste of Scotland establishments are growing in number and in quality each year.

For you, our reader, we are delighted that we have been able to bring to you a significant number of places, which are new to our Guide. We also see the return of many familiar places that have consistently, over the years, upheld their commitment to a quality Scottish dining experience.

Please tell us about your experiences, there is a form at the rear of the Guide, or e-mail us with your experiences. Most importantly, enjoy eating well in Scotland.

Amanda J Clark
Chief Executive

Credits

Editorial
Amanda Clark, Angela Nealon, Tracey Brown, Wendy Barrie

Published by
Taste of Scotland Limited
A non-profit making company limited by guarantee trading as Taste of Scotland

Design, Illustration and Typesetting
David Frame Creative, Edinburgh
Jim Middleton (Editorial), David Healy (Senior Designer), Euan Davidson (Production Manager)

Printed by
Edinburgh Press, East Lothian

Repro
Reproscan (Scotland) Ltd, Glasgow

Corporate Sponsorship, Sales and Marketing
Classic Concepts, Edinburgh
Sue Ireland, Grace Boyle, Theresa Donnelly, Kareen Lee

Trade Board Members
Laurie Black, Chairman Taste of Scotland Board, Fouters Bistro, Ayr
Annie Paul, Taychreggan Hotel
David Wilson, The Peat Inn
Nick Nairn, Nairns

Taste of Scotland is grateful for the continued support of
Scottish Tourist Board
Scottish Tourism Forum
Scotland the Brand

And all our corporate partners
Alexander Wines, Anta, Brodies, ASVA, Baxters of Speyside, Edinburgh Crystal, Historic Scotland, McLelland Cheese, Highlands and Islands Enterprise, The Macallan, National Trust for Scotland, Walkers Shortbread

We would also like to give special thanks to the following
Dorling Kindersley
Graham Lees Photography
Liz and Graham – Cover Photography
Tony Gorzkowski Photography

Contents

Welcome To The Guide 3
Credits..4
The Macallan Awards...6
Partner Profiles...8
Nairn's Cookery School 52
Map of Scotland...54
How To Use This Guide...56
List of Establishments 57
Association of Scottish Visitor Attractions................269
Scottish Tourist Board 270
Tourist Area Profiles 274
    Edinburgh & Lothian 274
    Grampian, Highlands, Aberdeen &
        the North East Coast 278
    Greater Glasgow & the Clyde Valley 282
    Highlands & Skye 286
    Outer Islands 290
    Perthshire, Angus & Dundee and the
        Kingdom of Fife 294
    South of Scotland 298
    West Highlands & Islands, Loch Lomond,
        Stirling & Trossachs 302
A Year in the Life of Taste of Scotland 306
Taste of Scotland Inspectors.......................................310
Feedback 311
Index..313

the macallan awards

The **2000 Winners** of the Macallan Taste of Scotland Awards are:

OVERALL EXCELLENCE AWARD
- Braidwoods, Dalry
  listed on page 99

CITY RESTAURANT AWARD
- Ubiquitous Chip, Glasgow
  listed on page 146

COUNTRY HOUSE AWARD
- Auchterarder House, Auchterarder
  listed on page 68

OUT OF TOWN RESTAURANT AWARD
- Livingston's Restaurant, Linlithgow listed on page 207

CHEF PROPRIETOR, FINE DINING IN A RURAL SETTING AWARD
- Braidwoods, Dalry
  listed on page 99

DEDICATION TO THE USE OF LOCAL SEASONAL PRODUCE AWARD
- Auchendean Lodge Hotel, Dulnain Bridge listed on page 103

SMALL RESIDENCE AWARD
- Cosses Country House, Ballantrae
  listed on page 73

COMMENDED ESTABLISHMENTS SHORTLISTED

CITY RESTAURANT
- Channings Restaurant, Edinburgh
- The Riverhouse Restaurant, Inverness

COUNTRY HOUSE
- Glenmorangie House at Cadboll, Fearn, by Tain
- Kilcamb Lodge Hotel, Strontian

OUT OF TOWN RESTAURANT
- Howgate Restaurant, Edinburgh Outskirts
- Loch Fyne Oyster Bar, Cairndow

CHEF PROPRIETOR, FINE DINING IN A RURAL SETTING
- The Cross, Kingussie
- Monachyle Mhor, Balquhidder

DEDICATION TO THE USE OF LOCAL SEASONAL PRODUCE
- Craigadam, Castle Douglas
- Handa, Isle of Lewis

SMALL RESIDENCE
- Lynwilg House, Aviemore
- Talisker House, Isle of Skye

NOW IN THEIR 13TH YEAR, these Awards were set up to encourage the pursuit of excellence and, by so doing, encourage others to emulate the winners. This ethos remains unchanged – with public nominations being the starting point, inspectors' nominations follow and then each shortlisted establishment is further judged by an expert panel. All the establishments listed here have consistently demonstrated their commitment to excellence.

The Macallan Single Malt is renowned for its unique character and unrivalled quality and as such makes a perfect partner for these Awards. This partnership certainly captures the imagination of the public as every year a record number of nominations are received.

The Awards are restricted to establishments which are listed in the previous Taste of Scotland Guide and thus are already highlighted as leaders in their specific category.

This year, once again, the judging for the Awards was an exceptionally difficult task with nominations coming in from all areas and for all types of establishments. It is particularly heartening that the standards encountered across Scotland are continually rising, resulting in a growing number of eligible contenders.

We again invite Taste of Scotland customers to nominate establishments in which you have received outstanding experiences this year. In addition, Taste of Scotland Inspectors are being asked to nominate their favourite places throughout the inspection season. Please use the feedback forms towards the back of this Guide to forward your nominations for The Macallan Taste of Scotland Awards 2001. Nomination cards are also available at some Taste of Scotland establishments. Letters and postcards are also welcome and taken into consideration.

Simply nominate an establishment which has impressed you greatly, tell us why and leave the rest to us. Closing date for entries – 30 June 2001.

The 2000 Winners are highlighted in the listings with this symbol:

ALEXANDER WINES is an independent, Glasgow-based fine wine merchant supplying wines from around the world to many of Scotland's best hotels and restaurants, including members of Taste of Scotland.

The company was founded in 1981 by the proprietor, Fraser Alexander. Just 23 at the time, and armed with a degree in Technology and Business Studies, Fraser had developed a passion for wine during a stint as a student in the vineyards of Baden, Germany. While his friends wrote their dissertations on more conventional subjects, Fraser submitted a paper comparing winemaking methods in Baden with those of the neighbouring French region of Alsace …

After graduating, Fraser spent a few months "sweeping tennis courts and wondering what to do", before landing his first job in the wine trade as regional representative for a wine company specialising in door-to-door sales. The wines were basic, to say the least, and the company's selling tactics were light years away from the 'softly softly' approach favoured by Alexander Wines today. Still, it was a start; and although Fraser soon left to start his own business, he took with him some very useful experiences, together with a firm belief in the future of wine-drinking in Scotland.

To begin with, the new company operated as a one man band out of a back room in the family home. There was no office and no staff. Undaunted, Fraser set off for the Loire Valley in a ramshackle old transit van, determined to seek out the best suppliers he could find. He struck gold with Domaine Henri Poiron, one of France's best producers of Muscadet and still, 20 years on, a key supplier for Alexander Wines. Other producers in the Loire Valley soon followed suit, and the region quickly became Fraser's speciality. He remembers those early days with nostalgic fondness, recalling the nights spent sleeping among the boxes in the back of the transit van "to save the cost of a hotel". Mechanical difficulties and a faltering command of French were another hazard of these improvised buying trips, but Fraser's evident enthusiasm for the region's wines was enough to win over even the most sceptical vigneron.

During the 1980s, business in Glasgow grew steadily as restaurants boomed and wine-drinking became more popular – and more democratic. Alexander Wines moved into "real" premises and rented space in a bonded warehouse. Staff were employed to man the office and deliver wine to restaurants and hotels across the city, and down into Ayrshire. In the early 1990s, the company moved again, this time to Hillington, where the proximity of the M8 motorway and extended warehousing facilities were guaranteed to make life easier for a rapidly expanding business.

The 1990s witnessed a huge increase in demand for wine which saw Alexander Wines promoted to the forefront of the on-trade in Glasgow. By this time, in line with consumer trends, Fraser was sourcing wines from every corner of the globe – South Africa, Australia, California, Spain, Hungary … – as well as from his traditional strongholds in France and Germany. Today, this impressive and varied portfolio includes such famous names as Laurent-Perrier Champagne, Marqués de Riscal Rioja, Château Kirwan, Simonsig Estate and Valdespino Sherry. Wherever possible, the wines are shipped direct from the supplier, thereby guaranteeing better control of stock – and a better price to the final consumer.

Alexander Wines' customer base is equally impressive, featuring a string of well-known restaurants such as 78 St. Vincent, Gamba, Eurasia and more than forty current Taste of Scotland members, including The Buttery and The Balmoral Hotel. Not surprisingly, the company continues to grow rapidly and now employs a team of nine full-time members, handling business in Glasgow, Edinburgh, Ayrshire and, increasingly, the east and north of Scotland.

Throughout its two decades of existence, Alexander Wines has remained firmly committed to its role as a supplier to restaurants, wine bars and hotels, believing that to diversify into the retail sector would detract from the standard of service provided to its on-trade customers. Similarly, the company has avoided any involvement in beers and spirits, preferring to focus its efforts on sourcing quality wines that offer consistent value for money.

With such a long history of involvement in the restaurant sector, it was perhaps inevitable that Alexander Wines should eventually become sponsors of Taste of Scotland.

The company's message to its customers has long been that food and wine go hand in hand: they are meant to be enjoyed together. It is a simple message, but one that is sometimes forgotten. The ongoing partnership between Alexander Wines and Taste of Scotland will, hopefully, go a long way towards reinforcing that message to members of the scheme and their customers.

Alexander Wines, Glasgow
Tel 0141 882 0039 Fax 0141 880 0041

anta design and make textiles and ceramics

anta is scottish and contemporary

TARTAN IS MORE OR LESS always fashionable. I understand, after a recent visit from Japanese Vogue, that tartan is to be "big" this Autumn. For fifteen years, since I have been in the business of designing, making and selling things tartan, its presence on the catwalks has not necessarily influenced cash-flow. I imagine the Queen Mother has owned a tartan skirt almost her entire life. She has certainly walked on tartan and sat upon it at Balmoral Castle where it has been since Queen Victoria's day. It is safe to say that beyond living memory tartan has always been fashionable.

No-one can claim to have invented tartan but at anta we have helped influence its continuing popularity. In the mid eighties, when tartan was almost exclusively the preserve of the pipe band, only worn outside the military by a handful of Highland families, it most frequently cropped up adorning shortbread tins. There remained in a few historic Highland houses, tartan furnishings in various states of decay. The degree to which they had faded indicated the date of their replacement over the last two centuries. The earlier and more faded were often the more beautiful. Very heavy tweed used as carpeting, finer worsted wool as upholstery and bed drapes. The combination of vegetable dyes and some chemical dyes used to weave the same piece of cloth caused the colours to fade at different rates. Red, which had to be a chemical derivative, remains stable, whereas blue, invariably made from indigo, fades quickly to a wonderful pale shade of violet. It was the unusual combination of vivid and subtle colours of these ancient furnishings that inspired the anta collections. The Highland Collection of upholstery and curtain fabrics and the Castle Carpet

Collection have no black, gaudy reds or yellows, but instead include pinks, mauves and violets not found in today's commercially produced tartans.

In my wanderings through Scottish country houses, galleries and museums in search of early tartan textiles, I noticed that tartan patterns had never been reproduced on ceramics. This was surprising – you would imagine the notion of eating from a tartan plate would have appealed to the Victorians.

There were carefully painted tartan plaids on Staffordshire figures of Highlanders, and Mauchlineware, the tiny tartan papier mâché trinkets made principally for the Victorian tourist, but no plates, cups, saucers or porridge bowls. Conscious of this, I developed a technique to reproduce clear colours in consistent bands over white glazed stoneware. Almost by accident I had invented the original tartan tableware. I soon realised that the shapes themselves had to be considered, too, as a tartan pattern, decorated in the round, was not as straightforward as I originally anticipated. The shape of the pot must be simple or the decoration could not easily be applied and the resulting pattern would compete with the form. (There are some messy first attempts in the anta archive of original designs!) I recruited architect Lachlan Stewart, my partner and husband. He designed the original range of shapes which were to become the basis of the Balloneware Collection of tartan stoneware. It is these same simple basic shapes we use for the new range of complementary plain coloured glazes. Serving plates, dinner plates and bowls can be put together in combinations of tartan and co-ordinating plain colours to achieve a uniquely-styled set to suit the contemporary Scottish dinner table. Stoneware, fired to a high temperature, can be safely used in dishwasher, microwave and conventional oven. The collection is named after Ballone, a 16th century castle on the shores of the Cromarty Firth which we bought as a ruin in 1990.

Now that it has been restored we live there with our three children, Lachie (13), Archie (9) and Stella (6). In the same year we set up the anta workshops at Fearn, north of Inverness where we now produce Balloneware, and it is here from the factory shop we sell it, the Highland collection of furnishing fabrics and the Castle Carpet Collection. anta also have a shop at 32 the High Street, the Royal Mile in Edinburgh and a website www.anta.co.uk

This autumn the anta carpet bag is back. It is part of a new collection of luggage which includes a holdall or overnight case, a large shopping bag and a hand bag available in a range of colours including tweeds and, of course, tartans. How fortunate that tartan is fashionable – again?

Annie Stewart, Design Director, anta

anta Scotland Limited
Head Office: Fearn, Tain
Ross-shire IV20 1XW
Tel 01862 832477
Fax 01862 832616
Email sales@anta.co.uk
www.anta.co.uk
Showroom: 32 High Street,
The Royal Mile, Edinburgh
Tel 0131 557 8300

baxters
of speyside

AFTER MORE THAN 130 YEARS, Baxters of Speyside take great pride in tradition, but don't be fooled into thinking they are old-fashioned. A company does not become a market leader – nor have the confidence to rebuff more than 180 take-over approaches along the way – by standing still.

Confidence in the Baxters brand is a crucial factor for shoppers in more than 30 countries. Whether they buy soups, preserves, chutneys or sauces, they know they'll take home a quality product. They know to expect the flavours and textures that other prepared foods simply can't match. This involves some fairly discerning shoppers – Royal Warrants from HM Elizabeth II, HM The Queen Mother and Gustav VI, King of Sweden, are not issued lightly.

Other than the precise details of the famous recipes themselves, there is no great secret about Baxters' success. The Chairman, Audrey Baxter, puts it simply: "We are passionate, at Baxters, about good food which means finding the finest ingredients and creating innovative recipes which are right for to-days highly discerning consumers throughout the world."

The business is run by the fourth generation of the same family in the same beautiful corner of north-east Scotland. Their insistence on only the finest ingredients and the avoidance of artificial additives, ensures consistently high quality, full of natural flavour. Many among the 800-strong workforce, recruited from the local community, have also been involved with Baxters for several generations.

The story begins in 1868 – construction of the Suez Canal was

nearing completion and Disraeli and Gladstone were fighting it out to be British Prime Minister. But George Baxter, a gardener on a local estate, had other things on his mind. He had just borrowed £100 from an uncle and other relatives to open a grocery store in Fochabers on the banks of the Spey.

Swelling the shop's merchandise were jams George's wife made from the fruits which grow in abundance in the local countryside. Margaret Baxter was beginning a distinguished tradition of invention, flair and innovation among the Baxter women, many of whose recipes have gone on to achieve world fame.

A generation later, son William Baxter travelled all over Scotland by train and bicycle, passionately advocating the quality of the mouth-watering recipes prepared by his wife Ethel who, in 1929, was responsible for their phenomenally successful Royal Game Soup. It was soon gracing the shelves of Harrod's and Fortnum & Mason.

Round about the same time, the

humble beetroot entered the story. William and Ethel spotted an opening in the market and quickly realised they had a winner. Baxters' beetroot continues to dominate the UK market.

Another generation on and grandson Gordon set out to conquer the great markets of America – and succeeded, helped in no small part by his wife Ena's now legendary recipe for Cock-a-leekie Soup. (That's chicken and leek with some extra special flavours which the highly creative Ena brought to the soup pot!)

Between 40 and 50 new recipes are introduced each year, but only once they have proved themselves worthy of inclusion in this extraordinary portfolio of products.

The first factory opened in 1914 beside the River Spey and production facilities have been expanding ever since. As sophisticated as these have become, the Baxter family has never lost sight of the natural, honest-to-goodness qualities that made their products so popular in the first place.

As well as being one of the great commercial successes of north-east Scotland, Baxters has its very own Highland Village which has become one of Scotland's major tourist attractions, drawing more than 200,000 visitors each year.

The centrepiece is a 19th century grocery store, complete with leather-bound ledgers and quill pens, a long mahogany counter, glass jars and bottles, and all the other shopkeeper's accoutrements of a bygone age. But it's much more than a quaint reconstruction of things past – this is the actual frontage, and much of the actual contents, of the shop in which George Baxter started the whole business.

There is, of course, a great deal more to Baxters Highland Village. Informal cookery demonstrations are held regularly and there are two restaurants serving the very best of Scottish produce. The Best of Scotland is very much at the forefront in the "village shops", too.

You can visit Baxters any time on their extensive website at www.baxters.co.uk. Because production requirements no longer permit factory tours, the website can provide you with its own virtual tour.

And it's real enough to enable you to order one of Baxters' sumptuous hampers over the Internet, as well as by conventional mail.

Baxters of Speyside
Fochabers, Moray
Tel 01343 820393 Fax 01343 821696

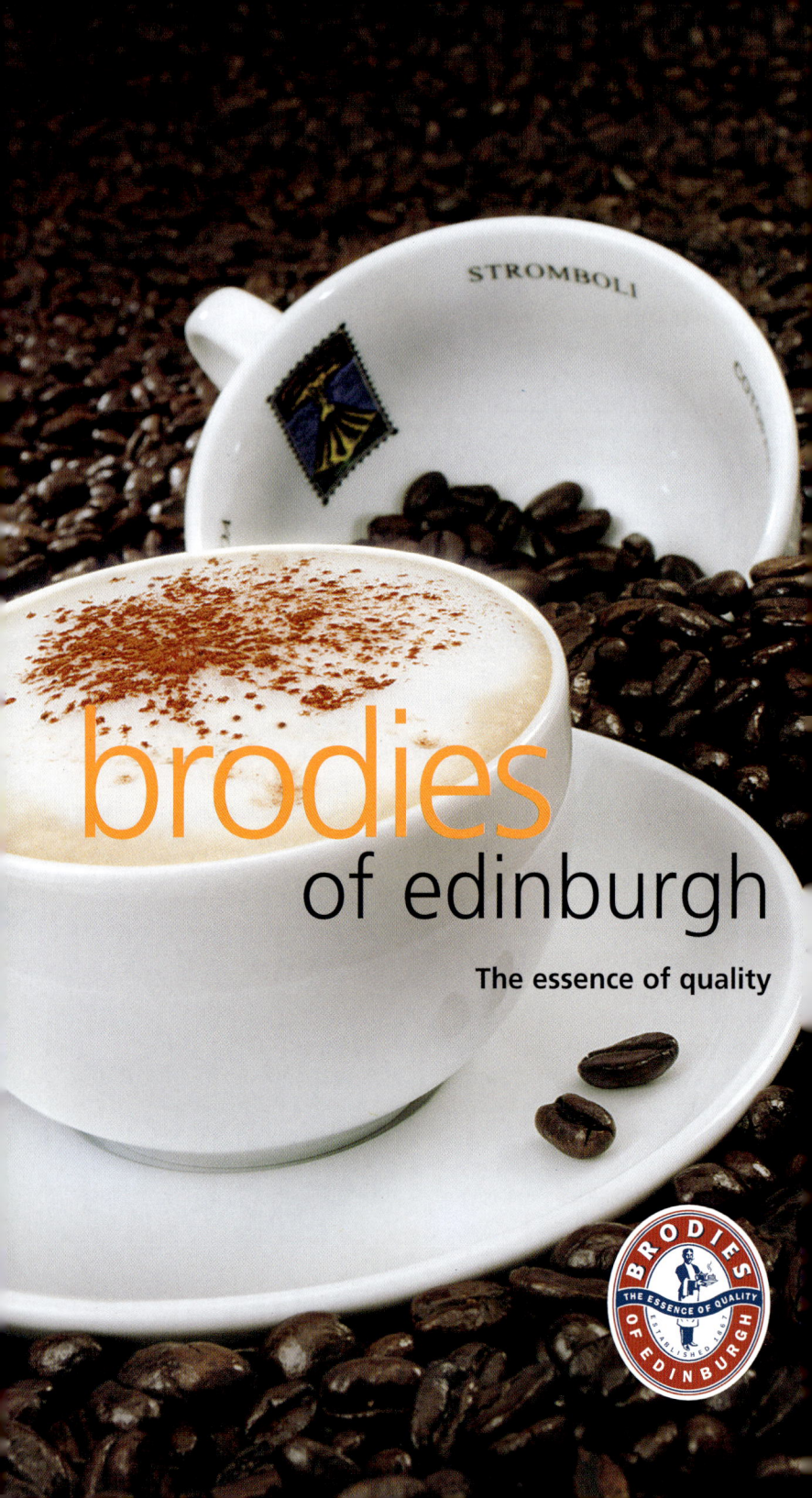

BRODIES... MASTERS OF COFFEE making since 1867 carry a comprehensive Catering Collection of Coffees, Teas, Chocolates, Fruit Cakes; Brewing Equipment (including cappuccino machines); Accessories (including Crockery, Personalised Menus, POS Material, Cafetieres); DaVinci Syrups, Herbal Teas, Sugars, Speciality Hot Drinks Mugs; Bedroom Packs, Biscuits, Disposables and more... as well as a Retail Range of Coffees, Teas, Chocolates, 4" Fruit Cakes and Luxury Gift Sets.

BRODIES QUALITY COFFEES

Since 1867 Brodies have sought out the best coffees from around the world, bringing them to Edinburgh to be expertly blended and roasted in a tradition that has hardly changed since the days of our founders. Specialising in Arabica coffees... only the best! We offer a full range of 20 coffees... from the mellow medium roast of High Mountain... to the rich and full roast of Old Mature Java or experience... Dynamic Volcanics™... our newest range of four highly roasted coffees packed with strength and character. Our coffees are available in beans or ground form in a variety of packs to suit individual needs.

Brodies continue to be at the forefront of the ever-changing face of coffee drinking in the UK. Along with our coffees we offer a full range of brewing equipment – specialising in espresso/cappuccino machines and their necessary accessories... from cups and chocolate shakers... to frothing jugs and thermometers... all so vital in today's coffee culture. We offer machines free on loan, to rent or purchase suiting any location, cup demand and budget, as well as a support and maintenance service to ensure you serve the perfect cup every time.

BRODIES FINEST TEAS

For over 125 years we have catered for the great British taste for tea, selecting the finest leaves to create a specialist range of loose leaf and tea bags (standard and tagged) all bearing the Brodies stamp of quality. Quality that not only matches our own very high standards, but also fulfils the stringent demands that give our tea blends full Tea Council Approval. Our choice of 16 teas is renowned for their flavour and fullness. Three of our most popular blends Scottish Breakfast,

Scottish Teatime and Famous Edinburgh are fine examples of TEA but we also produce more unusual blends including Gunpowder and Lapsang Souchang.

RICH FRUIT CAKES

Our range of speciality 4" retail or 9" catering fruit cakes are influenced from traditional Scottish recipes that have been adapted with Brodies flair for individuality. Made in small batches to specially created recipes all our cakes have a rich fruit base with additional flavours added.

For example our Highland Skeachan has added ginger molasses and ale, while our Exotic Fruit incorporates additional pineapple, fresh coconut, banana and mango laced with Jamaican Rum. Not forgetting our Scottish roots… we also offer three Whisky Fruit Cakes steeped with finest single malts.

CHOCOLATES

Every one of our luxury chocolates is handmade and individually checked by our small, dedicated team. We use only the finest top quality chocolate and natural ingredients producing unique chocolates with plenty of character. We have received recognition for their Innovation, Taste and Quality and are constantly developing new delicious centres.

We have 56 chocolate centres from… Traditional Scottish Desserts like Crannachan… a layered centre of succulent raspberry pieces blended in a white chocolate cream, topped off with vanilla mousse (mixed with toasted oats and scotch malt whisky) and finally encased in a dark bitter chocolate shell… to Brodies Gingers… crystallized ginger pieces and fine ground ginger, blended in a creamy white chocolate centre and covered in a rich dark chocolate topped with a

ginger piece. Our chocolates are available as part of our retail collection or loose as a range of banqueting chocolates. Please ask us for our Chocolate Menu.

WHY CHOOSE BRODIES?

TAILOR MADE

We take great pride in our resulting tailor-made range of quality gourmet foods, each with its own very particular character – a character you will grow to appreciate – with a consistency of quality you will find you can trust.

DEDICATED TO PERFECTION & FRESHNESS

Our main concession to modern times is the use of technology to seal in the freshness and flavour you'd expect of our all hand produced foods. Orders are packed and delivered daily throughout the UK. You can be sure you are buying only the best.

SERVICE

Whilst the best things in life are worth waiting for, we have an inkling that you may want them sooner! Our telesales and prompt delivery service mean that you need never be denied your favourite Brodies product.

BRODIES

And finally…because we are committed to taking care of you… we tailor our service – sometimes even our blends – for you. We are always interested to know more about your needs to ensure that our service is just the way you want it. Equally if you want to hear more about Brodies we'd be delighted to hear from you.

Brodies are proud to support Taste of Scotland and hope whether you're a consumer, retailer, barista, proprietor, caterer or hotelier, Brodies have something for you.

Brodie Melrose Drysdale & Co Ltd.
1 Dock Street
Edinburgh
EH6 6EY

For further information
Tel 0131 554 6331
Fax 0131 555 2584
Email sales@brodiemelrose.co.uk

EDINBURGH – a city whose art, architecture and history embody the essence of Scotland – is also home to the UK's No 1 crystal brand – Edinburgh Crystal. Established in 1867, the Edinburgh Crystal Glass Company developed the art of glass making, building on the techniques brought to the city by the Venetians four centuries earlier.

Using the elements of earth, air, fire and water, a dedicated team of craftsmen transform the molten glass into exquisite bowls, decanters and wine glasses finished with delicate hand engraving. At the initial stage, the skilled craftsmen melt the raw materials of sand, potage, litharge and cullet (rejected or broken glass) to a working temperature of 1100ºC. A ball of molten glass is gathered on the end of a hollow iron tube where it is rotated, tilted and swung before life is blown

into the glass. It is then swiftly transferred to the 'lehr' for gradual cooling before the pieces can be cut by the next members of the team, some of whom have been perfecting their art for nearly 30 years.

The dramatic mountains and tranquil lochs of the Scottish Highlands and Islands have been the inspiration for many of Edinburgh Crystal's designs, with the intricate cuts and swirls of the stem and glassware reflecting the Scottish landscape.

For over one hundred years the unique shape of the Thistle has embodied the company's high standards of design and Scottish craftsmanship.

Each individual glass passes through 33 pairs of careful hands prior to its completion. Another classic, the Star of Edinburgh, first introduced in 1948, takes its inspiration from the elegance of Scotland's capital city. Today it remains one of Edinburgh Crystal's most popular designs.

Edinburgh Crystal recognises that these unique skills are something to be shared and, in 1982, opened the Visitor Centre to let the public experience the crafts used to create these remarkable pieces. On the factory tour, visitors can experience the whole production process from the raw materials at the beginning to the finished product. For the adventurous, there is the 'hands on' tour (bookable in advance), which gives visitors the opportunity to try the age-old art of glassblowing for themselves and to cut their own crystal glass under the tutelage of the highly skilled glasscutters. The glass is then engraved with the visitor's name to be taken home as a lasting memento of their visit.

Visitors can stroll around the amazing display of Edinburgh Crystal and buy a gift for a friend or family member. For those seeking a bargain, the Factory Shop offers a chance to acquire some of the world's finest crystal at discounted prices. Happy shoppers and visitors can take a break at the relaxing on-site coffee shop.

Edinburgh Crystal is not only committed to creativity, quality and traditional craftsmanship, but also believes in investing in the latest technology in order to bring their customers the very best of the UK's leading crystal brand. On their recently launched website, www.edinburgh-crystal.com, visitors can browse around the virtual shelves from the comfort of their own home. For golf enthusiasts, top Scottish golfer Catriona Matthew will be adding her voice to a whole range of golfing products and offering tips and advice on how to better your game. In a first for Europe, people shopping online from Edinburgh Crystal will also be able to monitor their order from leaving the warehouse to arriving on their doorstep using the latest online technology.

So, whether shopping online or visiting the factory in person, Edinburgh Crystal's finely crafted products are sure to delight.

Edinburgh Crystal, Eastfield Industrial Estate, Penicuik. Tel 01968 675128

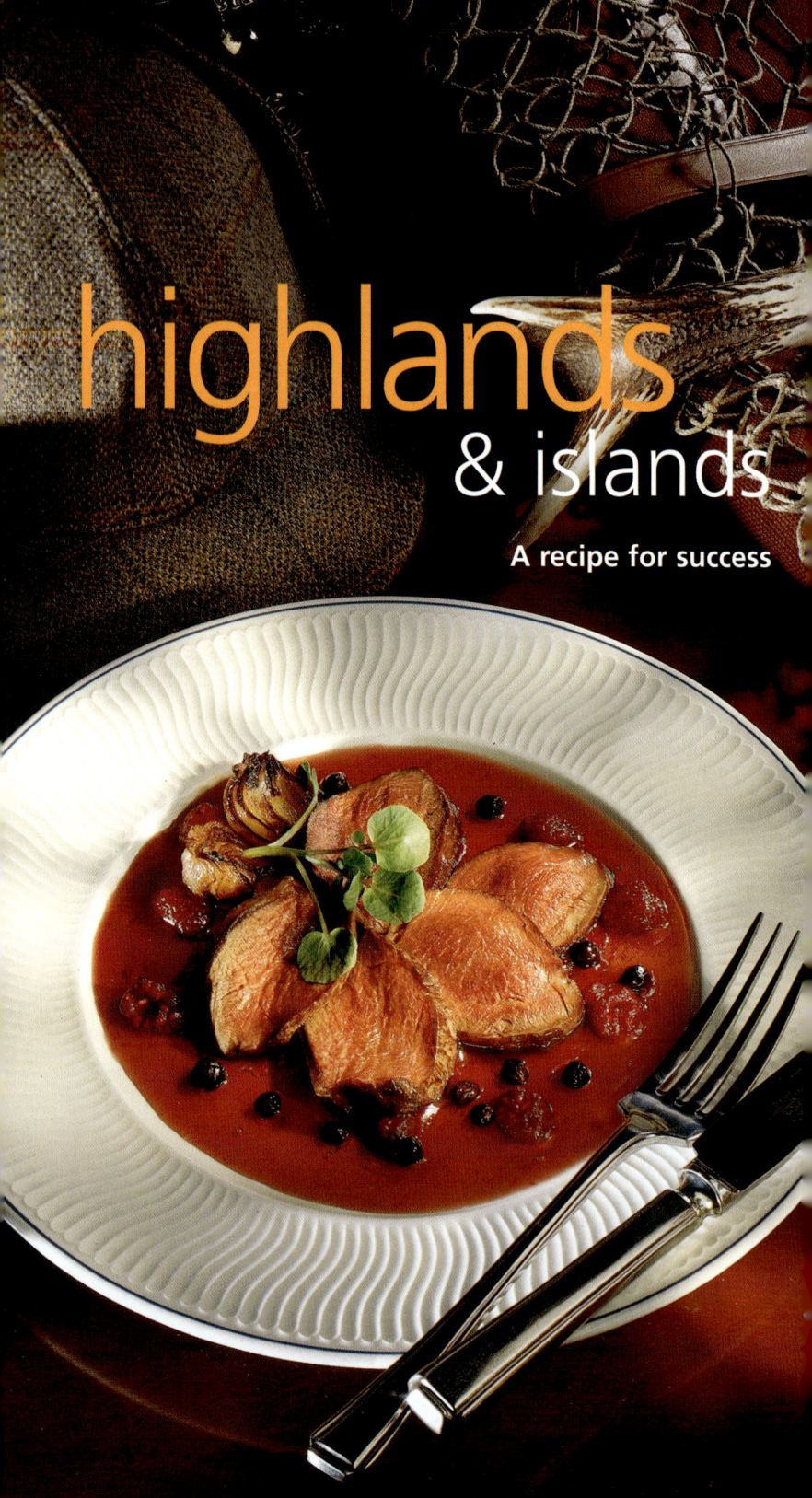

highlands
& islands

A recipe for success

A TASTE OF SCOTLAND

P AUSE FOR A SECOND... clear your mind... think of the Highlands and Islands of Scotland. No doubt images of high mountains, sweeping glens, crystal clear lochs and sparkling fast flowing rivers are flashing before your eyes.

The physical landscape of the north of Scotland is stunning and has gained a world-wide reputation for its clean and healthy environment. But how many of you, in your moment of reflection, looked beyond the geography of the area and saw the vibrant human landscape that colours this magnificent area?

Not only the rugged castle and ancient settlements of days gone by, but also the new and invigorated Highlands and Islands where traditional industries such as fishing and crofting sit alongside new high-tech businesses manufacturing computer components, carrying out data-processing for international companies, and undertaking high quality engineering. For it is communities which bring life to an area, through its people and their ability to earn a living to sustain themselves and their families.

Combining traditional skills and practices with new technology is what is happening in one of the major industries in the Highlands and Islands economy – food and drink production. This key sector employs a large part of the workforce in the area.

From the Mull of Kintyre to Shetland and the Western Isles to Strathspey, the Highlands and Islands covers half the land mass of Scotland, and is one of the most remote and unspoilt regions of Europe. Its 300 food and drink producers and manufacturers range from small speciality businesses

to large manufacturers such as Walkers Shortbread. They make the most of the area's natural resources to produce a diverse range of products – seafood, meat, game, cheese, bakery products, whisky, and a multitude of speciality products, including organic, to name but a few.

Helping these businesses and individuals to develop and to compete in national and international markets is the Highlands and Islands Enterprise (HIE) network, a government sponsored organisation with the task of helping to create a strong, diverse and sustainable economy.

This is achieved through a range of measures including finance for business, provision of factories and offices, skills development, assistance to cultural and community projects, and measures for environmental renewal. These measures are delivered by a front-line of 10 Local Enterprise Companies (LECs), locally based and private sector-led.

HIE's support for the food and drink sector incorporates all aspects of the food chain from the primary industries of agriculture, fishing and aquaculture through to the processing, manufacturing and marketing of produce.

New markets with growth potential are opening up as a result of changing consumption and lifestyles. Satisfying consumer and retail standards in terms of product quality, presentation and product innovation is a major challenge which HIE is supporting the food and drink sector in the Highlands and Islands to exploit.

So as you tour the Highlands and Islands, take time to observe, not just the beautiful scenery, but man's harvest of the land and sea to bring some of the finest produce to dinner tables not only in the Highlands and Islands but throughout the world.

There is the small colourful fishing boat across the bay lifting creels to retrieve the morning's catch of langoustines and lobsters. The orange-clad figures on distant fish farm cages tending to one of the many fish species farmed in the lochs and voes throughout the area. Very likely it is salmon, the king of fish, but it could also be trout, halibut, cod or turbot; mussels, oysters or scallops.

You may come across fresh milk from local farms being delivered to the creamery to be made into cheddar or a range of farmhouse cheeses. Or a combine harvester scything a field of golden barley destined for malting to be used in the production of the most Scottish product of all – Scotch whisky.

At the end of the day, the fruit of this toil is for you to enjoy. Whether dining in a Taste of Scotland establishment, buying something in one of our local stores, or receiving produce from one of our companies by mail order, take time to savour the flavour of the Highlands and Islands of Scotland.

For further information on food and drink from the Highlands and Islands of Scotland, please contact:

Food & Primary Products Team
Highlands & Islands Enterprise
20 Bridge Street
INVERNESS
IV1 1QR

Tel 01463 244484
Fax 01463 244241

Stuffed peacock, roast swan and spun sugar were all on the menu at Stirling Castle in mediaeval times...

a taste of scotland's past

Stirling Great Hall

A TASTE OF SCOTLAND

Edinburgh Castle

TODAY RECORDS OF THESE meals help bring the castle's history to life. The exotic dishes were uncovered by Historic Scotland researchers putting together a fascinating exhibition which visitors can see at the castle.

The vaulted Great Kitchens have been recreated as they would have been in the 16th century. The torch-lit tableaux provide a fascinating glimpse into below stairs life at Stirling, one of the grandest of all Scottish castles.

Cooking for Stirling's royal household was an extravagant business. In 1543, when the court moved to Stirling, it took 19 carriage horses to transport the contents of the great larder, the kitchen utensils and equipment for the wine cellar and bakehouse. Castle accounts for that year show that two bakers produced 464 loaves of bread each day and that oysters were extremely popular – 1000 could be consumed by the royal house in one day.

Stirling Castle is just one of over 300 enthralling sites cared for by Historic Scotland throughout the country. Some are featured in this Guide but there are many more... from prehistoric dwellings to stone circles, abbeys to cathedrals, castles to palaces, these properties represent over 5,000 years of Scottish history.

Of these, Edinburgh Castle is the best known and also Scotland's most visited tourist attraction. Perched on a towering volcanic rock, the castle dominates Edinburgh's skyline. Home to famous national icons: the Scottish Crown Jewels and the Stone of Destiny, the castle is a rich architectural mix of palace, fortress, barracks, chapel and war memorial. It's an evocative landmark which has dominated Scotland's history as a key stronghold and residence to many kings and queens.

Each property in Historic Scotland's care has its own story to tell. The 14th century tower of Lochleven Castle, on an island in Loch Leven, was the prison for Mary Queen of Scots for nearly a year before her dramatic escape in 1568. Now in summer months, visitors stream on and off the island on Historic Scotland's small ferry service from Kinross.

Tantallon Castle

Caerlaverock Castle, near Dumfries, quietly stands guard over the Solway Firth. It's everyone's idea of a real castle – an awe-inspiring, moated ruin full of nooks and crannies and has a distinguished history as lordly residence but also of war-time siege. During the great English siege of 1300, it was described as being "shaped like a shield". Today, you can take your children to play in the siege adventure park.

In a beautiful wooded riverside setting, Huntly Castle, in Aberdeenshire, provided shelter to Robert the Bruce at a crucial point in the Wars of Independence. The ancient seat of the Gordon family, the castle is famed for its surviving architecture.

The magnificent ruins of the royal palace of Linlithgow are beautifully set in its own park beside a loch. It was a favourite residence of the Stewart kings and the birthplace of James V and Mary, Queen of Scots. The impressive site of Dunstaffnage Castle overlooks what was probably the most important junction of sea lanes on the western seaboard. Built before 1275 by the MacDougall clan, the castle was captured by Robert the Bruce in 1309 and remained in royal possession for some years. During the ill-fated Jacobite risings of 1745-46 the castle was temporarily the prison of Flora MacDonald.

Tantallon Castle, started in the mid 14th century, was one of Scotland's most formidable strongholds and belonged to the powerful Douglas family. Set spectacularly on the edge of the cliffs looking out to the Firth of Forth, the castle's history illustrates the conflict between the Crown and one of Scotland's mightiest families.

Iona

The finest and most complete Renaissance townhouse in Scotland, Argyll's Lodging near Stirling Castle has been magnificently restored by Historic Scotland. The principal rooms have been furnished sumptuously, as they would have appeared when the 9th Earl of Argyll lived there around 1680.

Religious life in medieval Scotland can be experienced at a range of historic church centres including Historic Scotland's most recent addition, Iona Abbey – a celebrated

Iona Abbey

Christian site and burial place for many Scottish kings.

The island of Iona holds a unique place in the spiritual and cultural history of Scotland. Crossing by ferry from the neighbouring island of Mull, you are immediately struck by its sense of place. The abbey buildings dominate the island skyline and hold one of the most comprehensive collections of Christian carved stones in Scotland.

All this gives just a flavour of what there is to do and see. As added value, we offer a superb programme of battle re-enactments, drama, music, storytelling and other events to bring history to life.

Opening times and further information on sites are available by telephoning 0131 668 8800 or visit our website, www.historic-scotland.gov.uk

BECOME A FRIEND OF HISTORIC SCOTLAND

By becoming a Friend of Historic Scotland, you can help Historic Scotland preserve the future of these wonderful properties. Annual or lifetime membership offers free entry to all of the properties in Historic Scotland's care from as little as £26. There are many other benefits including:

- Discounted entry to English Heritage, Welsh Cadw and Manx National Heritage properties

- A quarterly colour membership magazine

- A 20 per cent discount in Historic Scotland shops

- Membership events and holidays

Memberships are available at all staffed Historic Scotland properties or call 0131 668 8999.

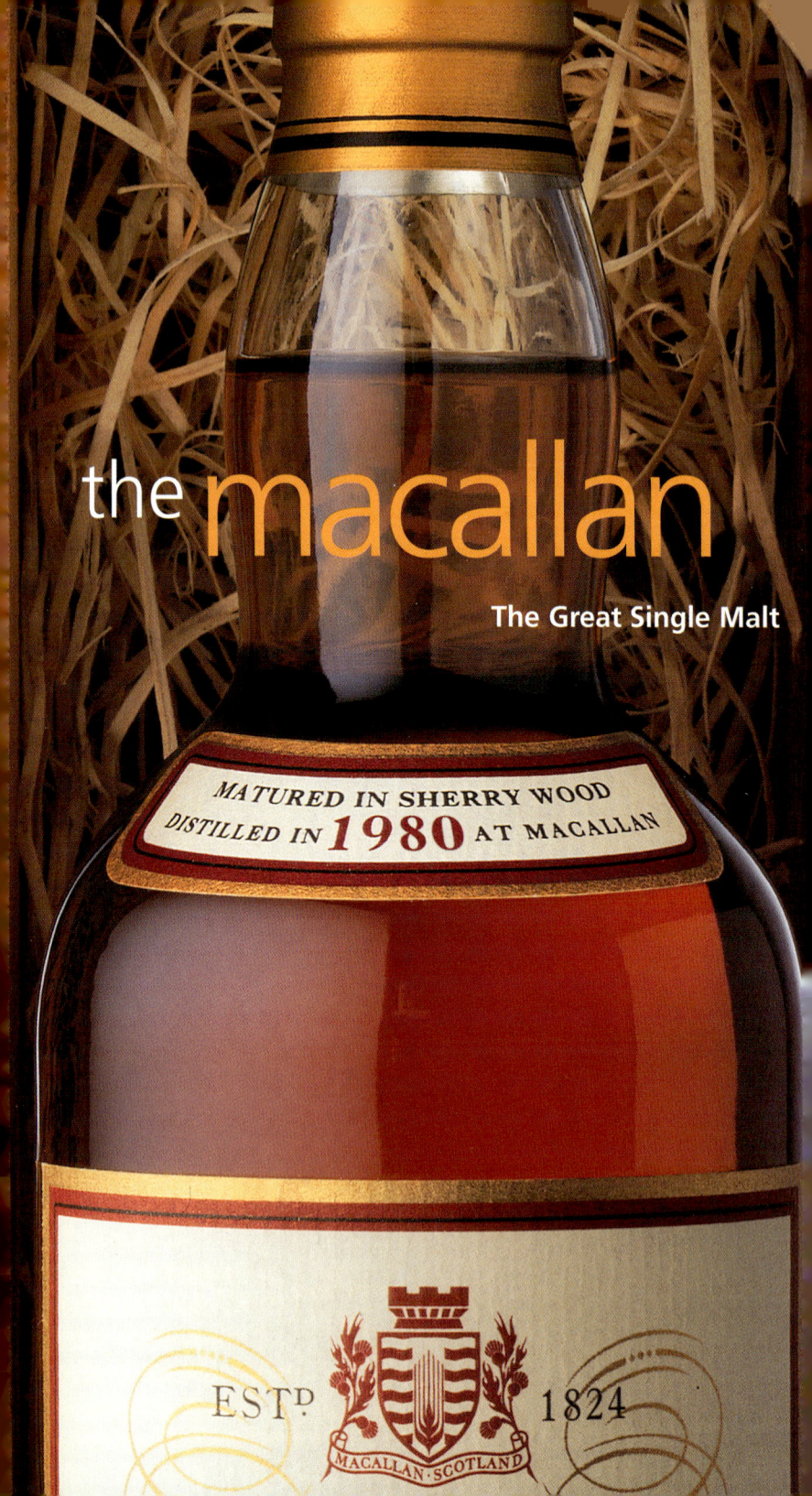

"...Macallan has become a byword for sleekness: it is a malt seemingly made from velvet couched in silk.
Ask any distillery manager his second favourite dram and, as often as not, The Macallan is it."

Jim Murray
'The Complete Guide to Whisky'

PERCHED HIGH ABOVE the banks of the River Spey, close to the village of Craigellachie, the distillery at Easter Elchies was, in 1824, one of the first to be licensed. Nine British Monarchs later, it is one of the few remaining operational distilleries that can trace its origins back to those first days of legal whisky making.

Upholding their long tradition of whisky making, the team at The Macallan labour long and hard to ensure that their malt whisky remains the malt against which all others must be judged. It is a dedication born of a passion to produce the very best.

THE PILLARS OF SPIRITUAL WISDOM

Within the walls of Easter Elchies House, "The Six Pillars of Spiritual Wisdom" are often discussed – those unique elements which combine to make The Macallan peerless. An absolute loyalty to these Pillars ensures that whatever else may occur in the world, The Macallan remains The Macallan.

1. THE BARLEY

The Macallan continues to use traditional Golden Promise Barley, a costly practice long abandoned by most other distilleries. It lends the spirit a rich, full fruity character, which balances with the wood and sherry flavours.

2. THE YEASTS

No less than four yeasts combine to create a more complex fermentation, which in turn creates a more complex whisky.

3. THE COPPER STILLS

The smallest direct gas fired stills

Easter Elchies House – home of The Macallan

on Speyside preserve the unique character of The Macallan spirit. By running them traditionally and slowly, the spirit remains complex and pure.

4. THE CUT

The cut of spirit taken from each distillation is exceptionally selective – the proportion of spirit deemed worthy of The Macallan name is smaller than even the most fastidious of its competitors.

5. THE NATURAL COLOUR

Unlike other malts, The Macallan does not have its colour enhanced by adding caramel. The deep rich golden glow of The Macallan is derived wholly from the marriage of carefully selected casks, which means its rich natural colour is matched by its rich natural taste.

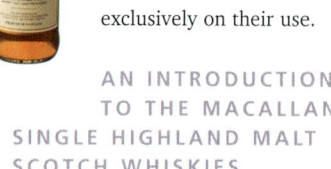

6. THE SHERRY CASKS

The Macallan continues to insist on maturing its whisky exclusively in Spanish Oak sherry casks. This creates a rich, resinous spicy character in the whisky. Due to the increasing expense and scarcity of these containers, it is many years since other distillers have insisted exclusively on their use.

AN INTRODUCTION TO THE MACALLAN SINGLE HIGHLAND MALT SCOTCH WHISKIES

A good many Taste of Scotland establishments offer a bewildering array of whisky from which to choose. To help ease your selection, we offer you here a guided tour around The Macallans' superlative range.

The Macallan 10 Years Old:
Deliciously smooth and well-rounded dried fruits flavour with a touch of sherry sweetness and wood.

The Macallan 12 Years Old:
Dried fruit and sherry flavours with a subtle toffee sweetness and a pleasant touch of spice.

The Macallan 18 Years Old:
Slightly nutty, aniseed flavour with classic Macallan rich spice and dried fruits with hints of orange.

The Macallan 18 Years Old Gran Reserve:
A full resinous, spicy character suffused with delicious citrus and dried fruit flavours.

The Macallan 25 Years Old:
Rich, full flavour reflecting the additional years of sherry oak ageing. Elegant dried fruits and full bodied with a lingering oak smoke aroma and silky complexity.

The Macallan 30 Years Old:
Rich dried fruit and sherry flavour with an orange note. A lingering spiciness and flavour of resinous wood give way to a long, spicy, orange aftertaste.

The Macallan 50 Years Old Millennium Decanter

VISIT EASTER ELCHIES – HOME OF THE MACALLAN

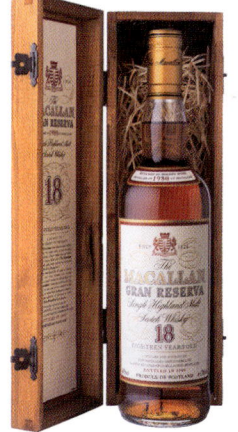

If you would like to visit Easter Elchies, home of the great single malt, simply call +44 (0)1340 871471 to make an appointment and we will be delighted to welcome you.

Alternatively make your booking via our website www.themacallan.com where you will also find more information about The Macallan and have the chance to win an exceedingly rare The Macallan 50 Years old Millennium Decanter worth £2,000 by completing our on-line questionnaire.

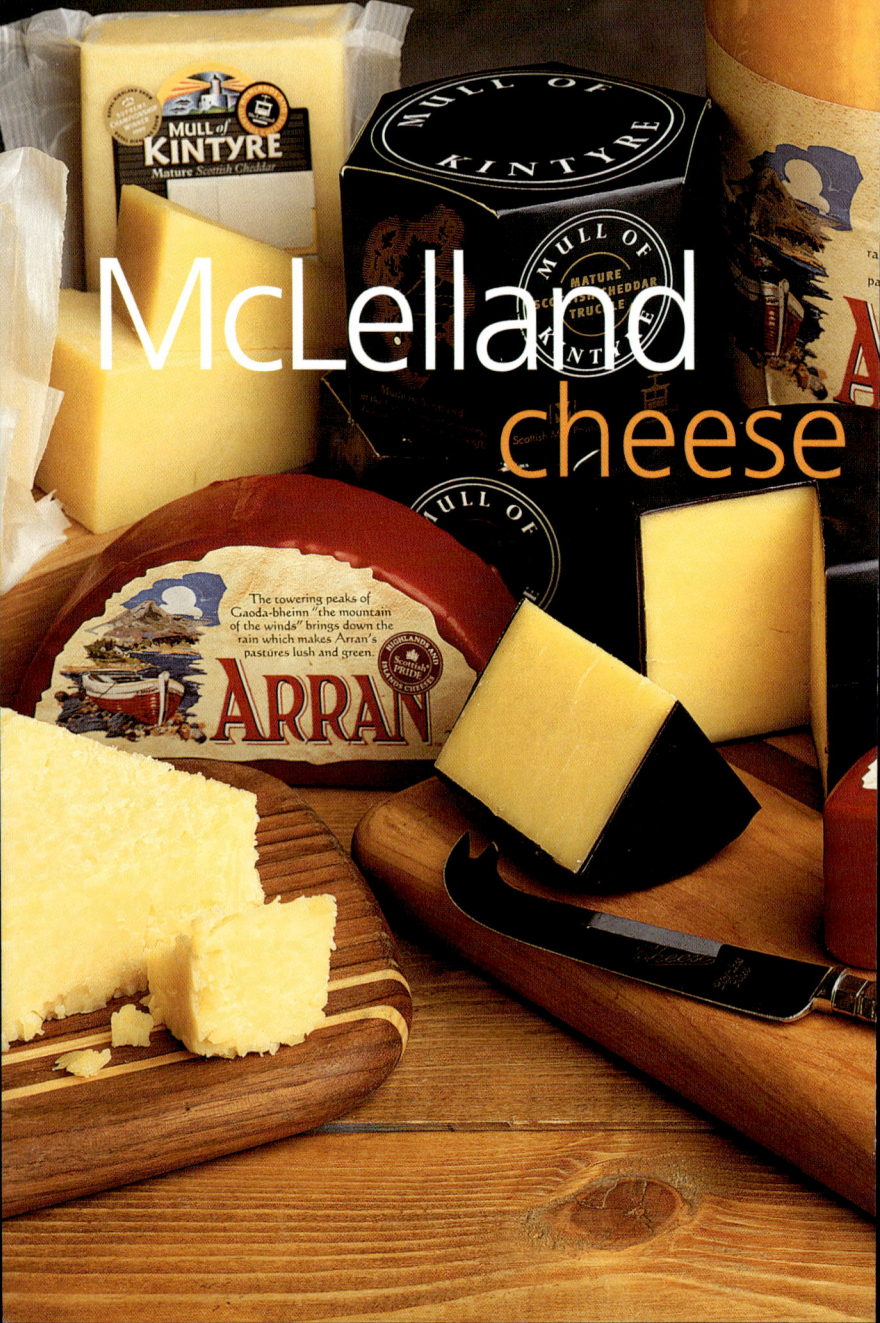

A McLELLAND & SON LTD is Scotland's oldest dairy trading company, having commenced as a family business in 1850, and now managed by 4th and 5th generation members of the family.

Originally the Cheese Market was situated in Candleriggs (near Glasgow Cross) but relocated to the Townhead area of Glasgow in 1989.

Since moving location, there have been several significant advances made by the company.

In 1995 McLellands secured a majority shareholding in the cheese making plant in Stranraer (The Caledonian Cheese Company) and they now produce the major selling cheddar cheeses in Scotland, namely Galloway, McLelland Mature and Seriously Strong as well as Galloway Butter. These products, as well as several own label cheeses for the supermarket chains, are all sold through A McLelland & Son Ltd.

In 1997, in conjunction with Scottish Milk, a new company was formed, Scottish Milk Products, with the aim of selling the Scottish Pride products as part of the McLelland portfolio, this includes the Arran, Rothesay and Campbeltown Creamery produced cheeses.

More recently, in 2000, a stake was taken in the cheese making plant in Kirkwall, (Orkney mainland) thus ensuring the continued production of cheese on the Island using locally produced milk.

McLelland's are constantly updating their products and packaging concepts to give customers the best possible range of dairy produce.

McLelland's have an interest in the Creameries on the Isle of Bute, Isle of Arran and the main island of Orkney, producing cheeses made from the high quality milk produced on the islands. The cheeses produced are marketed by

A McLelland & Son Ltd and small quantities are sold through the shops attached to the Creameries in Rothesay (Isle of Bute) and Torrylinn (Isle of Arran) where visitors are welcome to watch the expert cheesemakers at work. Orkney cheddar is a regular award winner at The Royal Highland Show in Edinburgh and medium, mature and vintage flavours are available in most major supermarkets and food outlets as a loose product and also pre-packed. The 454g coloured, white and smoked rounds make ideal gifts.

Rothesay Creamery was rebuilt in 1990 and produces cheese, mainly made from milk produced on the Isle of Bute, with a rounded, mellow, satisfying flavour.

Torrylinn Creamery on the Isle of Arran was opened in 1947 and still makes cheese using traditional methods in open vats. The result is a creamy soft textured medium mature Dunlop type cheese made in various sizes, many of which are waxed.

Campbeltown Creamery on the Mull of Kintyre has been manufacturing cheese on the site since 1919. Modern production methods are used to make prizewinning, top quality cheddar with a nutty aroma.

The Creamery was formerly a distillery, and according to the cheese maker, the quality and taste of the cheese owes a lot to the 'Angel's Share' of the whisky (the amount lost to evaporation) still lingering in the building. The Creamery handles all the milk produced on the Mull of Kintyre as well as the neighbouring Island of Gigha. The cheese is utilised in their branded products and their distinctive black waxed truckles are particularly sought after as gifts.

The main source of cheese for A McLelland & Son Ltd is the Caledonian Creamery in Stranraer where Galloway, McLelland Mature and Seriously Strong are made, along with Galloway and Scottish Pride butter. There has been a Creamery on the site since 1899, but the current buildings have been modernised several times, making it one of the most modern cheese making plants in Europe.

The Scottish Cheese Packing Centre and Store near Mauchline, in Ayrshire, part of the McLelland portfolio was rebuilt in 1998 and can meet the requirements of any customer. Cheese is packaged to order for McLelland's and also for supermarket 'own label' brands marketed through A McLelland & Son Ltd.

A McLelland & Son Ltd also assist in the marketing of speciality cheeses produced by independent cheesemakers.

Highland Fine Cheeses in Tain (Ross and Cromarty) produce Caboc and Galic from recipes reputed to date from the 16th Century as well as Highland Crowdie and Strathdon Blue (a blue, cows milk cheese).

The Inverloch Cheese Company in Campbeltown make fruit shaped cheeses with various flavours (Grand Marnier, Chives, Garlic etc) which are then waxed and known as Gigha Fruits, as well as small waxed truckles with various flavours (whisky, mustard, pickle etc) known as Taste of Gigha, both ideal as gifts.

Howgate Dairy Foods Ltd, Kinfauns near Perth produce Scottish Brie, St Andrews and other similar cheeses.

The National Trust for Scotland

Promoting Scotland's Quality

national trust
for scotland

...where the quality of the property is matched by the quality in the kitchen

Crathes Castle, Grampian

Hill House, Helensburgh

LONG FAMOUS FOR a traditionally warm welcome – and for its home baking – the National Trust for Scotland has this year set out to raise the quality of its food and service even further. It is a policy designed to enhance the Trust's presence in some of Scotland's most stunning locations, from the wilds of Glenfinnan to the sophistication of Charlotte Square.

This commitment to quality extends throughout, from the sourcing of local suppliers to the provision of resources and training. All of this effort is geared towards ensuring the best of Scotland's produce is available on every occasion. Whether you visit the properties for a day out, an event or an overnight stay, the Trust wants the experience to be enriched by the quality of our menus.

The National Trust for Scotland is the conservation charity whose purpose is to protect and promote Scotland's natural and cultural heritage for present and future generations to enjoy. Membership of the Trust quite literally opens some of the most famous doors in the country.

The diverse range of activities includes something for everyone – music recitals, fun days out for the family, holiday cottages in beautiful locations, volunteer work projects (e.g. St Kilda), ceilidhs, guided walks, sampling the ambience of historic properties or quite simply enjoying dinner in elegant surroundings. Information on any of these activities can be obtained from the Trust's headquarters at Charlotte Square in Edinburgh.

Many of our properties are listed in this book, taking in some of the most beautiful scenery and impressive buildings in Scotland. Culzean Castle in Ayrshire, for instance, has two separate entries, one for the prestigious Eisenhower Apartments and one for the

Brodick Castle, Isle of Arran

Glenfinnan, by Fort William

day visitor facilities. Enjoy afternoon tea amid the delights of Charles Rennie Macintosh's Hill House in Helensburgh, or Fyvie Castle's imposing structure in Aberdeenshire. The coffee bar at Glenfinnan, contrasting with the beautiful garden restaurant at Threave (Dumfriesshire), add to excellent days out with a difference. Charlotte Square Coffee House and No 27 Restaurant at the heart of Edinburgh's West End are a great way to find out about the Trust or enjoy dinner in elegant Georgian surroundings.

Brodick Castle on Arran, with Goat Fell as its backdrop, takes the breath away as one sails into Brodick Bay. Crathes Castle in Grampian offers a variety-packed day out for all the family. The battlefields of Scotland are well represented and, after taking in the scenes of ancient conflict, visitors will find that facilities at both Culloden and Bannockburn offer excellent food.

A culinary and cultural tour of Scotland would not be complete without a visit to Pollok House (Glasgow) or Haddo House

(Aberdeenshire) for lunch. Whatever your preference, by visiting these properties, eating there or even becoming a Trust member, you can celebrate Scotland's beauty and heritage whilst supporting the Trust's vital conservation work.

The properties, restaurants and tea rooms offer variety and menus which have been prepared to reflect the surroundings and local produce, put together skilfully by the local manager. You'll find traditional favourites such as:

- Tattie Drottle served with a cheese and herb scone
- Venison infused with blackberries and Heather Ale
- Savoury tart of spinach and Mrs Bonnet's Goat's cheese

along with such alternative offerings as

- Roasted tomato tarte tatin
- Sweet potato, Dunlop cheese and bramley apple in a cheese crust with fresh sage

Delicious soups are always available including pea, apple and mint, as well as the more traditional but no less tasty Scotch Broth and Cullen Skink. Many locations have speciality coffees – cappuccinos, lattés, cafetières and decaf. Teas range from Scottish Breakfast to soothing and satisfying herbal teas. You can also buy hot chocolate, Scottish mineral waters and soft drinks. Kids' lunch boxes, featuring the NTS detectives, make sure everyone is catered for, adding some fun and stimulation for younger family members.

A number of properties are licensed, especially where functions and evening meals are provided, with selections of Scottish Beers and fine wines.

Whatever the occasion, the attractions of the National Trust for Scotland have something to offer everyone. Most of the facilities can be hired for functions, with the kind of backdrop normally reserved for picture postcards. Self-catering holidays are available at many locations. With more than 40 shops throughout Scotland, you have easy access to retail 'therapy', beautifully complemented by Mail Order spring and autumn catalogues which celebrate both the variety and taste of the very best of Scotland.

Be sure to visit this year!

National Trust For Scotland
28 Charlotte Square
Edinburgh EH2 4ET
Tel 0131 243 9300
Fax 0131 243 9501

Bannockburn, Stirling

FROM HUMBLE BEGINNINGS to an internationally renowned business and flagship of Scottish foods, Walkers Shortbread is one of Scotland's success stories. The company was founded in 1898 by Joseph Walker, when he had to borrow enough money to buy some flour and rent a small baker's shop in the beautiful Speyside village of Aberlour, in the heart of the Scottish highlands. The company is still owned and managed by his three grandchildren and now the fourth generation of the Walkers family is involved in the company.

Despite becoming a household name, which supplies top stores such as Harrods and Fortnum & Mason, Walkers, is still based in the same village. It now employs almost 800 people and has three factories in Aberlour and one in Elgin, with entire families working at the firm. Many of its staff have spent all their working lives with the company.

Today the company's products are considered the definitive example of Scottish baking produced to the highest standards. It still specialises in traditional products baked to original family recipes, combining modern technology with age-old craftsmanship. Its' products are now available in over 60 countries world-wide. Their overseas sales have been so successful that Walkers was recently awarded the Queen's Award for Export Achievement for the third time, the only Scottish food manufacturer ever to have won the award on three occasions.

Walkers products are instantly recognisable, unashamedly packaged in traditional tartan, with luxury gifts and everyday treats in distinctive packaging and tins decorated with Scottish

paintings. Amongst the new gift tins recently introduced was a special commemorative tin to celebrate Her Majesty the Queen Mother's 100th birthday; and an elegant matt gold-embossed tin containing their popular home-bake range. The company has also launched two new novelty gift tins – an unusual three-sided tin, depicting some of Scotland's best-loved castles, and for the younger shortbread lover, a tin shaped like a Walkers delivery truck.

Always at the forefront of innovation and creativity, Walkers recently added a delicious melt-in-the-mouth vanilla shortbread, which is flavoured with real vanilla, to its product range while in honour of the new millennium, Walkers produced the very first champagne and malt whisky shortbread. Tastefully packaged in sophisticated silver cartons depicting images of famous Scots and achievements, the range also included an eye-catching domed shortbread tin which won several awards including the supreme gold award from the MPMA (Metal Packaging Manufacturers Association) for the best tin produced in the UK in 1999.

All of the shortbreads are made to Walkers famous all butter recipe which has been used for the last 100 years, with only natural ingredients and no additives, artificial colourings or flavourings. Each Walkers product is certified kosher (OUD), without animal fats and suitable for vegetarians.

Also recently introduced is the company's first organic range, baked to the traditional recipe but using only organic flour, butter and sugar. The range also includes organic wheat' n' oat biscuits, which are an ideal accompaniment to cheese. Both products are certified by the soil association.

Walkers also produces a range of organic products for Duchy Originals. Duchy Originals was established by HRH The Prince of Wales to help foster sustainable farming methods and natural food products to raise funds for the Prince of Wales' charitable foundation. The biscuits are baked using organic wheat and oats harvested from the Prince's Highgrove estate.

Walkers product range also includes traditional biscuits, cakes, oatcakes and meringues in addition to shortbread. Glenfiddich cake is crammed with fruit, deliciously rich and moist with a generous measure of malt whisky.

It is produced in co-operation with the famous distillery, situated near Walkers in the Spey Valley – an area known as 'Quality Corner' because of the many family companies producing goods which have become world famous because they are outstanding examples of what Scotland has to offer.

Walkers Shortbread
Aberlour, Speyside
Tel 01340 871555
Fax 01340 871055

nairn's cook school

GOOD NEWS FOR ALL FOODIES out there! Nick Nairn and his team have opened a new cook school in central Scotland.

The Lake of Menteith, an area of breathtaking natural beauty, provides a stunning setting for the school on the Lochend Estate. It has its own herb and salad garden supplying the school with the freshest herbs and a wide range of flavoursome and unusual salad leaves. The kitchen itself will really bowl you over, offering the ultimate in state-of-the-art kitchen facilities, with Falcon's sexy cooking ranges taking centre stage. It's the perfect opportunity to try for yourself the best equipment on the market. The kitchen just oozes style, with etched glass, stainless steel and natural woods throughout.

The classes on offer aim to share the experience and knowledge gained over half a century by the chefs Nick Nairn and John Webber. Nick is a familiar face to most Scots, and his passion for fresh produce and fantastic flavours is well documented. John Webber is the chef's chef, possibly the most respected and experienced in the country. Both have received Michelin stars during their culinary careers.

John and Nick share a passion for fresh produce and the quality of flavours they afford. This really comes through in the classes where they share their knowledge and skills in the form of a Masterclass, teaching not just to copy a recipe parrot fashion but instead their philosophy of cooking – the whys and hows.

The masterclasses take the form of a five-day residential course, and cover each section of the kitchen at different levels: introductory to intermediate and advanced. Having tackled just about everything from stocks and sauces to desserts, vegetables to fish and shellfish, the theory is that you'll leave with the knowledge and enthusiasm to create great dishes of your own.

Each subject is available as a day class, again at each level, allowing those with a hectic schedule to cover the masterclass in their own time. Recreational one-day classes will also be available, on topics such as dinner parties, and the Best of Island Harvest.

The school can accommodate up to 10 for hands-on cooking, and up to 20 for demonstrations or relaxed informal dining, and is available to hire for all occasions – whether for a tailor made class or a demonstrations dinner for colleges.

The day will be fun as well as informative, but let's leave it to one of the school's first visitors to say exactly how the day went, "I felt as if I have spent the whole day with friends and family. Friendly, informal atmosphere, great company, great food and great learning experience."

Nairn's Cook School
Telephone 01877 385603

OTHER TASTE OF SCOTLAND MEMBERS WHO RUN COOKERY SCHOOLS ARE:

- Lady Claire MacDonald, Kinloch Lodge, Isle of Skye
- Kinloch House, Blairgowrie
- Burrastow House, Isles of Shetland

Or contact Taste of Scotland for up-to-date information.

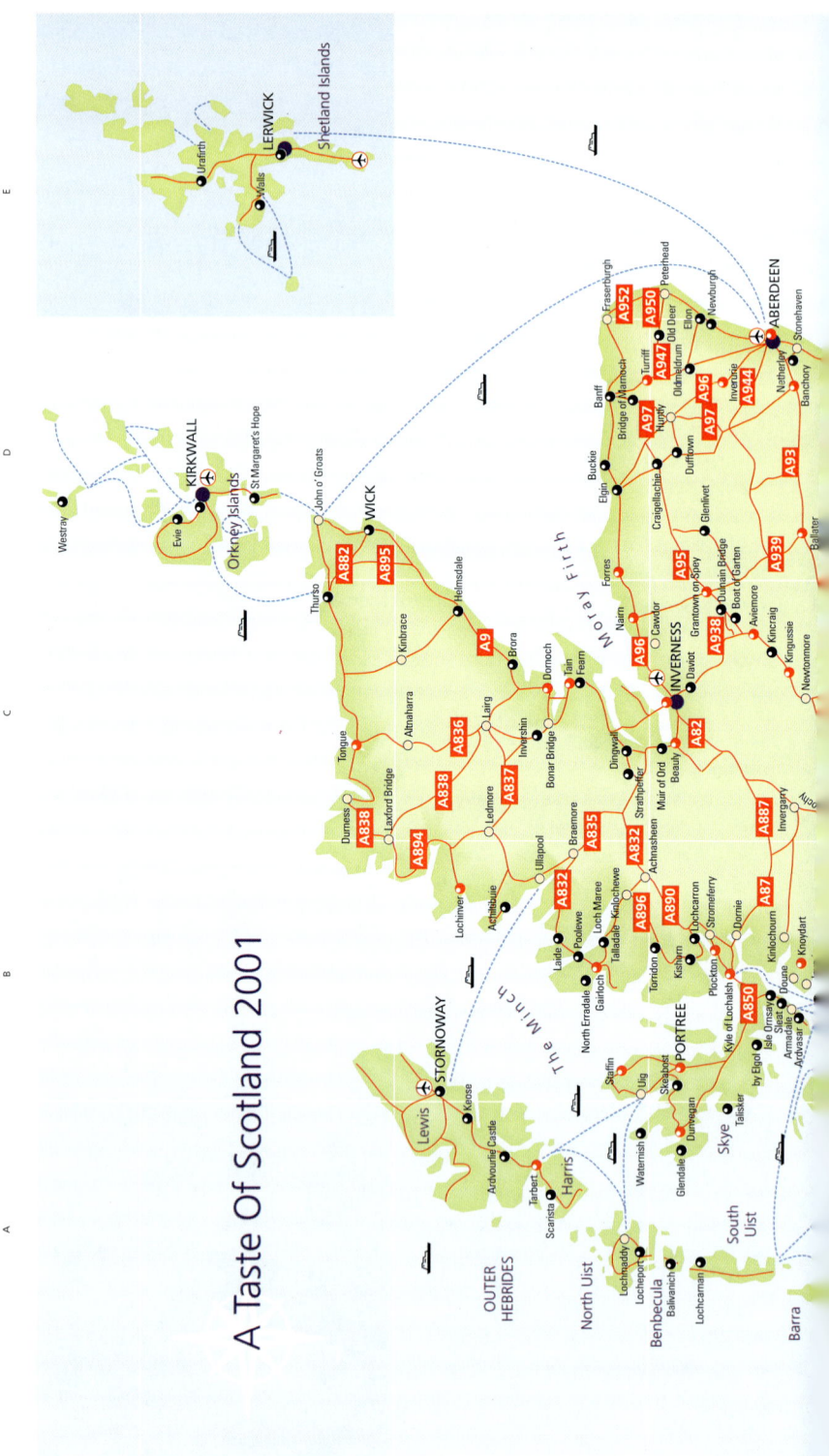

How to use this guide

All establishments listed in this Guide have exceeded an inspection conducted by a fully qualified Taste of Scotland Inspector. They are listed in alphabetical order under the nearest town or village. Island entries are shown under I for Isle. A full list of members is in the alphabetical index at the rear of the Guide or look at the map to see the locations of all Taste of Scotland establishments.

All the information included in the entry is accurate at time of printing – however we do urge customers to call and verify prices and opening times prior to setting off on a journey. Often seasonal variations may result in information included in the entry changing at short notice and a call will avoid disappointment.

Prices for accommodation are per person sharing a room and a guideline only. For single rates and special rates please call the establishment and verify these in advance.

At time of going to press the most up to date Scottish Tourist Board star ratings information available is included in the entry.

Visitor attractions are also graded by stars for the standard of customer care they provide – welcome, hospitality, service, and how the attraction itself is presented. Establishments with a concern for the environment take part in the Board's Green Tourism Business Scheme and their efforts are graded either Bronze, Silver of Gold.

We always welcome feedback on your experiences of Taste of Scotland both in using this Guide and the dining experience – please keep us informed.

Meal Prices

£ symbols indicate the price category which the establishment has told us they fall into. They are:

£	=	up to £10 per person
££	=	£11–£20 per person
£££	=	£21–£30 per person
££££	=	over £30 per person

◑	Opening arrangements
🏠	Number of rooms
🛏	Accommodation rates
SP	Special rates available
★	Scottish Tourist Board star rating
♀	Licensing information
UL	Unlicensed
✗	Information on meals
☕	Member of the Scotch Beef Club
V	Vegetarians welcome
⚓	Children welcome
♿	Facilities for disabled visitors
✄	Restrictions on smoking
🐾	Information on pets
£	Credit cards accepted
🔪	Owner/Proprietor/Manager/Chef

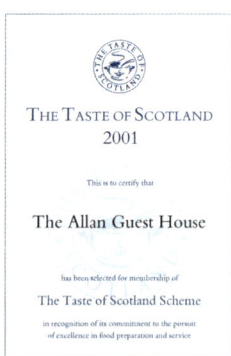

THE TASTE OF SCOTLAND
2001

This is to certify that

The Allan Guest House

has been selected for membership of
The Taste of Scotland Scheme

in recognition of its commitment to the pursuit
of excellence in food preparation and service

Taste of Scotland current members are identified by the 2001 Certificate of Membership (above) which should be prominently displayed.

ABERDEEN

Establishment	**The Allan Guest House**
Inspector's 2000 comment	• *"Guests staying here greatly benefit from the owners' enthusiasm for food and wine."*
Style of cooking	• *Modern Scottish cooking.*
Description	ALLAN GUEST HOUSE is run by Liz and Brian Taylor whose enthusiasm for good food and wine is evident throughout. Menus are a blend of the best of traditional with a modern twist, offering guests a varied choice. A suitable venue for families, holidaymakers or business guests and a most welcome addition to Taste of Scotland.
Menu specialities	*Cullen skink (fish soup). East meets West: Teryaki salmon, rooster potatoes from the Black Isle, selection of herb roast root vegetables. Upside down caramelised rice pudding with Armagnac soaked prunes.*
STB Rating	STB ★★★★ Guest House
Facilities and services	◐ *Open all year* ⌂ *Rooms: 7, 5 en-suite* ⌯ *DB&B £36.50–£58.50 B&B £25–£40* ✗ *Residents only Packed lunches by arrangement £ Dinner ££* Ⓥ *Vegetarians welcome* ⚹ *Children welcome* ▣ *Credit cards: Mastercard/Eurocard, Visa, Delta* ⍟ *Owner: Liz Taylor*
Address Contact details	*56 Polmuir Road Aberdeen AB11 7RT Tel: 01224 584484 Fax: 01224 595988 E-mail: allaninfo@camtay.co.uk Web: www.camtay.co.uk*
How to get there	*Polmuir Road is a T junction to Murray Terrace which is off Great Southern Road. [D4]*

ABERDEEN

Ardoe House Hotel

- *"Traditional country house elegance with fine food and a super leisure club – all combine to create an enjoyable visit.*
- *Modern and traditional Scottish cuisine."*

ARDOE HOUSE is a classic Scots baronial granite mansion with full leisure facilities. Dining is à la carte, from an extensive menu of unusually treated dishes and imaginative combinations, or table d'hôte. Chef Ivor Clark draws inspiration from classic French cooking, whilst using fresh Scottish produce. Full leisure facilities. 2 AA Rosettes.

Marinated fillet of sea bass with pickled vegetables, served with a seed mustard and herb dressing. Roast loin of lamb, with black pudding and leek cake, served with a port and rosemary jus. Warm oat and orange tart with a butterscotch sauce and cinnamon ice cream.

STB ★★★★ Hotel

◐ Open all year ⌂ Rooms: 112 en suite
🛏 DB&B from £70 B&B from £47.50 SP Special rates available ✗ Food available all day £££ Lunch ££ Dinner £££ Ⓥ Vegetarians welcome ✻ Children welcome ♿ Facilities for disabled visitors ⃠ No smoking in dining room 🗎 Credit cards: Mastercard/Eurocard, American Express, Visa, Diners Club, Switch ♦ General Manager: Ewan Kirkpatrick

South Deeside Road Aberdeen AB12 5YP
Tel: 01224 8606600 Fax: 01224 861283
E-mail: ardoe@macdonald-hotels.co.uk
B9077, 3 miles west of Aberdeen. Turn left at hotel sign and up driveway. [D4]

ABERDEEN

Atholl Hotel

- *"A well-placed hotel with good food being offered to suit the shopper, visitor or business clientele."*
- *Traditional Scottish cooking.*

THE ATHOLL HOTEL is under the personal supervision of Gordon Sinclair. The hotel has a comfortable and warm atmosphere. The cooking is simple and straightforward with high quality ingredients and there is much evidence of local quality produce. Menus change monthly with specials changing nightly depending upon availability.

Queen scallop pâté with chive scented jus. Halibut en croute: fresh halibut fillet with spring onion and soft cheese baked in puff pastry, with a lemon and lime sauce. Raspberry royale: fresh raspberries, cream topped with toasted oatmeal.

STB ★★★★ Hotel

◐ Open all year except New Year's Day
⌂ Rooms: 35 en suite 🛏 B&B £71–£89
SP Special rates available ✗ Lunch ££ Dinner ££
Ⓥ Vegetarians welcome ✻ Children welcome
🗎 Credit cards: Mastercard/Eurocard, American Express, Visa, Diners Club, Switch
♦ Managing Partner: Gordon Sinclair

54 Kings Gate Aberdeen AB15 4YN
Tel: 01224 323505 Fax: 01224 321555
E-mail: info@atholl-aberdeen.co.uk
Web: www.atholl-aberdeen.com
Follow signs for A96 north. Turn right at King's Gate roundabout, the hotel is situated ½ mile along King's Gate in the heart of the city's West End. [D4]

ABERDEEN

Craiglynn Hotel

- *"Enjoy a comfortable stay in Craiglynn by sampling quality food and service."*
- *Lovingly prepared Scottish cooking.*

CRAIGLYNN HOTEL is an impressive house, with many of its original features preserved. Service is friendly and attentive, where the guests are welcomed like part of the family. In the dining room menus are short, since everything is prepared from fresh local produce, and the cooking homely. The bedrooms are very comfortable and have unique en suite facilities.

Parsnip and apple soup. Lamb noisettes garnished with fresh rosemary. Freshly prepared desserts.

STB ★★★★ Small Hotel

◐ *Open all year except Christmas Day and Boxing Day* 🏨 *Rooms: 9 en suite* 🛏 *B&B £78* 🍷 *Restricted licence* ✗ *Non-residents – by reservation dinner ££* Ⓥ *Vegetarians welcome* ✗ *No smoking in dining room and bedrooms* 💳 *Credit cards: Mastercard/Eurocard, American Express, Visa, Diners Club, Switch, JCB, Solo* 🅝 *Partners: Hazel & Chris Mann*

36 Fonthill Road Aberdeen AB11 6UJ
Tel: 01224 584050 Fax: 01224 212225
E-mail: info@craiglynn.co.uk
Web: www.craiglynn.co.uk
On corner of Fonthill Road and Bon Accord Street, midway between Union Street and King George VI Bridge. Car park access from Bon Accord Street. [D4]

ABERDEEN

Lairhillock Inn & Crynoch Restaurant at Lairhillock

- *"Good atmosphere, charming staff and serving delicious food."*
- *Modern cooking with continental influences.*

LAIRHILLOCK is a traditional small coaching inn, set in the heart of beautiful countryside, which has a long and reputable reputation for offering good quality food and service. Friendly and helpful staff serve good freshly prepared food which has been carefully prepared using only the best local ingredients. Now under new ownership.

Terrine of woodpigeon and wild mushrooms. Layers of fillet of venison and wild boar with new potatoes and a heather honey, whisky and thyme jus. Toasted home-made banana bread.

◐ *Open all year except Christmas Day, Boxing Day, and 1, 2 Jan Crynoch Restaurant closed Tue* ✗ *Lunch (Inn) ££ (Crynoch Rest) Sun ££ Dinner (Inn) ££ (Crynoch Rest) except Tue £££* Ⓥ *Vegetarians welcome* ✱ *Children welcome* ♿ *Facilities for disabled visitors* ✗ *No smoking in the Conservatory* 🐾 *Dogs welcome in Snug Bar* 💳 *Credit cards: Mastercard/Eurocard, American Express, Visa, Diners Club, Switch, Delta* 🅝 *Proprietors: Roger Thorne & Angela Maddox*

Netherley by Stonehaven Aberdeenshire AB39 3QS
Tel: 01569 730001 Fax: 01569 731175
E-mail: lairhillock@breathemail.net
Web: www.lairhillock.co.uk
From Aberdeen take A90 to Stonehaven. After 6 miles take the Durris road – second right after Portleithen. Drive for 4 miles along this road. From the south, once on straight after Cammachmore, turn left at the Durris junction. [D4]

ABERDEEN

The Marcliffe at Pitfodels

- *"Guests are so well looked after that they are reluctant to leave!"*
- *Modern classic cooking with French influence.*

THE MARCLIFFE AT PITFODELS' atmosphere is luxurious, and enhances modern design with antiques and baronial detailing. There are two restaurants: the Conservatory, and the Invery Room. Menus in both are well-balanced and extensive; and the cooking is accomplished. Fresh lobster is available from May to October. 100 malt whiskies and 400 wines available.

Seared sea scallops with salad leaves and balsamic/basil dressing. Roast fillet Aberdeenshire beef with a confit of oxtail, panaché of garden vegetables. Crisp filo pastry layered with a sharp lemon mousseline, strawberries and a red fruit syrup.

STB ★★★★★ Hotel

◐ Open all year 🏨 Rooms: 42 en suite 🛏 DB&B £82.50–£150 B&B £52.50–£125 💷 Special rates available ✕ Lunch £££ Dinner £££ Ⓥ Vegetarians welcome ⚘ Children welcome ♿ Facilities for disabled visitors ✄ No smoking in Invery Room Restaurant 🐄 Member of the Scotch Beef Club 💳 Credit cards: Mastercard/Eurocard, American Express, Visa, Diners Club, Switch ⚑ Proprietor: Stewart Spence

North Deeside Road Aberdeen AB15 9YA
Tel: 01224 861000 Fax: 01224 868860
E-mail: reservations@marcliffe.com
Web: www.marcliffe.com
On A93 to Braemar. 1 mile from A92. 3 miles from city centre. [D4]

ABERDEEN

Norwood Hall Hotel

- *"A comfortable friendly hotel."*
- *Modern Scottish with international influences.*

THIS VICTORIAN mansion house hotel has been sympathetically restored to its former glory. It is run by a professional and dedicated team who offer true Scottish hospitality, together with the best of local produce. Food is presented pleasingly in the Victorian dining room and flavours do not disappoint.

Blue cheese and asparagus mousse on beef tomato with honey and orange dressing. Roulade of pork and venison wrapped in bacon, sliced onto a tarragon and apple jus. Iced hazelnut praline and white chocolate parfait.

STB ★★★ Hotel

◐ Open all year 🏨 Rooms: 21 en suite 🛏 DB&B £70–£102 B&B £50–£82 💷 Special rates available ✕ Lunch from ££ Dinner £££ Ⓥ Vegetarians welcome ⚘ Children welcome ♿ Limited facilities for disabled visitors ✄ No smoking in dining room 💳 Credit cards: Mastercard/Eurocard, American Express, Visa, Diners Club, Switch, Delta ⚑ General Manager: Morag MacIndoe

Garthdee Road Cults Aberdeen AB15 9FX
Tel: Tel: 01224 868951 Fax: 01224 869868
E-mail: info@norwood-hall.co.uk
Web: www.norwood-hall.co.uk
1 mile from the Bridge of Dee roundabout off the A90 and the A96. [D4]

ABERDEEN

Simpson's Hotel Bar/Brasserie

- *"Fine food and wine can be enjoyed in a relaxed atmosphere."*
- *Modern Scottish cuisine with international influences.*

MUCH OF Simpson's designer furniture and tiles come from Spain. The rich colour schemes of the vaulted ceiling restaurant extend to the sophisticated hotel; even the courtyard has a Mediterranean feel. Head chef Graham Mutch mixes traditional and original in innovative recipes using the best of Aberdeenshire products. Simpson's has 1 AA Rosette.

Dornoch black pudding and apple fritters with a spiced fruit chutney. Half rack of Scotch lamb with an Arran mustard crust served with a carrot and coriander mash. Caramelised rice pudding with mixed berry compote.

STB ★★★★ Hotel

◐ Open all year ✿ Rooms: 37 en suite ⌬ B&B £105-£140 ⓢ Special rates available ✖ Lunch ££ Dinner £££ Ⓥ Vegetarians welcome ✱ Children welcome ⚒ Facilities for disabled visitors ⚭ Rooms non smoking. Smoking area in Restaurant ⊞ Credit cards: Mastercard/ Eurocard, American Express, Visa, Switch, Delta ⛨ General Manager: Shona Stewart

59 Queens Road Aberdeen AB15 4YP
Tel: 01224 327777 Fax: 01224 327700
E-mail: address@simpsonshotel.co.uk
Follow signs for A96 North. Turn right at Queens Road Roundabout, hotel is 500 yards down the road on right-hand side. [D4]

ABERDEEN

The Victoria Restaurant

- *"Good food can be enjoyed in this little haven on busy Union Street."*
- *Modern and traditional cooking.*

THE VICTORIA has been a restaurant for over 50 years and is now owned by Gillian and Gordon Harold. Gillian is head chef and Gordon is in charge of the front of house. There is an evident commitment to quality with highly visible sourcing of Scottish produce and skilful cooking.

Home-made bread topped with Scottish Brie, baked in the oven and served with Gillian's apple chutney. Baked apple crêpe with butterscotch sauce and local ice cream. Traditional afternoon tea with fresh cream scones, cakes and cookies.

◐ Open all year except 2 weeks Jan Closed local holidays, Christmas and New Year Closed Sun ✖ Food available all day except Sun £ Lunch except Sun £ Ⓥ Vegetarians welcome ✱ Children welcome ⚭ No smoking in restaurant ⊞ Credit cards: Mastercard/ Eurocard, Visa, Switch, Delta ⛨ Proprietors: Gillian & Gordon Harold

140 Union Street Aberdeen AB10 1JD
Tel: 01224 621381
In the middle of the main street, on the first floor above Jamieson and Carry the Jewellers. [D4]

ABERDOUR

The Woodside Hotel

- *"First-class service and excellent food."*
- *Modern Scottish cooking.*

THE WOODSIDE HOTEL is run by Stewart and Lesley Dykes, experienced and professional hoteliers. The hotel is comfortable and popular, set as it is in this delightful seaside village. Dine formally or informally in the dining room or bistro. The food is well cooked and presented and served by friendly and attentive staff.

Prawn, tomato and lentil broth with a scallop ravioli. Maize-fed chicken, corn and potato cake, baby black pudding, and Madeira jus. Passion fruit mousse, kumquat marmalade and coconut ice cream.

STB ★★★ Hotel

◐ *Open all year* ▥ *Rooms: 20 en suite* ⊨ *DB&B £50–£65 B&B £25–£40* ⓢⓟ *Special rates available* ✘ *Food available all day ££ Lunch ££ Dinner ££* Ⓥ *Vegetarians welcome* ✻ *Children welcome* ♿ *Facilities for disabled visitors* ✄ *No smoking in dining room* ⌹ *Dogs welcome* ⊟ *Credit cards: Mastercard/Eurocard, American Express, Visa, Switch* ⓜ *Proprietor: Stewart Dykes*

High Street Aberdour Fife KY3 0SW
Tel: 01383 860328 Fax: 01383 860920
E-mail: reception@woodside-hotel.demon.co.uk
From north – cross Forth Road Bridge, take 2nd exit. Turn right under M90, follow signs to Kirkcaldy. Go through 4 roundabouts then into Aberdour. Hotel on left after garage. [D5]

ABERFELDY

Farleyer House Hotel

- *"Excellent food in beautiful surroundings."*
- *Sensational Scottish cuisine.*

ENLARGED twice since it was built as a croft in the 16th century, Farleyer stands in 34 acres of grounds. Its Bistro offers imaginative Scottish cooking in a relaxed and informal atmosphere. In the semi-formal Glenlyon Room, an à la carte menu reflects the outstanding quality of local game, meat and fish.

Hot Aberfeldy cheese parcel with red onion marmalade, walnut dressing, rocket salad and shaved Parmesan. Grilled wild sea trout served with a saffron mash, red wine jus and beetroot salsa. Parfait nougatine with a raspberry coulis and berry compote.

STB ★★★★ Hotel

◐ *Open all year* ▥ *Rooms: 19 en suite* ⊨ *DB&B £70–£85 B&B £45–£60* ⓢⓟ *Special rates available* ✘ *Food available all day ££ Lunch ££ Dinner ££* Ⓥ *Vegetarians welcome* ✻ *Children welcome* ♿ *Facilities for disabled visitors* ✄ *No smoking in Glenlyon Room* ♞ *Member of the Scotch Beef Club* ⊟ *Credit cards: Mastercard/ Eurocard, American Express, Visa, Diners Club, Switch, Delta* ⓜ *General Manager: Andy Cole*

Aberfeldy Perthshire PH15 2JE
Tel: 01887 820332 Fax: 01887 829430
E-mail: reservations@farleyer.com
Web: www.farleyer.com
Follow signs to the Castle Menzies and Weem on the B846. The hotel is situated 1 mile past the castle on right, approx 2 miles from Aberfeldy. [C5]

ABERFELDY

Guinach House

- *"Relax in the friendly and hospitable atmosphere with true Scottish hospitality and outstanding cooking!"*
- *Best Scottish sophisticated cuisine combining a range of national and international influences.*

GUINACH HOUSE is an ideal location for those who simply wish to relax in tranquil surroundings and indulge in gastronomic inspiration. Proprietors, the MacKays, are attentive and friendly hosts. Bert's culinary expertise allows him to create rich and varied menus, while maximising on fresh local produce. 2 AA Rosettes.

Salad of avocado with strawberries topped with marinated scallops in fresh lime juice and ginger. Noisettes of local venison set on French black pudding with a bramble and port wine sauce. Dark chocolate and Highland park mousse.

STB ★★★★ Hotel

◑ Open all year except Christmas Eve to 27 Dec 🛏 Rooms: 7 en suite 🍴 DB&B £68 B&B £45.50 ✕ Dinner 4 course menu £££ Ⓥ Vegetarians welcome ⚹ Children welcome ⚭ No smoking in dining room and bedrooms 💳 Credit cards: Mastercard/Eurocard, Visa 🍳 Proprietors: Mr & Mrs MacKay

by 'The Birks' Aberfeldy Perthshire PH15 2ET
Tel: 01887 820251 Fax: 01887 829607
On A826, south-west outskirts of Aberfeldy, on road to 'The Birks', Guinach is signposted from Urlar Road. [C5]

ACHARACLE

Dalilea House

- *"A peaceful friendly home where you can be assured of a well cooked meal."*
- *Innovative Scottish cooking.*

DALILEA HOUSE, is set in its own grounds and surrounded by farmland and farm animals. Mairi Macaulay has been gradually refurbishing the fabric of the house. Her cooking is well presented with use of Dalilea's own garden herbs and all produce is carefully sourced locally. Fishing/rowing boats on Loch Shiel are available.

Mussels with lemon and chive flower cream. Braised pheasant with chantrelles and wood sorrel on celeriac mash. Caramelised oranges and brambles with ginger ice cream.

STB ★★ Guest House

◑ Open 1 Mar to 30 Oct 🛏 Rooms: 6, 4 en suite 🍴 DB&B £40–£50 B&B £20–£30 Special rates available ⚐ Restricted hotel licence ✕ Food available all day £ Packed lunches £ Dinner ££ Non residents welcome at evening meals only – reservations necessary Ⓥ Vegetarians welcome – prior notice appreciated ⚹ Children welcome ⚭ No smoking in dining room ⚭ Dogs welcome 💳 Credit cards: Mastercard/Eurocard, Visa, Delta 🍳 Proprietor/Chef: Mairi Macaulay

Dalilea Acharacle Argyll PH36 4JX
Tel: 01967 431253 Fax: 01967 431364
E-mail: stay@dalilea.co.uk
Web: www.dalilea.co.uk
1½ miles off the A861 between Acharacle and Kinlochmondart. From Fort William on A830 towards Mallaig, take A861 at Lochailort or from Glencoe or Oban on the A82 cross the Corran/Ardgour ferry onto A861, through Strontian and Acharacle. [B4]

ACHILTIBUIE

Summer Isles Hotel

- *"Fine dining on exceptional food with elegant service."*
- *Innovative modern Scottish cooking.*

THE HOTEL overlooks the Summer Isles and beyond to the Hebrides. Chef Chris Firth-Bernard creates sumptuous dishes using the finest produce Scotland has to offer creating a unique experience for even the most discerning diner. All this and a wine list of over 400 bins means that everyone who goes there leaves reluctantly, determined to return.

Ravioli verdi stuffed with fresh local crabmeat, with shredded basil. Roast rib of Aberdeen Angus beef with caramelised garlic and roast red onion with a rich red wine sauce. Warm tarte tatin with hazelnut praline ice cream.

STB ★★★★ Hotel

◐ Open Easter to mid Oct ⌸ Rooms: 13, 12 with en suite facilities (plus log cabins adjacent to hotel) ⚑ DB&B £79–£110 B&B £44–£75 ✘ Food available all day £ Lunch £££ Dinner ££££ Ⓥ Vegetarians welcome ☘ Children welcome ⚠ No smoking in restaurant and bedrooms ▣ Credit cards: Mastercard/Eurocard, Visa, Switch ⍟ Proprietors: Mark & Gerry Irvine

Achiltibuie Ross-shire IV26 2YG
Tel: 01854 622282 Fax: 01854 622251
E-mail: summerisleshotel@aol.com
A835 to Ullapool and beyond – 10 miles north of Ullapool turn left onto single track road to Achiltibuie. Village is 15 miles on (i.e. 25 miles from Ullapool). [B3]

AIRDRIE

Bouzy Rouge

- *"Lively and enthusiastic offering good quality Scottish food with attention to detail."*
- *Light modern cuisine.*

BOUZY ROUGE is one of the very best in 'casual gourmet dining'. Ambient, stylish and relaxing, fantastic decor with cuisine to match. It uses the best fresh Scottish produce, skilfully prepared with a flare for the Mediterranean, and wines to appeal to even the most discerning diner. A stunning venue for families.

Carpaccio of Tay salmon, herb salad and aged balsamic. Breast of Perthshire pheasant filled with an apricot mousse with a Puy lentil risotto. Pannacotta with Blairgowrie berries.

◐ Open all year except New Year's Day ✘ Food available all day ££ Lunch £-££ Dinner ££ Ⓥ Vegetarians welcome ☘ Children welcome ♿ Facilities for disabled visitors ▣ Credit cards: Mastercard/Eurocard, American Express, Visa, Diners Club, Switch, Delta ⍟ Proprietors: Alan & Audrey Brown; Managers: Clare & Jocelynne

1 Rochsolloch Road Airdrie ML6 9BB
Tel: 01236 763853 Fax: 01236 770340
E-mail: reservations@bouzy-rouge.com
Web: www.bouzy-rouge.com
At junction of Rochsolloch Road and Deedes Street on A89 Glasgow-Airdrie Road. [C6]

AIRTH, BY FALKIRK

Radisson SAS Airth Castle Hotel

- *"Airth Castle offers the perfect venue for anything from demanding business needs to that special romantic occasion."*
- *Modern Scottish cooking.*

AT AIRTH CASTLE all rooms offer all modern amenities. There are two choices for dining – the Castle Restaurant offers a formal dining experience in elegant surroundings and can also offer private dining for a small party. The Conservatory Restaurant offers a less formal experience but to the same high standard.

Fresh king scallops with a white truffle infused coating on a bed of sautéed spinach and a mild garlic cream. Suprême of Barbary duck with a timbale of red cabbage and fig confit combined with an orange jus. Home-made cranachan.

STB ★★★★ Hotel

◗ Open all year Castle Restaurant closed Sun ⌂ Rooms: 122 en suite (23 in castle) ⌺ DB&B £70–£95 B&B £55–£65 ▣ Special rates available ✖ Food available all day Stables Bar £ Lunch Conservatory Restaurant ££ Dinner Conservatory Restaurant ££ Castle Restaurant ££££ Ⓥ Vegetarians welcome ✶ Children welcome ♿ Facilities for disabled visitors 🐕 Dogs welcome ▣ Credit cards: Mastercard/Eurocard, American Express, Visa, Diners Club, Switch ▣ General Manager: Mr Arco Buijs

*Airth by Falkirk FK2 8JF
Tel: 01324 831411 Fax: 01324 831419
E-mail: arco.buijs@radissonsas.com
Web: www.radissonsas.com
M9, follow signs to Kincardine Bridge. Castle on A905 on left hand side. [C5]*

ALVA

Farriers Country Hotel

- *"Hotel in attractive setting offering good food and a warm welcome."*
- *Good home cooking.*

THE RESTAURANT occupies a tastefully reformed stable block looking onto the cobbled courtyard. The atmosphere is complete with an impressive feature fireplace dividing the restaurant into two intimate dining rooms. The building offers tastefully decorated bedrooms, coffee shop, craft shop and the restaurant, where the finest local produce is served in modern-style.

Hot-smoked Tay salmon on a bed of rocket with a pesto and roasted garlic olive oil. Roast rack of lamb on a celeriac and potato rösti with a caramelised cherry tomato and balsamic essence. Warm chocolate and malt whisky tart served with home-made shortbread ice cream.

STB ★★ Small Hotel

◗ Open all year except Boxing Day ⌂ Rooms: 6 ⌺ DB&B £65–£90 B&B £50–£60 ▣ Special rates available ✖ Food available all day Lunch ££ Dinner £££ Ⓥ Vegetarians welcome ✶ Children welcome ♿ Facilities for disabled visitors 🐕 Dogs welcome ▣ Credit cards: Mastercard, American Express, Visa, Switch, Delta ▣ Chef Proprietor: Gary Turner

*Woodland Park Alva Clacks FK12 5HU
Tel: 01259 762702 Fax: 01259 769782
Web: scoot.co.uk/farriers-country-hotel
From Stirling take A91 through to Alva. As you leave Alva turn left at hotel sign, then drive ½ mile to end of road. [C5]*

ALYTH

'The Oven Bistro' At Drumnacree House

- *"Great food, reasonably priced, in atmospheric surroundings."*
- *Eclectic Scottish cuisine with continental influences.*

ALLAN CULL cooks at Tayside's only wood-burning oven which is located in the bistro. Menus are innovative and the results are really delicious and very succulent. Jenni Milne is professional and attentive front of house. There is an evident commitment to good food and freshness here. The hotel has its own vegetable and herb garden.

Home-cured salmon gravadlax served with dill mayonnaise. Braised lamb shanks slowly cooked in the oven with red wine and onions, served on a bed of chunky vegetables. Hot pear tart served with crème anglaise.

STB ★★★★ Hotel

◐ Open all year except New Year Closed Mon 🏨 Rooms: 6 ⛌ DB&B £60–£85 B&B £40–£65 ⓢⓅ Special rates available ✕ Lunch except Mon £ Dinner except Mon ££ Ⓥ Vegetarians welcome ⚸ Children welcome ♿ Facilities for disabled visitors 🐕 Dogs welcome ❦ Member of the Scotch Beef Club 🆔 Credit cards: Mastercard/Eurocard, American Express, Visa, Switch, Delta 🔑 Owner/Proprietor: Allan Cull

St Ninians Road Alyth Perthshire PH11 8AP
Tel: 01828 633355 Fax: 01828 632194
E-mail: allan.cull@virgin.net
Turn off A926 Blairgowrie-Kirriemuir to Alyth. Take first turning on left after Clydesdale Bank. Hotel 300 yards on right. [D5]

ARDNAMURCHAN

Feorag House

- *"Be spoiled in this beautiful home where Peter and Helen are both enthusiastic cooks."*
- *Skilful home cooking.*

FEORAG HOUSE, designed and built by Peter and Helen Stockdale themselves, is on the North shore of Loch Sunart. Stunning views are enjoyed from the dining rooms and bedrooms. Food is delicious and is cooked on Peter and Helen's Aga. Watch wildlife whilst enjoying a special afternoon tea from the sitting-room balcony.

Stuffed roast quail with apricot dressing. Fillet of baby sole with prawn and cream cheese filling on a bed of creamed potatoes and rich white wine sauce, served with selected seasonal vegetables. Poached nectarines under whipped cream and brûlée top.

STB ★★★★★ Guest House

◐ Open all year 🏨 Rooms: 3 en suite ⛌ DB&B £55–£65 B&B £35–£45 ⓢⓅ Special rates available ⓤⓛ Unlicensed – guests welcome to take own wine ✕ Dinner ££ Residents only Ⓥ Vegetarians welcome – by arrangement ⚸ Children over 10 years welcome ⚭ No smoking in dining room and bedrooms 🆔 Credit cards: Mastercard/Eurocard, Visa 🔑 Proprietors: Peter & Helen Stockdale

Glenborrodale Acharacle, Argyll PH36 4JP
Tel: 01972 500248 Fax: 01972 500285
E-mail: admin@feorag.demon.co.uk
Web: www.feorag.demon.co.uk
36 miles or 1 hour's drive from Corran Ferry. Take A861 then B8007 to Glenborrodale. 200 yards beyond school on left. [B5]

ARDNAMURCHAN

Water's Edge

- *"A secluded spot for two where your every comfort is catered for."*
- *Homely Scottish cooking.*

WATER'S EDGE has a very comfortable room for two, overlooking the water, where you may even take dinner if you wish. Alternatively, dinner is served in a traditionally furnished dining room. Rob and Joan serve good, homely Scottish cooking making best use of their own garden herbs. Good hospitality in wonderful surroundings.

Leek, pear and watercress soup with home-made wholemeal bread. Prime rump steak cooked in Guinness with orange, Orkney clapshot, broccoli with almonds. Fresh applemint mousse with home-made shortbread.

STB ★★★★ B&B

◐ Open from mid Feb to mid Nov ⌂ Rooms: 1 en suite ⌨ DB&B £46–£51 ⓤ Unlicensed – guest welcome to take own wine ££ Ⓥ Vegetarians welcome ✂ No smoking throughout ✦ Dogs welcome by arrangement 🆔: No credit cards ⛳ Proprietors: Rob & Joan Thompson

Kilchoan Ardnamurchan Argyll PH36 4LL
Tel: 01972 510261
E-mail: rob@ardnamurchan75.co.uk
Web: www.ardnamurchan.com/watersedge
From Corran Ferry (8 miles south of Fort William) take A861 to Salen, then B8007 to Kilchoan. In village, pass school on left, follow road round bay to ferry stores: take cul-de-sac straight ahead. Water's Edge is bungalow with flagpole. [B5]

ARISAIG

Old Library Lodge & Restaurant

- *"Very good food and a high degree of comfort – a 'must do' on the Road to the Isles'."*
- *Good, fresh food, seafood a speciality.*

THE OLD LIBRARY LODGE and Restaurant enjoys an attractive situation on the waterfront in Arisaig. Guests may choose from an à la carte menu with a choice of five of everything – starters, main courses and puddings. Alan does most of the cooking, and everything possible is sourced locally. Breakfast is something to really look forward to.

Pan-fried cous cous coated goats cheese. Grilled local scallops on a celeriac purée. Caramelised lemon tart with home-made elderflower ice cream.

STB ★★★ Restaurant with Rooms

◐ Open 24 Mar to end Oct Closed Tue lunch ⌂ Rooms: 6 en suite ⌨ DB&B from £60 B&B from £38 ⓢⓟ Special rates available ⚑ Refreshment licence ✗ Lunch except Tue £-££ Dinner £££ Ⓥ Vegetarians welcome – prior notice required 🆔 Credit cards: Mastercard/ Eurocard, American Express, Visa, Switch, Delta ⛳ Proprietors: Alan & Angela Broadhurst

Arisaig Inverness-shire PH39 4NH
Tel: 01687 450651 Fax: 01687 450219
E-mail: reception@oldlibrary.co.uk
Web: www.oldlibrary.co.uk
In centre of village on waterfront, next to Post Office. [B4]

AUCHENCAIRN

Balcary Bay Hotel

- *"Experience seriously good food whilst enjoying the views at Balcary Bay."*
- *Modern Scottish cooking.*

AT BALCARY BAY enjoy lunch in the delightful conservatory overlooking the bay or take afternoon tea in the drawing room. Dinners are special and formal with menus carefully created by Chef Graham Oxley. The expectations which arise from the hotel's magnificent setting are more than met by the excellent standards set within.

Seared pavé of foie gras with a balsamic jus and spiced fig chutney. Peppered escalope of venison and roast strawberries, with a bitter chocolate glaze, crisp leeks and fondant potato. Warm mulberry soufflé with a cinnamon fool and raspberry compote.

STB ★★★★ Hotel

☽ Open Mar to end Nov ☷ Rooms: 20 en suite ⚭ DB&B £54–£80 B&B £54–£61 ⓈⓅ Special rates available ✗ Lunch Sun – booking advisable £: Lunch Mon to Sat – by prior reservation only ££ Bar Lunches daily Dinner £££ Ⓥ Vegetarians welcome ⚘ Children welcome ♿ Facilities for disabled visitors ⚘ Smoking discouraged in dining areas 🆎 Credit cards: Mastercard/ Eurocard, American Express, Visa, Switch, Delta ⚑ Proprietors: The Lamb Family

Auchencairn nr Castle Douglas Dumfries & Galloway DG7 1QZ
Tel: 01556 640217 Fax: 01556 640272
E-mail: reservations@balcary-bay-hotel.co.uk
Web: www.balcary-bay-hotel.co.uk
A711 Dalbeattie-Kirkcudbright to Auchencairn. Then take 'no through road' signposted Balcary (single track) for 2 miles. [C7]

AUCHTERARDER

Auchterarder House: Winner 2000 – Country House

- *"One of Scotland's finest country house hotels where culinary skills and hospitality are second to none."*
- *Outstanding country house cooking with modern influences.*

AUCHTERARDER HOUSE is set in 17 acres of beautifully maintained grounds which include herb gardens, of which some of the produce can be found in the magnificent dining room. Menus are created by chef Willie Deans using only the finest Scottish produce, prepared with great skill and imagination. Service is warm and friendly without being intrusive.

Pressed terrine of ham hough and foie gras, with parsley juices, raisin vinaigrette and pressed girolles. Braised turbot, lime leaves, crisp fried salmon sausage, fricassee of peas, cardamom creamed leeks. Quartet of lemon – chef's surprise.

STB ★★★★ Hotel

☽ Open all year ☷ Rooms: 15 en suite ⚭ B&B £90–£200 ⓈⓅ Special rates available ✗ Food available all day £ Lunch ££ Dinner ££££ Ⓥ Vegetarians welcome ⚘ No smoking in dining room ⚘ Member of the Scotch Beef Club 🆎 Credit cards: Mastercard/ Eurocard, American Express, Visa, Diners Club, Switch, Delta ⚑ Owned by The Wrens Hotel Group

Auchterarder Perthshire PH3 1DZ
Tel: 01764 663646 Fax: 01764 662939
E-mail: auchterarder@wrensgroup.com
Web: www.wrensgroup.com
B8062 from Auchterarder to Crieff. Hotel is 1 mile from village. [C5]

AUCHTERARDER

Denfield House

- *"Excellent cooking, charming hosts and every comfort thought of."*
- *Creative modern Scottish.*

DENFIELD HOUSE is a charming house set in the most beautiful part of Perthshire. Owner, Ailsa Reynolds is a skilled and committed cook and the meals are highly accomplished with interesting and innovative menus. On arrival guests are offered afternoon tea with home baking, cakes and biscuits. A delightful, relaxing and very hospitable place.

Thai-style timbale of Arbroath crab, served on a cucumber plate with tomato and cucumber salsa. Hickory smoked gigot of Tombuie lamb with beetroot marmalade, baked baby vegetables and new potatoes. Roasted apricots with praline semi fredo.

◐ Open 2 Jan to 21 Mar and 24 Apr to 23 Dec Closed Christmas Day and Boxing Day ⌂ Rooms 5, 2 en suite ⇌ DB&B £60 B&B £35 ⓢⓟ Special rates available ⓤ Unlicensed ✗ Picnic hampers on request £ Dinner £££ Ⓥ Vegetarians welcome – by prior arrangement ✷ Children welcome ⌿ No smoking in the dining room ⌇ Dogs welcome ⊞ Credit cards: Mastercard, Visa, Delta ⊠ Owners: Ailsa & Jamie Reynolds

Trinity Gask Auchterarder Perthshire PH3 1LH
Tel: 01764 683474 Fax: 01764 683776
E-mail: ailsa@denfieldhouse.com
Web: www.denfieldhouse.com
Take B8062 from Auchterarder towards Crieff. Take a right turn immediately after Kinkell Bridge. Denfield House approx 1½ miles on left. [C5]

AUCHTERARDER

The Dormy Clubhouse

- *"This '19th hole' offers hearty traditional Scottish fare with views onto the famous Gleneagles King's and Queen's courses."*
- *Excellent hearty Scottish.*

DORMY has an attractive bar-style of service, excellently trained staffed in refined surroundings with top notch bar food. Menus offer honest, traditional and enticing fare. Runner-up (Category 2) in The Taste of Scotland Scotch Lamb Challenge Competition 1999. Runner-up (Category 1) in The Taste of Scotland Scotch Lamb Challenge Competition 2000.

Black pudding fritter with apple chutney. Roast chicken and sage stuffing. Apple and cinnamon crumble.

◐ Open all year Closed Oct 17 to Mar 15 (dinner) Closed Christmas Day (dinner) and New Year's Eve (dinner) Open 7 days a week all day (summer) ✗ Food available all day ££ Lunch ££ Dinner ££ Ⓥ Vegetarians welcome ✷ Children welcome ♿ Facilities for disabled visitors ⚉ Member of the Scotch Beef Club ⊞ Credit cards: Mastercard/Eurocard, American Express, Visa, Diners Club, Switch, Delta ⊠ Restaurant Manager: Karen Sharp

Gleneagles Hotel Auchterarder PH3 1NF
Tel: 01764 662231 (ext 4359)
Web: www.gleneagles.com/
By Auchterarder follow the signs to Gleneagles and the Dormy Clubhouse is on your left on the main driveway to the hotel. [C5]

AUCHTERHOUSE

Old Mansion House

- *"A most welcome return to Taste of Scotland."*
- *Modern Scottish cooking.*

THIRTEENTH Century castle converted to a 16th Century baronial mansion. The public rooms and bedrooms are comfortable and elegant. The cooking is skilled and menus are varied and interesting and the service is equally attentive but not intrusive in this unique, well-run establishment. 2 AA Rosettes.

Timbale of Loch Fyne crab and crayfish, with a seared fillet of john dory; lemon and basil dressing. Fillet of Aberdeen Angus beef, set on rösti potato, glazed with scallop and coriander mousse, served with a ragoût of woodland mushrooms. Iced Drambuie and oatmeal parfait.

STB ★★★★ Hotel

◐ *Open all year* ⌂ *Rooms: 8, 6 en suite plus lodge house* ⌯ *DB&B £80 B&B £55–£65* ⓢⓅ *Special rates available* ✘ *Lunch ££ Dinner £££* Ⓥ *Vegetarians welcome* ✼ *Children welcome* ⓐ *Facilities for disabled visitors* ⌫ *No smoking in the dining room* ⌦ *Dogs – by arrangement* ⓒ *Credit cards: Mastercard/ Eurocard, American Express, Visa, Diners club, Switch, Delta* Ⓝ *Proprietors: Jannick & Maxine Bertschy*

*Auchterhouse By Dundee Angus DD3 0QN
Tel: 01382 320366 Fax: 01382 320400
E-mail: oldmansionhouse@netscapeonline.co.uk
Web: www.visitscotland.com/oldmansionhouse
North-west of Dundee – 5 miles from Kingsway, take the A923 Coupar Angus road off the Kingsway, through Birkhill village and join the B954 road. Hotel situated 2 miles on left. [D5]*

AVIEMORE

Corrour House Hotel

- *"It is always a delight to return to Corrour. The food, hospitality and Sheana's delicious pastry are all exceedingly good."*
- *Imaginative country house cooking.*

THIS IS a charming family-run hotel which offers true Highland hospitality from accomplished hosts, David and Sheana Catto. This elegant house stands in four acres of garden and woodland and enjoys fine views of the Cairngorm Mountains. The cooking is excellent making best use of local produce whatever the meal.

Shetland Isles crab tart. Breast of wild duck with a red wine, raspberry and garden herb sauce. Banana, coconut and heather honey cheesecake.

STB ★★★★ Small Hotel

◐ *Open 27 Dec to 31 Oct* ⌂ *Rooms: 8 en suite* ⌯ *DB&B £65 B&B £40* ⓈⓅ *Winter rates available* ✘ *Dinner 4 course menu ££* Ⓥ *Vegetarians welcome* ✼ *Children welcome* ⌫ *No smoking in dining room and some bedrooms* ⓜ *Member of the Scotch Beef Club* ⓒ *Credit cards: Mastercard/Eurocard, Visa* Ⓝ *Proprietors: Mr & Mrs Catto*

*Rothiemurchus, by Aviemore PH22 1QH
Tel: 01479 810220 Fax: 01479 811500
Web: www.corrourhouse.co.uk
Rothiemurchus is a ½ mile from Aviemore, on road to Glenmore and Cairngorms. [C4]*

AVIEMORE

Lynwilg House: Finalist The Macallan Taste of Scotland Awards 2000

- *"One of the best guest houses in the land with excellent food and home comforts."*
- *Traditional Scottish cooking.*

MARJORIE CLEARY presents a set menu at Lynwilg each evening; her inventiveness and flair in the kitchen mean that every meal is special. There is an obvious dedication to Scottish produce, home produce and cooking in general at Lynwilg. Winner The Macallan Taste of Scotland Special Merit Award Outstanding Hospitality 1994.

Lynwilg ceps filled with chicken mousse with a tarragon sauce. Sole and salmon parcel with a vermouth and chive sauce, home-grown asparagus, dill hollandaise and saffron potatoes. Passion fruit and mango mousse with a mango and lime coulis.

STB ★★★★ Guest House

◐ Open New Year to 31 Oct 🏨 Rooms: 3 en suite 🛏 DB&B £48–£58 B&B £28–£35 🆂 Special rates available 🆄 Unlicensed – guests welcome to take own wine ✘ Dinner 4 course menu ££–£££ Residents only Ⓥ Vegetarians welcome ☧ Children welcome ✗ No smoking in restaurant 💳 Credit cards: Mastercard/Eurocard, Visa 🅝 Proprietors/Owners: Alan & Marjory Cleary

Lynwilg, By Aviemore PH22 1PZ
Tel: 01479 811685 Fax: 01479 811685
E-mail: marge@lynwilg.co.uk
Web: http://www.lynwilg.co.uk
A9 Perth-Inverness, take Lynwilg road, 1 mile south of Aviemore. [C4]

AVIEMORE

The Old Bridge Inn

- *"Good food in a friendly relaxed atmosphere ensures new owners uphold Old Bridge traditions."*
- *Hearty pub food.*

THE OLD BRIDGE INN offers pub food as it should be – freshly prepared and cooked. Innkeeper Iain MacRury and chef Norma Hutton concentrate on fresh local produce for their extensive and imaginative menu. There is a special children's menu. In the evenings, the menu is based on food cooked on a large chargrill.

Salad of mixed seafood with horseradish and dill sauce. Medallions of Rothiemurchus venison with glazed shallots, juniper and red wine sauce. Ecclefechan tart with fresh Highland cream.

◐ Open all year ✘ Lunch £ Dinner ££ Ⓥ Vegetarians welcome ☧ Children welcome ♿ Facilities for disabled visitors 💳 Credit cards: Mastercard/Eurocard, Visa 🅝 Owners: Dr William J Cox & Robin Playfair

23 Dalfaber Road, Aviemore PH22 1PU
Tel: 01479 811137 Fax: 01479 811372
At south end of Aviemore, take B970 ski road (Cairngorms) for 300 yards then take turning on left for another 300 yards. [C4]

AYR

The Eisenhower Apartment, Culzean Castle, National Trust for Scotland

- *"An utterly unique place – majestic surroundings and superb food."*
- *Traditional Scottish.*

TO STAY in the Apartment is a very special experience. The apartments are located on the top floor of the castle and lead off the astoundingly beautiful oval staircase/balcony. The rooms are extremely spacious and have fantastic views. Guests are encouraged to mingle and meet, and afternoon tea is served with astonishing antique silver-service.

Seared fresh and smoked salmon topped with crème fraîche on a tartare potato pancake. Roast fillet of Scottish beef with a green peppercorn and whisky sauce served with fresh seasonal vegetables. Poached pears with a fresh raspberry sauce.

◐ Open Apr to Oct ⌂ Rooms: 6 (5 en suite, 1 with private bathroom) ⊠ B&B £140–£265 (incl tea) ⓢⓟ Special rates available for group booking of whole apartment ⚱ licensed – complimentary drinks cupboard ✘ Non-resident dinner parties – by prior notice Dinner ££££ ✸ Children welcome (prior notice for under 10 years) ♿ Facilities for disabled visitors ⌇ No smoking in dining room and bedrooms ▣ Credit cards: Mastercard/Eurocard, American Express, Visa ⓝ Administrator: Jonathan Cardale

Culzean Castle Maybole Ayrshire KA19 8LE
Tel: 01655 884455 Fax: 01655 884503
E-mail: culzean@nts.org.uk
Web: www.aboutscotland.com
www.nts.org.ukCulzean
Take A77 to Stranraer then A719 – Maybole to Culzean (signposted). [C6]

AYR

Fouters Bistro

- *"If you are in Ayr don't miss the opportunity to sample the friendly atmosphere and superb cooking at this gem of a bistro."*
- *Modern Scottish cooking.*

THIS YEAR Fouters has an up-to-date new look. A bustling, friendly atmosphere makes one feel like a 'regular'. Laurie's food is modelled on the best of French ethics of simplicity married to the very best ingredients. With skilful cooking and the best ingredients from around Scotland, no wonder Fouters has 2 AA Rosettes.

Ayrshire game terrine. Seared scallops with a sweet chilli sauce. Iced Drambuie parfait.

◐ Open all year except 25 to 27 Dec and 1 to 3 Jan Closed Sun ✘ Lunch except Sun £ Dinner except Sun £££ Ⓥ Vegetarians welcome Special diets catered for ✸ Children welcome ♛ Member of the Scotch Beef Club ▣ Credit cards: Mastercard/Eurocard, American Express, Visa, Diners Club, Switch, Solo ⓝ Owners: Laurie & Fran Black

2A Academy Street Ayr KA7 1HS
Tel: 01292 261391 Fax: 01292 619323
E-mail: qualityfood@fouters.co.uk
Web: www.fouters.co.uk
Town centre, opposite Town Hall. [C6]

AYR

Visitor Centre Restaurant, Culzean Castle & Country Park, National Trust for Scotland

- *"An excellent visitor experience in stunning surroundings."*
- *Traditional Scottish.*

THE VISITOR CENTRE RESTAURANT, Culzean Castle & Country Park is set in the most perfect location and is well worth seeing. A National Trust establishment, its grounds and property are maintained to an exceptionally high standard. The restaurant serves Scottish home cooking, baking and light refreshments, all prepared on site and to a high standard.

Dunsyre pâté served with oatcakes and seasonal leaves. Glazed fillet of venison with blackcurrant and cranberry jus. Culzean Garden fresh raspberry cheesecake with clotted cream.

STB Highly Commended

☽ *Open 1 Apr to 31 Oct* ♟ *Licensed* ✘ *Food available all day* £ *Lunch* £ Ⓥ *Vegetarians welcome* ✹ *Children welcome* ♿ *Facilities for disabled visitors* ✂ *No smoking throughout* ✱ *Dogs welcome in grounds only* 🏦 *Credit cards: Mastercard, Visa, Switch* 🅝 *Catering Manager: Bill Hudson*

Maybole Ayrshire KA19 8LE
Tel: 01655 884502 Fax: 01655 884521
Web: www.nts.org.uk
12 miles south of Ayr on the A719, 4 miles west of Maybole on A77. [C6]

BALLANTRAE

Cosses Country House: Winner 2000 – Small Residence

- *"Cosses remains a firm favourite with repeat visitors – a sure sign of a very special place!"*
- *Gourmet country house cooking.*

AT COSSES they grow their own vegetables, herbs and some fruit. Susan who is a Cordon Bleu Chef creates menus that are unique and moreover quite delicious. Flavours are nurtured and treated with great respect. All breads, rolls even teacakes are home-made as are preserves and yoghurt. Cosses is a treasury of good food.

Mini Tobermory cheddar soufflés. Ballantrae lobster with garden herb mayonnaise, strawberry and cucumber salad, Cosses new potatoes and vegetable salad. Home-grown blackcurrant crème Brûlée.

☽ *Open Feb to Nov* 🏨 *Rooms: 3 en suite* ⚭ *DB&B £57–£80 B&B £32–£48* 🆂 *Special rates available* ✘ *Dinner £££ Dinner for non-residents – by reservation only* Ⓥ *Vegetarians welcome* ✹ *Children welcome* ✂ *No smoking in dining room* 🏦 *Credit cards: Mastercard, Visa* 🅝 *Proprietors: Susan & Robin Crosthwaite*

Cosses Ballantrae Ayrshire KA26 OLR
Tel: 01465 831363 Fax: 01465 831598
E-mail: cosses@compuserve.com
From A77 at southern end of Ballantrae, take inland road at Caravan sign. Cosses is c. 2 miles on right. [B6]

BALLATER ROYAL DEESIDE

Balgonie Country House Hotel

- *"A memorable visit offering first class cuisine, hospitality and scenery."*
- *Traditional and innovative recipes using fresh local produce.*

BALGONIE's proprietors, John and Priscilla Finnie, pride themselves on maintaining a friendly but unobtrusive service. The dining room is the heart of Balgonie providing excellent cuisine using locally sourced fish and game. When in season, herbs and soft fruits from the garden are always found on the menu. 2 AA Rosettes.

Black pudding topped with Orkney scallops, finished with red onion vinaigrette. Rack of spring lamb with wild mushrooms and asparagus, served with a thyme-scented jus. Madeira crème brûlée with Bramley Apple compote.

STB ★★★★ Hotel

◐ Open 12 Feb to 5 Jan ⌂ Rooms: 9 en suite ⋈ DB&B £85–£95 B&B £55–£70 ▣ Special rates available ✕ Lunch – by reservation only ££ Dinner 4 course menu – non-residents by reservation £££ Ⓥ Vegetarians welcome – prior notice required ⚹ Children over 5 years welcome at dinner ⌀ No smoking in dining room ▣ Credit cards: Mastercard/Eurocard, American Express, Visa, Switch, Delta ⚐ Proprietor: John G Finnie

Braemar Place Ballater AB35 5NQ
Tel: 013397 55482 Fax: 013397 55482
Off A93 Aberdeen-Perth, on outskirts of village of Ballater. [D4]

BALLATER ROYAL DEESIDE

Darroch Learg Hotel

- *"Excellent food, fabulous views and a high degree of comfort make Darroch Learg a very special place."*
- *Modern Scottish cooking.*

THE HOTEL sits high up on a rocky hillside, with excellent views. The dining room and spacious conservatory allow diners to enjoy the wonderful outlook of the hills of Glen Muick. The short table d'hôte menu offers top quality local meat, confidently and expertly prepared in unusual combinations and sauces. 3 AA Rosettes.

Ravioli of foie gras and Parma ham, with onion jam, crispy potatoes and a Parmesan cream. Loin of lamb with a tian of summer vegetables, roast lamb kidney and rosemary sauce. Iced vanilla parfait with langues du chat and spiced red wine pear.

STB ★★★★ Hotel

◐ *Open Feb to Dec closed Christmas* ⌂ *Rooms: 18 en suite* ⋈ *DB&B £56–£82 B&B £37.50–£57.50* ✕ *Food available all day £££ Lunch £££ Dinner ££££* Ⓥ *Vegetarians welcome – prior notice required* ⚹ *Children welcome* ♿ *Facilities for disabled visitors – ground floor* ⌀ *No smoking in dining room* ♞ *Member of the Scotch Beef Club* ▣ *Credit cards: Mastercard/Eurocard, American Express, Visa, Diners Club, Switch* ⚐ *Proprietors: Nigel & Fiona Franks*

Braemar Road Ballater Aberdeenshire AB35 5UX
Tel: 013397 55443 Fax: 013397 55252
E-mail: nigel@darroch-learg.demon.co.uk
Web: www.royal-deeside.org.uk/darroch.htm
½ mile from centre of village of Ballater, off A93. [D4]

BALLATER ROYAL DEESIDE

Deeside Hotel

- *"This hotel lives up to its reputation – good food, served well."*
- *Traditional Scottish cooking with modern twist.*

THE DEESIDE is a family-run establishment. In the evening, meals are available in both the restaurant and bar where you can also sample a good selection of Scottish real ales and malt whiskies. The dining room has had a spacious sunny conservatory added recently extending the appeal of this well-run hotel.

Creamy seafood and dill chowder. Roast rack of lamb with a herb and pepper crust. Clootie dumpling.

STB ★★★ Hotel

◐ Open 10 Feb to 2 Jan except Christmas Day and Boxing Day 🏠 Rooms: 9 en suite 🛏 DB&B £37.50–41.50 B&B £22–£26 ⓢ Special rates available ✗ Dinner ££ Ⓥ Vegetarians welcome ✤ Children welcome ♿ Facilities for disabled visitors ⌦ No smoking in restaurant 💳 Credit cards: Mastercard/Eurocard, Visa, Switch 🔑 Directors: Donald & Alison Brooker

Braemar Road Ballater AB35 5RQ
Tel: 013397 55420 Fax: 013397 55357
E-mail: deesidehotel@talk21.com
Web: www.royal-deeside.org.uk/deeside.htm
On west side of Ballater, set back from A93 Braemar road. [D4]

BALLATER ROYAL DEESIDE

Glen Lui Hotel

- *"Good food and a warm welcome."*
- *Modern Scottish cooking, with distinct French influences.*

AT THE Glen Lui, service is friendly and menus are well-presented and varied. The wrap-around conservatory/restaurant offers an extensive à la carte menu with a distinct French influence. There is a comprehensive wine list. Glen Lui has 1 AA Rosette and is a member of the Certified Aberdeen Angus Scheme. Investor in People Award.

Isle of Gigha goats cheese wrapped in Parma ham, baked and set on salad leaves. Roasted local venison saddle topped with black pudding parfait on a garlic croûton finished with a red wine jus. Scottish bramble frangipane tart with crème fraîche.

STB ★★★★ Hotel
Green Tourism Three Leaf Gold Award

◐ Open all year 🏠 Rooms: 19 en suite 🛏 DB&B £46–£62 B&B £30–£46 ⓢ Special rates available ✗ Lunch £Dinner £–££ Ⓥ Vegetarians welcome ✤ Children welcome ♿ Facilities for disabled visitors ⌦ No smoking in restaurant and bedrooms 🦢 Member of the Scotch Beef Club 💳 Credit cards: Mastercard/Eurocard, American Express, Visa, Switch, Delta 🔑 Proprietors: Serge & Lorraine Geraud

Invercauld Road Ballater Aberdeenshire
AB35 5RP
Tel: 013397 55402 Fax: 013397 55545
E-mail: infos@glen-lui-hotel.co.uk
Web: www.glen-lui-hotel.co.uk
Off A93 at western end of Ballater at end of Invercauld Road. [D4]

BALLATER ROYAL DEESIDE

The Green Inn Restaurant With Rooms

- *"A truly gastronomic experience!"*
- *Modern regional Scottish cooking, with good use of international influences.*

JEFF PURVES' cooking is innovative and imaginative, and he applies this to the excellent local produce available on Deeside and combining flavours with assured confidence. Jeff uses cream only when necessary, replacing sugar with honey. 2 AA Rosettes. Winner of The Macallan Taste of Scotland Restaurant of the Year Award 1995.

Assiette of wild salmon. Grilled fillet of beef topped with a Strathdon Blue cheese soufflé and shallot juslie. Warm chocolate and banana bread pudding with white chocolate ice cream.

STB ★★★★ Restaurant with Rooms

◐ Open all year except 2 weeks Oct, Christmas Day and 26 to 28 Dec Closed Sun Oct to Mar ⌂ Rooms: 3 en suite ⌂ DB&B £54.50–£59.50 ⓢⓟ Special rates available ✘ Dinner £££ Ⓥ Vegetarians welcome ⚹ Children welcome ⌂ Disabled access only ✿ Smoking permitted at coffee stage only ⚘ Member of the Scotch Beef Club ⌂ Credit cards: Mastercard/Eurocard, American Express, Visa, Diners Club, Switch ⚘ Proprietors: J J & C A Purves

9 Victoria Road Ballater AB35 5QQ
Tel: 013397 55701 Fax: 013397 55701
In centre of Ballater on village green. [D4]

BALLATER ROYAL DEESIDE

Hilton Craigendarroch Hotel & Country Club

- *"Craigendarroch offers the complete package of food, sport and leisure facilities."*
- *Modern grand hotel with fine dining and bistro cooking.*

BUILT in the 19th century for the Keiller family the hotel now caters for a wider audience and has facilities to match. The Oaks is a classy formal restaurant serving interesting and imaginative dishes prepared by executive chef, Paul Moran. There is also the Clubhouse Restaurant for bistro style dining.

Home-cured salmon fillet in grapefruit and Pernod, with curly endive and salmon egg dressing. Venison loin wrapped in Parma ham, morel mousse, red onion compote and port wine sauce. Tart of dark chocolate, espresso ice cream and raspberry coulis.

STB ★★★★ Hotel

◐ Open all year ⌂ Rooms: 45 en suite ⌂ DB&B £39–£89 B&B £29–£65 ⓢⓟ Special rates available ✘ Lunch (Clubhouse Restaurant) £–££ Dinner (Clubhouse Restaurant) from ££–£££ Dinner (The Oaks) from ££–£££ Ⓥ Vegetarians welcome ⚹ Children welcome ✿ No smoking in The Oaks ⌂ Credit cards: Mastercard/Eurocard, American Express, Visa, Diners Club, Switch, Delta ⚘ General Manager: Andrew Murphie

Braemar Road Ballater Aberdeenshire AB35 5XA
Tel: 013397 55858 Fax: 013397 55447
E-mail: general.manager@craigendarroch.stakis.co.uk
Web: www.hilton.com
On A93 western end of Ballater, near Balmoral. [D4]

BALLATER ROYAL DEESIDE

Loch Kinord Hotel

- *"Good food and a warm welcome in this traditional village hotel."*
- *Innovative Scottish cooking.*

NEW OWNERS, Andrew and Jenny Cox, have refurbished this Victorian hotel and restaurant creating a new, friendly atmosphere. There is formal dining in the restaurant; wholesome yet fairly sophisticated bar food; or an alternative pub atmosphere in the Holly Tree. The owners are an enthusiastic and knowledgeable couple.

Savoury profiteroles stuffed with North Sea prawns and crab meat with a lime dressing. Collops of fillet steak coated in oatmeal and sauteed with onions and tomatoes in brandy, finished with cream. 'Glean Talisker' – dried fruit soaked in whisky and mixed with whipped cream.

STB ★★★ Hotel

◐ Open all year ⌂ Rooms: 15, 9 en suite ⇌ DB&B £35–£50 B&B £20–£35 ✘ Lunch ££ Dinner ££ Ⓥ Vegetarians welcome ⚹ Children welcome ♿ Facilities for disabled visitors ⌇ No smoking in dining room ⌇ Dogs welcome by arrangement only ⊞ Credit cards: Mastercard/Eurocard, American Express, Visa, Switch, Delta ⌇ Partners: Andrew & Jenny Cox

Ballater Road Dinnet by Ballater Royal Deeside Aberdeenshire AB34 5JY
Tel: 013398 85229 Fax: 013398 87007
E-mail: info@loch-kinord-hotel.com
Web: www.loch-kinord-hotel.com
On main A93 Aberdeen to Braemar road situated midway between village of Aboyne (5 miles) and from Ballater (5 miles). Hotel is on the right heading towards Ballater from Aboyne. [D4]

BALLATER ROYAL DEESIDE

Ravenswood Hotel

- *"A Victorian villa where the owners place great store on traditional, welcoming hospitality."*
- *Traditional Scottish hotel cooking.*

RAVENSWOOD HOTEL is a splendid period building retaining many of its original features. The Fyfes offer simple good food; local produce well-cooked. Family-service meals are offered in the dining room, with fireplace, while the lounge bar offers a selection of alternative dishes. A lovely place to explore Royal Deeside from.

Cream of tomato soup with basil. Pan-fried Ayrshire pork fillet with a cider and apple sauce set on a bed of local spinach. Fresh fruit filled brandy snap cones with a raspberry coulis.

STB ★★★ Hotel
Green Tourism One Leaf Bronze Award

◐ Open all year except 10 Nov to 5 Dec ⌂ Rooms: 7, 5 en suite ⇌ DB&B £32.50–£47.50 B&B £20–£35 ⓢ Special rates available ✘ Dinner ££ Ⓥ Vegetarians welcome ⚹ Children welcome ⌇ No smoking in dining room ⊞ Credit cards: Mastercard/Eurocard, American Express, Visa ⌇ Owners: Scott & Cathy Fyfe

Braemar Road Ballater Aberdeenshire AB35 5RQ
Tel: 013397 55539 Fax: 013397 55539
Web: www.royal.deeside.org.uk
On the A93, western end of Ballater – a 10 minute walk from centre of village. [D4]

BALLOCH

Sheildaig Farm

- *"Enjoy Sheildaig – from delightful courtyard bedrooms to a thoughtfully prepared dinner."*
- *Modern Scottish fare.*

SHEILDAIG is not a working farm. It has been stylishly converted with a courtyard leading to the bedrooms. Everything is cooked by Lesley – a skilled and accomplished cook – and guests are asked to order in advance where possible, if not every effort will be made to accommodate late booking requirements.

Wild mushroom and herb cheese parcel. Fillet of Scottish salmon with a honey, mustard and orange glaze. Baked peaches with cinnamon and crunchie cream.

STB ★★★★ B&B

☾ open all year ♨ Rooms: 3 en suite ⇌ DB&B £40–£50 B&B £25–£35 ☒ special rates available ✗ Residents only Lunch by arrangement £ Dinner ££ Ⓥ Vegetarians welcome ★ Children welcome ♿ Facilities for disabled visitors ⌇ No smoking in dining room ⊟ Credit cards: Mastercard/Eurocard, Visa, Switch ⓝ Owner: Lesley McLellan

Upper Stoneymollen Road Balloch Alexandria G83 8QY
Tel: 01389 752459 Fax: 01389 753695
E-mail: sheildaig@talk21.com
Web: www.scotland2000.com/sheildaig or www.aboutscotland.com/central/sheildaig.htm
Driving north on the A82, take the first exit on the Balloch A82-A811 roundabout and proceed for approximately ½ mile – following the farmhouse B&B signs to Sheildaig farm. [C5]

BALQUHIDDER

Monachyle Mhor: Finalist The Macallan Taste of Scotland Awards 2000

- *"Straight from a fairy tale: past Rob Roy's grave, along the lochside to this rose-washed country home set amidst farmland where fine food awaits you!"*
- *Modern Scottish cooking.*

THE LEWIS' fully deserve their reputation for hospitality and comfort. Both the restaurant and cosy bar serve imaginative, good food offering game from the estate, fish from the West Coast and the finest Scottish meat cooked with a French influence by Chef Tom. Interesting, discerning wine list. 2 AA Rosettes.

Mallaig scallops with smoked cod wild rice kedgeree. Pan-fried breast of Monachyle grouse and loin of rabbit, served with cabbage, bacon, pinhead oatmeal, Balquhidder chanterelles and a sage and game jus. Duo of Amaretto and dark chocolate mousse pots with soured cream.

STB ★★★ Hotel

☾ Open all year ♨ Rooms: 10 en suite ⇌ B&B £32.50–£45 ✗ Food available all day £-£££ Lunch ££ Dinner £££ Ⓥ Vegetarians welcome ⌇ No smoking in restaurant ⚘ Member of the Scotch Beef Club ⊟ Credit cards: Mastercard/ Eurocard, Visa, Switch ⓝ Proprietors: Jean Lewis & Tom Lewis

Balquhidder Lochearnhead Perthshire
FK19 8PQ Tel: 01877 384 622
Fax: 01877 384 305
E-mail: info@monachylemhor.com
Web: www.monachylemhor.com
11 miles north of Callander on A84. Turn right at Kingshouse Hotel – 6 miles straight along glen road. [C5]

BANAVIE

Glen Loy Lodge Hotel

- *"Enjoy this interesting home and the wonderful home baking."*
- *Quality local produce.*

GLEN LOY LODGE HOTEL, originally built in the 1920s, has been refurbished into a charming country house hotel furnished to recreate the elegance of the era. The cooking adds innovative modern twists to traditional items, from dinner menus to interesting choices for breakfast. Meals are complemented by a well chosen and unusual wine list.

Trio of monkfish, salmon and scallops with a watercress cream sauce. Rack of Lochaber lamb with a fresh mint crust, served with a raspberry and rosemary sauce and potato, leek and Crowdie mash. Lemon tart.

STB ★★★ Small Hotel

◑ Open all year except Nov 🏨 Rooms: 9 en suite 🛏 DB&B £52-£60 B&B £30-£38 💷 Special rates available 🍷 Restricted licence ✗ Lunch ££ Dinner £££ Ⓥ Vegetarians welcome ⚹ Children welcome ⌦ No smoking throughout 🐕 Dogs welcome 💳 Credit cards: Mastercard/Eurocard, Visa, Switch, Delta 👤 Proprietors: Pat & Gordon Haynes

Banavie Nr Fort William Inverness-shire
PH33 7PD
Tel: 01397 712 700 Fax: 01397 712 700
E-mail: glenloy.lodge@virgin.net
Web:
www.smoothhound.co.uk/hotels/glenloyl.html
4 miles north of Banavie on the B8004. [B4]

BANCHORY

The Horsemill Restaurant, Crathes Castle, National Trust for Scotland

- *"Extremely good home baking in interesting historic surroundings."*
- *Quality meals, snacks and home baking.*

THE ORIGINAL 'horse mill' has been tastefully converted into a very fresh and sunny tea-room and restaurant. Wicker chairs and pine tables reflect the restaurant's commitment to high standards of food presentation and hygiene. Food is served in a modern and imaginative way and everything is made on the premises. Staff are delightful.

Courgette and red pepper soup, served with a cheese and herb scone. Howgate Brie with grapes on maize bread, served with seasonal leaves. Fresh raspberry tart.

STB Highly Commended

◑ Open all year Closed from Christmas Eve for 2 weeks 🍷 Licensed ✗ Food available all day from £ Lunch £ Ⓥ Vegetarians welcome ⚹ Children welcome ♿ Facilities for disabled visitors ⌦ No smoking throughout 💳 Credit cards: Mastercard, Visa 👤 Catering Manager: Alison Martin

Banchory AB31 3QJ
Tel: 01330 844525 Fax: 01330 844797
Web: www.nts.org.uk
On A93, 3 miles east of Banchory and 15 miles west of Aberdeen. [D4]

BANCHORY

The Old West Manse

- *"Hospitality at its best with food and surroundings to match."*
- *Home cooking with flair.*

JAYNE AND JOHN Taylor have established themselves as offering exceptional quality to their guests. Skill and dedication is evident in the cooking – plus some of those extra special touches often only found in larger establishments – from a turn down service to fresh milk in your room for that bedtime cuppa!

New season cauliflower soup flavoured with Strathdon Blue. Breast of Grampian chicken stuffed with haggis, wrapped in smoked bacon and served with a malt whisky and shallot sauce. Fresh lime and lemon meringue roulade with a mango and passion fruit coulis.

STB ★★★★★ B&B

☾ *Open all year* ⌂ *Rooms: 3 (2 en suite, 1 private facilities)* ⚭ *DB&B from £46 B&B from £27.50* ✗ *Packed lunch on request £ Dinner residents only ££ Residents only* Ⓥ *Vegetarians welcome* ⚹ *Children welcome* ⚞ *No smoking in bedrooms and dining room* ⚑ *Dogs by prior arrangement* ⊞ *Credit cards: Mastercard/Eurocard, Visa, Switch, Delta* ⚑ *Owners: Jayne & John Taylor*

71 Station Road Banchory Aberdeenshire AB31 5UD
Tel: 01330 822202 Fax: 01330 822202
Situated on the A93 Aberdeen to Braemar road. Car park entrance is approx 60 metres past A980 junction on right (travelling from Aberdeen). [D4]

BANCHORY

Raemoir House Hotel

- *"This country house hotel offers quality throughout!"*
- *Imaginative Scottish Cooking.*

RAEMOIR HOTEL, set in 3500 acres of beautiful grounds, is a stunning building furnished to the highest standard. Chef John Barbour prepares food to a very high standard with skill and imagination. Raemoir, under the experienced new ownership of Roy and Lesley Bishop-Milnes, is undertaking a complete refurbishment programme.
2 AA Rosettes.

Lobster timbale with fennel and vermouth dressing. Fillet of Aberdeen Angus beef with caramelised beetroot and marrow gratin dauphinoise potatoes. Orange and Grand Marnier crème brûlée with honeycomb tuille and vanilla ice cream.

STB ★★★★ Hotel

☾ *Open all year* ⌂ *Rooms: 21 en suite* ⚭ *DB&B £65–£85 B&B £40–£60* ⓢⓟ *Special rates available* ✗ *Lunch ££ Dinner £££* Ⓥ *Vegetarians welcome* ⚹ *Children welcome* ♿ *Facilities for disabled visitors* ⚞ *No smoking in dining room* ⚑ *Dogs welcome* ⊞ *Credit cards: Mastercard/Eurocard, American Express, Visa, Diners Club, Switch, Delta* ⚑ *Director: Lesley & Roy Bishop-Milnes*

Banchory Royal Deeside AB31 4ED
Tel: 01330 824884 Fax: 01330 822171
At the junction of B977 and A980 – 17 miles west of Aberdeen. [D4]

BANFF

Banff Springs Hotel

- *"A warm welcome and friendly staff await the guests."*
- *Traditional Scottish cooking.*

WITH wonderful views of the Buchan coastline, Banff Springs is in a superb location. The restaurant is a particularly good place to enjoy the views. The cooking uses only good local fresh ingredients, presented and prepared by a chef who cares and understands his subject. In this pleasant atmosphere, staff are keen to ensure guests enjoy their stay.

Arbroath smokies, mayonnaise and cream laced with malt whisky, served with yoghurt dill dressing and oatcakes. Medallions of beef fillet topped with a Stilton soufflé surrounded by Madeira essence and roasted shallots. Baileys and cinnamon brûlée with vanilla shortbread.

STB ★★★ Hotel

◐ *Open all year except Christmas Day* 🛏 *Rooms: 31 en suite* 🛌 *DB&B £44–£70.45 B&B £29–£52.50* 💷 *Special rates available* ✕ *Lunch £ Dinner ££* Ⓥ *Vegetarians welcome* ✝ *Children welcome* ♿ *Facilities for disabled visitors* 🚭 *No smoking in restaurant* 💳 *Credit cards: Mastercard/Eurocard, American Express, Visa, Switch, Delta* ⚑ *Proprietor: Nicola Antliff*

Golden Knowes Road Banff AB45 2JE
Tel: 01261 812881 Fax: 01261 815546
E-mail: info@banffspringshotel.co.uk
Web: www.banffspringshotel.co.uk
On the western outskirts of Banff on the A98 Fraserburgh to Elgin road. [D3]

BANKFOOT

Perthshire Visitor Centre

- *"A lovely spot to break the journey, interesting for all ages, and good food besides."*
- *Home cooking.*

THE MACBETH EXPERIENCE is the focus of this visitor centre which includes a friendly restaurant with a new conservatory, waitress service and a varied selection of meals, desserts and home baking. Sunday lunches and high teas served. Good, fresh coffee also available here! Shop includes a food hall, gifts and leisure wear.

Chicken liver pâté, with chutney and home-made oatcakes. Roasted loin of Perthshire lamb, finished in a minty gravy. Sticky toffee pudding served with Orkney cream.

STB ★★★★ Visitor Attraction

◐ *Open all year except Christmas Day and New Year's Day* ✕ *Food available all day £* 🍷 *Table licence* Ⓥ *Vegetarians welcome* ✝ *Children's play area* ♿ *Facilities for disabled visitors* 💳 *Credit cards: Mastercard/Eurocard, Visa* ⚑ *Proprietors: Wilson & Catriona Girvan and Calum MacLellan*

Bankfoot Perth PH1 4EB
Tel: 01738 787696 Fax: 01738 787120
E-mail: wilson@macbeth.co.uk
8 miles north of Perth on A9. Follow signs for Bankfoot. [D5]

BEAULY

Lovat Arms Hotel

- *"Good quality food is served in this friendly hotel."*
- *Modern Scottish cooking.*

THE LOVAT ARMS is a stylish family-owned hotel in the centre of a picturesque small market town. The food is very well cooked and presented by head chef Donald Munro who uses his skills to present local produce in innovative ways for good value for money. Afternoon Tea and High Tea available.

Trio of Scottish pudding, (haggis, black, white in puff pastry with Inverness sauce). 8oz fillet of Torachilty Angus beef, wrapped in smoked salmon topped with melted Dunsyre Blue cheese. Balvraid strawberries folded into whipped cream flavoured with Pernod and green peppercorns.

◐ *Open all year* ⌂ *Rooms: 22 en suite* ⇌ *DB&B £40–£75 B&B £35–£55* ⓢⓟ *Special rates available* ✘ *Food available all day £-££ Lunch £-££ Dinner £-£££* Ⓥ *Vegetarians welcome* ⚭ *Children welcome* ♿ *Facilities for disabled visitors – please telephone* ⚠ *No smoking in dining room* 💳 *Credit cards: Mastercard/Eurocard, Visa* ⚐ *Proprietor: William Fraser*

Beauly Inverness-shire IV4 7BS
Tel: 01463 782313 Fax: 01463 782862
E-mail: lovat.arms@cali.co.uk
On A862, 11 miles from Inverness in Beauly centre. [C4]

BEAULY

Made In Scotland

- *"Browse in the craft shop then relax while the friendly staff serve you in the restaurant."*
- *Scottish cooking.*

MADE IN SCOTLAND is located in a well designed, modern and spacious restaurant. It is a child friendly, welcoming place to enjoy a range of light snacks and meals all freshly prepared on the premises. There is also a range of high quality Scottish crafts and gifts.

Home-made soups. Flaky smoked salmon from the Western Isles served with prawns and dill. Home-made treacle and Eyemouth tart, served with crème fraîche from the West Highland Dairies.

STB ★★★ Tourist Shop

◐ *Open all year except Christmas Day, Boxing Day, 1 and 2 Jan* ✘ *Food available all day £ Lunch £* Ⓥ *Vegetarians welcome* ⚭ *Children welcome* ♿ *Facilities for disabled visitors* ⚠ *No smoking throughout* 💳 *Credit cards: Mastercard/Eurocard, American Express, Visa, Switch* ⚐ *Retail Manager: Anne Boyd*

Station Road Beauly IV4 7EH
Tel: 01463 782578 Fax: 01463 782409
E-mail: mis@enterprise.net
Web: www.made-in-scotland.co.uk
Only ¼ hour by road from Inverness, on the south edge of Beauly on the A862. [C4]

BIGGAR

Hartree Country House

- *"A friendly hotel offering fresh home cooking."*
- *Good Scottish cooking.*

HARTREE is a charming house and has retained many baronial features in its interior. The grand dining room offers an interesting menu composed by new owner/chef Mike Scotford, which makes best use of local produce skilfully prepared and presented. Jacqui Scotford is front of house and is a most welcoming hostess.

Tain of West Coast lobster resting on a chervil jelly. Loin of Sutherland venison resting on crushed potatoes and parsnips, topped with a game sauce. Chocolate tear drop filled with a raspberry and Champagne mousse.

STB ★★★ Small Hotel

◐ Open all year ⌂ Rooms: 15 en suite ⇌ DB&B £50–£65 B&B £35–£50 ⓢ Special rates available ✗ Dinner £-££ Ⓥ Vegetarians welcome ⚹ Children welcome ⊞ Credit cards: Mastercard, American Express, Visa, Switch, Delta ⋈ Proprietors: Michael & Jacqueline Scotford

Biggar Lanarkshire ML12 6JJ
Tel: 01899 221027 Fax: 01899 221259
E-mail: hartree@dialstart.net
Web: www.hartreehouse.com
Just off A702 on western outskirts of Biggar. [C6]

BIGGAR

Shieldhill

- *"A welcoming, unstuffy castle hotel where outstanding service and cuisine can be relied upon."*
- *Modern Scottish.*

SHIELDHILL is a true country house hotel. The cooking here is completely in keeping with the surroundings, with a team of highly skilled chefs making best use of local produce in an imaginative way. Shieldhill also has a highly acclaimed wine list to complement the à la carte dinner menu. 2 AA Rosettes.

Courgette Charlotte served with a light sauté of chanterelle mushrooms scented with truffle. Braised shank of Shieldhill lamb glazed with heather honey and thyme, set on a wild garlic risotto. Light chocolate pudding complemented with a banana parfait and white chocolate sauce laced with Baileys liqueur.

STB ★★★★ Hotel

◐ Open all year ⌂ Rooms: 16 en suite ⇌ B&B £57-£195 ⓢ Special rates available ✗ Food available all day £ Lunch ££ Dinner £££ Ⓥ Vegetarians welcome ⚹ Children welcome ♿ Facilities for disabled visitors 🐾 Dogs welcome ⊞ Credit cards: Mastercard/Eurocard, Visa, Switch, Delta ⋈ Proprietors: Bob & Christina Lamb

Quothquan Biggar ML12 6NA
Tel: 01899 220035 Fax: 01899 221092
E-mail: enquiries@shieldhill.co.uk
Web: www.shieldhill.co.uk
Turn off A702 on to B7016 Biggar to Carnwath road in middle of Biggar. After 2 miles turn left into Shieldhill road, hotel is on right. [C6]

BIGGAR

Skirling House

- *"A perfect little place, the sort one always hopes to find and so rarely does."*
- *Excellent home cooking.*

THIS FASCINATING house is the home of Bob and Isobel Hunter. Bob presents a four course set menu each evening cooked with a light, well executed touch and served in the new conservatory extension. The house cellar is well stocked. A gem of an architectural find where hospitality is warm and genuine.

Wild mushroom ragoût with wilted rocket. Peppered loin of Stobo lamb with red pepper infused sauce. White chocolate and summer berry mille feuille.

STB ★★★★★ B&B

◐ *Open 1 Mar to 31 Dec* ♞ *Rooms: 3 en suite* ⚑ *DB&B £57–£67 B&B £35–£45* ♟ *Restricted hotel licence* ✘ *Dinner 4 course menu ££* Ⓥ *Vegetarians welcome* ♿ *Restricted access* ⚕ *No smoking throughout* ▣ *Credit cards: Mastercard, Visa, Switch, Delta* ♚ *Proprietors: Bob & Isobel Hunter*

*Skirling Biggar Lanarkshire ML12 6HD
Tel: 01899 860274 Fax: 01899 860255
E-mail: enquiry@skirlinghouse.com
Web: www.skirlinghouse.com
In Skirling village overlooking the village green. 2 miles from Biggar on A72. [C6]*

BLAIR ATHOLL

The House of Bruar

- *"A busy self-service restaurant."*
- *A good selection of popular dishes.*

THE HOUSE OF BRUAR is a large, splendidly designed 'emporium' selling the best of Scottish country products – cashmere, cloth, wildflowers, country wear – with a golf shop, mail order, food hall and 350-seater restaurant. The lengthy blackboard menus offer snacks and full meals, with many classic Scottish dishes; the cooking is fresh and accomplished.

Grilled salmon with lemon and parsley butter. Pan-fried strips of pork fillet in a creamy mushroom sauce. Treacle tart and fresh whipped cream.

◐ *Open all year except Christmas Day, Boxing Day and New Year's Day* ✘ *Food available all day* Ⓥ *Vegetarians welcome* ♣ *Children welcome* ♿ *Facilities for disabled visitors* ⚕ *No smoking throughout* ▣ *Credit cards: Mastercard/Eurocard, American Express, Visa, Switch, Delta* ♚ *Chef: Hugh Cuthbertson Restaurant Manager: David Coupar*

*Bruar Falls by Blair Atholl Perthshire PH18 5TW
Tel: 01796 483236 Fax: 01796 483218
E-mail: office@houseofbruar.demon.co.uk
Web: www.houseofbruar.com
7 miles north of Pitlochry on the side of A9 at Bruar. Restaurant services A9. [C4]*

BLAIR ATHOLL

The Loft Restaurant

- *"A great place for a light home-made lunch or more substantial evening meal – 'a true friend' on the A9."*
- *Elegant Scottish.*

WITH ITS twisted old beams, stone walls and oak flooring this is a great setting to sample the excellent cuisine of Head Chef Graham Horne. Menus are refreshing and appealing to suit all. The Loft has a conservatory bar and roof terrace. Booking essential.
2 AA Rosettes.

Terrine of pressed Guinea fowl, shallots and fennel with chanterelles. Roast rack of lamb with spinach and tomato and thyme jus with fondant potatoes. Hot chocolate soufflé with chocolate ganache and cinnamon ice cream.

◐ Open all year ✕ (Morning coffee to late dinner available) Lunch £ Dinner ££
Ⓥ Vegetarians welcome ⚥ Children welcome ⌁ No smoking in restaurant ▩ Credit cards: Mastercard/Eurocard, American Express, Visa, Diners Club, Switch, Delta, JCB ⚑ Partner: Mrs P M Richardson

Golf Course Road Blair Atholl by Pitlochry PH18 5TE
Tel: 01796 481377 Fax: 01796 481511
Take B8079 off A9, 5 miles north of Pitlochry. In village take golf course road by Tilt Hotel, the Loft is 50 yards on right. [C4]

BLAIRGOWRIE

Altamount House

- *"Relaxing country house offering good food and warm hospitality."*
- *Modern Scottish cooking.*

ALTAMOUNT HOTEL is a lovely Georgian house, owned by Robert Glashan – an accomplished host. The cooking at Altamount is in a modern style, well-presented using the best local produce with well-balanced menus, complemented by a comprehensive wine list. The hotel garden provides an assortment of vegetables and herbs.
2 AA Rosettes.

Char-grilled East Coast scallops with a citrus salad, sweet chilli jam and saffron oil. Best end of lamb served with dauphinoise potatoes, ratatouille gâteau and a redcurrant and garlic sauce. Hot Grand Marnier soufflé with lemon sorbet and poppy seed biscuits.

STB ★★★ Hotel

◐ Open all year ⌂ Rooms: 7 en suite ⛌ DB&B £50–£75 B&B £35–£60 ▦ Special rates available and golf packages ✕ Food available all day £ Lunch £-££ Dinner £££ Ⓥ Vegetarians welcome ⚥ Children welcome ♿ Facilities for disabled visitors ⌁ No smoking in dining room ☻ Member of the Scotch Beef Club ▩ Credit cards: Mastercard/Eurocard, American Express, Visa, Diners Club, Switch, Delta ⚑ Proprietors: Robert & Sally Glashan

Coupar Angus Road Blairgowrie PH10 6JN
Tel: 01250 873512 Fax: 01250 876200
E-mail: althotel@netcomuk.co.uk
Web: www.s-h-systems.co.uk/hotels/altamoun.html
A923 to Coupar Angus from town centre. The hotel is 500 yards on right-hand side [D5]

BLAIRGOWRIE

Cargills Restaurant & Bistro

- *"A lively informal bistro offering excellent food and friendly service."*
- *Modern Scottish cooking with some European influence.*

CHEF/PROPRIETOR Willie Little creates an impressive selection of high quality dishes all very reasonably priced. A blackboard shows daily specials in addition to the menu. A carefully chosen wine list complements the food. Ideal for a relaxed lunch or dinner followed by a short riverside stroll to Cargills Leap! Sunday brunch has also become a firm favourite.

Root vegetable rösti with beetroot salad and chive crème fraîche. Roast haunch of local roe deer with mushy peas and fondant potato. Pineapple polenta upside down cake with maple syrup.

◗ Open all year Closed Tue ✘ Lunch £-££ Dinner ££ Ⓥ Vegetarians welcome ✸ Children welcome ♿ Facilities for disabled visitors 💳 Credit cards: Mastercard/Eurocard, Visa, Switch, Delta ⚙ Chef/Proprietor: Willie Little

Lower Mill Street Blairgowrie Perthshire
PH10 6AQ
Tel: 01250 876735 Fax: 01250 876735
E-mail: exceed@btconnect.com
Web: www.exceed.co.uk
At the Square in the centre of Blairgowrie, turn left off A93 Perth-Braemar road into Mill Street. Cargills is behind the car park, 200 yards down on the left. [D5]

BLAIRGOWRIE

Kinloch House Hotel

- *"This is a superb hotel where guests' comfort is the top priority."*
- *Outstanding Scottish cuisine.*

SET IN 25 acres, Kinloch House Hotel is a fine example of a Scottish country house. Service is impeccable yet unobtrusive in an elegant dining room. Menus offer the finest Scottish produce, carefully prepared by head chef Bill McNicoll who also runs cookery courses. The hotel has a fine health and fitness centre and 3 AA Rosettes.

Kyle scallops set on herb risotto with a cheese and garlic sauce. Loin of lamb wrapped in tarragon mousse, with potato galette, creamed Savoy cabbage and a lamb reduction. Warm blueberry and almond tart served with Mascarpone and candied zest.

STB ★★★★★ Hotel

◗ Open 29 Dec to 18 Dec 🛏 Rooms: 20 en suite 🛌 B&B £74.45-£81.25 ✘ Lunch ££ Dinner £££ Ⓥ Vegetarians welcome ✸ Children welcome – over 7 years only at dinner ♿ Facilities for disabled visitors 🚭 No smoking in dining room 🐄 Member of the Scotch Beef Club 💳 Credit cards: Mastercard/Eurocard, American Express, Visa, Diners Club, Switch, Delta ⚙ Proprietors: The Shentall Family

By Blairgowrie Perthshire PH10 6SG
Tel: 01250 884 237 Fax: 01250 884 333
E-mail: reception@kinlochhouse.com
Web: www.kinlochhouse.com
On A923, 3 miles west of Blairgowrie. [D5]

BOAT OF GARTEN

Boat Hotel

- *"A warm welcome and good food in the osprey village of Boat of Garten."*
- *Modern/traditional Scottish cuisine.*

IAN AND SHONA Tatchell are committed and welcoming hosts. They have upgraded the hotel to a high standard and this same commitment to customer care is evident. Chef Peter Woods prepares meals combining traditional and modern techniques using only the very best ingredients. 2 AA Rosettes.

Light Shetland shellfish broth with new season vegetables, pasta and lightly cooked fishes with Parmesan and langoustine 'fluffies'. Rack of Scottish spring lamb, flash roasted with ramsons and sliced over a confit of summer vegetables, doused with a rosemary jus and served with dauphinoise potatoes. Dark chocolate bread and butter pudding drizzled with a white chocolate sauce.

STB ★★★ Hotel

◐ *Open all year* ♠ *Rooms: 32 en suite* ⚬ *DB&B £65–£80 B&B £43.50–£58.50* ⓢ *Special rates available* ✖ *Lunch ££ Dinner £££* Ⓥ *Vegetarians welcome* ✱ *Children welcome* ✂ *No smoking in dining room* ⌇ *Dogs welcome (not in public areas)* ⊞ *Credit cards: Mastercard/Eurocard, Visa, Switch, Delta* ⚑ *Owners: Ian & Shona Tatchell*

Boat of Garten Inverness-shire PH24 3BH
Tel: 01479 831258 Fax: 01479 831414
E-mail: holidays@boathotel.co.uk
Web: www.boathotel.co.uk
From Aviemore take A95 to Grantown-on-Spey and turning to Boat of Garten. After 1 mile turn right into Boat of Garten. The hotel is adjacent to the Strathspey Steam Railway. [C4]

BOTHWELL

The Grape Vine Restaurant

- *"Popular informal restaurant and wine bar with extensive and interesting wine selection."*
- *Modern Scottish cooking.*

THE GRAPE VINE, in the centre of the attractive conservation village of Bothwell, is run by Morris Inns who have developed the business to suit customers' particular tastes. Customers can enjoy anything from a light snack to more formal dining, where a good choice of menu items is on offer, yet still enjoy a relaxed atmosphere.

Arbroath smokie fish cakes with a smoked Orkney sabayon. Roast haunch of venison set on Arran mustard mash with a red wine and bitter chocolate jus. Sweet glazed honey apples complemented by butterscotch cream.

◐ *Open all year except 1 and 2 Jan* ✖ *Food available all day £ Lunch £ Dinner ££* Ⓥ *Vegetarians welcome* ✱ *Children welcome* ♿ *Restricted access for disabled visitors* ⊞ *Credit cards: Mastercard/Eurocard, American Express, Visa, Diners Club, Switch, Delta* ⚑ *Proprietor: Morris Inns Group*

27 Main Street Bothwell G71 8RD
Tel: 01698 852014 Fax: 01698 854405
E-mail: colin@morris-inns.com
Web: www.morris-inns.com
On main street in conservation village of Bothwell, ½ mile off M74 (East Kilbride exit). [C6]

BRIDGE OF ORCHY

Bridge of Orchy Hotel

- *"On a main tourist route – enjoy excellent fine dining in the evenings, or freshly cooked quality bar meals throughout the day."*
- *Modern and stylishly presented Scottish fare.*

THIS COMFORTABLE hotel, with warm log fires and delightful candlelit dining room, makes a very enjoyable place from which to explore this stunning part of the Highlands and to relax after a long day. Equally this is a good spot to stop and enjoy good Scottish cooking with a modern twist. 1 AA Rosette.

Ballotine of salmon on fine leaves with a citrus dressing. Pan-fried loin of venison on a bed of spinach complemented with a balsamic jus. Orange and passion fruit parfait accompanied with a mixed berry coulis.

STB ★★★★ Hotel

◐ *Open all year except Christmas Day and New Year* ♜ *Rooms: 10 en suite* ⚭ *B&B £30–£45* ⓈⓅ *Special rates available* ✘ *Food available all day ££ Lunch – by arrangement in dining room: Bar lunches served daily ££ Dinner £££* Ⓥ *Vegetarians welcome* ⚹ *Children welcome* ✄ *No smoking in dining room* 💳 *Credit cards: Mastercard/Eurocard, American Express, Visa, Diners Club, Switch, Delta*

Bridge of Orchy Argyll PA36 4AD
Tel: 01838 400208 Fax: 01838 400313
E-mail: bridgeoforchy@onyxnet.co.uk
Web: www.scottish-selection.co.uk
On main A82 road to Fort William. 6 miles north of Tyndrum. [C5]

BRIDGE OF WEIR

The Lochnagar

- *"An interesting and innovative restaurant and coffee shop where quality is the number one priority."*
- *Modern Scottish cooking.*

PREPARATION of the compact lunch menu, made with quality ingredients, is careful and sensitive. A wide range of coffees is on offer to enjoy with the delicious home baking, available all day. A small indoor children's play area includes tables for parents to enjoy coffee or lunch. The reputation of this small establishment is growing, so booking is advisable.

Twice baked goat's cheese soufflé. Locally smoked haddock kedgeree, served with fresh parsley and hot buttered toast. Lochnagar's lemon meringue pie.

◐ *Open 8 Jan to 29 Dec Closed Sun* ♇ *Licensed* ✘ *Food available all day £ Lunch except Sun ££ Dinner – party bookings, minimum of 14, welcome by arrangement* Ⓥ *Vegetarians welcome* ⚹ *Children welcome* ♿ *Facilities for disabled visitors* ✄ *No smoking throughout* 💳 *Credit cards: Mastercard/Eurocard, Visa, Switch, Delta, Solo, Visa Electron, JCB* ⓟ *Partners: John & Mary-Ann Rankin/Hamish & Kate Rankin*

Main Street Bridge of Weir Renfrewshire PA11 3LA
Tel: 01505 613410 Fax: 01505 613410
In centre of village of Bridge of Weir. Car parking to rear of building. 5 miles from Glasgow Airport. [C5]

BRORA

Royal Marine Hotel

- *"This place has real Scottish country house style."*
- *Traditional with a modern influence.*

THE ROYAL MARINE HOTEL was built in 1913 and overlooks the mouth of the River Brora and is adjacent to Brora's 18 hole James Braid Links Golf Course. Guests may also fish from the hotel's own boat on Loch Brora. The hotel has a leisure complex and conference and meeting facilities. 1 AA Rosette.

Pan-seared Orkney king scallops with carrot and courgette linguine and a light lemon grass and saffron velouté. Pan-seared loin of Highland venison roasted with a poppy seed crust served with wilted pak choi and a lemon oil and truffle dressing. Hot chocolate fondants with honeycomb ice cream.

STB ★★★★ Hotel

◐ Open all year ⌂ Rooms: 22 en suite 🛏 DB&B £50–£80 B&B £40–£65 SP Special rates available ✘ Food available all day ££ Lunch £ Dinner £££ Ⓥ Vegetarians welcome ✸ Children welcome ♿ Facilities for disabled visitors ✁ No smoking in restaurant ☙ Member of the Scotch Beef Club ⊞ Credit cards: Mastercard/Eurocard, American Express, Visa, Diners Club, Switch ⚅ Managing Director: Robert Powell

Golf Road Brora Sutherland KW9 6QS
Tel: 01408 621252 Fax: 01408 621181
E-mail: highlandescape@btinternet.com
Web: www.highlandescape.com
On the A9 from Golspie to Helmsdale. At Brora cross bridge over River Brora and take Golf Road on right. Hotel is on left. [C3]

BROUGHTY FERRY

South Kingennie House

- *"A restaurant that creates innovative dishes from the best of local produce."*
- *Skilful, traditional Scots cooking.*

SOUTH KINGENNIE is owned and run by Peter and Jill Robinson who serve inexpensive and imaginative table d'hôte meals in a long, elegant dining room. Peter's stylish and imaginative cooking is matched by Jill's supervision front of the house. Atmosphere and service are relaxed and friendly. The wine list is comprehensive.

Avocado, sliced duck and orange salad with port and redcurrant sauce. Grilled fillet of Shetland salmon glazed with a basil crust. Baked lemon roulade with citrus sauce.

◐ Open all year except Boxing Day, 1 Jan, last week Jan and first week Feb Closed Sun evening and Mon ✘ Lunch except Mon £-££ Dinner except Sun Mon ££-£££ Ⓥ Vegetarians welcome ✸ Children welcome ♿ Facilities for disabled visitors ✁ No smoking in restaurant ⊞ Credit cards: Mastercard/Eurocard, American Express, Visa, Switch, Delta, Diners Club ⚅ Proprietors: Peter & Jill Robinson

Kellas by Broughty Ferry DD5 3PA
Tel: 01382 350 562
From A92 Dundee–Arbroath, take B978 to Kellas then road to Drumsturdy to signpost for South Kingennie, 2 miles. [D5]

BUCKIE

The Old Monastery Restaurant

- *"Calum and Val make great efforts to source produce – staying as local as possible without compromising quality and flavour."*
- *Classical European in a modern style.*

UNDER THE caring ownership of Val and Calum Buchanan the Old Monastery has developed its own reputation for quality. Menus change regularly and feature locally-sourced Scottish produce. Calum is a great wine enthusiast and has compiled an eclectic wine list to complement the menus. The Old Monastery has 2 AA Rosettes.

Crab and langoustine cake, tomato and ginger salsa, herb salad. Saddle of hill lamb on rosemary scented vegetables and Jersey Royals. Candied rhubarb, clementines and strawberries with Mascarpone sorbet.

◐ Open all year except 3 weeks Jan – Phone for festive hours Closed Sun evening and all day Monday ✕ Lunch except Mon ££ Dinner except Sun Mon £££ Ⓥ Vegetarians welcome ✻ Children welcome (over 8 years in evening is preferred) ⌦ No smoking in restaurant ⊞ Credit cards: Mastercard/Eurocard, American Express, Visa, Switch, Delta ⚑ Proprietors: Calum & Valerie Buchanan

Drybridge Buckie Moray AB56 5JB
Tel: 01542 832660 Fax: 01542 839437
E-mail: buchanan@oldmonasteryrestaurant.freeserve.co.uk
Web: www.scottishholidays.net/oldmonastery
Turn off A98 opposite main Buckie Junction onto Drybridge road. Continue up hill for 2½ miles. [D3]

CAIRNBAAN

Cairnbaan Hotel

- *"Cairnbaan is a lively and bustling hotel, with good fresh food, served by friendly staff."*
- *Imaginative Scottish.*

THE CAIRNBAAN HOTEL has recently changed hands and is now run by Darren Dobson who is very much 'at the helm'. The restaurant has been very tastefully refurbished resembling that of a ship's deck. This is a busy and lively hotel offering good home made food using fresh local produce.

Sweet-marinated herring with a pear, watercress and walnut salad. Roast breast of pheasant on skirlie toast with rowan jelly. Compote of sweet oranges topped with fresh cream flavoured with home-made marmalade and Drambuie.

STB ★★★★ Small Hotel

◐ Open all year 🛏 Rooms: 11 en suite ⚐ DB&B £50–£75 B&B £45–£55 ⓢ Special rates available ✕ Lunch ££ Dinner ££ Ⓥ Vegetarians welcome ✻ Children welcome ♿ Facilities for disabled visitors ⌦ No smoking in the dining room ⊞ Credit cards: Mastercard/Eurocard, Visa, Switch, Delta ⚑ Owner: Darren Dobson

Cairnbaan By Lochgilphead Argyll PA31 8SJ
Tel: 01546 603668 Fax: 01546 606045
E-mail: cairnbaan.hotel@virgin.net
Web: www.canalhotel.com
Two miles north of Lochgilphead on the Oban road. [B5]

CAIRNDOW

Loch Fyne Oyster Bar: Finalist The Macallan Taste of Scotland Awards 2000

- *"Enjoy what the chef prepares for you and then, having been inspired, buy some more to prepare at home. "*
- *Fresh seafood.*

THE RESTAURANT here eschews 'haute cuisine'; dishes are very simply prepared, so the fresh natural flavour of the seafood can be enjoyed. The adjacent shop features an extensive chilled cabinet displaying all their products in an attractive layout. Permits 'carry-outs'. Winner of The Macallan Taste of Scotland Special Merit Award for Achievement 1995.

Fresh rock oysters from Loch Fyne. Queen scallops roasted with bacon. Bradan roast (salmon smoked in a hot kiln) served hot with a whisky sauce. Shellfish platter – fresh oysters, langoustines, queen scallops, brown crab and clams.

◐ Open all year except Christmas Day and New Year's Day ✗ Food served all day ££ Ⓥ Vegetarians welcome 🖃 Credit cards: Mastercard/Eurocard, Visa, Diners Club, Switch, Delta ⋈ Proprietors: Loch Fyne Oysters Ltd

Clachan Cairndow Argyll PA26 8BL
Tel: 01499 600 236 Fax: 01499 600 234
E-mail: info@loch-fyne.com
Web: www.lochfyne.com
At head of Loch Fyne on A83 Arrochar to Inveraray Road. Well signposted on right-hand side 10 miles before Inveraray. [C5]

CALLANDER

Roman Camp Country House Hotel

- *"An adventurous and inspiring food experience."*
- *Modern Scottish cuisine.*

ROMAN CAMP offers the peace of the past alongside every possible modern convenience. In the dining room, the best of fresh local produce is imaginatively used to create the finest Scottish cuisine, complemented by an excellent wine list. Service is unhurried and impeccable, the food is first class. 3 AA Rosettes.

Cold ratatouille soup with basil oil, melon and cucumber. Red wine-poached turbot with squat lobster and caviar fricassée. Vanilla and passion fruit bavarois with caramelised pineapple syrup.

STB ★★★★ Hotel

◐ Open all year 🏨 Rooms: 14 en suite 🛏 DB&B £78.50–£113.50 B&B £44.50–£79.50 🅢🅟 Special rates available ✗ Lunch ££ Dinner 4 course menu ££££ Ⓥ Vegetarians welcome ⚤ Children welcome ♿ Facilities for disabled visitors ⚭ No smoking in dining room 🖃 Credit cards: Mastercard/Eurocard, American Express, Visa, Diners Club, Switch, Delta ⋈ Proprietors: Eric & Marion Brown

Callander FK17 8BG
Tel: 01877 330003 Fax: 01877 331533
E-mail: mail@roman-camp-hotel.co.uk
Web: www.roman-camp-hotel.co.uk
At the east end of Callander main street from Stirling, turn left down 300 yard drive to hotel. [C5]

CAMPBELTOWN

Low Cattadale Farm

- *"A comfortable farmhouse with delicious food, attractively presented."*
- *Skilled home cooking.*

LOW CATTADALE is a two minute drive from beautiful sandy bays, places of historic interest and a 18 hole golf course. The dining room is comfortable and the food offered is accomplished Scottish cooking, making use of the best locally sourced ingredients. Dinner is served at 6 pm, leaving the evening free for exploration.

Brie in pastry served with green dressed salad and a cranberry sauce. Sirloin steak with haggis and grain mustard Crowdie, served with a selection of fresh vegetables and potatoes. Bread and butter pudding with fromage frais.

STB ★★★ B&B

◐ Open Mar to Nov 🏨 Rooms: 3 en suite 🛏 DB&B from £28 B&B from £18 🅤 Unlicensed ✕ Residents only Dinner ££ Ⓥ Vegetarians welcome ☆ Children welcome ⌘ No smoking in dining room 🐕 Dogs welcome 🗎 Credit cards: No credit cards ♜ Owner: Mrs Elizabeth Semple

*Southend by Campbeltown Argyll PA28 6RN
Tel: 01586 830205
Take B842 road from Campbeltown to Southend for 8 miles, to road sign 'Mull of Kintyre single track road'. Low Cattadale 1 mile along this road. [B6]*

CARNOUSTIE

11 Park Avenue

- *"11 Park Avenue offers excellent food in this famous golfing town."*
- *Modern Scottish cooking.*

11 PARK AVENUE offers a stunning eating experience. The restaurant is small, thoughtfully laid out and intimate. Everything here is home-made and prepared with the style and skill of Stephen Collinson, whose commitment to quality and food knows no bounds.

Seared West Coast scallops with crispy bacon, oyster mushrooms and a balsamic vinegar dressing. Pan-fried fillet of beef on a Stilton and polenta crouton, with a salsa and Madeira sauce. A trio of: crème caramel, crème brûlée, and caramelised rice pudding.

◐ Open all year except 1st 2 weeks Jan Closed Sun Mon ✕ Lunch – by arrangement ££ Dinner except Sun Mon ££-£££ Ⓥ Vegetarians welcome ☆ Children welcome ♿ Facilities for disabled visitors ⌘ No smoking in dining room 🗎 Credit cards: Mastercard/Eurocard, American Express, Visa, Diners Club, Switch, Delta, JCB ♜ Chef/Proprietor: Stephen Collinson

*11 Park Avenue Carnoustie Angus DD7 7JA
Tel: 01241 853336 Fax: 01241 853336
E-mail: parkavenue@genie.co.uk
Web: www.carnoustie.co.uk/11parkavenue.htm
Park Avenue runs from the main street in Carnoustie towards the railway and beach. [D5]*

CARNOUSTIE

Carnoustie Hotel, Golf Resort & Spa

- *"Tackle the most challenging golf course in the world and experience the delights of this excellent hotel."*
- *Modern Scottish cooking.*

CARNOUSTIE is a new and luxurious resort hotel, with outstanding views over the championship course, which has quickly established its reputation for quality. It is a highly elegant hotel which is professionally run and finished to the highest standard. Cooking here is of the highest calibre.

Ravioli of lobster and shellfish velouté. Prime fillet of Aberdeen Angus beef, oxtail brandade, carlos potato, and garlic soubise. Cranachan parfait with soused Perthshire berries.

STB ★★★★ Leisure Centre

◐ Open all year ⊞ Rooms: 85, 75 en suite and 10 suites ⌨ DB&B £95–£131.50 B&B £57.50–£102.50 ⓢ Special rates available ✗ Food available all day from £££ Lunch ££ Dinner £££ Ⓥ Vegetarians welcome ⚹ Children welcome ♿ Facilities for disabled visitors ⊻ No smoking in dining room ⚐ Dogs welcome ⊞ Credit cards: Mastercard/Eurocard, American Express, Visa, Diners Club, Switch, Delta ⚑ Chairman: Mr Michael A Johnston

The Links Carnoustie DD7 7JE
Tel: 01241 411999 Fax: 01241 411998
E-mail: enquiries@carnoustie-hotel.com
Web: www.carnoustie-hotel.com
From Dundee travel east on A92 towards Arbroath, after 7 miles turn right at first signpost for Carnoustie. Follow road for 1½ miles to main street. Turn left for 500m, turn right at signpost for beach and golf course. [D5]

CARRADALE

Carradale Hotel

- *"Menus feature local produce and modern presentation."*
- *Innovative/traditional cooking.*

THIS FAMILY hotel attracts golfers and tourists to this pretty village in the heart of Kintyre. Fresh, local produce in abundance is featured on the menus, and dining can be either formal or informal. Ongoing refurbishment is taking place in public areas and bedrooms showing a commitment to continuous improvement here.

Carradale-landed scallops with two salsas, and lobster chilli oil. Medallions of Scottish beef, lamb and venison with a herb mustard mash and a port and juniper reduction. Duo of chocolate and butterscotch pots, minted shortbread and Drambuie cream.

STB ★★★ Hotel

◐ Open all year except 23 to 26 Dec ⊞ Rooms: 9 en suite ⌨ DB&B £41.50–£51.50 B&B £25–£35 ⓢ Special rates available ✗ Lunch £ Dinner ££ Ⓥ Vegetarians welcome ⚹ Children welcome ⊻ No smoking in restaurant ⊞ Credit cards: Mastercard/Eurocard, Visa ⚑ Proprietors: Marcus & Morag Adams

Carradale nr Campbeltown Argyll PA28 6RY
Tel: 01583 431 223 Fax: 01583 431 223
E-mail: carradaleh@aol.com
Web: www.carradalehotel.com
From Tarbert (Loch Fyne) 26 miles via A83, B8001 and B842. From Campbeltown about 17 miles on B842. [B6]

CASTLE DOUGLAS

Craigadam: Finalist The Macallan Taste of Scotland Awards 2000

- *"A fine Scottish welcome, exceptional home cooking and congenial surroundings."*
- *Delightful home cooking.*

CRAIGADAM is a large and elegant farmhouse. The dining room and drawing room are filled with family treasures and the cooking is carefully balanced, presented with great attention to detail and the flavours are delightful. Dinner is enjoyed in the oak-panelled dining room, drinks and coffee served in the drawing room.

Smoked haddock mousseline with prawn and hollandaise sauce, and home-made bread. Noisettes of Galloway lamb on a bed of spinach with a mint sauce. Lemon meringue roulade with mango and passion fruit sauce.

STB ★★★★ B&B

◐ Open all year except Christmas Eve to 2 Jan ⌂ Rooms: 6 en suite ⊨ DB&B £40 B&B £25 ♀ licensed ✗ Dinner ££ Ⓥ Vegetarians welcome ✽ Children welcome ⊁ No smoking in bedrooms ▣ Credit cards: Mastercard/Eurocard, Visa, Switch, Delta, JCB, Solo, Visa Electron ⋈ Partner: Celia Pickup

Castle Douglas DG7 3HU
Tel: 01556 650233 Fax: 01556 650233
E-mail: inquiry@craigadam.co
Web: www.craigadam.com
2 miles north of Crocketford on the A712. [C7]

CASTLE DOUGLAS

Threave Garden, National Trust for Scotland

- *"Relaxing pleasant surroundings, ideal for lunch or coffee/tea with good home baking."*
- *Skilful home cooking with local produce.*

THE RESTAURANT at Threave Garden is at the entrance to some 26 hectares of one of the finest gardens in the country. Kate McBurnie and her team prepare innovative dishes using local game, fish, vegetables and fruit, all served by enthusiastic staff. Some excellent examples of home baking and Scottish fayre.

Spicy lentil pâté served with traditional oatcakes. Venison and orange casserole on a bed of creamed parsnips and served with seasonal vegetables. Meringue roulade served with seasonal local fruits and cream.

STB Commended

◐ Open 1 Apr to 31 Oct ⓢⓟ Special rates available ♀ Licensed ✗ Food available all day £ Lunch £ Ⓥ Vegetarians welcome ✽ Children welcome ♿ Facilities for disabled visitors ⊁ No smoking throughout 🐕 Dogs welcome in the grounds but not in the restaurant ▣ Credit cards: Mastercard/Eurocard, Visa ⋈ Catering Manager: Kate McBurnie

Threave Castle Douglas Kirkcudbrightshire DG7 1RX
Tel: 01556 502575 Fax: 01556 502683
Web: www.nts.org.uk
Off A75, 1 mile west of Castle Douglas, follow signs to Threave Garden. [C7]

CHIRNSIDE

Chirnside Hall Country House Hotel

- *"Friendly hosts in a relaxing and very comfortable Scottish country house hotel."*
- *Modern Scottish.*

CHIRNSIDE HALL is a delightful country house full of original features which has been sensitively refurbished in recent years. Cooking here is of a very high standard with interesting menus – only the best of locally sourced ingredients is used. Mr and Mrs Korsten are the new owners.

Warm tartlet of smoked salmon and leeks, with a grain mustard sauce. Roast loin of lamb with skirlie and black pudding. Iced chocolate parfait with orange compote.

STB ★★★★ Hotel

◐ Open all year 🏨 Room: 10 en suite 🛏 DB&B £62.50-£80 B&B £50-£70 💷 Special rates available ✖ Light snack lunch – for residents Dinner £££ Ⓥ Vegetarians welcome ☘ Children welcome ⚞ No smoking in dining room 🐕 Dogs welcome 💳 Credit cards: Mastercard/ Eurocard, Visa, Switch 👤 Proprietors: Christian & Tessa Korsten

Chirnside nr Duns Berwickshire TD11 3LD
Tel: 01890 818219 Fax: 01890 818231
E-mail: chirnsidehall@globalnet.co.uk
Web: www.chirnsidehallhotel.com
Between Chirnside and Foulden on the A6105, 1 mile east of Chirnside. [D6]

CLACHAN BY TARBERT

Balinakill Country House Hotel

- *"An interesting house in a very peaceful setting with friendly service."*
- *Simple Scottish Fayre.*

BALINAKILL HOUSE is a grand mansion house set in parkland grounds which is now benefiting from the caring new owners' attentions. All bedrooms are en suite, offering modern conveniences in traditional surroundings. Menus are prepared by Angus, focusing greatly on using only the freshest and best local produce – particularly local game, seafood and Gigha cheese.

Melon with citrus segments and ginger syrup with a glazed sabayon. Pan-fried venison with juniper sauce and mille feuille of celeriac. Brandy snap basket filled with exotic fruits and sorbet.

STB ★★ Hotel

◐ Open all year 🏨 Rooms: 11 en suite 🛏 DB&B £45–£59.95 B&B £35–£40 💷 Special rates available ✖ Food available all day £ Lunch £ Dinner ££ Ⓥ Vegetarians welcome ☘ Children welcome ♿ Facilities for disabled visitors ⚞ No smoking in dining room 🐕 Dogs welcome 💳 Credit cards: Mastercard, Visa, Switch, Delta 👤 Proprietors: Angus & Susan Macdiarmid

Clachan By Tarbert Argyll PA29 6XL
Tel: 01880 740206 Fax: 01880 740298
E-mail: info@balinakill.com
Web: www.balinakill.com
Heading south: on A83 between Tarbert and Campbeltown. As you approach the village of Clachan, Balinakill is on the left. [B6]

COLDINGHAM BAY

Dunlaverock Country House

- *"A charming guest house in a stunning seaside setting; good fresh food and a warm welcome."*
- *Innovative home cooking.*

AT DUNLAVEROCK HOUSE every effort has been taken to make guests as comfortable as possible. Proprietors Mari and Ronnie Brown are very friendly, attentive hosts. Scottish produce is evident on the menu, including a range of cheeses from the Scottish Borders, all freshly prepared with excellent flavours. Standards are high throughout this relaxing hotel.

Double-baked smoked salmon soufflé. Roast leg of Border lamb, with mint gremolata sauce. Bread and butter pudding, with apricot compote.

STB ★★★★ Guest House

Open 1 Feb to 2 Jan except 22 to 26 Dec Rooms: 6 en suite DB&B £48–£60 Special rates available Dinner ££ Vegetarians welcome Children over 9 years welcome Facilities for disabled visitors No smoking in dining room Credit cards: Mastercard/Eurocard, Visa, JVC Proprietors: Mari & Ronnie Brown

*Coldingham Bay Eyemouth Berwickshire TD14 5PA
Tel: 018907 71450 Fax: 018907 71450
E-mail: dunlaverock@lineone.net
Web: www.cometo/dunlaverock
Take A1107 to Coldingham and then follow signs to Coldingham Bay. [D5]*

CRAIGELLACHIE

Craigellachie Hotel

- *"Excellent food with hospitality to match."*
- *Modern Scottish cuisine.*

CRAIGELLACHIE is located at the heart of Whisky Country, within the attractive Speyside village of Craigellachie. The kitchen uses fresh produce as far as possible, skilfully prepared by Chef Antony Allcott. The hotel has three dining areas each unique in style but all with a warm, welcoming atmosphere and professional, yet unobtrusive service. 2 AA Rosettes.

Wild duck and goose liver galantine with sweet chestnut and brandied apricots. Canon of Highland lamb on a fricassee of young leeks. Iced malt whiskey and grape soufflé with sweet ginger Viennese butter biscuits.

STB ★★★★ Small Hotel

Open all year Rooms: 26 en suite B&B £57.50–£72.50 Special seasonal rates available Lunch £-£££ Dinner 4 course menu £-££££ Vegetarians welcome Children welcome No smoking in restaurants Member of the Scotch Beef Club Credit cards: Mastercard/Eurocard, American Express, Visa, Diners Club, Switch, Delta, JCB General Manager: Duncan Elphick

*Craigellachie Speyside Banffshire AB38 9SR
Tel: 01340 881 204 Fax: 01340 881 253
E-mail: sales@craigellachie.com
Web: www.craigellachie.com
On A941/A95, 12 miles south of Elgin. [D4]*

CRIEFF

The Bank Restaurant

- *"Creative cooking and friendly service in a tastefully converted bank building."*
- Modern Scottish cooking.

THE BANK RESTAURANT is run by Bill and Lilias McGuigan and was cleverly renovated from a bank hall to its current guise. Bill is chef/proprietor, whose cooking is skilful and talented. Lilias is very hospitable front of house. All dishes are cooked to order making the dining experience a leisurely and relaxed one. The Bank has 1 AA Rosette.

Smoked bacon, mussel and Brie tartlet with mixed leaves and a balsamic dressing. Rib-eye of 'Buccleuch Estate' beef, with colcannon potatoes and a rosemary and garlic sauce. Lemon tart with prune and Armagnac ice cream.

◐ Open all year except 2 weeks Jan Closed Sun evening and Mon ✕ Lunch £ Dinner ££-£££ Ⓥ Vegetarians welcome �童 Children welcome ▩ Credit cards: Mastercard/Eurocard, American Express, Visa, Switch, Delta ▨ Proprietors: Bill & Lilias McGuigan

32 High Street Crieff Perthshire PH7 3BS
Tel: 01764 656575 Fax: 01764 656575
In Crieff town centre opposite tourist office and town clock. [C5]

CRIEFF

Crieff Hydro Hotel

- *"Superb hotel facilities for all ages!"*
- Scottish produce with modern influences.

CRIEFF HYDRO HOTEL is a unique resort hotel with excellent facilities. The Brasserie at the Hydro is stylish and designed to a high standard with menus which are interesting and innovative. The dining room offers the more formal dining experience with sophisticated menus. The happy smiling faces in this busy establishment tell the story.

Gâteau of Brie and Feta topped with crisp crouton of brioche and sun-dried tomatoes. Breast of chicken accompanied by a timbale of basmati rice and a cordon hoisin sauce. Compote of Thai fruit with Midori liqueur and vanilla ice cream.

STB ★★★★ Hotel

◐ Open all year ▦ Rooms: 221 en suite (and 23 self-catering units) ⊨ DB&B £59–£212 B&B £55–£108 ▩ Special rates available ✕ Lunch £-££ Dinner ££ Ⓥ Vegetarians welcome ✦ Children welcome ♿ Facilities for disabled visitors ⌦ No smoking in brasserie ⚑ Kennels available for dogs of hotel guests ▩ Credit cards: Mastercard/Eurocard, American Express, Visa, Switch, Delta ▨ Food & Beverage Manager: William Lindsay

Crieff Perthshire PH7 3LQ
Tel: 01764 655555 Fax: 01764 653087
E-mail: enquiries@crieffhydro.com
Web: www.crieffhydro.com
1 hour from either Edinburgh or Glasgow. Follow A85 from Perth to Crieff (signposted Crianlarich) for 20 minutes. From Crieff town centre – up on the hill overlooking the town. [C5]

CRIEFF

Glenturret Distillery

- *"A popular venue offering a choice of dining experiences and very good self service food!"*
- *Traditional Scottish fare.*

THE SMUGGLERS RESTAURANT, situated on first floor of the converted warehouse, is self-service, with high standards of cooking. The Pagoda Room offers a more formal setting. The menus feature Highland venison, beef, lamb and salmon. Coffee, afternoon tea and home baking are also available during the day.

Glenturret hot smoked salmon in barley, whisky and woodchips dressed with honey and brown sugar. Local venison served with a pickled walnut sauce. Cranachan: oatmeal, cream and raspberries flavoured with The Glenturret Original Malt Liqueur.

STB Highly Commended

◐ Open all year except 25, 26 Dec, 1 2 Jan ✖ Food available all day £ Lunch ££ Dinner – by private arrangement only ££££ Ⓥ Vegetarians welcome ✱ Children welcome ♿ Facilities for disabled visitors ✂ Complete facilities are no smoking but a smoking area is provided in Smugglers Restaurant ☷ Credit cards: Mastercard/Eurocard, American Express, Visa, Switch ⦿ Brand Heritage Manager: Tracy McCafferty

The Hosh Crieff Perthshire PH7 4HA
Tel: 01764 656565 Fax: 01764 654366
E-mail: glenturret@highlanddistillers.co.uk
Web: www.glenturret.com
Approx 1 mile outside Crieff on A85 Crieff to Comrie road. Just over 1 hour from Edinburgh (M9) and Glasgow (M8). [C5]

CRINAN

Crinan Hotel

- *"A one-off setting with assured culinary skills and an excellent wine list – something for everyone here."*
- *Fresh imaginative fine cooking.*

LOCATED by the famous Crinan canal the main restaurant, the Westward, offers a delicious table d'hôte menu and an à la carte lunch is available in the bar. The exclusive and celebrated Lock 16 Restaurant is on the top storey of the hotel. Winner of The Macallan Taste of Scotland Hotel of the Year Award 1998.

Duck, foie gras and Puy lentil terrine with winter truffle and sweet shallot dressing. Pan-fried tranche of halibut with shellfish risotto, roasted salsify and saffron velouté. Baked fig tarte tatin with vanilla ice cream and marsala wine syrup.

STB ★★★★ Hotel

◐ Open all year ⌂ Rooms: 22 en suite ⊨ DB&B £105–£120 B&B £75–£90 ⓢⓟ Special winter rates available ✖ Lunch £ Dinner (Westward Restaurant) ££££ Dinner (Lock 16 mid Apr to end Sep only) except Sun Mon booking essential ££££ Ⓥ Vegetarians welcome ✱ Children welcome ♿ Facilities for disabled visitors ☷ Credit cards: Mastercard/Eurocard, American Express, Visa, Switch ⦿ Proprietors: Nick & Frances Ryan

Crinan Lochgilphead Argyll PA31 8SR
Tel: 01546 830261 Fax: 01546 830292
E-mail: nryan@crinanhotel.com
Web: www.crinanhotel.com
A82 Glasgow-Inveraray, then A83 to Lochgilphead. Follow A816 (Oban) for c.5 miles, then B841 to Crinan. [B5]

CUPAR

Ostlers Close Restaurant

- *"The best of quality food served in a delightful restaurant."*
- *Elegant Scottish cuisine using fresh Scottish produce.*

CHEF/PROPRIETOR Jimmy Graham and wife Amanda deserve the excellent reputation they have earned here over the past 19 years. Jimmy's treatment of fish and shellfish is outstanding, but he applies the same flair to Scottish meat and game, organic vegetables, fruit, herbs and wild mushrooms. 3 AA Rosettes.

Seared fillet of Pittenweem monkfish with Glamis asparagus risotto. Roast roe venison with chanterelles on a game sauce. Trio of summer fruit desserts.

◐ *Open all year except Christmas Day, Boxing Day, 1 Jan and first 2 weeks early summer Closed Sun Mon* ✕ *Lunch Tue, Fri, Sat only – booking essential Dinner except Sun Mon £££* Ⓥ *Vegetarians welcome – please mention at booking* ✶ *Children welcome* ⚹ *Smoking restricted until all diners at coffee stage* ☙ *Member of the Scotch Beef Club* 🎫 *Credit cards: Mastercard/Eurocard, American Express, Visa, Switch, Delta* ⚑ *Proprietors: Jimmy & Amanda Graham*

Bonnygate Cupar KY15 4BU
Tel: 01334 655574
Web: www.ostlersclose.co.uk
Small lane directly off A91 main road through town. [D5]

DALRY

Braidwoods: Winner 2000 – Overall Excellence; Chef Proprietor; Fine Dining in a Rural Setting

- *"Keith and Nicola continue to offer a stunning culinary experience, ensuring guests have a memorable occasion."*
- *Innovative modern Scottish cooking.*

THE FOOD at Braidwoods is of the highest standard. Menus change daily to account for the very best quality available produce and are composed with real skill and delicacy to create highly imaginative dishes. Booking is essential – table is yours for the duration of your meal. The Macallan Taste of Scotland Special Merit Award for Newcomers 1995.

Warm tart of Parmesan with rocolla leaves, crispy Parma ham and roast red pepper coulis. Roast breasts of squab pigeon on spiced red cabbage, crisp pommes anna and Madeira jus. A chilled apple crumble with iced vanilla parfait.

◐ *Open last week Jan to first week Sep and 3rd week Sep to 31 Dec except Christmas Day Closed Sun pm, Mon and Tue lunch* 🍷 *Table licence* ✕ *Lunch except Mon Tue ££ Dinner except Sun Mon £££* Ⓥ *Vegetarians welcome – prior notice required* ✶ *Children over 12 years welcome* ⚹ *No smoking throughout* ☙ *Member of Scotch Beef Club* 🎫 *Credit cards: Mastercard/Eurocard, American Express, Visa, Switch, Delta* ⚑ *Owners: Keith & Nicola Braidwood*

Drumastle Mill Cottage By Dalry KA24 4LN
Tel: 01294 833544 Fax: 01294 833553
Web: www.braidwoods.co.uk
A737 Kilwinning-Dalry. On southern outskirts of Dalry, take road to Saltcoats for 1 mile and follow signs. [C6]

DAVIOT NR INVERNESS

Daviot Mains Farm

- *"Margaret Hutcheson continually endeavours to find the best produce to tempt her guests."*
- *Creative home cooking.*

THE FARMHOUSE at Daviot Mains is built in the traditional style of a Highland lodge and is the warm and welcoming home of Margaret, Alex and Rachel Hutcheson. Margaret's excellent home cooking uses ingredients which are meticulously sourced to provide only the very best of Highland produce and served in generous portions.

According to season: home-made soups, fresh local salmon and trout, Aberdeen Angus beef, Scotch lamb, vegetables and cheeses. Local fruits and home-made puddings.

STB ★★★★ B&B

◐ Open all year except Christmas Eve and Christmas Day Note: Dinner served Mon to Fri Apr to Sep incl, thereafter Mon to Sat incl ££ – booking essential ⌂ Rooms: 6 en suite ⇌ DB&B £38–£45 B&B £25–£30 ⓢ Special rates available – Nov to Mar ♥ Licensed Ⓥ Vegetarians welcome – prior notice required Special diets on request ⚹ Children welcome ⌦ No smoking throughout ⊞ Credit cards: Mastercard/Eurocard, Visa ⌇ Owners: Alex & Margaret Hutcheson

Inverness IV2 5ER
Tel: 01463 772215 Fax: 01463 772099
E-mail: taste@daviotmainsfarm.co.uk
Web: www.daviotmainsfarm.co.uk
On B851 (B9006) to Culloden/Croy, 5 miles south of Inverness. Ignore signs for Daviot East and Daviot West. [C4]

DINGWALL

Kinkell House

- *"Excellent food in lovely peaceful surroundings."*
- *Country house cooking.*

MARSHA AND STEVE Fraser are generous hosts who make guests feel instantly welcome and relaxed. The excellence of Marsha's cooking is presented in interesting and well-balanced à la carte menus with both classic and innovative treatments. The restaurant is popular, and non-residents are asked to book in advance.
1 AA Rosette.

Warm tart of forest mushrooms with saffron. Fillets of monkfish wrapped in Argyll smoked ham with a sorrel dressing. Blueberry and apple meringue pie with home-made Calvados ice cream.

STB ★★★★ Small Hotel

◐ Open all year ⌂ Rooms: 9 en suite ⇌ DB&B £55–£65 B&B £35–£45 ⓢ Special rates available ✗ Lunch – by reservation ££ Dinner – by reservation ££ Ⓥ Vegetarians welcome ⚹ Children welcome ♿ Facilities for disabled visitors ⌦ No smoking in dining room and bedrooms ⊞ Credit cards: Mastercard/Eurocard, Visa ⌇ Proprietors: Marsha & Steve Fraser

Easter Kinkell by Conon Bridge Dingwall Ross-shire IV7 8HY
Tel: 01349 861270 Fax: 01349 865902
E-mail: kinkell@aol.com
Web: www.kinkell-house.co.uk
1 mile from A9 on B9169, 10 miles north of Inverness. [C3]

DIRLETON

The Open Arms Hotel

- *"A welcoming hotel in a pretty setting offering excellent cuisine."*
- *Modern Scottish.*

THE OPEN ARMS offers a warm friendly atmosphere with a fine dining restaurant open for lunch and dinner and also The Brasserie, Deveaus, which is less formal. Local salmon is a particular favourite served with East Lothian vegetables. There is a good accompanying wine list, with thoughtfully selected vintages, fairly priced. 2 AA Rosettes.

Warm salad of pigeon breast served on an Ayrshire bacon and Puy lentil broth. Roast turbot and smoked salmon paupiette with baby vegetable fondue and garden rhubarb confit. Poached peach flavoured with rosewater and cinnamon served on creamed rice and warm raspberry sauce.

STB ★★★★ Small Hotel

◐ *Open all year* 🏨 *Rooms: 10 en suite* 🛏 *DB&B £70–£110 B&B £50–£90* 💲 *Special rates available* ✕ *Lunch £-££ Dinner ££-£££* Ⓥ *Vegetarians welcome* ✤ *Children welcome* ♿ *Limited facilities for disabled visitors* 🚭 *Smoking discouraged: cigars and pipes not permitted* 💳 *Credit cards: Mastercard/ Eurocard, Visa, Switch, Delta* 👤 *Proprietors: Tom & Emma Hill*

Dirleton East Lothian EH39 5EG
Tel: 01620 850241 Fax: 01620 850570
E-mail: openarms@clara.co.uk
Web: http://home.clara.net/openarms
From Edinburgh take coast road to Gullane and North Berwick. Dirleton is 2 miles between them. [D5]

DORNOCH

Mallin House Hotel

- *"Comfort and value are to be found here – and good hearty food."*
- *Scottish cooking with seafood a speciality.*

THE HOTEL is a mere 200 yards from the Royal Dornoch Golf Course. It offers an exceptionally good range of bar meals. An extensive à la carte menu offers a good choice of local produce with superb, locally caught seafood as something of a speciality. Food is imaginatively prepared with unusual sauces and accompaniments.

King scallops and crab claws (pan-fried with spring onion, ginger, ceps, clams, and a hint of garlic.). Venison Bordelaise. Linda's crème caramel.

STB ★★ Hotel

◐ *Open all year* 🏨 *Rooms: 10 en suite* 🛏 *DB&B £48–£55 B&B £30–£35* ✕ *Lunch ££ Dinner £-££* Ⓥ *Vegetarians welcome* ✤ *Children welcome* ♿ *Facilities for disabled visitors* 💳 *Credit cards: Mastercard/Eurocard, American Express, Visa, Switch, Delta* 👤 *Proprietors: Malcolm & Linda Holden*

Church Street Dornoch IV25 3LP
Tel: 01862 810335 Fax: 01862 810810
E-mail: mallin.house.hotel@zetnet.co.uk
Web: www.users.zetnet.co.uk/mallin-house
Down to centre of town, turn right. [C3]

DORNOCH

The Royal Golf Hotel

- *"The perfect blend of traditional and modern interior design – it certainly has a wow about it!"*
- *Innovative Scottish cooking.*

THE ROYAL GOLF HOTEL is a traditional Scottish hotel which has been completely and sumptuously refurbished. Meals are served daily in the picture-windowed extension, which overlooks the golf course and the sandy beaches of the Dornoch Firth beyond. Head Chef Jeanette Weatheritt creates wonderful dishes using the fresh local produce available.

Gâteau of smoked salmon and prawns, topped with an Arran mustard cream cheese. Duo of pigeon and pheasant wrapped in smoked bacon and set on a herb pancake with a redcurrant and juniper jus. Crisp filo tartlet filled with raspberries and Mascarpone crème.

STB ★★★ Hotel
Green Tourism Two Leaf Silver Award

◐ Open 1 Mar to 31 Dec ⌂ Rooms: 25 en suite ⊨ DB&B £76–£96 B&B £51–£70 ㉠ Special rates available ✗ Lunch £ Dinner 4 course menu £££ Ⓥ Vegetarians welcome ⚹ Children welcome ⚞ No smoking in restaurant ⊟ Credit cards: Mastercard/Eurocard, Visa, Diners Club, Switch ⚐ General Manager: Joanne Urquhart

The First Tee Dornoch Sutherland IV25 3LG
Tel: 01862 810283 Fax: 01862 810923
E-mail: rooms@morton-hotels.com
Web: www.morton-hotels.com
From A9, 2 miles into Dornoch town square, straight across crossroads, 200 yards on right. [C3]

DOUNE PERTHSHIRE

Mackeanston House

- *"Mackeanston offers Scottish hospitality in a relaxed family home atmosphere."*
- *Scottish home cooking.*

THIS is a real family home where Fiona Graham offers a warm, hospitable welcome combining informality and a relaxing atmosphere with efficient service and food of a high standard. Many ingredients used in the kitchen are organically grown in Fiona's garden which may be viewed from the conservatory dining room.

Roasted red peppers with basil and Aga-baked Mediterranean loaf. Garden herb roulade with salmon and Ricotta, new potatoes and fresh tomato sauce. Home-made strawberry ice cream with Mackeanston shortbread.

◐ Open all year except Christmas Day ⌂ Rooms: 4 – 3 en suite, 1 private facilities (2 in house, 2 in cottage) ⊨ DB&B £58–£63 B&B £33–£38 ㉠ Special rates available ㉅ Unlicensed ✗ Dinner £££ Non-residents – dinner only Ⓥ Vegetarians welcome ⚹ Children welcome ⚞ No smoking throughout ⊟ Credit cards: Mastercard/Visa ⚐ Proprietors: Colin & Fiona Graham

Doune Perthshire FK16 6AX
Tel: 01786 850213 Fax: 01786 850414
E-mail: mackean.house@cwcom.net
Web: www.aboutscotland.com/stirling/mackeanston
Take junction 10 off M9 motorway to Stirling/Perth. Follow A84 to Doune for 5 miles, turn left on to B826 to Thornhill. Take farm road on left after 2 miles then private road before farmyard. [C5]

DUFFTOWN

A Taste of Speyside Restaurant

- *"Quality scottish food combined with traditional setting in the centre of the malt whisky capital."*
- *Good wholesome Scottish food.*

ONE OF the major attractions is the superb selection of Speyside malt whiskies on offer here. The menu makes the most of local ingredients and is enhanced by a well-chosen wine list.

Speyside platter (between two as a starter): smoked salmon, whiskied chicken liver pâté, smoked venison, local farmhouse cheese, sweet-cured herring, salad, oatcakes and home-made bread. Noisettes of lamb with a redcurrant and red wine sauce. Heather honey and malt whisky cheesecake.

◐ Open 1 Mar to 1 Nov ✕ Food available all day £ Lunch £ Dinner ££ Ⓥ Vegetarians welcome ✶ Children welcome ☒ Credit cards: Mastercard/Eurocard, American Express Visa, Switch ⋈ Partners: Raymond McLean & Peter Thompson

10 Balvenie Street Dufftown Banffshire AB55 4AB
Tel: 01340 820860 Fax: 01340 820860
50 yards from the Clock Tower on the road to Elgin. [D4]

DULNAIN BRIDGE

Auchendean Lodge Hotel: Winner 2000 – Dedication to Use of Local Seasonal Produce

- *"Enjoy the view, enjoy the expertly cooked food and hospitality, then relax in front of the log burning fire."*
- *Original, talented, eclectic cooking.*

OWNERS Eric Hart and Ian Kirk, are convivial professionals who give their guests a memorable dining experience. They share the cooking; Eric being a mycologist finds over 30 varieties of edible wild mushrooms locally. The hotel's garden provides many vegetables along with many local specialities, complemented by an excellent wine list.

Home-cured beef with garden rocket salad and St Andrews cheese. Breast of wild pigeon with Madeira sauce. Blackcurrant, liquorice and vanilla ripple ice cream.

STB ★★★★ Hotel

◐ Open most of the year ⌂ Rooms: 5 en suite ⛌ DB&B £46–£84 B&B £26–£59 ⓢⓟ Special rates available ✕ Pre-booked packed lunch £ Dinner £££ Ⓥ Vegetarians welcome – advise on booking ✶ Children welcome ♿ Facilities for non-residents only ⌦ No smoking in dining room and one lounge ☒ Credit cards: Mastercard/Eurocard, Visa ⋈ Proprietors: Eric Hart & Ian Kirk

Dulnain Bridge Grantown-on-Spey Inverness-shire PH26 3LU
Tel: 01479 851 347 Fax: 01479 851 347
E-mail: hotel@auchendean.com
Web: www.auchendean.com
On A95, 1 mile south of Dulnain Bridge. [C4]

DUNBLANE

Cromlix House

- *"Award-winning food served in luxurious surroundings!"*
- *Outstanding modern Scottish cuisine.*

DAVID AND AILSA ASSENTI exemplify the true traditions of country house hospitality – each guest is cherished. Everything here is of the highest standard. Head chef Paul Devonshire produces imaginative meals for the discriminating palate. Menus change daily using seasonally available produce. The wine list is discerning and extensive. 2 AA Rosettes.

Pavé of salmon with a smoked haddock and chive risotto. Loin of lamb with hasselback potatoes, fine beans and a tomato jus. Sable of summer berries layered with a drambuie sabayon.

STB ★★★★★ Hotel

◑ Open mid Jan ⌂ Rooms: 14 en suite (incl 8 suites) ⇌ DB&B from £131.50 B&B £92–£150 SP Special rates available – Oct to mid May ♇ Residents and diners licence only ✗ Lunch Mon to Fri – Oct to mid May pre-booked only; Sat Sun ££-£££ Dinner ££££ Ⓥ Vegetarians welcome ⚹ No smoking in dining room ⌇ Dogs in bedrooms only ⌑ Member of the Scotch Beef Club ⊞ Credit cards: Mastercard/Eurocard, American Express, Visa, Diners Club, Switch ⌧ Proprietors: David & Ailsa Assenti

Kinbuck By Dunblane Perthshire FK15 9JT
Tel: 01786 822125 Fax: 01786 825450
E-mail: reservations@cromlixhouse.com
Web: www.cromlixhouse.com
5 minutes off the A9. North of Dunblane Exit A9 to Kinbuck (B8033). Through Kinbuck village, cross narrow bridge and drive is 2nd on left. [C5]

DUNFERMLINE

Davaar House Hotel and Restaurant

- *A comfortable-family run hotel bursting with enthusiasm."*
- *Good home cooking.*

DAVAAR HOUSE is centrally situated in a residential area of Dunfermline and stands in lovely gardens. The food is cooked by Doreen Jarvis and her daughter Karen who create traditional dishes with intuitive flair, using the best fresh local produce which is abundant in the coastal East Neuk of Fife.

Smoked haddock and mustard grain fish cakes with chive cream. Fine Scottish sirloin grilled to order and garnished with Fife Valley vegetables. Baked rice brûlée with bramble sauce.

STB ★★★ Hotel

◑ Open all year except 23 Dec to 6 Jan Closed Sun ⌂ Rooms: 10 en suite ⇌ DB&B £54–£68 B&B £35–£50 SP Special rates available ♇ Restricted licence ✗ Lunch (Dec only) except Sun ££ Dinner except Sun £££ Ⓥ Vegetarians welcome ⚹ Children welcome ⚙ Facilities for disabled visitors ⚹ No smoking in restaurant and 1st floor bedrooms ⊞ Credit cards: Mastercard/Eurocard, Visa, Switch, Delta ⌧ Proprietors: Doreen & Jim Jarvis

126 Grieve Street Dunfermline KY12 8DW
Tel: 01383 721886 Fax: 01383 623633
From M90, junction 3, A907 Dunfermline. Straight on through town, over Sinclair Gardens roundabout, right into Chalmers Street at 4th set of traffic lights, 2nd left into Grieve Street. [D5]

Dunfermline

Garvock House Hotel

- *"Definitely Dunfermline's best kept secret."*
- *Modern Scottish cooking.*

GARVOCK HOUSE is an elegant house dating back over 200 years and retaining many original features, lovingly restored by its present owners. The cooking is excellent – a blend of innovative Scottish modern with traditional and, more recently available, Scottish ingredients. Much attention to detail – from turndown service to the care given to the presentation of your meal.

A smooth chicken and goose liver parfait with tomato chutney and toasted brioche. Seared Shetland salmon with coriander risotto and a chilli, caramel and lime oil. Iced raspberry ripple terrine with raspberry coulis and coconut tuille.

STB ★★★★ Small Hotel

◐ Open all year Closed Sun evening ⌂ Rooms: 11 en suite ⌘ B&B from £42.50 ▣ Special rates available ✕ Lunch ££ Dinner £££ except Sunday Ⓥ Vegetarians welcome ✼ Children welcome ♿ Facilities for disabled visitors ✗ No smoking in dining room ⌘ Small dogs welcome ⌸ Credit cards: Mastercard/Eurocard, Visa, Switch, Delta ⚜ Proprietors: Rui & Pamela Fernandes

*St John's Drive Transy Dunfermline KY12 7TU
Tel: 01383 621067 Fax: 01383 621168
E-mail: sales@garvock.co.uk
Web: www.garvock.co.uk
Exit junction 3, M90 and follow A907 into Dunfermline. After football stadium turn left into Garvock Hill and first right into St John's Drive. Hotel is 500m on right-hand side. [D5]*

Dunkeld

The Pend

- *"Warm and friendly hosts, good food and home comforts."*
- *Scottish home cooking.*

THE PEND is a delightful house with plenty of character, tasteful decorations and owner/chef Marina Braney is eager to provide guests with an optimum level of service. Dinner is served at a set time, special diets and requests are catered for, and everyone is seated around one table.

Dunkeld smoked salmon with lemon and horseradish creams. Roast Scottish lamb with redcurrant and wine gravy served with rosemary and garlic roast potatoes, creamed spinach, carrots and sugar snap peas. Peaches cardinal in raspberry purée.

STB ★★★★ B&B

◐ Open all year ⌂ Rooms: 3 ⌘ DB&B £50–£60 B&B £30–£35 ▣ Special rates available ✕ Dinner ££ Residents only Ⓥ Vegetarians welcome ✼ Children welcome ⌘ Dogs welcome ⌸ Credit cards: Mastercard/Eurocard, American Express, Visa, Diners Club, Switch, Delta, JCB ⚜ Owner/Chef: Marina Braney

*5 Brae Street Dunkeld Perthshire PH8 0BA
Tel: 01350 727586 Fax: 01350 727173
E-mail: react@sol.co.uk
Web: www.thepend.com
In the town centre, on Brae Street, off the High Street. Opposite the turning to the cathedral. [C5]*

DUNKELD

The Royal Dunkeld Hotel

- *"A comfortable stay in a delightful small town."*
- *Scottish cooking.*

THE ROYAL DUNKELD HOTEL is a former coaching inn now fully modernised with all modern amenities and offering a friendly welcome. There is a choice of dining here – either informally in the Gargoyles Lounge Bar or in the more formal restaurant. Food here is traditional, freshly prepared and well presented.

Seared West Coast scallops in a filo tartlet with basil, tomato and roasted shallots. Pan-fried noisettes of lamb served between potato galettes with roasted peppers and spinach, glazed with a mint hollandaise. Poached peach and vanilla mousse with nectarine sorbet.

STB ★★★ Hotel

◐ Open all year ⌂ Rooms: 35 en suite ⚏ DB&B £45–£55 B&B £30–£37.50 ⦿ Special rates available ✘ Lunch ££ Dinner £££ Ⓥ Vegetarians welcome ⚘ Children welcome ⚐ Facilities for disabled visitors ⚞ No smoking in dining room ⚑ Dogs welcome ⊟ Credit cards: Mastercard/Eurocard, American Express, Visa, Switch, Delta ⚏ Proprietor: Neil Menzies

Atholl Street Dunkeld Perthshire PH8 0AR
Tel: 01350 727322 Fax: 01350 728989
E-mail: royaldunkeldhotel@compuserve.com
Web: www.ourworld.compuserve.com/home pages/royaldunkeldhotel
www.see-scotland.com
Just off A9, on the main street of Dunkeld. 15 miles north of Perth. [C5]

DUNOON

The Anchorage Hotel & Restaurant

- *"A delightful establishment run by charming and welcoming hosts."*
- *Scottish food imaginatively cooked.*

PROPRIETORS, Tony and Dee Hancock have carefully renovated the Anchorage and the large conservatory restaurant overlooks the immaculate pretty gardens. Dining here you have the impression of eating outside. Comfortable lounge and breakfast rooms take in the stunning lochside scenery. A very appealing hotel, and Dee and Tony are amiable hosts.

Haggis tower: haggis topping a tower of neeps and tatties with a pool of Drambuie cream sauce. Berwickshire ostrich in a rice red wine, thyme and green peppercorn sauce. Dessert is always a surprise.

STB ★★★★ Hotel

◐ Open all year ⌂ Rooms: 5 en suite ⚏ DB&B £42.50–£55 B&B £27.50–£60 ✘ Lunch £ Dinner £££ Ⓥ Vegetarians welcome ⚘ Children welcome ⚐ Facilities for disabled visitors ⚞ No smoking throughout ⊟ Credit cards: Mastercard/Eurocard, Visa, Delta ⚏ Owners: Dee & Tony Hancock

Shore Road Sandbank Dunoon Argyll PA23 8QG
Tel: 01369 705108 Fax: 01870 7061099
E-mail: info@anchorage.co.uk
Web: www.anchorage.co.uk
3 miles out of Dunoon on A815 heading north. [B5]

DUNOON

Chatters Restaurant

- *"Cooking here is perfectly balanced, carefully crafted and presented with flair. Do go!"*
- *Traditional French-influenced Scottish cooking.*

IN THE CAPABLE hands of Rosemary MacInnes, Chatters combines excellence with a friendly informal atmosphere. The chefs are enthusiastic and extremely competent. Well balanced à la carte menus are presented for lunch and dinner – all food is home-made. 1 AA Rosette. Winner of The Macallan Taste of Scotland Special Merit Award for Enterprise 1994.

Warm roulade of spinach filled with woodland mushrooms on a red pepper and tomato coulis. Loin of local venison with a confit of carrot and celery and a rowan jelly reduction. Chocolate and whisky torte on an elderflower sabayon with a quenelle of Belgian chocolate mousse.

◐ Open Mar to mid Jan except Christmas Day, Boxing Day and New Year's Day Closed Sun Mon Tue ♀ Table licence ✕ Lunch except Sun Mon Tue £-££ Dinner except Sun Mon Tue ££-£££ ✍ Smoking in lounge only ⊞ Credit cards: Mastercard/Eurocard, Visa ⚑ Proprietor: Rosemary Anne MacInnes

58 John Street Dunoon Argyll PA23 8BJ
Tel: 01369 706402
E-mail: oldmill@cwcom.net
Web: www.oldmill.mcmail.com/chatters
Approach John Street from mini-roundabout on the sea front road. Restaurant opposite the cinema. [B5]

DUNOON

Enmore Hotel

- *"A lovely, well-run, hotel on the seafront."*
- *Modern Scottish cooking.*

THIS IS a friendly family-run hotel. David Wilson, Chef/Proprietor, pays good attention to sourcing local produce and presents a short menu cooked most competently, using home-baked bread and preserves. His wife, Angela, offers warm and genuine hospitality. Herbs and vegetables are grown in the hotel's garden. 1 AA Rosette.

Grilled smoked salmon escalope served with a garden sorrel sauce. Noisette of Scotch lamb with garden rosemary-enhanced jus. Porridge and raspberry crème brûlée.

STB ★★★★ Hotel

◐ Open all year except 20 Dec to 20 Jan
⌂ Rooms: 9 en suite ⇌ B&B £39–£75
☼ Special rates available ✕ Snack food available all day £-£££ Lunch – booking preferred ££-£££ Dinner – booking essential £££
Ⓥ Vegetarians welcome ☆ Children welcome
♿ Facilities for disabled visitors – non-residents only ✍ No smoking in dining room ⊞ Credit cards: Mastercard/Eurocard, American Express, Visa, Switch, Delta ⚑ Proprietors: Angela & David Wilson

Dunoon PA23 8HH
Tel: 01369 702230 Fax: 01369 702148
E-mail: enmorehotel@btinternet.com
Web: www.enmorehotel.co.uk
On seafront near Hunters Quay Ferry, approx 1 mile from town centre. Situated between the 2 ferries serving Dunoon. [B5]

EDINBURGH

36

- *"A gastronomic experience matched with exemplary service and atmosphere."*
- Best contemporary Scottish cooking.

A STUNNINGLY different modern restaurant. The minimalist, beautifully designed interior with modern yet comfortable furniture makes for a delightful atmosphere. The staff are all well-trained and professional. The cooking is skilful, by Chef Malcolm Warham, who uses the best fresh ingredients and his imagination to come up with inspired dishes.

A canelloni of Achiltibuie smoked haddock and sole with a tomato and tarragon salsa. Pan-fried fillet of Scotch beef with a braised oxtail ravioli, turnip sauerkraut and roasted shallots. A hot cherry and Caledonian ale soufflé with a walnut cookie.

◐ Open all year ✕ Lunch Sun only £-££ Dinner £££ Ⓥ Vegetarians welcome ✍ No smoking in restaurant ☙ Member of the Scotch Beef Club ▣ Credit cards: Mastercard/Eurocard, American Express, Visa, Diners Club, Switch, Delta ▯ Restaurant Manager: Patricia Toland; Head Chef: Malcolm Warham

36 Great King Street Edinburgh EH3 6QH
Tel: 0131 556 3636 Fax: 0131 556 3663
E-mail: 36@thehoward.com
Web: www.thehoward.com
Great King Street is off Dundas Street, the continuation of Hanover Street – 5 minutes from Princes Street. [D5]

EDINBURGH

A Room In The Town

- *"Excellent bistro with informal atmosphere offering good value for all tastes."*
- Modern Scottish cooking.

THE RESTAURANT offers a unique atmosphere with its simple, yet effective decor. Menus adorn the walls, describing the daily dishes. The cooking here is modern, innovative Scottish by Chef Steve Dickson. Diners are also welcome to take their own wine, although the restaurant is licensed. A busy city bistro well worth a visit.

Scottish salmon fillet cured in whisky, dill and demerara sugar, served with Highland oatcakes and sour cream. Pot-roasted silverside of beef with clapshot and burnt onion gravy. Upside down pear and gingerbread pudding with cardamom custard.

◐ Open all year except Christmas Day, Boxing Day, and 1, 2 Jan ✕ Lunch £ Dinner £££ Ⓥ Vegetarians welcome ▣ Credit cards: Mastercard/Eurocard, Visa, Switch, Delta, JCB, Solo ▯ Proprietors/Directors: John Tindal & Peter Knight; Head Chef: Steve Dickson

18 Howe Street Edinburgh EH3 6TG
Tel: 0131 225 8204 Fax: 0131 225 8204
Turn off Princes Street up Frederick Street – Howe Street is a continuation of Frederick Street – over the hill, down towards Stockbridge. [D5]

EDINBURGH

Atrium

- *"A striking modern restaurant achieving consistently high levels of excellence in its food."*
- *Outstanding modern Scottish cooking.*

THE IMAGINATIVE cooking is as distinctive as the restaurant it serves. Neil Forbes, Head Chef, offers an à la carte menu based on fresh local produce. Menus are inspired, creative and well-balanced, as befits one of Edinburgh's foremost restaurants. Andrew Radford chef/proprietor was recipient of The Macallan Personality of the Year 1994.

Sautéed scallops, globe artichoke and crab salad, dill hollandaise. Breast of Gressingham duck, bok choi, sticky belly pork, lentil and coriander sauce. Nougat glace with cherry syrup, almond tuille.

◐ *Open all year except 1 week Christmas Closed Sun* ✕ *Lunch except Sun ££ Dinner except Sun £££* Ⓥ *Vegetarians welcome* ⚸ *Children welcome* 🄲 *Credit cards: Mastercard/Eurocard, American Express, Visa, Diners Club, Switch, Delta* ⚑ *Proprietors: Andrew & Lisa Radford*

*10 Cambridge Street Edinburgh EH1 2ED
Tel: 0131 228 8882 Fax: 0131 228 8808
Within Saltire Court, sharing entrance with Traverse Theatre, adjacent to Usher Hall. [D5]*

EDINBURGH

The Balmoral Hotel

- *"A variety of impeccable cuisines."*
- *A grand hotel in the traditional style with exceptional standards.*

THE BALMORAL has it all – No. 1 for outstanding classically orientated cooking; less formal meals at Hadrian's; not to mention NB's Bar and Palm Court. 2 AA Rosettes. The Macallan Taste of Scotland Hotel of the Year 1995, Hotel Dining 1999. Category 1 and Overall Winner – The Taste of Scotland Scotch Lamb Challenge Competition 2000.

Marinated salmon terrine with mustard oil and tomato confit. Roast fillet mignon of beef with grain mustard mash and shallot sauce. Mandarin crème brûlée with blood orange ice cream.

STB ★★★★★ Hotel

◐ *Open all year* 🛏 *Rooms: 188 en suite* 🍽 *DB&B £120–£1120 B&B £90–£1000* ㊙ *Special rates available* ✕ *Food available all day £££ Lunch £££–££££ Dinner £££–££££* Ⓥ *Vegetarians welcome* ⚸ *Children welcome* ♿ *Facilities for disabled visitors* 🚭 *No smoking area in restaurants* 🐄 *Member of the Scotch Beef Club* 🄲 *Credit cards: Mastercard/Eurocard, American Express, Visa, Diners Club, Switch, Delta* ⚑ *Hotel Manager: Matthew Dixon*

*1 Princes Street Edinburgh EH2 2EQ
Tel: 0131 556 2414 Fax: 0131 557 3747
Web: www.rfhotels.com
Princes Street at the corner of North Bridge at East End of Princes Street. [D5]*

EDINBURGH

blue bar cafe

- *"Fresh and simple food using only the best local produce."*
- *Modern fusion bistro style.*

BLUE aims to cater for the discerning diner looking for a more informal, whilst still exceptionally high quality, experience. David Haetzman, Head Chef, is a highly skilled, innovative chef committed to the use of fresh local produce. The menus offer great choice, from light snacks to main meals.

Crayfish risotto with crab and leek wonton. Roast lamb rump with pea purée and bubble and squeak, with balsamic shallot dressing. Apple fritter with apple crumble sorbet.

◐ *Open all year except 1 week Christmas* ✗ *Food available 12 noon–3 pm, 6 pm–11 pm* £ *Lunch* ££ *Dinner* ££ Ⓥ *Vegetarians welcome* ⚹ *Children welcome* ♿ *Facilities for disabled visitors* 💳 *Credit cards: Mastercard/Eurocard, American Express, Visa, Diners Club, Switch* 👤 *Proprietors: Andrew & Lisa Radford*

10 Cambridge Street Edinburgh EH1 2ED
Tel: 0131 221 1222 Fax: 0131 228 8808
Adjacent to the Usher Hall. On the first floor of Saltire Court, above the Atrium and Traverse Theatre box office. [D5]

EDINBURGH

Bouzy Rouge

- *"Busy West End basement restaurant to suit the gourmet or casual diner."*
- *Modern Scottish.*

OPEN THE DOOR and you cannot fail to be impressed by the interior. The cooking is modern Scottish and as with all Bouzy Rouge restaurants, menus are compiled by both Alan Brown, proprietor, and the chef. Prices vary which allows great customer choice – from business lunches and casual dining to a gourmet menu.

Saffron risotto with sauteed chicken livers and reduced balsamic. Breast of Borders pigeon, set on a wild mushroom and asparagus tartlet with port gravy. Butterscotch mousse with toasted praline crust and caramel sauce.

◐ *Open all year except New Year's Day* ✗ *Food available all day* £-££ *Lunch* £-££ *Dinner* £-££ Ⓥ *Vegetarians welcome* ⚹ *Children welcome* 💳 *Credit cards: Mastercard/Eurocard, American Express, Visa, Diners Club, Switch* 👤 *Proprietors: Alan & Audrey Brown; Manager: Allison Beatty*

1 Alva Street Edinburgh EH2 4PH
Tel: 0131 225 9594 Fax: 0131 225 9593
E-mail: reservations@bouzy-rouge.com
Web: www.bouzy-rouge.com
Corner of Queensferry Street at Alva Street. Located on basement level. [D5]

EDINBURGH

Cafe Hub

- *"Modern, informal, all-day dining with influences from around the globe."*
- *Light, innovative and above all fresh.*

THIS OLD CHURCH has been carefully and sensitively redesigned internally and restored externally. Casual dining with neighbourhood cafe feel. The fine food experience at Cafe Hub is headed up by Craig Winning. The Hub has two wonderful rooms available for private use; the Dunard Library and Main Hall which accommodate up to 600 people.

King prawns with hot and sour sauce. Rib-eye on a bed of mustard mash, served with roast beetroot. Coffee pavlova, served with caramelised banana.

◐ *Open all year except Christmas Day* ✕ *Food available all day £ Lunch ££ Dinner ££* Ⓥ *Vegetarians welcome* ✱ *Children welcome* ♿ *Facilities for disabled visitors* ✍ *Facilities for smoking on terrace area* 💳 *Credit cards: Mastercard/Eurocard, American Express, Visa, Diners Club, Switch, Delta* ▤ *Cafe Manager: Craig Winning; Chef: Nick Bryan*

Castlehill Royal Mile Edinburgh EH1 2NE
Tel: 0131 473 2067 Fax: 0131 473 2016
E-mail: thehub@eif.co.uk
Web: www.eif.co.uk
A landmark church at the top of the Royal Mile, where Castlehill meets the Lawnmarket and Johnston Terrace. [D5]

EDINBURGH

Caledonian Hilton Hotel

- *"Classic, elegant surroundings and superb modern cooking make dining here a treat not to be missed."*
- *Fresh, lively and world class.*

THE 'CALEY' is an Edinburgh institution. The Pompadour Restaurant has been completely renovated and offers some of the best views and food in the city. The food is complex, intricate and deftly handled. Service is state-of-the-art; the wine list exceptional. Downstairs there is Chisholm's – a modern brasserie-style restaurant.

Compote of Western Isle seafood with fine leaves, saffron vinaigrette and basil oil. Pan-fried medallions of Aberdeen Angus beef with quails eggs, celeriac purée and red wine mushroom jus. Chocolate and pink grapefruit parfait, caramelised citrus fruits and Glenkinchie syrup.

STB ★★★★★ Hotel

◐ *Open all year* 🛏 *Rooms: 249 en suite* 🛌 *B&B £100–£200* 🆂 *Special rates available* ✕ *Lunch (Chisholm's) ££ Dinner (Chisholm's) ££ Lunch (The Pompadour) Tue to Fri ££ Dinner (The Pompadour) Tue to Sat £££* Ⓥ *Vegetarians welcome* ✱ *Children welcome in Chisholm's* ♿ *Facilities for disabled visitors* ✍ *Smoking area in Chisholm's, no smoking in The Pompadour* 💳 *Credit cards: Mastercard/Eurocard, American Express, Visa, Diners Club, Switch, Delta* ▤ *Resident Manager: Peter Hales*

Princes Street Edinburgh EH1 2AB
Tel: 0131 459 9988 Fax: 0131 225 6632
West end of Princes Street at junction with Lothian Road. [D5]

EDINBURGH

Channings Restaurant: Finalist The Macallan Taste of Scotland Awards 2000

- *"Don't miss this excellent establishment just off the beaten track."*
- *Innovative modern Scottish and continental cooking.*

THE SERVICE at Channings is superb, attentive and discreet yet friendly and relaxed. The cuisine is fresh and innovative but full of style and passionate flavours – Chef Richard Glennie really 'feels' his flavours so the food tastes even better than it looks – and it looks fantastic!

Canelloni filled with woodland mushrooms and chicken mousseline, fried risotto cake and truffle flavoured cappuccino. Fillet of turbot poached in a five spice infused consommé, crab tortellini, seared scallop and wilted greens. Assiette of apple desserts.

STB ★★★★ Hotel

◐ Open all year except 23 to 27 Dec incl and 7 Jan ▥ Rooms: 46 en suite ⊟ DB&B on request B&B £125–£198 ▩ Special rates available ✗ Lunch £ Dinner ££ Ⓥ Vegetarians welcome ⚘ Children welcome ✂ No smoking in restaurant ⊟ Credit cards: Mastercard/Eurocard, American Express, Visa, Diners Club, Switch, Delta ▨ Head Chef: Richard Glennie; Restaurant Manager: David McCourt

*12-16 South Learmonth Gardens Edinburgh EH4 1EZ
Tel: 0131 315 2225 Fax: 0131 332 9631
E-mail: restaurant@channings.co.uk
Web: www.channings.co.uk
From West End, cross Dean Bridge into Queensferry Road, then right, just after pedestrian lights, into South Learmonth Avenue and then right at the bottom. [D5]*

EDINBURGH

Daniel's Bistro

- *"A unique dining experience with a successful combination of Scottish, French and Pan-European dishes."*
- *Modern Scottish and French Provincial.*

DANIEL'S is an old converted bonded warehouse and is a feat of architectural design blended with simple furnishings. All this makes for a relaxed and friendly atmosphere created and pursued by Patron Daniel. Menus range from classic Scottish dishes to more continental choices – all skilfully prepared and presented – there is something to suit everyone here.

Tarte Flambee: milk bread dough with a topping of crème fraîche, fromage frais, onions and bacon lardons. Slow cooked duck confit served with paysanne sauteed potatoes. Daniel's special bread and butter pudding.

◐ Open all year except Christmas Day, Boxing Day, 1 and 2 Jan ✗ Lunch £-££ Dinner ££ Ⓥ Vegetarians welcome ⚘ Children welcome ♿ Facilities for disabled visitors ✂ Separate smoking dining area ⊟ Credit cards: Mastercard/Eurocard, American Express, Visa, Switch, Delta ▨ Owner: Daniel J. Vencker

*88 Commercial Street Edinburgh EH3 6SF
Tel: 0131 553 5933 Fax: 0131 553 3966
Web: www.edinburghrestaurants.co.uk
Located in Leith near the harbour. The building is opposite the new Scottish Executive and near HMS Britannia. [D5]*

EDINBURGH

Dubh Prais Restaurant

- *"A real taste of Scotland in a genuine Scottish restaurant where the cream of fresh local produce is served in style."*
- *Contemporary Scottish cooking.*

CHEF/OWNER James McWilliams presents a well-balanced à la carte menu which devotes itself entirely to Scottish seasonal produce and regional recipes. The dishes are described with patriotic fervour and are cooked using simple methods as the freshest produce requires. Seating is limited and in such a central location tables are often hard to come by.

Cullen skink. Collops in the pan. Atholl brose parfait.

◐ Open all year except 2 weeks Christmas and 2 weeks Easter Closed Sun Mon ✖ Lunch except Sun Mon £ Dinner except Sun Mon £££ Ⓥ Vegetarians welcome ⚹ Children welcome ⚸ Guests are asked not to smoke cigars or pipes 🖃 Credit cards: Mastercard/Eurocard, American Express, Visa, Switch, Delta, JCB ⚐ Chef/Proprietor: James McWilliams; Proprietor: Heather McWilliams

123b High Street Edinburgh EH1 1SG Tel: 0131 557 5732 Fax: 0131 557 5263 Edinburgh Royal Mile, opposite Crowne Plaza hotel. [D5]

EDINBURGH

Duck's at Le Marché Noir

- *"Relax in the welcoming atmosphere of Duck's where the food, wine and service will add to an exceptional dining experience."*
- *Excellent modern French/Scottish cuisine.*

IN THIS stylish New Town restaurant, award-winning chefs produce innovative and excellent Scottish-style cooking from fresh, local ingredients. The exceptional menus are well-presented with French undertones. Malcolm Duck takes justifiable pride in his extensive and spectacular wine list. A private dining room and special menus also available. 2 AA Rosettes.

Boudin of langoustine with mizuna salad and langoustine sauce. Roast loin of lamb coated with a roast garlic mousse, thyme and lentil du Puy sauce. Chocolate tart with a Cognac parfait and coffee custard.

◐ Open all year except 25 and 26 Dec ✖ Lunch ££ Dinner £££ Ⓥ Vegetarians welcome ⚹ Children welcome ♿ Facilities for disabled visitors ⚸ No smoking room in restaurant 🖃 Credit cards: Mastercard/Eurocard, American Express, Visa, Diners Club, Switch, Delta, JCB ⚐ Proprietor: Malcolm Duck

2/4 Eyre Place Edinburgh EH3 5EP Tel: 0131 558 1608 Fax: 0131 556 0798 E-mail: bookings@ducks.co.uk Web: www.ducks.co.uk At the northern end of Dundas Street lies Eyre Place. Duck's lies near the junction of the two. [D5]

EDINBURGH

Grain Store Restaurant

- *"Delicious, freshly prepared food, served with genuine hospitality."*
- *Modern Scottish.*

A MODERN staircase opens into a series of chambers, with attractive bare stone walls, superb arched windows, wood floors, with wood furniture and fittings. The cooking is accomplished, innovative and delicious, with a menu that changes with the seasons, all complemented by excellent service. Look out for the cheeseboard as Ian Mellis' famous shop is right next door.

Velouté of fresh fish and seafood, seagrass and a hint of Pernod. Saddle of lamb, sage and lemon crust, caramelised garlic. Almond meringue, nougat glacé, strawberry syrup.

● Open all year except Boxing Day ✕ Lunch £-££ Dinner ££-£££ Ⓥ Vegetarians welcome ✱ Children welcome 🖸 Credit cards: Mastercard/Eurocard, American Express, Visa, Switch, Delta, JCB, Solo ■ Partner/Manager: Paul MacPhail; Partner/Chef: Carlo Coxon

30 Victoria Street Edinburgh EH1 2JN
Tel: 0131 225 7635 Fax: 0131 622 7313
Web: www.preorderit.co.uk
2 minutes walk from the castle. Victoria Street is between the Grassmarket and George IV Bridge. [D5]

EDINBURGH

The Grange Hotel

- *"A well maintained and attractively furnished city hotel, with good quality food."*
- *Contemporary Scottish.*

A RELAXED atmosphere with comfort and style awaits at this Victorian mansion in its own gardens. Only a few minutes by car from the centre, it is able to offer a real country house atmosphere. Lunch and dinner are served in the conservatory overlooking the gardens to the rear. Menus are modern, innovative and seasonally changing.

Thai style crab and ginger cakes with buttered spinach and lemon mayonnaise. Baked loin of pork stuffed with a pigeon and black pudding farce, with braised cabbage and apple rösti. The Grange banoffee pie.

STB ★★★ Hotel

● Open all year ⌂ Rooms: 15 en suite ☒ B&B £60-£75 ▦ Special rates available ✕ Food available all day ££ Lunch ££ Dinner ££ Ⓥ Vegetarians welcome ✱ Children welcome ⚞ No smoking in restaurant 🖸 Credit cards: Mastercard/Eurocard, American Express, Visa, Switch, Delta ■ General Manager: Garry Field

8 Whitehouse Terrace Edinburgh EH9 2EU
Tel: 0131 667 5681 Fax: 0131 668 3300
E-mail: grange-hotel@talk21.com
Web: www.grange-hotel-edinburgh.co.uk
From Princes Street (West End), travel up Lothian Road onto Melville Drive. Turn right into Marchmont Road, continue up through Kilgraston Road then right into Whitehouse Terrace. [D5]

EDINBURGH

Haldanes Restaurant

- *"Charming surroundings of traditional style sits well with modern and creative Scottish cooking."*
- *Innovative Scottish cuisine.*

HALDANES has established itself as one of the foremost Edinburgh restaurants. Proprietor George Kelso creates Scottish cuisine in his own unique style while his wife Michelle, as front of house, gives excellent service to diners – a truly professional combination. In summer diners may enjoy the terraced garden to the rear.

Seared West Coast scallops with crispy bacon, leeks and balsamic dressing. Saddle of Highland venison with a wild mushroom mousse and red wine and celeriac sauce. Caramelised lemon tart with berry compote and crème fraîche.

◑ Open all year ✖ Lunch except Sun Sat ££ Dinner £££ Ⓥ Vegetarians welcome ♣ Children welcome ✱ No smoking in restaurant ☙ Member of the Scotch Beef Club ⊞ Credit cards: Mastercard/Eurocard, American Express, Visa, Switch, Delta ◙ Proprietor/Chef: George Kelso

*39a Albany Street Edinburgh EH1 3QY
Tel: 0131 556 8407 Fax: 0131 557 6633
E-mail: info@haldanesrestaurant.com
At the east end of the city centre – off Broughton Street on the corner of Albany Street and York Lane. [D5]*

EDINBURGH

Henderson's Salad Table

- *"Popular informal bistro, walking distance from the centre of town, with an interesting selection of vegetarian dishes. Healthy eating in relaxing and interesting surroundings."*
- *Innovative and interesting vegetarian cuisine.*

HENDERSON'S, still actively run by the family, appeals to all ages proving that wholefoods can be fun, especially Monday to Saturday nights when 'real' musicians enliven the wine bar. Vegetarian salads, savouries, quiches and puddings are freshly prepared and eagerly consumed throughout the day with an unusual selection of real ales and wines.

Broccoli and Dunsyre Blue cheese soup with freshly baked nutty malt bread. Vegetarian haggis filo parcels with honey and Drambuie sauce. Walnut pie with crème fraîche.

◑ Open all year except Christmas Day, Boxing Day, 1 and 2 Jan Closed Sun except during Edinburgh Festival ✖ Food available all day except Sun £ Lunch except Sun £ Dinner except Sun £-££ Ⓥ Vegans welcome ♣ Children welcome ✱ No smoking in main restaurant and wine bar areas ⊞ Credit cards: Mastercard/Eurocard, American Express, Visa, Switch, Delta, JCB ◙ Proprietors: The Henderson Family

*94 Hanover Street Edinburgh EH2 1DR
Tel: 0131 225 2131 Fax: 0131 220 3542
Web: www.hendersonsofedinburgh.co.uk
2 minutes from Princes Street under Henderson's wholefood shop, at the junction with Thistle Street. [D5]*

EDINBURGH

Howies Restaurant

- *"Friendly and efficient staff serving innovative dishes."*
- *Modern Scottish with Mediterranean influences.*

HOWIES has successfully gained a niche in the market with its innovative, reasonably priced, menu. Great care is taken over the daily changing menus to create appealing choices. Howies now offer a limited, but good quality, and very fairly priced wine list. The option to take your own wine is still available (£2 corkage charge).

Cappuccino of wild mushrooms. Rump of lamb on roast olive polenta with a shallot confit, basil oil and Parmesan crackling. Caramelised lemon tartlet.

◐ *Open all year except 25, 26 Dec and 1, 2 Jan Closed Mon lunch only* ✖ *Lunch except Mon £ Dinner ££* Ⓥ *Vegetarians welcome* ✱ *Children welcome* ♿ *Facilities for disabled visitors* 💳 *Credit cards: Mastercard/Eurocard, American Express, Visa, Diners Club, Switch, Delta*

*63 Dalry Road Edinburgh EH11 2BZ
Tel: 0131 313 3334 Fax: 0131 313 3334
On the south side of Dalry Road, between Richmond Terrace and Caledonian Road, 2 minutes from Haymarket. [D5]*

EDINBURGH

Howies Stockbridge

- *"A bustling popular restaurant serving innovative menus in a relaxed style."*
- *Modern Scottish.*

HOWIES Stockbridge is situated in the heart of Stockbridge. This is a lively, buzzing bistro where great attention has been given to design. The two or three course menus represent excellent value for money as do the house wines. The food here is exciting and delicious with the best of Scottish produce being used innovatively.

Smoked haddock and crab timbale wrapped in spinach, dressed with wasabi and ginger. Noisette of lamb on warm butter bean purée flavoured with garlic and rosemary, served with a minted Asian pear and ginger sauce. Howies banoffie pie.

◐ *Open all year except 25, 26 Dec and New Year's Day* ✖ *Food available all day Sat Sun £ Lunch £ Dinner ££* Ⓥ *Vegetarians welcome* ✱ *Children welcome* ♿ *Facilities for disabled visitors* 🚭 *No smoking room in restaurant* 🐕 *Guide dogs only* 💳 *Credit cards: Mastercard/Eurocard, American Express, Visa, Diners Club, Switch, Delta, JCB*

*4-6 Glanville Place Edinburgh EH3 6SZ
Tel: 0131 225 5553 Fax: 0131 225 5553
Located by the Stockbridge, on the corner of Hamilton Place. [D5]*

EDINBURGH

Igg's Restaurant

- *"A vibrant restaurant, with finest Scottish produce, skilfully prepared and the charisma of Spain!"*
- *Spanish dishes with Scottish produce.*

IGG'S is a small, friendly, owner-run restaurant in the heart of Edinburgh's Old Town which has been extended into the premises next door and has been elegantly refurbished. At lunchtime a tapas menu is available as well as a good priced three/four course table d'hôte and à la carte evening menu. 2 AA Rosettes.

Warm tart tatin of beetroot topped with a quenelle of Mascarpone and a tomato chive dressing. Fillet of Stobo Estate beef topped with a blue cheese crust on a rösti potato with a whisky sauce. Hot chocolate pudding with a warm chocolate sauce and vanilla ice cream.

◐ *Open all year except 1 to 3 Jan Closed Sun* ✕ *Lunch except Sun ££ Dinner except Sun £££* Ⓥ *Vegetarians welcome* ⚹ *Children welcome* ♿ *Wheelchair access* ❤ *Member of the Scotch Beef Club* 🄱 *Credit cards: Mastercard/Eurocard, American Express, Visa, Diners Club, Switch, Delta, JCB* ⚑ *Owner: Iggy Campos*

15 Jeffrey Street Edinburgh EH1 1DR Tel: 0131 557 8184 Fax: 0131 441 7111 Jeffrey Street lies between the Royal Mile and Market Street, behind Waverley Station. [D5]

EDINBURGH

Jackson's Restaurant

- *"Bags of Celtic charm – all in the best possible taste!"*
- *Modern Scottish cooking.*

JACKSON'S is open for both lunch and dinner, offering table d'hôte and à la carte menus, and its central location attracts both visitors and locals. The 'business' lunch is creative and very well-priced; the à la carte majors on Scottish ingredients, treated in unusual and original ways. A private room is also available.

King prawns, flash-fried with lime essence set on a spaghetti of seasonal vegetables. Marinated wild venison haunch, sautéed in rosemary butter and sloe gin with plum and red onion confit. Drambuie spiked crème brûlée served with a cinnamon shortbread.

◐ *Open all year except Christmas Day and Boxing Day Extended hours during Edinburgh Festival* ✕ *Lunch £ Dinner £££* Ⓥ *Vegetarians welcome* 🄱 *Credit cards: Mastercard/Eurocard, American Express, Visa, Switch, Delta, JCB* ⚑ *Proprietor: Lyn MacKinnon*

209 High Street Royal Mile Edinburgh EH1 1PE Tel: 0131 225 1793 Fax: 0131 220 0620 On the north side of the upper Royal Mile near to Cockburn Street. [D5]

EDINBURGH

Keepers Restaurant

- *"Good Scottish cooking in relaxing and cosy cellar surroundings."*
- *Traditional Scottish cooking.*

KEEPERS specialises in game – supported by fish, shellfish and prime meat. The cooking is traditional and the wine list is well-chosen and reasonably priced. The restaurant serves lunch and dinner on a table d'hôte (five starters, five main courses) and à la carte basis. Individual rooms (or, indeed, the entire place) can be reserved.

Sautéed scallops with a sauce of bacon and saffron cream. Stuffed breast of pheasant with pistachio nuts and ginger. Drambuie crème brûlée with fresh raspberries.

◗ *Open all year Closed Sun Mon and Sat lunch unless by prior arrangement Note: Parties by prior arrangement ✖ Lunch except Sun Mon Sat £ Dinner except Sun Mon ££ Ⓥ Vegetarians welcome ⚹ Children welcome ⚹ No smoking area by request ▭ Credit cards: Mastercard/Eurocard, American Express, Visa, Switch ▯ Proprietors: Keith & Mairi Cowie*

13B Dundas Street Edinburgh EH3 6QG
Tel: 0131 556 5707 Fax: 0131 556 5707
E-mail: keithcowie@keepers.sagehost.co.uk
Web:www.keepers.sagehost.co.uk
At the southern end of Dundas Street, near the junction with Abercromby Place. [D5]

EDINBURGH

Le Café Saint-Honoré

- *"The Auld Alliance of great Scottish food cooked in a French style."*
- *Scottish produce with French influence.*

CAFÉ ST-HONORÉ has a Gallic charm although Chef/Proprietor Chris Colverson favours a more Scottish style of cooking with French influences in the preparation. Menus change daily and are à la carte, and very reasonably priced. The cooking is adventurous and highly professional; interesting combinations and fresh, innovative sauces appear regularly.

Home-made noodles, with braised squid and olives. Shank of lamb, garlic confit, spinach, boudinnoir. Crème brûlée.

◗ *Open all year except Christmas Day, Boxing Day, and 2 days over New Year Closed Sun (except during Edinburgh Festival) and Sat Lunch ✖ Lunch ££ Pre and Apres Theatre Suppers Dinner £££ Ⓥ Vegetarians welcome ⚹ Children welcome ⚹ 2 non-smoking dining areas and 1 smoking dining area No parking ▭ Credit cards: Mastercard/Eurocard, American Express, Visa, Diners Club, Switch, Delta, JCB ▯ Chef/Proprietor: Chris Colverson & Gill Colverson*

34 North West Thistle Street Lane Edinburgh EH2 1EA
Tel: 0131 226 2211
Centre of Edinburgh, just off Frederick Street, 3 minutes from Princes Street. At Frederick Street end of lane. [D5]

EDINBURGH

The Marque

- *"This is a real jewel in Edinburgh – a superb dining experience."*
- *Modern Scottish with European influences.*

THE MARQUE is jointly owned and run by Lara Kearney, John Rutter and Glyn Stevens. The Marque has special menus for pre-theatre suppers as well as the usual interesting menus at lunch and dinner. The Marque's reputation is firmly established – as the cooking and hospitality served here is of the highest quality.

Duck breast, sweet potato and chilli mash, spinach and tomato jus. Olive oil-roasted halibut, baba ganouj, prawn dumpling, miso noodle broth. White, dark and milk chocolate terrine with caramel ice cream.

◐ *Open 7 Jan to 31 Dec Closed 25, 26 Dec, New Year's Day and first week in Jan Closed Mon* ✘ *Lunch except Mon ££ Dinner except Mon £££* Ⓥ *Vegetarians welcome – prior notice advised* ✝ *Children welcome* ✄ *Smoking in lounge only* 💳 *Credit cards: Mastercard/Eurocard, American Express, Visa, Switch, Delta* ⋈ *Restaurant Manager/Partner: Lara Kearney*

19-21 Causewayside Edinburgh EH9 1QF
Tel: 0131 466 6660 Fax: 0131 466 6661
E-mail: themarque@claramail.com
100 yards from the Dick Vet and the Meadows.
[D5]

EDINBURGH

No 3 Royal Terrace

- *"Choice of informal or formal dining in bistro or restaurant, with Scottish produce served in an interesting style. A true dining experience."*
- *Modern Scottish.*

NO 3 ROYAL TERRACE is a tastefully refurbished town house with many of the original features retained. The eating experience here is second to none with Scottish produce served in an innovative style. Diners may enjoy a relaxed informal meal in the bistro, or the more formal setting of the dining room.

Seared West Coast scallops with chive mash and caramelised onions. Border fillet of ostrich with pak-choy and pave potatoes veiled with an oriental sauce. Brioche bread and butter pudding with maple syrup ice cream.

◐ *Open all year except Christmas Day and Boxing Day* ✘ *Lunch ££ Dinner £££* Ⓥ *Vegetarians welcome* ✝ *Children welcome* 💳 *Credit cards: Mastercard/Eurocard, American Express, Visa, Diners Club, Switch* ⋈ *Proprietor: Nigel Hogg; Head Chef: Steven Worth*

Edinburgh EH7 5AB
Tel: 0131 477 4747 Fax: 0131 477 4747
E-mail: nigel@howgate.f9.co.uk
Web: www.howgate.f9.co.uk
From east end of Princes Street travel down Leith Walk. At first roundabout after the Playhouse Theatre take 2nd left onto London Road then sharp right onto Blenheim Place/Royal Terrace. [D5]

EDINBURGH

No 27 Charlotte Square, National Trust for Scotland

- *"A superb flagship for The National Trust, with a fast growing reputation as a haunt for discerning locals and tourists."*
- *Modern and traditional Scottish cooking served in style.*

NO 27 is the headquarters of 'The Trust'. It has a super gift shop with a splendid showcase. The Coffee Shop offers food all day, from porridge with cream in the morning; delicious cakes and scones; light lunches; and formal dining in the fine Georgian rooms for evenings. Painstakingly restored in all its glory.

Bowl of creamy crab soup flavoured with brandy. Saddle of venison, pan-fried with Perthshire berries – presented with roasted shallots. Home-made Highland toffee cake with a caramel sauce.

❶ *Open all year except 25, 26 Dec and 1, 2 Jan* ♞ *Licensed* ✘ *Food available all day £-££ Lunch £ Dinner ££* Ⓥ *Vegetarians welcome* ✱ *Children welcome* ♿ *Facilities for disabled visitors* ✔ *No smoking throughout* ▣ *Credit cards: Mastercard, Visa, Diners Club, Switch, Delta* ⧖ *Restaurant Manager: Lesley Fair*

27 Charlotte Square Edinburgh EH2 4ET
Tel: 0131 243 9339 Fax: 0131 243 9595
E-mail: catering@nts.org.uk
Web: www.nts.org.uk
In Edinburgh city centre, 2 minutes from West End of Princes Street. [D5]

EDINBURGH

The Potting Shed Restaurant At The Bruntsfield Hotel

- *"A friendly restaurant serving beautifully presented food, exceeding expectations."*
- *Innovative Scottish cooking.*

THE BRUNTSFIELD HOTEL is a town house hotel located opposite Bruntsfield Golf Links and incorporates the Potting Shed Restaurant which offers good food in a friendly, relaxed atmosphere. Food prepared by chef Martyn Dixon offers two and three course lunch menus on Saturday and Sunday and three course dinner every evening, which are very good value for money.

Fresh asparagus spears glazed with hollandaise sauce and set on a puff pastry pillow. Hot smoked salmon with wild mushroom risotto and chervil oil. Dark chocolate torte set on a purée of raspberries and served with dark chocolate ice cream.

STB ★★★★ Hotel

❶ *Open all year* ⌂ *Rooms: 75 en suite* ⚯ *DB&B £45–£77.50 B&B £42.50–£98* ▣ *Special rates available* ✘ *Food available all day (Kings Bar) £ Lunch £ Dinner (Kings Bar) £ Dinner (Potting Shed) ££* Ⓥ *Vegetarians welcome* ✱ *Children welcome* ♿ *Facilities for disabled visitors* ✔ *Smoking in bar area of restaurant only* ▣ *Credit cards: Mastercard/Eurocard, American Express, Visa, Diners Club, Switch, Delta* ⧖ *Hotel Manager: Andrea Whigham*

69 Bruntsfield Place Edinburgh EH10 4HH
Tel: 0131 229 1393 Fax: 0131 229 5634
E-mail: bruntsfield@queensferry-hotels.co.uk
Web: www.thebruntsfield.co.uk
1 mile south of Edinburgh city centre on A702, overlooking Bruntsfield Links. [D5]

EDINBURGH

The Reform Restaurant

- *"Stylish and minimalist, a great place to sample Scottish food with an innovative twist!"*
- *Modern stylish fusion cooking.*

REFORM has captured the old town setting with its decor of white and warm yellow giving an elegant but relaxed atmosphere. Here you will find the best of Scottish produce, presented in an original style – a truly modern dining experience in the Old Town.

Marinated Scottish salmon with lemon capers and horseradish crème fraîche wrapped in ribbons of cucumber. Oven-roasted rack of lamb on a sweet potato rösti with roast parsnip and pear with a cranberry jus. Roasted peppered strawberries with Grand Marnier in a brandy snap basket and a sweetened crème fraîche.

◐ *Open all year except Christmas Day and New Year's Day* ✘ *Lunch £* Ⓥ *Vegetarians welcome* ✹ *Children welcome* 🖃 *Credit cards: Mastercard/Eurocard, American Express, Visa, Switch, Delta* ◫ *Manager: N Lacaze*

267 The Canongate Royal Mile Edinburgh EH8 8BQ
Tel: 0131 558 9992 Fax: 0131 558 1718
Located just up from the New Scottish Parliament building, on the left-hand side as you go down the Royal Mile. [D5]

EDINBURGH

Restaurant At The Bonham

- *"The place to be seen in Edinburgh – a seriously modern and funky hotel."*
- *Modern Scottish/new Californian cooking.*

SERIOUSLY trendy, minimalist and striking – in stunning contrast with the Victorian building, the Bonham is a very spacious and chic hotel using the highest standards of fabric and furnishings. The management also has a commitment to professionalism and training. With chef Pelham Hill in the kitchen quality dining experience is complete.

Home-smoked Cailzie ostrich with baby leek salad and beetroot chutney. Medallions of Highland venison with wild boar and apple sausages, rosemary and port jus. White chocolate and raspberry trifle with dark chocolate cookies.

STB ★★★★ Hotel

◐ *Open all year except 3 to 7 Jan incl* 🛏 *Rooms: 48 en suite* 🛏 *B&B £135–£295* ⓢⓡ *Special rates available* ✘ *Food served all day £ Lunch ££ Dinner £££* Ⓥ *Vegetarians welcome* ✹ *Children welcome* ♿ *Facilities for disabled visitors* ⚟ *Smoking area in restaurant* 🖃 *Credit cards: Mastercard/Eurocard, American Express, Visa, Diners Club, Switch, Delta* ◫ *Head Chef: Pelham Hill*

35 Drumsheugh Gardens Edinburgh EH3 7RN
Tel: 0131 623 9319 Fax: 0131 226 6080
E-mail: restaurant@thebonham.com
Web: www.thebonham.com
Drumsheugh Gardens is in the heart of the West End. The Bonham lies at the junction with Rothesay Place. [D5]

EDINBURGH

The Rock

- *"Good modern Scottish cooking with exciting presentation."*
- *Modern Scottish cooking.*

THE ROCK RESTAURANT is run by John Mackay, an accomplished chef. It offers exceptionally good food, freshly prepared and presented in a contemporary style. The menu offers delights for the gourmet using interesting combinations of spices and influences from other corners of the world. The restaurant is elegant, tasteful and modern in decor with friendly staff.

Open ravioli of seared sea bass with salsa. Rump of Scottish lamb on garlic and goats cheese, flageolet beans with roast shallots and garlic, and a rosemary-scented jus. Strawberry and green peppercorn parfait served with Champagne-poached strawberries.

◐ *Open all year Closed Sun lunch* ✕ *Lunch except Sun £-££ Dinner ££-£££* Ⓥ *Vegetarians welcome* ⒸⒹ *Credit cards: Mastercard/Eurocard, American Express, Visa, Switch* 🄼 *Owner & Head Chef: John Mackay*

78 Commercial Street Leith Edinburgh EH6 6LX Tel: 0131 555 2225 Fax: 0131 555 1116 From city centre follow signs to Leith. At bottom of Leith Walk take left into Junction Street, right at traffic lights to Commercial Street. Turn first left to Dock Place then left into Commercial Quay. [D5]

EDINBURGH

Sheraton Grand Hotel

- *"The Grill room offers an oasis of traditional style service and superb dining."*
- *Scottish/international.*

THE SHERATON GRAND HOTEL has two restaurants; The Grill Room and The Terrace. The latter overlooks Festival Square and offers a sophisticated brasserie style menu. The former is formal and intimate: Executive Chef, Nicolas Laurent, brings international expertise to the finest raw ingredients. 3 AA Rosettes.

Caramelised scallops with spring vegetables, orange and vanilla-scented oil. Roast rack of lamb with Provençale crust, black olive sauce. Almond macaroon with Mascarpone cream, roasted pineapple, pina colada parfait.

STB ★★★★★ Hotel
Green Tourism Two Leaf Silver Award

◐ *Open all year* 🛏 *Rooms: 260 en suite* 🛌 *DB&B £114.50–£182 B&B £82.50–£150* ✕ *Lunch (The Terrace) ££ (The Grill Room) £££ Dinner (The Terrace) ££ (The Grill Room) ££££* Ⓥ *Vegetarian menus available in both restaurants* ✶ *Children welcome with special menu available* ♿ *Facilities for disabled visitors* ✂ *Pipes and cigars after 9 pm in The Grill Room No smoking area in both restaurants* 🐄 *Member of the Scotch Beef Club* ⒸⒹ *Credit cards: Mastercard/Eurocard, American Express, Visa, Diners Club, Switch* 🄼 *Executive Chef: Nicolas Laurent; Restaurant Manager: Jean-Philippe Maurer*

1 Festival Square Edinburgh EH3 9SR Tel: 0131 221 6422 Fax: 0131 229 6254 E-mail: sue_finlay@sheraton.com Web: www.starwood.com Vehicle access adjacent from western approach road. Pedestrian entrance off Festival Square. [D5]

Edinburgh

Stac Polly

- *"Enticing menus and charming style make this a very appealing restaurant."*
- *Modern/Scottish cuisine.*

THE STRENGTH of Stac Polly's menu is its originality and its charm. Chef Steven Harvey compiles menus which take full advantage of Scotland's glorious larder – thus providing exciting interpretations of modern and traditional Scottish cuisine. From a full to a light meal, choice and service are excellent. The wine list is small but selective.

Baked filo pastry parcels of haggis, served on a sweet plum sauce. Oven-roasted loin of lamb on a horseradish mash with a cider and honey glaze. Chocolate Marquise with coffee bean sauce and cinnamon ice cream.

① *Open all year incl Sun* ✕ *Lunch £ Dinner ££* Ⓥ *Vegetarians welcome* ✼ *Smoking area in restaurant* ⊞ *Credit cards: Mastercard/Eurocard, American Express, Switch Visa, Diners Club* ⓝ *Proprietor: Roger Coulthard*

29-33 Dublin Street Edinburgh EH3 6NL
Tel: 0131 556 2231 Fax: 0131 557 9779
Web: www.stacpolly.co.uk
At the east end of Queen Street, Dublin Street runs down hill off Queen Street. [D5]

Edinburgh

Tower Restaurant

- *"The Tower is an exciting eating experience set in modern stylish surroundings with outstanding views of the city."*
- *Stylish cuisine.*

THE RESTAURANT looks out over the rooftops of Old Edinburgh. A fine menu is on offer here with skilled, well-trained staff on hand to ensure that your experience is a memorable one. Everything is cooked with great care and attention to detail and the food is complemented with a well balanced wine list to suit all tastes.

Duck liver parfait with toasted brioche. Fillet of Aberdeen Angus beef with smoked garlic broth. Glazed lemon tart with a lime and ginger sorbet.

① *Open all year except Christmas Day and Boxing Day* ✕ *Food available all day ££ Lunch ££ Dinner £££* Ⓥ *Vegetarians welcome* ⚹ *Children welcome* ♿ *Facilities for disabled visitors* ✼ *No Smoking throughout* ⊞ *Credit cards: Mastercard/Eurocard, American Express, Visa, Diners Club, Switch* ⓝ *Proprietor: James Thomson General Manager: Stuart Thom; Head Chef: Steven Adair*

Museum of Scotland Chambers Street Edinburgh EH1 1JF
e-mail: reservations@tower-restaurant.com
Web: www.tower-restaurant.com
Tel: 0131 225 3003 Fax: 0131 247 4220
Museum of Scotland, level 5. [D5]

EDINBURGH

The Witchery by the Castle

- *"A beautiful atmospheric restaurant, providing some of the best food Edinburgh has to offer."*
- *Stylish modern Scottish cuisine.*

THE WITCHERY has a 'Secret Garden' which is one of the most romantic dining spots in the city. An à la carte menu and theatre supper menu are available in the evening, all with a choice of stylish and interesting dishes. James Thomson's wine list is spectacular, incorporating excellent wines from all over the World.

Lobster salad with a new potato and dill rémoulade. Aberdeen Angus with smoked garlic broth. Almond sable with Grampian raspberries.

◐ Open all year except Christmas Day and Boxing Day ⊞ Rooms: 2 en suite ✗ Lunch ££ Theatre Supper £ Dinner £££ ⊞ Credit cards: Mastercard/Eurocard, American Express, Visa, Diners Club, Switch ⦿ Proprietor: James Thomson

*Castlehill Royal Mile Edinburgh EH1 2NF
Tel: 0131 225 5613 Fax: 0131 220 4392
E-mail: reservations@thewitchery.com
Web: www.the witchery.com
At the Castle end of the Royal Mile, just a few feet from the castle entrance, opposite Camera Obscura. [D5]*

EDINBURGH OUTSKIRTS

Caerketton Restaurant

- *"An excellent example of fresh produce, freshly and skilfully prepared."*
- *Modern Scottish cooking.*

THE DECOR at the Caerketton Restaurant is simple and effective with terracotta walls and green chairs giving a calm and relaxing atmosphere. Proprietors Bob and Susan Woodman, with Chef Scott Donaldson, ensure that fresh produce is served in an innovative style. A true example of Scottish food at its best.

Grilled whole langoustines with garlic and chilli over a lemon rocket salad. Pan-fried supreme of duck marinated in orange and honey, on a piquant plum compote, with Cointreau jus. Brandy snap filled with Edinburgh Fog, on a rich raspberry coulis.

◐ Open all year except Christmas Day, New Year's Day and 2 Jan Closed Mon ✗ Lunch except Mon £ Dinner except Mon ££ Ⓥ Vegetarians welcome ✶ Children welcome ♿ Facilities for disabled visitors ⊘ No smoking in dining room ⊞ Credit cards: Mastercard/Eurocard, American Express, Visa, Switch, Delta ⦿ Director/Proprietor: Bob Woodman

*Mauricewood Mains Mauricewood Road Penicuik Midlothian EH26 0NJ
Tel: 01968 670800 Fax: 01968 672670
E-mail: caerketton@mains72.freeserve.co.uk
From the Edinburgh city bypass take the A702 (Lothianburn junction) for 3.7m, turn left at sign (Mauricewood, Belwood, Glencorse) the restaurant is on the right hand side (after 500 yards). Or take A701 (Straiton junction) for 3.6m, turn right into Belwood road at Glencorse crossroads, and continue to top, restaurant is opposite. [D6]*

EDINBURGH OUTSKIRTS

Dalhousie Castle

- *"Authentic Scottish castle with a unique dining experience."*
- *Traditional Scottish and French cooking.*

A UNIQUE dungeon restaurant: the cooking is traditional Scottish with French influences serving local produce at its best. The new Orangery Conservatory dining area will serve 'modern' Scottish and Mediterranean cooking. There is also the addition of a new Spa planned for opening late 2000. Extensive classical function and conference rooms.

Warm salad of wild mushrooms and shallots topped with lightly grilled Border goats cheese. Pan-fried loin of Highland estate venison, timbale of haggis, traced by a red wine and raspberry sauce finished with chocolate. Orange and Drambuie parfait with heather honey and raspberry syrup.

STB ★★★★ Hotel

◐ Open all year except 2 weeks Jan ▣ Rooms: 34 en suite (inc 5 in lodge) ⊨ DB&B £99.50–£129.50 B&B £72.50–£102.50 ⓢ Special rates available ✕ Food available all day ££ Lunch from ££ Dinner £££ Orangery Restaurant: lunch from £ Dinner from ££ Ⓥ Vegetarians welcome ✴ Children welcome ⌇ No smoking in Dungeon Restaurant or bedrooms ▣ Credit cards: Mastercard/ Eurocard, American Express, Visa, Diners Club, Switch, Delta ▣ Managing Director: Neville Petts

*Bonnyrigg nr Edinburgh EH19 3JB
Tel: 01875 820153 Fax: 01875 821936
E-mail: enquiries@dalhousiecastle.co.uk
Web: www.dalhousiecastle.co.uk
A7, 7 miles south of Edinburgh. From traffic lights on A7 at B704 junction. [D6]*

EDINBURGH OUTSKIRTS

Houstoun House Hotel

- *"A very comfortable historic hotel with every modern luxury and excellent cuisine."*
- *Country house cuisine.*

T HE RESTAURANT at Houstoun House is situated in the former drawing room, library and great hall on the first floor – all delightful rooms and beautifully furnished with antiques and pictures. The chef presents a sophisticated and well-balanced table d'hôte menu at lunch and an à la carte menu at dinner – his cooking is first-class.

Trout tartar with poached quails eggs with a chilled gazpacho dressing. Roast pigeon and baby vegetables nestling on a red onion and carraway tarte tartare, served with a port essence. Rhubarb and ginger crème caramel with golden sugar and fresh mint.

STB ★★★★ Hotel

◐ Open all year ▣ Rooms: 72 en suite ⊨ DB&B £75–£95 B&B £50–£70 ⓢ Special rates available ✕ Lunch except Sat ££ Dinner ££££ Ⓥ Vegetarians welcome ✴ Children welcome ♿ Facilities for disabled visitors ⌇ No smoking dining room available ❦ Member of the Scotch Beef Club ▣ Credit cards: Mastercard/ Eurocard, Visa, Diners Club, Switch ▣ General Manager: Ann Yuille

*Uphall West Lothian Edinburgh EH52 6JS
Tel: 01506 853831 Fax: 01506 854220
Just off M8 motorway at Junction 3. [D6]*

ELGIN

Mansfield House Hotel

- *"A high degree of comfort, charming staff and very good food."*
- *Traditional Scottish cooking, with some French influences.*

CLOSE to the centre of Elgin, this completely refurbished and restored former manse provides a comfortable retreat for business and leisure visitors alike. Head Chef, Craig Halliday, presents a well-priced à la carte menu made up of classic Scottish dishes, using market available fish, meat and vegetables. 1 AA Rosette.

Smoked trout, tomato and spring onion salad with a horseradish dressing. North Sea halibut baked en papillote with white wine and pink peppercorns. White chocolate parfait on a pool of prune and Armagnac coulis.

STB ★★★★ Hotel

◐ Open all year ⌂ Rooms: 21 en suite ⇌ DB&B £60–£90 B&B £40–£70 ⓢⓟ Special rates available ✗ Lunch £ Dinner £££ Ⓥ Vegetarians welcome ⚹ Children welcome ♿ Facilities for disabled visitors ✖ No smoking in restaurant ▣ Credit cards: Mastercard/Eurocard, American Express, Visa, Switch ⑪ Owners: Mr & Mrs T R Murray

Mayne Road Elgin IV30 1NY
Tel: 01343 540883 Fax: 01343 552491
E-mail: mansfieldelgin@bun.com
Web: www.mansfieldhouse.com
Just off A96 in Elgin. From Inverness, drive towards town centre and turn right at first roundabout. At mini-roundabout, hotel on right. [D3]

ELLON

**Haddo House,
National Trust for Scotland**

- *"Watch the waistline – follow a light sandwich with a whopping cream cake! mmmm!"*
- *Light lunches, snacks and home baking.*

HADDO HOUSE has the very welcoming Stables tea-room which is high ceilinged, simply decorated and light and airy. A fine example of the high standards set at National Trust properties. Home baking and cooking feature highly on the menu making Haddo house an ideal place to spend the day.

Soups: Broccoli and Stilton; traditional Scotch Broth. Hot Highland fudge cake with toffee sauce and locally produced luxury ice cream. Wide range of bakes from local recipes and baked on premises.

STB Commended Visitor Attraction

◐ Open weekends only Apr and Oct Daily 1 May to 30 Sep ⓢⓟ Special rates available ⚇ Licensed – pre-arranged events only ✗ Food available all day £ Lunch £ Ⓥ Vegetarians welcome ⚹ Children welcome ♿ Facilities for disabled visitors ✖ No smoking throughout ⌇ Dogs welcome ▣ Credit cards: Mastercard, Visa ⑪ Property Manager: Craig Ferguson

Tarves Ellon Aberdeenshire AB4 0ER
Tel: 01651 851440 Fax: 01651 851888
Web: www.nts.org.uk
On the Old Meldrum–Tarves road, take road on left 1 mile outside Tarves. Along 1½ miles drive to Haddo House. [D4]

FAIRLIE

Fins Seafood Restaurant

- *"You don't get much fresher than this – and cooked to perfection."*
- *Imaginative, modern fish cookery.*

FINS, and Fencebay Fisheries, is now quite a complex. Many make frequent pilgrimages to enjoy the deft, light cooking of Gillian Dick, head chef – oysters, squat lobsters, bass, sole, langoustines and fresh trout. A conservatory, in which light meals are available between lunch and dinner during the summer months, has been recently added.

Seared squid with a chilli pepper marinade. Monkfish and salmon in ginger, lime, coconut and coriander. Rhubarb cheesecake with a strawberry and rhubarb compote.

◐ Open all year except Christmas Day, Boxing Day and New Year's Day Closed Mon ⌂ Rooms: 2 ✗ Lunch except Mon ££ Dinner except Mon £££ Ⓥ Vegetarians welcome ★ Children welcome – lunch only ♿ Facilities for disabled visitors ✄ No smoking in restaurant ⊞ Credit cards: Mastercard/Eurocard, American Express, Visa, Switch, Delta ⊠ Owner: Jill Thain

Fencefoot Fairlie Ayrshire KA29 OEG Tel: 01475 568989 Fax: 01475 568921
E-mail: fencebay@aol.com
Web: www.fencebay.co.uk
On A78, 1 mile south of Fairlie near Largs. [C6]

FALKIRK

The Grange Manor Hotel

- *"A relaxed family-run hotel with attention to detail and delicious dishes."*
- *Modern Scottish cooking.*

BILL WALLACE enjoys personally greeting his guests, ensuring that they feel at home in this comfortable hotel. Chef Colin Legget offers complex Scottish cooking of high modern standards. Both à la carte and table d'hôte eating are provided where game and fish feature with light, imaginative sauces, alongside traditional meats and poultry. 1 AA Rosette.

Saladette of Puy lentil and foie gras with truffle and Muscat wine dressing. Red mullet on a cèpe and tomato tart, spiced tapenade and roasted chilli oil. Pear William parfait, sesame seed lacy tuile with hazelnut caramel and a quenelle of rice pudding.

STB ★★★★ Hotel

◐ Open all year ⌂ Rooms: 37 en suite ⛁ DB&B £83.50–£98.50 B&B £60–£75 ⓢ Special rates available ✗ Food available all day £££ Lunch ££ Dinner £££ Ⓥ Vegetarians welcome ★ Children welcome ♿ Facilities for disabled visitors ⊞ Credit cards: Mastercard/Eurocard, American Express, Visa, Diners Club, Switch, Delta ⊠ Proprietors: Bill & Jane Wallace

Glensburgh Road Grangemouth FK3 8XJ
Tel: 01324 474836 Fax: 01324 665861
E-mail: info@grangemanor.co.uk
Web: www.grangemanor.co.uk
Just off M9. To Stirling – exit at junction 5, follow A905 for 2 miles (to Kincardine Bridge). To Edinburgh – exit at junction 6, turn right, 200 metres on right. [C5]

FALKIRK

Inchyra Grange Hotel

- *"I totally agree with* The Inchyra Blessing – *'Good food, rich comfort and friendly attention'."*
- Choice of Italian Bistro and fine dining restaurant.

THERE ARE two restaurants at Inchyra; the Priory Restaurant with a daily changing menu based on the availability of local produce – dinner is à la carte; and Peligrino's Italian Bistro for a light meal. Bar meals are available in the Earl Lounge. Centrally located it is popular with locals and visitors alike.

Warm tartlet of creamed leek and Finnan haddock. Roast rib of Donald Russell beef with Yorkshire puddings and classic chasseur sauce. Chocolate and Cointreau torte served with a chantilly cream and a sauce anglaise.

STB ★★★★ Hotel

◗ Open all year ⌂ Rooms: 109 en suite ⌸ DB&B £55–£65 B&B £40–£50 ✖ Food available all day £££ Lunch except Sat ££ Dinner £££ Ⓥ Vegetarians welcome ⚹ Children welcome ♿ Facilities for disabled visitors ⚱ No smoking in restaurant ☙ Member of the Scotch Beef Club 🖃 Credit cards: Mastercard/ Eurocard, American Express, Visa, Diners Club, Switch ⍟ General Manager Steven McLeod

*Grange Road Polmont Falkirk FK20 OYB
Tel: 01324 711911 Fax: 01324 716134
From Edinburgh and the east – leave motorway at junction 5, take junction with Bo'ness sign (A905) on left. Travel ½ mile to roundabout, turn right into Wholeflats Road. After 400 yards take first right for Polmont. Hotel is 400 yards on right. [C5]*

FALKIRK

La Bonne Auberge Brasserie

- *"Attractively served and carefully cooked cuisine."*
- Modern Scottish with French influences.

PART OF the Park Lodge Hotel, La Bonne Auberge Brasserie is a popular local restaurant serving a sound Scottish menu, with French influences, in an attractive setting. Menus incorporate items from, a more informal contemporary light meal and grill to more traditional main courses. Staff are well trained, friendly and helpful.

Grilled asparagus with Parmesan cheese and balsamic vinegar dressing. Roast breast of duck with a horseradish potato rösti on plum gravy. Port wine trifle, with wild berries and rum ice cream.

STB ★★★ Hotel

◗ Open all year ⌂ Rooms: 55 ⌸ DB&B £44–£80 B&B £34.50–£65 ⓢⓟ Special rates available ✖ Food available all day ££ Lunch £ Dinner ££ Ⓥ Vegetarians welcome ⚹ Children welcome ♿ Facilities for disabled visitors 🖃 Credit cards: Mastercard/Eurocard, American Express, Visa, Diners Club, Switch, Delta ⍟ General Manager: David Lochans

*The Park Lodge Hotel Camelon Road
Falkirk FK1 5RY
Tel: 01324 628331 Fax: 01324 611593
E-mail: park@queensferry.hotels.co.uk
Web: www.theparkhotel.co.uk
Situated on Camelon Road directly opposite Dollar Park. [C5]*

FALKIRK

Quenelles Restaurant

- *"Nothing is too much trouble in this friendly restaurant."*
- *Modern Scottish cooking.*

QUENELLES offers only the best Scottish produce cooked with flair and imagination by chef/proprietor Andy Bell. Joint Partner, Julia Thomas looks after front of house. This is a family-run restaurant whose policy is to use good raw materials from local producers. There is an extended lunchtime menu and a chef 's specials board.

Sliced pigeon breast on a mound of caramelised onion surrounded by a port and thyme jus. Wild brown trout filled with chanterelle mushrooms, chive and malt whisky glaze, served with honey and rosemary carrots and horseradish mashed potato cake. Drambuie flavoured raspberry cranachan.

◐ *Open all year except first 2 weeks Jul Closed Sun Mon* ✕ *Lunch except Sun Mon £ Dinner except Sun Mon ££* Ⓥ *Vegetarians welcome* ⚹ *Children welcome* ⊞ *Credit cards: Mastercard/Eurocard, Visa, Switch, Delta, Solo, JCB* ⚑ *Chef/Proprietor: Andy Bell*

4 Weir Street Falkirk FK1 1RA
Tel: 01324 877411 Fax: 01324 632035
North side of town centre. Visible from roundabout at main post office. From High St, (pedestrian only) turn into Kirk Wynd at Steeple, continue to far end of Vicar Street, restaurant is on right. [C5]

FALKLAND

Kind Kyttock's Kitchen

- *"A visit to Fife should involve a visit to Kind Kyttock's Kitchen."*
- *Excellent home baking.*

KIND KYTTOCK's is charming. Bert Dalrymple's baking is divine – he also preserves his own fruits, jams, pickles and chutneys and makes his own soups and more! Winner of The Macallan Taste of Scotland Special Merit Award for Best Tea-Room 1997 and received the Tea Council's Award of Excellence 2000.

Kind Kyttock's Scotch broth served with Kind Kyttock's 'famous' home-made brown bread. Delicious salads freshly prepared with the finest ingredients. Scots pancake filled with fresh strawberries and cream.

◐ *Open all year except Christmas Eve to 5 Jan Closed Mon* ✕ *Food available all day except Mon £* Ⓥ *Vegetarians welcome* ⚹ *Children welcome* ⌫ *No smoking throughout* ⊞ *Credit cards: Mastercard/Eurocard, American Express, Visa, Switch* ⚑ *Owner: Bert Dalrymple*

Cross Wynd Falkland Fife KY15 7BE
Tel: 01337 857477 Fax: 01337 857379
A912 to Falkland. Centre of Falkland near the Palace, turn up at the Square into Cross Wynd. [D5]

FALKLAND

Malt Barn Inn

- *"A high standard of service and hospitality with food to match."*
- *Scottish produce, Scandinavian-style!*

THE MALT BARN is a small roadside inn where the best Scottish produce is presented Scandinavian-style by hosts Mark and Monica Henderson. A speciality is gravlax. There is also the Beer Garden – when weather permits! In addition all the produce can be either vacuum-packed or bottled for you.

'Scandinavian delight': A medley of hot smoked Scottish trout, gravlax, and blackcurrant and vodka-marinated herring, accompanied by a frosted chilli-pepper schnapps. A fillet steak with a border of duchess potatoes, topped with bearnaise sauce on a sizzling hot oak plank. Hot blueberry soup with cinnamon and vanilla ice cream, served with almond macaroons.

◐ Open all year except 1 to 5 Jan ✘ Food available all day £-££ Lunch £-££ Dinner ££-£££ Ⓥ Vegetarians welcome ☆ Children welcome – lunchtime only and up to 8pm ♿ Facilities for disabled visitors ⚐ Smoking area ▣ Credit cards: Mastercard/Eurocard, Visa, Switch, Delta ▌ Proprietors: Mark & Monica Henderson

Main Street Newton of Falkland Fife KY15 7RZ
Tel: 01337 857589 Fax: 01337 857589
E-mail: mhhenz@aol.com
½ mile outside Falkland which is off Junction 8 on M90. 20 Minutes south of St Andrews. [D5]

FEARN BY TAIN

Glenmorangie House at Cadboll: Finalist The Macallan Taste of Scotland Awards 2000

- *"Relaxed ambience, fine dining and exceptional service – what a gem."*
- *Scottish cuisine.*

GLENMORANGIE HOUSE offers the ultimate in hospitality in a beautiful part of Scotland. Professionally run by Michael Andrews, the house offers comfort, modern amenities and warmth. Menus are presented in classical style with modern influences, using the finest of locally-sourced and home-grown produce. Wine included in price for dinner.

Mille feuille of Cadboll salmon and Moray Firth crab and lobster. Fillet of Ross-shire beef, creamy leeks and peppercorns spiced cabbage. Chocolate truffle cake with fresh strawberries and sorbet.

STB ★★★★★ Small Hotel

◐ Open all year ▥ Rooms: 9 en suite ⛌ DB&B £85–120 B&B £60–£75 ⓢⓟ Special rates available ✘ Food available all day – with prior booking Lunch from ££ Dinner from ££ Non residents – with prior booking Ⓥ Vegetarians welcome ☆ Children welcome ⚐ No smoking in dining room ⛨ Pets welcome in cottage rooms ▣ Credit cards: Mastercard, American Express, Visa, Switch ▌ House Manager: Michael Andrews

Fearn by Tain Ross-shire IV20 1XP
Tel: 01862 871 671 Fax: 01862 871 625
E-mail: relax@glenmorangieplc.co.uk
Web: www.glenmorangie.com
33 miles north of Inverness on A9. Turn right at roundabout for B9175 Nigg. Drive 2 miles to left turn for Balintore and Hilton. 5 miles through village of Hilton to end of lane. [C3]

FORRES

**Brodie Castle,
National Trust for Scotland**

- *"Relax for a day sampling walks, absorbing the history of the castle and refreshments at the coffee shop."*
- Scottish.

SURROUNDED by farmland, which provides wholesome local produce, Brodie Castle welcomes visitors whether they wish to explore its extensive grounds, enjoy the art treasures within the castle or admire its architectural splendours. The friendly tea-room offers excellent Scottish home baking and cooking and light refreshments using the best ingredients and all cooked on the premises.

Home-made spicy parsnip soup served with crusty roll. Crispy baguette topped with melted Cheddar cheese, bacon and tomato, served with seasonal salad and home-made coleslaw. Brodie's seasonal fruit crumble with cream or Mackie's ice cream.

STB Commended

◐ Open daily 1 Apr to 30 Sep and weekends only in Oct ▩ Special rates available ▥ Unlicensed ✗ Food available during Castle's opening hours £ day £ Lunch £ Ⅴ Vegetarians welcome ⚘ Children welcome ⚒ Facilities for disabled visitors ⚕ No smoking throughout ⚐ No credit cards ⚑ Catering Manager: Wendy Guild

Brodie Forres Moray IV36 2TE
Tel: 01309 641371 Fax: 01309 641600
Web: www.nts.org.uk
On A96 between Forres and Nairn. 3 miles west of Forres. [D3]

FORRES

Knockomie Hotel

- *"Fine surroundings, a fine wine list and a very fine meal!"*
- The best of Scottish cooking with French influences.

KNOCKOMIE HOTEL offers first-rate accommodation and dining. Part of the landscaped gardens are used to supply herbs and salad; vegetables are grown locally. On the daily changing table d'hôte menu, food is local and fresh. The Bistro is more casual than the traditional dining room. The wine list is of especial interest. Knockomie Hotel has 2 AA Rosettes.

John dory wrapped in Parma ham, served with a tomato and basil salad. Rack of lamb with a courgette and fennel tart, pomme purée, baby spinach and a thyme jus. Warm caramelised pear with a parfait of vanilla and bitter chocolate sorbet.

STB ★★★★ Hotel
Green Tourism Two Leaf Silver Award

◐ Open all year except Christmas Day ▩ Rooms: 15 en suite ▣ Special rates available ✗ Lunch £ Dinner 5 course menu £££ Ⅴ Vegetarians welcome ⚘ Children welcome ⚒ Facilities for disabled visitors ⚕ No smoking in dining room ⚛ Member of the Scotch Beef Club ⚃ Credit cards: Mastercard/Eurocard, American Express, Visa, Diners Club, Switch, Delta, JCB ⚑ Resident Director: Gavin Ellis

Grantown Road Forres Moray IV36 2SG
Tel: 01309 673146 Fax: 01309 673290
E-mail: stay@knockomie.co.uk
Web: www.knockomie.co.uk
1 mile south of Forres on A940. 26 miles east of Inverness. [D3]

FORRES

Ramnee Hotel

- *"Bustling town hotel – popular with the locals."*
- *Fresh local produce well-presented in modern style.*

THE RAMNEE HOTEL is a lively and bustling town hotel set in two acres of beautiful gardens. Food in Hamblin's Restaurant is characterised by generous portions imaginatively presented. The accompanying wine list is extensive and well-chosen. Lighter, more informal meals are available in 'Tipplings' cocktail lounge. Staff are friendly and helpful. 1 AA Rosette.

Chowder of Moray Firth mussels presented with a lobster ravioli. Char-grilled Angus beef served with a parsnip mash, roasted shallot, bacon and tarragon butter. Scottish summer berries served with a lemon, and basil sorbet.

STB ★★★★ Hotel

◑ Open all year except Christmas Day and 1 to 3 Jan ⌂ Rooms: 20 en suite ⌂ DB&B £55–£77.50 B&B £32.50–£55 ⓢⓟ Special rates available ✕ Lunch £ Dinner ££–£££ Ⓥ Vegetarians welcome ✱ Children welcome ⌫ No smoking in restaurant ⌸ Credit cards: Mastercard/Eurocard, American Express, Visa, Diners Club, Switch, Delta ⌸ Director: Garry W Dinnes

Victoria Road Forres Moray IV36 3BN
Tel: 01309 672410 Fax: 01309 673392
E-mail: ramneehotel@btconnect.com
Web: www.tartancollection.co.uk
A96 Inverness-Aberdeen, off bypass at roundabout at eastern side of Forres – 500 yards on right. [D3]

FORT WILLIAM

An Crann

- *"Carefully prepared, delicious food and very good value for early birds!"*
- *Imaginative Scottish cooking.*

AN CRANN, located in an impressive barn conversion full of character, has unique views of Ben Nevis and the surrounding Braveheart country. The emphasis is very much on good food, creatively prepared, using high quality local produce. Home-made daily specials, soups, vegetarian dishes and fresh seafood are always on the menu. Food available from 5pm – 9pm (the early bird option 5pm – 6.30 pm).

Local langoustines with lemon grass cream, roasted red pepper and tomato soup. Highland lamb served with a Madeira, garlic and rosemary sauce. Clootie dumpling with whisky cream.

◑ Open 25 Mar to mid Oct ✕ Dinner except Sun ££ Ⓥ Vegetarians welcome ✱ Children welcome ♿ Facilities for disabled visitors ⌸ Credit cards: Mastercard, Visa ⌸ Owner/Chef: Sine Marie Ross

Seangan Bridge Banavie Fort William PH33 7PB
Tel: 01397 772 077/228
10 minutes drive from Fort William. Take A82 north, then at lights take A830 for Mallaig. Turn right towards Banavie B8004, 2 miles to An Crann. [B4]

FORT WILLIAM

Crannog Seafood Restaurant

- *"Skilfully prepared seafood presented with detail and care."*
- *Fresh seafood, cooked simply.*

CRANNOG is a converted bait store on the end of a short pier in Fort William. Diners can sometimes watch the catch being landed direct into the kitchen – and enjoy the freshest imaginable seafood. There is a small reception area for pre-dinner drinks. Meat eaters welcome.

Warm home-made seafood tart accompanied by sweet dill mustard. The Crannog Fisherman's feast: a mouth watering selection of West Coast seafood; scallops, smoked mussels, langoustines, rainbow trout, oakroast salmon, oysters and monkfish. Local cheeses presented with home-made warmed oatcakes, celery and fruit.

◐ Open all year except Christmas and New Year ✘ Lunch £ Dinner ££ Ⓥ Vegetarians welcome ✳ Children welcome ♿ Facilities for disabled visitors ✁ Smoking area in restaurant 💳 Credit cards: Mastercard/Eurocard, Visa, Switch, Solo 🎩 Managing Director: Finlay Finlayson

*Town Pier Fort William PH33 7PT
Tel: 01397 705589 Fax: 01397 705026
E-mail: crannogallan@msn.com
Web: www.crannog.net
Fort William town pier – off A82 Fort William town centre bypass. [B4]*

FORT WILLIAM

The Moorings Hotel

- *"Friendliness and a hearty meal are evident at the Moorings."*
- *Bold and imaginative Scottish cooking.*

THE MOORINGS is a coaching inn, set in lovely grounds and run by Managing Director, Stewart Leitch. The cooking here is bold, using good local produce, and the chefs are keen to innovate and experiment. There is a commitment here to quality – equally to be found in the service, surroundings and the cooking.

Soufflé of West Coast seafood on a pool of saffron sauce with pan-seared scallops. Noisette of Mamore lamb in a wild garlic coat set on a shallot and rhubarb marmalade. Home-made nougat truffle ice cream parfait set on a butterscotch sauce.

STB ★★★★ Hotel

◐ Open all year except Christmas week 🛏 Rooms: 21 en suite 🛌 DB&B £62–£78 B&B £36–£52 💲 Special rates available ✘ Food available all day ££ Lunch ££ Dinner £££ Ⓥ Vegetarians welcome ✳ Children welcome ♿ Facilities for disabled visitors ✁ No smoking in dining room 🐕 Dogs welcome 💳 Credit cards: Mastercard/Eurocard, American Express, Visa, Diners Club, Switch, Delta, JCB 🎩 Managing Director: Stewart Leitch

*Banavie Fort William PH33 7LY
Tel: 01397 772797 Fax: 01397 772441
E-mail: moorings@lochaberhotels.freeserve.co.uk
On the outskirts of Fort William. From Fort William, take A830 Mallaig road for approx 1 mile. Cross the Caledonian Canal and take first right into the village of Banavie. [B4]*

FORT WILLIAM

No 4 Cameron Square

- *"Elegant little restaurant serving skilfully prepared fresh quality produce, including a very good value business lunch."*
- *Stylish Scottish cuisine.*

THIS IS an elegant little restaurant with delightful gardens, with a few tables outside for sunny days, that overlook the new extension to the restaurant. This restaurant demonstrates a real commitment to quality under Executive Chef Alasdair Robertson. Coffee and cake is served between lunch and evening service. 1 AA Rosette.

Warm salad of pigeon breast with a blackcurrant vinaigrette. Ballantyne of Guinea fowl on a bed of fresh herb risotto with wild garlic leaves and a red wine jus. Home-made sticky fig pudding with butterscotch sauce.

◐ Open all year except Sun during winter
✗ Food available all day ££ Lunch £ Dinner ££
Ⓥ Vegetarians welcome ✹ Children welcome
♿ Facilities for disabled visitors ✂ No smoking dining area 💳 Credit cards: Mastercard/Eurocard, American Express, Visa, Diners Club, Switch, Delta ⚙ Managing Director: Stewart Leitch

Cameron Square Fort William Inverness-shire PH33 6AJ
Tel: 01397 704222 Fax: 01397 704448
Web: www.no4-fortwilliam.co.uk
Centrally located in Fort William, Cameron Square is just off the pedestrianised High Street. 'No 4' is next to the Tourist Information Office. [B4]

GAIRLOCH

Charleston House

- *"A warm welcome and hearty home cooking awaits the guest here."*
- *Good Scottish cooking with Mediterranean and Far Eastern influences.*

CHARLESTON HOUSE is an imposing, Listed house of character on the shore of Flowerdale Bay at the edge of Gairloch. Morag Walmsley is an accomplished cook serving delicious and excellent produce cooked with style. John, her husband, is a charming host, and ensures that your stay is a relaxed and comfortable one. Dining room open to non-residents.

Freshly landed Gairloch crab, dressed by ourselves, served in the shell with a mixed leaf salad. Salmis of Pheasant with redcurrants and glazed chestnuts. Fresh raspberry and almond torte.

STB ★★ Guest House

◐ Open all year except 1st and 2nd week Dec
🛏 Rooms: 7 ⚏ DB&B £44–£48 B&B £22–£26
🅢🅟 Special rates available 🚭 Unlicensed ✗ Dinner £££ Ⓥ Vegetarians welcome ✹ Children welcome ✂ No smoking in the dining room
🐕 Dogs welcome by arrangement only
💳 Credit cards: Mastercard/Eurocard, Visa, Switch, Delta, JCB ⚙ Proprietors: Morag & John Walmsley

Charleston Gairloch IV21 2AH
Tel: 01445 712497 Fax: 01445 712689
E-mail: holidays@charleston-house.ndirect.co.uk
Web: www.charleston-house.ndirect.co.uk
Turn first left before the harbour when approaching from South. [B3]

GAIRLOCH

Creag Mor Hotel

- *"Whether feasting on their carefully prepared food or walking in the gardens you will have a good stay at the Creag Mor."*
- *Modern Scottish cooking*

RAY AND BARBARA Leaver-Hill preside professionally over this attractive hotel set in a most spectacular location. In the elegant Mackenzie restaurant Chef Gordon Gillespie and his team offer carefully crafted food by candlelight. The cooking here is skilfully executed using the best available locally sourced produce. A very special place.

Sole and chive mousse topped with strands of smoked salmon, fresh leaves and lemon balm dressing. Fillet of turbot with roast plum tomatoes and a herb and sorrel sauce. Poached spiced pears accompanied with Amaretto parfait and mixed berry coulis.

STB ★★★★ Hotel

◐ Open 1 Mar to 11 Nov ⌂ Rooms: 17 en suite
⛌ DB&B £75–£85 B&B £50–£70 ⓢ Special rates available ✘ Food available all day £ Lunch £ Dinner £££ Ⓥ Vegetarians welcome
✯ Children welcome ♿ Facilities for disabled visitors ⚞ No smoking in restaurant 🐾 Dogs welcome ⊞ Credit cards: Mastercard/Eurocard, American Express, Visa, Switch, Delta
ⓜ Proprietors: Ray & Barbara Leaver-Hill

*Charleston Gairloch Wester Ross IV21 2AW
Tel: 01445 712068 Fax: 01445 712044
E-mail: enquiries@creagmor-hotel.co.uk
Web: www.creagmor-hotel.co.uk
Situated in Charleston, ½ mile south of Gairloch. First turning on right when entering Charleston on A832 from Inverness. [B3]*

GAIRLOCH

Little Lodge

- *"A truly memorable experience."*
- *Innovative menus with excellent local and home-made produce.*

THE COMMITMENT of Di Johnson and Inge Ford is outstanding – from their own hens, sheep and goats to the garden providing vegetables and herbs. Di's imaginative marinades and sauces enhance local produce, while Inge's home-made bread, oatcakes, yoghurt and preserves make breakfast a special treat. Winner The Macallan Taste of Scotland Special Merit Award Hospitality 1996.

Gairloch crab and shitake cakes with tomato and ginger sauce. Saddle of Aberdeenshire organically-reared lamb, claret and rosemary sauce, rösti potatoes and braised fennel with cardamom. Chocolate roulade with garden raspberry and sloe gin coulis.

◐ Open May to Sept ⌂ Rooms: 3 en suite
⛌ DB&B £55 (minimum stay 2 nights)
Ⓤ Unlicensed – guests welcome to take own wine and spirits ✘ Non-residents welcome – by prior arrangement Dinner £££ ✶ No children
⚞ No smoking throughout ⊞ No credit cards
ⓜ Proprietors: Di Johnson & Inge Ford

*North Erradale Gairloch IV21 2DS
Tel: 01445 771237
Take B8021 from Gairloch towards Melvaig for 6 miles, situated ¼ mile beyond turning to North Erradale. [B3]*

GAIRLOCH

Myrtle Bank Hotel

- *"Enjoy the expansive views from Myrtle Bank's amazing seafront position."*
- *Traditional Scottish cooking.*

MYRTLE BANK HOTEL is popular with both locals and visitors to the area. Local produce and home-made cooking are the basis of the menu which is balanced and well-priced. Guests have the choice between bar and dining room eating. Seafood is particularly tasty given the local catch!

Warm salad of Loch Ewe scallops with a wine and saffron cream sauce, resting on mixed salad leaves. Medallions of west coast venison with caramelised shallots and roasted garlic, surrounded by a red wine jus. Orange cake with a caramel sauce.

STB ★★★ Hotel

◐ *Open all year except New Year's Day* 🛏 *Rooms: 12 en suite* 🍽 *DB&B £56–£62 B&B £36–£44* 💷 *Special rates available* ✕ *Lunch from £ Dinner from £* 🅥 *Vegetarians welcome* ✻ *Children welcome* ♿ *Facilities for disabled visitors* 🚭 *No smoking in dining room* 💳 *Credit cards: Mastercard, American Express, Visa, Switch,* ⊠ *Proprietors: Iain & Dorothy MacLean*

Low Road Gairloch Wester Ross IV21 2BS
Tel: 01445 712004 Fax: 01445 712214
E-mail: myrtlebank@email.msn.com
Web: www.hotelgairloch.com
Close to the centre of Gairloch, just off B2081.
[B3]

GAIRLOCH

The Old Inn

- *"A comfortable inn serving a wide range of delicious dishes with care and charm."*
- *Traditional Scottish cooking.*

AT THE Old Inn Alastair and Ute Pearson provide a warm welcome for an enjoyable holiday. Food plays an important role at The Old Inn – West Coast seafood, Highland game and carefully sourced meat. Special touches at this establishment set it apart from others. There is something for the whole family here.

Beef carpaccio served with a dressing of virgin olive oil, capers and lemon topped with Parmesan shavings. Seared scallops in lime, ginger, and garlic butter, served on tossed salad with a sunflower and wasabi dressing. Chef's home-made tiramisu.

STB ★★ Inn

◐ *Open all year* 🛏 *Rooms: 14 en suite* 🍽 *B&B £20–£30* 💷 *Special rates available* 🍷 *Licensed* ✕ *Food available all day £ Lunch £ Dinner £* 🅥 *Vegetarians welcome* ✻ *Children welcome* 🚭 *No smoking in the dining room* 🐕 *Dogs welcome* 💳 *Credit cards: Mastercard/ Eurocard, Visa, Switch, Delta* ⊠ *Proprietor: Mr A Pearson*

Gairloch Ross-shire IV21 2BD
Tel: 01445 712006 Fax: 01445 712445
E-mail: nomadscot@lineone.net
Web: www.theoldinn.co.uk
Travelling from Inverness take the A9 north over the Kessock Bridge. At the Tore roundabout take the A835 to Garve. Just north of Garve take the A832 to Achnasheen, continue on the A832, at the Achnasheen roundabout to Gairloch. On the right hand side of the A832 opposite Gairloch Harbour. [B3]

GLASGOW

Babbity Bowster

- *"A lively inn, in the heart of the Merchant City."*
- *Scottish cooking.*

BABBITY BOWSTER is known as one of the 'in places' in Glasgow's city centre. The hotel today has a lively bar on the ground floor, with garden outside; the Schottische Restaurant for more formal dining. Quality food, drink and intellectual conversation is the key to the success of this place, together with Fraser Laurie's personal supervision.

Scottish oysters poached with fish stock and vermouth and topped with breadcrumbs. Fillet of beef on a croûton with a rich port and foie gras sauce. Black and white chocolate terrine with more than a hint of Glayva.

◐ *Open all year except Christmas Day and New Year's Day Note: Restaurant closed Sun evening/ Sat lunch* 🏨 *Rooms: 7 en suite* 🍴 *DB&B £60–£85 B&B £50–£70* ✖ *Food available all day £ Lunch £ Dinner ££-£££* Ⓥ *Vegetarians welcome* ✱ *Children welcome* 💳 *Credit cards: Mastercard/Eurocard, American Express, Visa* 🔑 *Owner: Fraser Laurie*

16-18 Blackfriars Street Glasgow G1 1PE
Tel: 0141 552 5055 Fax: 0141 552 7774
E-mail: babbitybowster@gofornet.co.uk
In the heart of Glasgow's Merchant City – at the East End of city centre. [C6]

GLASGOW

Bouzy Rouge

- *"A very pleasant and enjoyable dining out experience."*
- *Scottish with international influence.*

THE MENU at Bouzy Rouge complements the unique designer (specially made) furniture. It offers many options for both special occasions and day-to-day business and whilst using the best Scottish produce introduces international dishes and themes. Also look out for the speciality nights. Despite being open all day and evening – booking essential. 2 AA Rosettes.

Gâteau of Scottish puddings: Lewis haggis, white and black, buttered shallots and served with an Orkney cheese sabayon. Saddle of Rannoch venison, roasted pink with caramelised shallots and a juniper berry reduction. Raspberry crème brûlée with burnt cream and shortbread fingers.

◐ *Open all year except New Year's Day* ✖ *Food available all day ££ Lunch £-££ Dinner ££* Ⓥ *Vegetarians welcome* ✱ *Children welcome* ♿ *Facilities for non-wheelchair visitors only* 💳 *Credit cards: Mastercard/Eurocard, American Express, Visa, Diners Club, Switch, Delta, Solo, Electron* 🔑 *Proprietors: Alan & Audrey Brown; Managers: Andy & Murray*

111 West Regent Street Glasgow G2 2RU
Tel: 0141 221 8804 Fax: 0141 221 6941
E-mail: reservations@bouzy-rouge.com
Web: www.bouzy-rouge.com
City centre location on corner of West Regent and Wellington Street. Approach via M8 from Charing Cross and follow one-way system from Sauchiehall Street. [C6]

GLASGOW

The Buttery

- *"Chef Ian Mackie continues a great tradition here – presenting the best Scottish produce with skill and flair."*
- *Gourmet, Scottish, contemporary.*

THE BUTTERY dates back to 1869 when it was Scotland's first premier restaurant. Stained glass doors lead to the Victorian wood-panelled dining room. Service is impressive. Under chef Ian Mackie, Scottish dishes are exquisitely presented with unusual combinations and lots of interesting textures and flavours. The luncheon menu is excellent value. The Buttery has 2 AA Rosettes.

Open ravioli of flaked salmon and seared langoustine with sweet vermouth and cream. Sliced roulade of pork fillet stuffed with herb and spinach parfait, haggis timbale, grape chutney, and brandy and green peppercorns. 'The Buttery Grand Dessert' – every dessert on offer miniaturised.

◐ *Open all year except Christmas Day and New Year's Day Closed Sun* ✗ *Lunch except Sun Sat ££ Dinner except Sun £££* Ⓥ *Vegetarians welcome* ✁ *Smoking of pipes and cigars is preferred in the bar* ☙ *Member of the Scotch Beef Club* 🖃 *Credit cards: Visa, Diners Club, Switch, Delta* ⓜ *Manager: Fraser Campbell*

652 Argyle Street Glasgow G3 8UF
Tel: 0141 221 8188 Fax: 0141 204 4639
Argyle Street, just below M8 overpass – Westside. Take Elderslie Street, turn left at mini-roundabout at southern end of street. Restaurant at bottom of street on left. [C6]

GLASGOW

The Cabin Restaurant

- *"Commitment to fresh produce comes through in the superb flavours."*
- *Modern Scottish with Irish influences.*

THE ATMOSPHERE is informal and cheerful. Dishes from the table d'hôte menu are cooked to order; the cooking technique is creative, confident and to a very high standard; menus change daily, according to what is available in the market. A very friendly, fun restaurant where the quality of the food shines through.

Pan-seared woodpigeon breast on puréed beetroot and orange with game jus. Grilled turbot with fresh herb crust on a bed of braised summer vegetables. Mixed fresh Blairgowrie berries set in red wine jelly accompanied by a mango coulis.

◐ *Open all year except 1 to 14 Jan and 15 to 30 Jul Closed Sun Mon* ✗ *Lunch except Sun Mon Sat £ Dinner except Sun Mon £££* Ⓥ *Vegetarians welcome* ✱ *Children welcome* ♿ *Facilities for disabled visitors* ✁ *Pipes and cigars not permitted* 🖃 *Credit cards: Mastercard/Eurocard, Visa* ⓜ *Proprietors: Mohammad Abdulla & Denis Dwyer*

996 Dumbarton Road Whiteinch Glasgow G14 9UJ
Tel: 0141 569 1036
From Glasgow city take Clyde expressway, pass Scottish Exhibition & Conference Centre to Thornwood Roundabout. Follow sign to Whiteinch (½ mile). Restaurant on right-hand side at junction with Haylynn Street. [C6]

GLASGOW

Café Gandolfi

- *"A vibrant meeting place with loads of character and excellent food."*
- *Modern Scottish cooking.*

THE CAFE GANDOLFI has been a Glasgow institution for years. Seumas MacInnes' commitment to Scottish quality has never changed. This is somewhere you can be sure of the best, from good coffee and a piece of caramel shortcake, to a full meal. The cafe is informal, excellent and well worth visiting.

Cullen skink. Smoked venison with gratin dauphinoise. Lemon tart.

◐ Open all year except 25, 26 Dec and 1, 2 Jan ✗ food available all day ££ Lunch £ Dinner ££
Ⓥ Vegetarians welcome ⚹ Children welcome
🆎 Credit cards: Mastercard, Visa, Switch, Delta
🅜 Owner/Manager: Seumas MacInnes

64 Albion Street Glasgow G1 1NY
Tel: 0141 552 6813 Fax: 0141 552 8911
Centrally located in Albion Street, within walking distance of George Square in the Merchant City. [C6]

GLASGOW

City Merchant Restaurant

- *"An enthusiastic welcome always awaits at the City Merchant – together with exciting Scottish seafood cooking."*
- *Modern Scottish.*

THE CITY MERCHANT RESTAURANT, having doubled its capacity, specialises in seafood, but also offers game, prime Scottish steaks and vegetarian dishes. Daily fish market 'extras' change daily, sometimes hourly. The wine list has over 60 bins, and a 'bin-end' blackboard offers excellent value. Gallery area and function room available for private parties. Booking advisable.

Thai cured salmon with pickled ginger and lime pickle. Venison escalopes, black pudding mousse and thyme gravy. Crannachan ice cream with home-made shortbread.

◐ Open all year except Christmas Day, 1 and 2 Jan ✗ Food available all day £-££ Lunch £-££ Dinner ££-£££ Ⓥ Vegetarians welcome
⚹ Children over 6 years welcome ♿ Facilities for disabled visitors 🚭 No smoking area in restaurant 🆎 Credit cards: Mastercard/Eurocard, American Express, Visa, Diners Club, Switch 🅜 Executive Head Chef: Andrew Cumming, Proprietors: Tony & Linda Matteo

97 Candleriggs Glasgow G1 1NP
Tel: 0141 553 1577 Fax: 0141 553 1588
E-mail: citymerchant@btinternet.com
Web: www.citymerchant.co.uk
Facing City Halls in Candleriggs, in Glasgow's Merchant City. Candleriggs on right going east along Ingram Street. [C6]

GLASGOW

GLASGOW

Drum and Monkey

- *"Enjoy the buzz of a busy city pub or the bistro – offering a fine range of fresh Scottish dishes."*
- *Modern Scottish.*

THE DRUM AND MONKEY has a warm and comfortable ambience. Bar food is available, with a menu of freshly prepared-to-order sandwiches and wholesome salads. But for the real food experience the adjoining bistro provides more elaborate menus, which are carefully balanced and produced from locally sourced ingredients, highlighting our finest Highland beef, Border lamb and Scottish seafood.

Warm tartlet of wild Scottish mushrooms and Mozzarella cheese on fine herb leaves. Seared Guinea fowl stuffed with crab, pickled ginger and coriander, shitake mushrooms, and fine herbs, with oven-roasted vegetables and chervil jus. Clootie dumpling with ice cream.

◐ *Open all year except 25, 26 Dec, 1 and 2 Jan* ✘ *Food available all day ££ Sun brunch available in bar Lunch except Sun ££ Dinner ££* Ⓥ *Vegetarians welcome* ♿ *Facilities for disabled visitors* ▣ *Credit cards: Mastercard/Eurocard, American Express, Visa, Diners Club, Switch, Delta* ◗ *Manager: Kevin D F Dow*

93/95 St Vincent Street Glasgow G2 5TL
Tel: 0141 221 6636 Fax: 0141 229 5902
On corner of St Vincent and Renfield Street – approx 100 yards from Central Station. [C6]

Glasgow Moat House

- *"Soak up the atmosphere of the riverside and enjoy good food in this busy hotel."*
- *Modern international cuisine.*

THE GLASGOW MOAT HOUSE has two restaurants both of which provide standards not often encountered in large international hotels. The Mariner (1 AA Rosette) is the fine dining experience whilst No 1 Dockside is informal with extensive buffet and à la carte menus.

Tartare of Loch Fyne oak smoked salmon, glazed salmon and fine capers. Rack of Borders lamb, fondant potato and fine beans. Warm clootie dumpling, clotted cream, and whisky syrup.

STB ★★★★ Hotel

◐ *Open all year* ▦ *Rooms: 283 with private facilities* ⊨ *DB&B from £80 B&B £70–£146* ✘ *Food available all day (Quarterdeck) Note: Extensive buffet available at dinner ££ Lunch (No 1 Dockside) £-££ Dinner (Mariner) except Sun ££-£££* Ⓥ *Vegetarians welcome* ♣ *Children welcome* ♿ *Facilities for disabled visitors* ✴ *No smoking areas in restaurants* ▣ *Credit cards: Mastercard/Eurocard, American Express, Visa, Switch, Delta* ◗ *General Manager: Mrs Jela Stewart*

Congress Road Glasgow G3 8QT
Tel: 0141 306 9988 Fax: 0141 221 2022
E-mail: gmgla@queensmoat.co.uk
Situated on the banks of the River Clyde, next to the SECC and Clyde Auditorium (Armadillo). [C6]

GLASGOW

Hilton Glasgow (Camerons Restaurant)

- *"An oasis of elegance and superb dining in a busy city central setting."*
- *Exquisite international cuisine.*

CAMERONS RESTAURANT has been newly refurbished and offers a stylish and soothing ambience. The service is in a class of its own. The flavours of an international brasserie can be experienced in the less formal Minsky's Restaurant. Raffles Bar transports you to the Far East to sip cocktails. 2 AA Rosettes.

Collops of Scottish lobster on asparagus and fennel salad with lemon thyme butter salad. Wild venison cutlets and spiced pear compote resting on sweet potato chorizo cake with light spring onion jus. Baked cardamom cheesecake served with Grand Marnier sorbet.

STB ★★★★★ Hotel

◐ *Open all year* 🏨 *Rooms: 319 en suite* 🛏 *B&B from £120* ✘ *Lunch (Camerons) except Sun Sat ££–£££: (Minsky's) from £ Dinner (Camerons) except Sun ££–£££: (Minsky's) from £* Ⓥ *Vegetarians welcome* ✶ *Children welcome* ♿ *Facilities for disabled visitors* 🐄 *Member of the Scotch Beef Club* 💳 *Credit cards: Mastercard/Eurocard, American Express, Visa, Switch* 🎩 *General Manager: Klaus Zsilla*

1 William Street Glasgow G3 8HT
Tel: 0141 204 5555 Fax: 0141 204 5004
Web: www.hilton.com
Access from M8 junction 18, or via Waterloo Street from city centre. [C6]

GLASGOW

The Inn On The Green

- *"A stylish hotel with well established restaurant."*
- *Scottish with contemporary twist.*

A BEAUTIFUL townhouse hotel with individually styled designer bedrooms with an independently renowned restaurant in a unique art gallery setting. The menus are extensive, with daily specials making best use of local sourced quality produce, with a Scottish slant. In the evenings enjoy good food accompanied by light jazz piano/vocals.

Traditional Cullen skink. Grilled fillet of Hebridean oak-smoked salmon. Banana and pineapple filo with Cointreau and butterscotch sauce.

STB ★★★ Hotel

◐ *Open all year N.B. Please telephone to ensure restaurant is open during Festive Season* 🏨 *Rooms: 18 en suite* 🛏 *Room Rate £75–£90* 🆂🅿 *Special rates available* ✘ *Lunch – please telephone ahead £ Dinner £££* Ⓥ *Vegetarians welcome* ✶ *Children welcome* ♿ *Facilities for disabled visitors* 🚭 *Smoking discouraged in dining areas* 💳 *Credit cards: Mastercard/Eurocard, American Express, Visa, Switch, Delta* 🎩 *General Manager: Philip Raskin*

25 Greenhead Street Glasgow G40 1ES
Tel: 0141 554 0165 Fax: 0141 556 4678
E-mail: sales@theinnonthegreen.co.uk
Web: www.theinnonthegreen.co.uk
Located on the edge of Glasgow Green, close to the Peoples' Palace and just off the main london road arterial route from M74 to city centre. [C6]

GLASGOW

La Bonne Auberge

- *"A place to enjoy skilfully cooked Scottish fare in the friendly atmosphere of a French brasserie."*
- *Modern Scottish.*

LA BONNE AUBERGE is privately franchised within the city centre Holiday Inn, offering French flair in Parisian style and comfortable surroundings. Guests can relax in L'Orangerie Conservatory. Master Chef Gerry Sharkey demonstrates great skill in his hand-crafted dishes, using Scottish produce.

Tender grilled asparagus with pancetta, tomato and chive butter sauce. Roasted loin of Highland venison with a timbale of black pudding, shallot confit and rich rosemary jus. Banana crème brûlée with hot fudge sauce and chocolate brownies.

STB ★★★★ Hotel

◐ Open all year except Christmas Day and New Year's Day 🛏 Rooms: 113 en suite 🛌 DB&B £127.95 B&B £107.95 💰 Special rates available ✗ Food available all day Lunch £ Dinner £ Ⓥ Vegetarians welcome ✝ Children welcome ♿ Facilities for disabled visitors 💳 Credit cards: Mastercard/Eurocard, American Express, Visa, Diners Club, Switch, Delta ⁜ General Manager: Tony Wright

161 West Nile Street Glasgow G1 2RL
Tel: 0141 352 8310 Fax: 0141 332 7447
E-mail: tw@holidayinn.demon.co.uk
Web: www.labonneauberge.co.uk
Diagonally opposite Glasgow Royal Concert Hall. [C6]

GLASGOW

Lux

- *"A gourmet's delight – exquisite cuisine and well-informed excellent service."*
- *Innovative modern Scottish.*

SITUATED in a quiet West End corner, Lux reflects the simplicity of modern establishments but retains the atmosphere of JJ Burnet's 19th century architecture. Menus are carefully composed by chef Stephen Johnson who adds his own special touches and secret ingredients, all enhanced by a well-balanced wine list. Regular tasting dinners take place at Lux, phone for details.

Mexican spiced julienne of beef with a sweetcorn, lentil and sun-dried tomato salsa. Pan-fried scallops on saffron mash with spinach olive oil. Lux crème brûlée.

◐ Open all year except 25, 26 Dec Closed Sun Mon ✗ Lunch by arrangement only Dinner except Sun Mon £££ Ⓥ Vegetarians welcome ✝ Children welcome 💳 Credit cards: Mastercard/Eurocard, Visa, Switch, Delta ⁜ General Manager: Julia Hutton

1051 Great Western Road Glasgow G12 0XD
Tel: 0141 576 7576 Fax: 0141 334 9491
E-mail: info@luxstazione.com
Web: www.luxstazione
c2 miles from city centre at entrance to Gartnavel Hospital. Lux is on the first floor above Bar Stazione. [C6]

GLASGOW

Nairns

- *"Wonderful gourmet dining with dishes devised from the freshest ingredients."*
- *Innovative fusion food.*

THIS IS Nick Nairn's flagship. On two floors with the upstairs dining room more classically formal and downstairs more contemporary in style. Menus are carefully inspired and changed daily. All dishes are cooked to order and created under the watchful eye of Scotland's best known celebrity chef. A testament to his energy and dedication.

Glazed confit duck on Puy lentil salad, plum sauce. Fillet of halibut with grain mustard and new potatoes, bok choi and citrus vinaigrette. Caramel parfait, brandy snap basket.

STB ★★★★★ Restaurant with Rooms

◐ Open all year except 25, 26 Dec and 1, 2 Jan ♠ Rooms: 4 en suite ⊨ Room rate £110–£140 ✗ Lunch Tue to Sat ££ Dinner £££
Ⓥ Vegetarians welcome ⚘ Children welcome (if they can eat from menu) ⌇ Diners requested to refrain from smoking until coffee. Cigar and pipe smoking are not permitted ⚘ Member of the Scotch Beef Club ⊞ Credit cards: Mastercard/Eurocard, American Express, Visa, Diners Club, Switch, Delta ⚘ General Manager: Jim Kerr

*13 Woodside Crescent Glasgow G3 7UL
Tel: 0141 353 0707 Fax: 0141 331 1684
E-mail: info@nairns.co.uk
Web: www.nairns.co.uk
At Charing Cross. Woodlands Crescent is off Sauchiehall Street. [C6]*

GLASGOW

Nº Sixteen

- *"Relaxed, informal atmosphere with excellent cooking and value for money."*
- *Modern Scottish cooking.*

Nº SIXTEEN is simple in style and decor with white-painted walls and sanded floors which are a palate for the stylish food served here. Chef Rupert Staniforth prepares modern-style dishes in an innovative style. His wife Aisla and team, look after the front of house in this busy, popular restaurant.

Crisp confit duck leg on grilled black pudding with creamed leeks and a red wine sauce. Pan-fried fillet of john dory on tagallini with warm black olive vinaigrette and a red pepper pesto. Saffron and coconut iced terrine with glazed fresh fruit.

◐ Open all year except Christmas Day and Boxing Day Closed Sun ✗ Lunch Sat only £ Dinner except Sun ££ Ⓥ Vegetarians welcome ⚘ Children 12 years and over welcome
⊞ Credit cards: Mastercard/Eurocard, Visa, Switch, Delta ⚘ Proprietors: Rupert & Aisla Staniforth

*16 Byres Road Glasgow G11 5JY
Tel: 0141 339 2544 Fax: 0141 576 1505
Byres Road runs from Great Western Road to Dumbarton Road. Nº Sixteen is at the Dumbarton Road end. [C6]*

GLASGOW

Pollok House, National Trust for Scotland

- *"Delightful freshly cooked food in interesting historic surroundings."*
- Good quality Scottish cuisine.

POLLOK HOUSE is a very fine example of the quality visitor experience available at National Trust properties. It is a most beautiful house set amidst spectacular gardens in Pollok Park. The Edwardian Kitchen Restaurant offers good home baking, light refreshments and delightful traditional Scottish dishes – all created fresh on the premises.

Green pea and apple soup with fresh mint and a crusty roll. Savoury tart of spinach with Ayrshire goats cheese served with seasonal leaves and walnut bread. Hot Highland toffee cake served with Mackie's traditional ice cream.

◐ Open all year except Christmas Day, Boxing Day, 1 and 2 Jan ⓤ Unlicensed ✘ Food available all day £ Lunch £ Dinner – pre-arranged functions only ££ Ⓥ Vegetarians welcome ✷ Children welcome ♿ Facilities for disabled visitors ⌇ No smoking throughout ▣ Credit cards: Mastercard, Visa, Switch, Delta ⓜ Catering Manager: Fiona McLean

Pollok Country Park 2060 Pollokshaws Road Glasgow G43 1AT
Tel: 0141 616 6410
Off M77, junction 1, follow signs for Burrell Collection. 3 miles south of Glasgow city centre. Frequent bus and rail (Pollokshaws West station) from city centre. [C6]

GLASGOW

The Puppet Theatre

- *"Wonderful gourmet food and service in this unique and stylish restaurant."*
- Modern Scottish cooking.

THE PUPPET THEATRE has become one of the best restaurants in Glasgow with booking required weeks in advance for the weekends. The cooking is produced with great skill with best Scottish produce presented in modern Scottish style which looks great and with tastes that match expectation! A unique restaurant.

Grilled duck breast fillet, crispy polenta with a plum and star anise compote. Stew of mixed West Coast fish, turned vegetables with an infused saffron sauce. Pineapple ravioli with nuts and fruits minestrone, Jamaica pepper ice cream.

◐ Open all year except Boxing Day, New Year's Day and 2 Jan Closed Mon ✘ Lunch except Mon Sat £-££ Dinner except Mon £££ Ⓥ Vegetarians welcome ✷ Children 12 years and over welcome ♿ Facilities for disabled visitors ⌇ Smoking area, if requested ▣ Credit cards: Mastercard/Eurocard, American Express, Visa, Switch, Delta ⓜ General Manager: Geraldine McDonald; Head Chef: Herve Martin

11 Ruthven Lane Glasgow Hillhead G12 9BG Tel: 0141 339 8444 Fax: 0141 339 7666
E-mail: puppet@bigbeat.co.uk
Web: www.bigbeat.co.uk
In Ruthven Lane – off Byres Road in Glasgow's West End. Ruthven Lane opposite Hillhead underground station. [C6]

GLASGOW

Restaurant Rococo

- *"An exciting restaurant offering tastes and sights to thrill the most sophisticated palate."*
- *World class modern cuisine.*

ONE OF Glasgow's new quality venues for outstanding cuisine and service, Rococo is set in sumptuous surroundings. No expense has been spared in blending the atmosphere and style into one of Glasgow's top restaurants where you can enjoy a superb wine list of over 300 bins. Service is impeccable.

Trio of livers: goose, chicken, and foie gras, served with a chantrelle and Zinfandel jus. Fillet of sea bass, with a herb crust, crunchy greens and a hollandaise sauce. Belgian chocolate and praline tart with Armagnac and prune ice cream.

◗ *Open all year except New Year's Day Closed Sun except special occasions* ✘ *Lunch except Sun ££ Dinner except Sun £££* Ⓥ *Vegetarians welcome* ✱ *Children welcome* ♿ *Facilities for disabled visitors* 💳 *Credit cards: Mastercard/Eurocard, American Express, Visa, Diners Club, Switch, Delta* ⓜ *Manager: Ross Forsyth*

West George Street Glasgow G2 2NR
Tel: 0141 221 5004 Fax: 0141 221 5006
E-mail: res@rococoglasgow.com
Web: www.rococoglasgow.com
City centre location on corner of West George and Wellington Street. Approach via M8 from Charing Cross and follow one-way system from Sauchiehall Street. [C6]

GLASGOW

Stravaigin

- *"Stravaigin continues to be one of the pioneering restaurants in Glasgow offering the best food, with innovative preparation and presentation."*
- *Inspired Scottish eclectic menus.*

COLIN CLYDESDALE continues to collect new ideas and ingredients and adds them to naturally produced local ones. The menus are eclectic and offer excellent value for money. The cooking is highly-skilled and dishes are presented with flair. 2 AA Rosettes. Winner of the Macallan Taste of Scotland City Restaurant Award 1999.

Pan-fried sesame coated mullet on mooli, carrot and beansprout salad with Japanese style sherry dressing. Saddle of Argyllshire rabbit on Caceras style chorizo, jambon lentils, Rioja gravy and matchstick potatoes. Cider apple jelly with calvados sabayon and muscavado polenta shortbread.

◗ *Open all year except Christmas Day, Boxing Day, 31 Dec and 1 Jan Closed Mon* ✘ *Food available all day, 7 days (Cafe bar) ££ Lunch (restaurant) Fri and Sat only £ Dinner (restaurant) except Mon ££* Ⓥ *Vegetarians welcome* ✱ *Children welcome* 💳 *Credit cards: Mastercard/Eurocard, American Express, Visa, Diners Club, Switch, Delta* ⓜ *General Manager: Carol S Wright*

28 Gibson Street Hillhead Glasgow G12 8NX
Tel: 0141 334 2665 Fax: 0141 334 4099
E-mail: bookings@stravaigin.com
Web: www.stravaigin.com
From M8 junction 17. From city centre take A82, Great Western Road. Turn left down Park Road, right onto Gibson Street. 200 yards on right hand side. [C6]

GLASGOW

Ubiquitous Chip: Winner 2000 – City Restaurant

- *"The Chip is a classic! Ever-evolving yet never losing its original appeal – innovation with integrity."*
- *Modern Scottish cooking.*

THE 'CHIP' is situated in a cobbled mews in Glasgow's West End. It has a spectacular courtyard area, with trickling pool, and more traditional dining room. The cuisine marries the traditional and original in innovative recipes, and this variety is complemented by a wine list rated among the top ten in Britain for quality and value.

Ayrshire Guinea fowl terrine studded with pistachio and peppers, Blairgowrie raspberry vinaigrette. Free-range Perthshire pork wrapped in Ayrshire bacon, fondant potato, Rothesay black pudding and apple strudel. Blairgowrie raspberry parfait with raspberry tuille and eau de vie de framboise sabayon.

◐ Open all year except Christmas Day, 31 Dec and 1 Jan ✗ Food available all day Lunch ££ Dinner £££ ⓥ Vegetarians welcome ⚹ Children welcome ♿ Facilities for disabled visitors ⊞ Credit cards: Mastercard/Eurocard, American Express, Visa, Diners Club, Delta ⚒ Proprietor: Ronnie Clydesdale

*12 Ashton Lane Glasgow G12 8SJ
Tel: 0141 334 5007 Fax: 0141 337 1302
E-mail: mail@ubiquitouschip.co.uk
Web: www.ubiquitouschip.co.uk
Behind Hillhead underground station, in a secluded lane off Byres Road in the heart of Glasgow's West End. [C6]*

GLASGOW

YES Restaurant, Bar & Café

- *"An exciting city restaurant with exceptional standards in modern food and service."*
- *Best modern Scottish.*

YES has both a very stylish informal brasserie at ground level with a bustling atmosphere and a more formal contemporary and sophisticated restaurant downstairs. Service in both is discreet and professional. The food here is modern and intuitive – original and creative, with a real flair for flavours and outstanding presentation.

Pressed terrine of rabbit with wild mushrooms, potatoes, mixed herb salad and a walnut dressing. Loin of lamb with lamb's kidneys, Savoy cabbage, rosemary fondant potatoes and a mint jus. Brioche and ginger bread pudding with bananas, caramel sauce and marshmallow ice cream.

◐ Open all year except 25, 26 Dec and 1, 2 Jan Closed Sun ✗ Lunch except Sun Sat ££ Dinner except Sun ££££ ⓥ Vegetarians welcome ⚹ Children welcome ⊞ Credit cards: Mastercard/Eurocard, American Express, Visa, Diners Club, Switch, Delta ⚒ General Manager: Gordon McNeil

*22 West Nile Street Glasgow G1 2PW
Tel: 0141 221 8044 Fax: 0141 248 9159
City centre. M8 exit for George Square, turn left at 2nd lights into Port Dundas Road which joins West Nile Street. [C6]*

GLASGOW OUTSKIRTS

The Beardmore Hotel

- *"Amazing style and comfort, yet informal and relaxed, offering superb food."*
- *Imaginative cuisine in an imaginative setting.*

THE BEARDMORE HOTEL has two dining areas: Citrus with its 'funky' retro furnishing and presenting a combination of well-cooked produce, and B Bar Café, with fresh food served quickly from 10 am–10 pm. Investor in People Award. Winner of The Macallan Taste of Scotland Restaurant of the Year Award 1996.

Terrine of marinated chicken and leek with aged balsamic. Pan-fried halibut with smoked salmon, served with a lime and ginger butter. Mango and coconut tartlet.

STB ★★★★ Hotel

◐ *Open all year* ⊞ *Rooms: 168 en suite* ⊨ *DB&B £50–£135 B&B £35–£120* ▦ *Special rates available* ✕ *Food available all day from £ Lunch from ££ Dinner from ££* Ⓥ *Vegetarians welcome* ★ *Children welcome* ⊁ *Smoking area in lounge bar* ⊞ *Credit cards: Mastercard/ Eurocard, American Express, Visa, Diners Club, Switch* ▮ *Director & General Manager: David Clarke*

Beardmore Street Clydebank Glasgow G81 4SA Tel: 0141 951 6000 Fax: 0141 951 6018 E-mail: beardmore.hotel@hci.co.uk Web: www.beardmore.hotel.co.uk Between Glasgow and Loch Lomond. Off A82, 8 miles from M8 Junction 19 over Erskine Bridge or approach from Glasgow along Dumbarton Road. [C6]

GLASGOW OUTSKIRTS

The Cook's Room

- *"Tom is an inspired cook and this is a very special restaurant."*
- *Modern Scottish cooking.*

THIS GASTRONOMIC gem, The Cook's Room, is one of 'the' places to eat in Glasgow. It has been converted into a restaurant in the Arts and Crafts style. The menus offer the finest of Scottish ingredients and are colourful, imaginative, confident and mouth-watering. One of the friendliest restaurants in the friendliest of cities.

Borders woodpigeon with a rich Puy lentil and spinach cassoulet. Fillet of sea bream with stir-fried spring vegetables, with a yellow pepper and saffron dressing. Rum and raisin steamed pudding with butterscotch sauce and home-made vanilla ice cream.

◐ *Open all year except Christmas Day and New Year's Day* ✕ *Brunch Sun Mon ££ Dinner £££* Ⓥ *Vegetarians welcome* ★ *Children welcome* ⊞ *Credit cards: Mastercard/Eurocard, Visa, Switch, Delta* ▮ *Cook: Tom Battersby*

205 Fenwick Road Giffnock Glasgow G46 6JD Tel: 0141 621 1903 Fax: 0141 621 1903 Tiny shop front in the middle of terrace on main A77 road between Shawlands and Newton Mearns. Ample free parking at rear in Giffnock Station car park. [C6]

GLASGOW OUTSKIRTS

East Lochhead

- *"Excellent example of Scottish cooking and hospitality, with a charming relaxing atmosphere."*
- *Accomplished Scottish cooking.*

EAST LOCHHEAD is a traditional Scottish stone-built farmhouse renovated to the highest modern standards with many delightful touches. Janet and Ross Anderson are accomplished and friendly hosts. Janet is an accomplished cook who uses fruit and vegetables from her own garden and honey from her own bees – fabulous home cooking.

Aubergine, red pepper and goats cheese parcels with fresh herb dressing. Grilled chicken breast with braised pearl barley, lemon, thyme and honey-glazed carrots and green beans. Iced cranachan parfait with red berries.

STB ★★★★ B&B

● Open all year ⌂ Rooms: 6, 5 en suite ⇌ DB&B £50–£52.50 B&B £32.50 ⓢⓟ Special rates available ⓤⓛ Unlicensed ✖ Food available all day ££ Lunch ££ Dinner ££ Dinner/Lunch parties with prior booking Ⓥ Vegetarians welcome ⚹ Children welcome ⌧ No smoking throughout ⊞ Credit cards: Mastercard, American Express, Visa ⓝ Proprietor: Janet Anderson

*Largs Road Lochwinnoch Renfrewshire
PA12 4DX
Tel: 01505 842610 Fax: 01505 842610
E-mail: winnoch@aol.com
Web: www.eastlochhead.co.uk
Exit junction 28a from M8 (A737 Irvine). Turn right on A760. East Lochhead is situated 2 miles on left-hand side. [C6]*

GLASGOW OUTSKIRTS

Gavins Mill Restaurant

- *"A welcome newcomer to the Guide – 21st Century Scottish cooking and service."*
- *Innovative modern Scottish.*

GAVINS MILL is a 15th Century flour mill that has been sensitively restored, with original elements of the building used as new functional features. The restaurant upstairs is a testimonial to modern design. Cooking is original; staff and management are accomplished; and the chef is highly skilled.

West Coast langoustines grilled in garlic butter. Trio of native seafood with saffron beurre blanc. Raspberry brûlée.

● Open all year ✖ Food available all day £££ Lunch ££ Dinner £££ Ⓥ Vegetarians welcome ⚹ Children welcome ♿ Facilities for disabled visitors ⊞ Credit cards: Mastercard/Eurocard, American Express, Visa, Diners Club, Switch, Delta ⓝ General Manager: Mr Ryan James

*Gavins Mill Road Milngavie Glasgow G62 6NB
Tel: 0141 956 2255 Fax: 0141 943 2488
E-mail: gavinsmill@icscotland.co.uk
Web: www.gavinsmill.co.uk
Near town centre – Gavins Mill is at the bottom of the Tesco car park, off the Glasgow road. [C6]*

GLASGOW (OUTSKIRTS)

Gleddoch House Hotel & Country Estate

- *"Redolent of a bygone age – classic surroundings and stylish cooking."*
- Modern Scottish cooking.

GLEDDOCH HOUSE HOTEL's 360-acre estate has an 18-hole golf course, horse riding, clay pigeon shooting and off-road driving. The restaurant is spacious and gracious; the four-course, table d'hôte menu is superbly cooked and presented by chef Brian Graham. The whole food experience is excellent. The hotel has conference and private dining facilities, and 2 AA Rosettes.

Seared king scallops on a filo parcel of roasted root vegetables traced with Oban mussels in white wine pan jus. Roast saddle of Highland venison, sliced pink on a bed of red cabbage and pear compote with blackberry, poivrade sauce. Drambuie parfait on a gratin of winter berries with rich strawberry coulis.

STB ★★★★ Hotel

◐ Open all year 🛏 Rooms: 38 en suite 🍽 DB&B £75-£127.50 B&B £99-£180 💷 Special rates available ✖ Food available all day £-££££ Lunch ££ Dinner ££££ Ⓥ Vegetarians welcome ⁂ Children welcome ☙ Member of the Scotch Beef Club ⊞ Credit cards: Mastercard/Eurocard, American Express, Visa, Diners Club, Switch ⚑ General Manager: Leslie W Conn

*Langbank Renfrewshire PA14 6YE
Tel: 01475 540711 Fax: 01475 540201
E-mail: gleddochhouse@ukonline.co.uk
M8 towards Greenock. Take B789 Langbank/Houston exit. Follow signs to left and then right after ½ mile – hotel is on left. [C6]*

GLASGOW (OUTSKIRTS)

Uplawmoor Hotel

- *"A warm, friendly and comfortable establishment rightly popular with locals."*
- Good Scottish cooking.

UPLAWMOOR HOTEL provides excellent meals in a relaxed, comfortable environment. The lounge bar provides quality bar meals at lunchtime and evenings. The restaurant and adjoining cocktail bar open in the evening. The à la carte menu, together with the fortnightly changing table d'hôte, provide a wide choice. Runner-up (Category 2), Taste of Scotland Scotch Lamb Challenge Competition 1999.

Hot smoked Fencebay salmon with an avocado and tomato salsa. Pan-fried breast of Gressingham duck with a confit of leg and a rosemary jus. Armagnac and poppy seed parfait with a warm rhubarb compote.

STB ★★★ Hotel

◐ Open all year except Boxing Day and New Year's Day 🛏 Rooms: 14 en suite 🍽 DB&B £45-£65 B&B £30-£45 💷 Special rates available ✖ Food available all day Sun Sat £ Lunch £ Dinner ££ Ⓥ Vegetarians welcome ⁂ Children welcome ⊘ No smoking in restaurant ⊞ Credit cards: Mastercard/Eurocard, Visa, Switch, Delta ⚑ Proprietor: Stuart Peacock

*Neilston Road Uplawmoor Glasgow G78 4AF
Tel: 01505 850565 Fax: 01505 850689
E-mail: enquiries@uplawmoor.co.uk
Web: www.uplawmoor.co.uk
Just off the A736 Glasgow to Irvine Road. Approx 4 miles from Barrhead. [C6]*

GLENCOE

GLENDARUEL

The Holly Tree Hotel, Seafood & Game Restaurant

- *"Idyllic location where diners can witness fresh live shellfish being landed on the hotel jetty."*
- *Skilled handling of seafood.*

LOVINGLY RESTORED in the classical 'Charles Rennie Mackintosh' style. The comfortable restaurant overlooks the floodlit gardens. A varied choice of superb fresh seafood is skilfully prepared; the atmosphere is friendly; the hospitality excellent, all combine to make this a most relaxing place to enjoy the astounding scenery and location.

Grilled oysters topped with Isle of Mull cheese. Venison set on ginger parsnip purée with redcurrant and Moniack wine sauce. Glayva and oatmeal iced parfait.

◐ Open all year ⌂ Rooms: 10 en suite ⌘ DB&B £50–£78 B&B £30–£57.50 ▦ Special rates available ✘ Food available all day Lunch from £ Dinner from £££ Ⓥ Vegetarians welcome ✶ Children welcome ♿ Facilities for disabled visitors ⌇ No smoking in restaurant ▭ Credit cards: Mastercard/Eurocard, Visa, Switch, Delta ▣ Manager: Annette McFatridge

Kentallen by Appin Argyll PA38 4BY
Tel: 01631 740292 Fax: 01631 740345
E-mail: mail@hollytreehotel.co.uk
Web: www.hollytreehotel.co.uk
From Glasgow take the A82 to Glencoe, continue towards Ballachulish Bridge, then take the A828 Oban road to Kentallen. Hotel is 2 miles down this road on right hand side beside loch. [B5]

Dunans Castle

- *"Experience this delightful castle in a family environment."*
- *Homely Scottish fare.*

DUNANS CASTLE is a delightful, recently restored castle personally run by the Lord and Lady of Marr, who are accomplished hosts. All guests here are welcomed as one of the family. The cooking is skilful with menus clearly reflecting locally sourced produce and prepared and presented to a very high standard.

Loch Fyne bradan rost served on a bed of crisp lettuce with oatmeal cakes. Haunch of venison served with a fruit sauce, creamed baton carrots, bacon tossed beans, breaded cauliflower, dill butter new potatoes. Fresh fruit in a brandy snap basket laced with Madeira, served with honeycomb ice cream.

STB ★★★★ Guest House

◐ Open all year ⌂ Rooms: 6 en suite ⌘ DB&B from £60 B&B from £45 ▦ Special rates available ✘ Lunch – pre-book only ££ Dinner – pre-book only £££ Ⓥ Vegetarians welcome ✶ Children welcome ⌇ No smoking throughout ⌇ Dogs welcome by arrangement ▭ Credit cards: Mastercard/Eurocard, American Express, Visa, Diners Club, Switch, Delta ▣ Owner: Lady Marr

Glendaruel Argyll PA22 3AD
Tel: 01369 820380 Fax: 01369 820213
E-mail: marr@dunans-castle.co.uk
Web: www.dunans-castle.co.uk
A82 Glasgow to Tarbert, then A83 to Inveraray road – once over the 'Rest and be Thankful'. Take A815 to Strachur then A886 to Glendaruel. Dunans Castle is signposted on left, few miles down this road. [B5]

GLENDEVON BY DOLLAR

Tormaukin Hotel

- *"The wide repertoire of dishes available offers something for everyone."*
- *Accomplished Scottish cooking.*

TORMAUKIN was built in the 18th century but has been well restored/refurbished retaining original features. It is very popular with locals and visitors alike. There are two menus available – bar meals and a la carte – with excellent choices and value for money. Tormaukin is suitable for families and offers consistent quality to its guests.

King prawns grilled with fresh lime, served with angel hair pasta tossed in chilli and garlic. Saddle of hare (Maukin) roasted with bacon, served with a Madeira wine sauce. Sticky gingerbread pudding with ginger wine sauce.

STB ★★★ Small Hotel

◐ Open all year except Christmas Day and 8 to 11 Jan ⌂ Rooms: 10 en suite ⊨ B&B £32.50–£55 ⊠ Special rates available ✘ Food available all day Sun £ Lunch ££ Dinner £££ Ⓥ Vegetarians welcome ⚹ Children welcome ⚹ Facilities for disabled visitors ⚹ Dogs welcome by arrangement ⊞ Credit cards: Mastercard/Eurocard, American Express, Visa, Diners Club, Switch, Delta ⚹ General Manager: Mrs Michele Philp

Glendevon By Dollar FK14 7JY
Tel: 01259 781 252 Fax: 01259 781 526
E-mail: enquiries@tormaukin.co.uk
Web: www.tormaukin.co.uk
By the roadside at Glendevon village on A823 between Auchterarder and Muckhart. [C5]

GLENFINNAN

Glenfinnan Monument,
National Trust for Scotland

- *"A friendly team at Glenfinnan who take pride in their home baking."*
- *Wholesome Scottish fayre.*

THIS IS a neat little coffee bar with open-plan servery. It has a friendly atmosphere as staff – while on view to customers – chat, serve and prepare the next day's baking. Everything here is with the customer in mind e.g. tables are placed around the window with all seating facing the view.

Traditional pea and ham soup served with crusty bread. Fresh smoked salmon and dill savoury tart served with seasonal leaves. Citrus lemon cake with a zesty lemon icing.

STB Commended

◐ Open 1 Apr to 31 Oct ⊠ Special rates available ⓤ Unlicensed ✘ Food available all day £ Lunch £ Ⓥ Vegetarians welcome ⚹ Children welcome ⚹ Facilities for disabled visitors ⚹ No smoking in snack bar ⊞ Credit cards: Mastercard, Visa, Switch ⚹ Property Manager: Lillias Grant

Information Centre Inverness-shire PH37 4LT
Tel/Fax: 01397 722250
E-mail: Web: www.nts.org.uk
A830, 18½ miles west of Fort William. [B4]

GLENLIVET

Minmore House

- *"Guests are totally cosseted at Minmore House – and the procedure is just to 'rebook' the next visit."*
- *Classic contemporary style using the best of Scottish produce.*

MINMORE HOUSE is run by new team Chef Victor Janssen and his wife Lynne. They are enthusiastic hosts who set high standards of hospitality and cooking. The ambience is delightful and a very friendly atmosphere exists here. The best use of Scottish ingredients in an innovative way – menus are delightful. An excellent place to relax.

Scampi à l'escargots. Roast Gressingham duckling with a passion fruit and green peppercorn sauce. Home made cassata with praline of hazelnuts and Frangelico liqueur.

STB ★★★ Hotel

◐ *Open mid Apr to end Oct and December* 🛏 *Rooms: 10 en suite* 🍴 *DB&B £75 B&B £50* ᴿ *Special rates available* ✗ *Packed Lunch on request Lunch ££ Dinner £££* Ⓥ *Vegetarians welcome* ⚘ *Children welcome* ✌ *No smoking in restaurant* 💳 *Credit cards: Mastercard/Eurocard, Visa, Switch, Delta* ⚑ *Victor & Lynne Janssen*

Glenlivet Banffshire AB37 9DB
Tel: 01807 590378 Fax: 01807 590472
E-mail: minmorehouse@ukonline.co.uk
Web:
www.SmoothHound.co.uk/hotels/minmore.html
Take the A95 from Grantown-on-Spey. Right after 15 miles take B9008 – follow signs to The Glenlivet Distillery. [D4]

GLENROTHES

Balbirnie House Hotel

- *"The Russell family are consummate professionals and make every experience at Balbirnie a pleasure."*
- *Original and accomplished.*

THE RUSSELL family have a true commitment to excellence which is evident throughout – from housekeeping to the very high standard of cooking. 2 AA Rosettes. Winner of the Macallan Taste of Scotland Hotel of the Year Award 1996. Runner-up (Category 1) in The Taste of Scotland Scotch Lamb Challenge Competition 1999.

Hot home oak roasted salmon with marinated local mushrooms and an Arran mustard dressing. Pan-fried loin of venison, with red cabbage, glazed red apple, garlic mash and bramble gravy. Heather honey and Drambuie parfait.

STB ★★★★ Hotel

◐ *Open all year* 🛏 *Rooms: 30 en suite* 🍴 *DB&B £82.50–£142 B&B £85–£112.50* ᴿ *Special rates available* ✗ *Lunch £ Dinner £££* Ⓥ *Vegetarians welcome* ⚘ *Children welcome* ♿ *Facilities for disabled visitors* 🐄 *Member of the Scotch Beef Club* 💳 *Credit cards: Mastercard/Eurocard, American Express, Visa, Diners Club* ⚑ *Proprietors: The Russell Family*

Balbirnie Park Markinch Fife KY7 6NE
Tel: 01592 610066 Fax: 01592 610529
E-mail: balbirnie@btinternet.com
Web: www.balbirnie.co.uk
½ hour equidistant from Edinburgh and St Andrews. Just off A92 on B9130. Follow directions to Markinch Village then Balbirnie Park. [D5]

GLENSHEE

Dalmunzie House Hotel

- *"A comfortable hotel – offering a warm welcome and a relaxed informal stay."*
- *Traditional Scottish cooking.*

DALMUNZIE HOUSE HOTEL's 6,500-acre estate has a 9-hole golf course, fishing, stalking, grouse shooting, pony-trekking, and the Glenshee ski slopes are close by. The menu is table d'hôte (four/five choices) with a couple of à la carte supplements. The cooking is homestyle but imaginative. Dalmunzie House Hotel has 1 AA Rosette.

Caramelised red onion tart with sea scallops, smoked bacon and garlic chives. Pan-fried breast of Guinea fowl with Mediterranean vegetables, nanna potatoes and a port and black olive jus. Rhubarb and oatmeal parfait with crumble topping and vanilla sauce.

STB ★★★ Hotel

◐ Open 28 Dec to 28 Nov ♜ Rooms: 17, 16 en suite ⊨ DB&B £64-£72 (3 to 6 days) B&B £42-£55 ⓢⓟ Special rates available ✘ Lunch £ Dinner ££-£££ Ⓥ Vegetarians welcome ⚹ Children welcome ⚹ Limited facilities for disabled visitors ⊞ Credit cards: Mastercard/Eurocard, Visa, Switch ⚹ Owners: Simon & Alexandra Winton

Spittal of Glenshee Blairgowrie Perthshire PH10 7QG
Tel: 01250 885224 Fax: 01250 885225
E-mail: dalmunzie@aol.com
Web: www.welcome.to/dalmunzie
Approx 20 miles from Blairgowrie on A93 at Spittal of Glenshee – then follow signs. [C4]

GRANTOWN-ON-SPEY

Ardconnel House

- *"Ardconnel House offers luxury accommodation, good food and hospitality to match."*
- *French cooking using Scottish produce.*

ARDCONNEL HOUSE is elegantly furnished and decorated in keeping with the Victorian style. Run by owners Barbara and Michel Bouchard, Michel is French and brings flair and skill to very good local produce, whilst Barbara skilfully tends to guests' needs. A carefully selected wine list complements the excellent food.

Cider and Stilton soup served with Parmesan croutons. Scottish pheasant with sherry and port sauce. Panettone and banana sticky toffee pudding.

STB ★★★★★ Guest House

◐ Open Easter to 31 Oct ♜ Rooms: 6 en suite ⊨ DB&B £43-£50 B&B £25-£32 ⓢⓟ Special rates available ✘ Dinner – by arrangement ££ Residents only ⚹ Children over 8 years welcome ⚹ No smoking throughout ⊞ Credit cards: Mastercard/Eurocard, Visa ⚹ Proprietors: Michel & Barbara Bouchard

Woodlands Terrace Grantown-on-Spey PH26 3JU
Tel: 01479 872104 Fax: 01479 872104
E-mail: enquiry@ardconnel.com
Web: www.ardconnel.com
On A95, south west entry to town. [C4]

GRANTOWN-ON-SPEY

Culdearn House Hotel

- *"Be completely spoiled by the excellent hospitality and cuisine offered at Culdearn."*
- *Innovative, imaginative cooking.*

THIS CHARMING establishment has achieved many accolades and Alasdair and Isobel Little are enthusiastic hosts, and look after their guests very well. Isobel is a talented chef and prepares local produce in classic Scots ways. Over 70 malt whiskies are offered and an interesting wine list.
1 AA Rosette.

West Coast scallops, pan-fried, served on a bed of watercress, and topped with crispy bacon. Roast loin of Scotch lamb, sliced on a sweet potato mash with a red wine and rosemary jus. Raspberry meringue roulade on a raspberry coulis.

STB ★★★★ Hotel
Green Tourism Three Leaf Gold Award

◐ Open 1 Mar to 30 Oct ⌂ Rooms: 9 en suite ⌘ DB&B £65–£75 SP Special rates available ♊ Restricted licence ✘ Non-residents – reservations essential Picnic lunches to order Dinner 4 course menu £££ ✄ No smoking in dining room ⚑ Member of the Scotch Beef Club ⊞ Credit cards: Mastercard/Eurocard, American Express, Visa, Diners Club, Switch, Delta, JCB ⚐ Proprietors: Isobel & Alasdair Little

*Woodlands Terrace Grantown-on-Spey Morayshire PH26 3JU
Tel: 01479 872106 Fax: 01479 873641
E-mail: culdearn@globalnet.co.uk
Web: www.culdearn.com
Entering Grantown on A95 from south west, turn left at 30 mph sign. Culdearn faces you. [C4]*

GRANTOWN-ON-SPEY

Muckrach Lodge Hotel & Restaurant

- *"Highland hospitality together with fine wines and food at Muckrach Lodge."*
- *Modern Scottish cooking with continental influence.*

COOKING is 'the' priority here, with the emphasis on interesting and flavoursome combinations. The chef is young and enthusiastic about his subject. There are two restaurants here – the bistro bar and the Conservatory. Proprietors James and Dawn Macfarlane are very much 'hands on', ensuring that their guests enjoy their stay at Muckrach. 1 AA Rosette.

Sauteed duck livers on crushed garlic potatoes with Parmesan wafers and a balsamic jus. Venison fillet on a rosemary rösti with a jus of ginger, juniper and orange. Belgian chocolate terrine with Amaretto ice cream.

STB ★★★★ Hotel

◐ Open all year ⌂ Rooms: 13, 12 en suite ⌘ DB&B £72–£82 B&B £49.50–£59.50 SP Special rates available ✘ Lunch £ Dinner £££ Ⓥ Vegetarians welcome ♣ Children welcome ♿ Facilities for disabled visitors ✄ No smoking in restaurants ⚑ Member of the Scotch Beef Club ⊞ Credit cards: Mastercard/Eurocard, American Express, Visa, Diners Club, Switch, JCB ⚐ Proprietors: James & Dawn Macfarlane

*Dulnain Bridge Grantown-on-Spey Morayshire PH26 3LY
Tel: 01479 851 257 Fax: 01479 851 325
E-mail: muckrach.lodge@sol.co.uk
Web: www.muckrach.com
3 miles from Grantown-on-Spey on A938 Dulnain Bridge – Carrbridge Road, 400 yards from Dulnain Bridge. [C4]*

GRANTOWN-ON-SPEY

The Pines

- *"Michael and Gwen are committed to giving their guests comfort, hospitality and food of a very high standard."*
- *Modern Scottish cooking.*

THE EXPERIENCE at The Pines is one of real Scottish hospitality. Many antiques, fine furnishings and family portraits are to be found here together with interesting 'objets d'art'. Michael and Gwen Stewart make their guests welcome in their fine home with its large landscaped garden in a delightful woodland setting.

Fillet of lemon sole with ginger and sesame on cumin roasted carrots. Breast of chicken with a mushroom and white wine sauce on a bed of green lentils. Chocolate torte with home-made vanilla ice cream and raspberry coulis.

STB ★★★★ Small Hotel

◐ Open 1 Mar to 31 Oct – or by special arrangement ⌂ Rooms: 8 (7 en suite, 1 with adjacent private facilities) ⇌ DB&B £43–£55 B&B £25–£35 ⊞ Special rates available ✘ Dinner ££ Residents only Ⓥ Vegetarians welcome ✴ Children over 12 years welcome ⌇ No smoking throughout ⊞ Credit cards: Mastercard/Eurocard, Visa, Delta ⋈ Owners: Gwen & Michael Stewart

Woodside Avenue Grantown-on-Spey PH26 3JR
Tel: 01479 872092 Fax: 01479 872092
E-mail: enquiry@pinesgrantown.freeserve.co.uk
Web: www.pinesgrantown.freeserve.co.uk
On entering the town take A939 road to Tomintoul. 1st right. [C4]

GULLANE

Greywalls

- *"One always feels it such a privilege to enjoy such good food and service in such an enchanting setting as Greywalls."*
- *Refined country house cuisine.*

THIS historic hotel's lovely walled garden complements the serenity of the house itself. Chef Simon Burns' excellent menus are table d'hôte and his cooking is quite inspirational. The wine list is exceptional. Greywalls retains its position as one of Scotland's very special places. Greywalls has 2 AA Rosettes. Winner of The Macallan Taste of Scotland Country Lunch Award 1999.

Seared fillet of sea bass 'en papiotte' with ginger, tomato and wild mushrooms. North Berwick lobster, hot smoked over hickory chips, with a lime butter. Fine apple tart with thick vanilla cream and caramel sauce.

STB ★★★★ Hotel

◐ Open mid Apr to mid Oct ⌂ Rooms: 23 en suite ⇌ B&B £90–£110 ✘ Lunch ££ Dinner ££££ Ⓥ Vegetarians welcome – prior notice required ✴ Children welcome ♿ Facilities for disabled visitors ⌇ No smoking in dining room ⊞ Credit cards: Mastercard/Eurocard, American Express, Visa, Diners Club, Switch ⋈ Manager: Sue Prime

Muirfield Gullane East Lothian EH31 2EG
Tel: 01620 842144 Fax: 01620 842241
E-mail: hotel@greywalls.co.uk
Web: www.greywalls.co.uk
At the eastern end of Gullane village (on the A198), signposted left as a historic building. [D5]

HAWICK

Mansfield House Hotel

- *"Charming restaurant lovingly restored to its former Victorian glory."*
- *Traditional Scottish and contemporary cooking.*

A VICTORIAN mansion owned and run by the MacKinnon family. Under their supervision Chef David Tate presents well-priced à la carte and 'business lunch' menus in the formal dining room, and bar meals are also available. As well as the usual grills, the à la carte menu features some unusual combinations.

Local haggis and black pudding served hot on turnip pancake with cheese sauce. Loin of lamb wrapped in mint and smoked bacon, sweet potato, vegetables, sauce bourguignonne. Gooseberries in elderflower jelly, shortbread cigars and Borders clotted cream.

STB ★★★ Hotel

◐ Open all year except 26, 27 Dec, 1 and 2 Jan 🏠 Rooms: 12 en suite 🛏 DB&B £45–£75 B&B £30–£55 💷 Special rates available ✗ Lunch £-££ Dinner ££-£££ Ⓥ Vegetarians welcome ⚹ Children welcome ♿ Facilities for disabled visitors ⚕ No smoking area in restaurant 💳 Credit cards: Mastercard/Eurocard, American Express, Visa, Diners Club ♛ Owners: Ian & Sheila MacKinnon

Weensland Road Hawick TD9 8LB
Tel: 01450 360400 Fax: 01450 372007
E-mail: ian@mansfield-house.com
Web: www.mansfield-house.com
On the A698 Hawick to Kelso road. On the outskirts of the town. [D6]

HELENSBURGH

Hill House, National Trust for Scotland

- *"Impeccable and detailed attention to quality which exceeded expectations."*
- *Scottish.*

HILL HOUSE is internationally renowned for being the creation of Charles Rennie Mackintosh and is a wonderful example of this architect's talent. It has been maintained to the highest standard and is worth making a special effort to see. In the tearoom Scottish home bakes, and light refreshments are served by friendly and enthusiastic staff.

Wickedly tempting cakes, biscuits and home-baked Scottish fare, along with a variety of teas and coffees.

STB Commended

◐ Open 1 Apr to 31 Oct 🚫 Unlicensed ✗ Food available all day £ Lunch £ Ⓥ Vegetarians welcome ⚹ Children welcome ♿ Facilities for disabled visitors ⚕ No smoking throughout 💳 No credit cards ♛ Property Manager: Anne Ellis

Upper Colquhoun Street Helensburgh G84 9AJ
Tel: 01436 673900 Fax: 01436 674685
Web: www.nts.org.uk
Off B832, between A82 and A814, 23 miles north-west of Glasgow. [C5]

HELENSBURGH

Kirkton House

- *"Converted farmhouse with beautiful elevated views of the River Clyde from a delightful garden."*
- *Accomplished home cooking.*

KIRKTON HOUSE, a converted, late 18th century farmhouse, is a residential farmstead hotel. Stewart and Gillian set out to make your stay as pleasant as possible. Meals are normally chatty events, like a house party but at separate tables. Kirkton House has all the facilities of a small hotel, serves a homely dinner and a wonderful breakfast.

Haggis 'n' neeps sampler with whisky cream sauce. Baked halibut with bacon and vegetables. Banana flambé with ice cream.

STB ★★★★ Guest House

◐ Open all year except Dec and Jan 🏨 Rooms: 6 en suite ⌑ DB&B £42.50–£54.75 B&B £30.50–£45 ▦ Special rates available ⚐ Restricted licence ✗ Dinner 4 course menu ££ – advance booking required Ⓥ Vegetarians welcome ⚹ Children welcome ⚭ Facilities for disabled visitors – downstairs rooms only ⚞ No smoking in dining room ▣ Credit cards: Mastercard/Eurocard, American Express, Visa, Diners Club, Delta, JCB ◪ Proprietors: Stewart & Gillian Macdonald

Darleith Road Cardross Argyll & Bute G82 5EZ Tel: 01389 841 951 Fax: 01389 841 868 E-mail: tos@kirktonhouse.co.uk Web: www.kirktonhouse.co.uk Cardross is mid way between Helensburgh and Dumbarton on the north bank of the Clyde. At west end of Cardross village turn north off A814 up Darleith Road. Kirkton House drive ½ mile on right. [C5]

HELMSDALE

Navidale House Hotel

- *"Country house Hotel in a beautiful setting offering good Scottish fayre."*
- *Excellent home cooking with flair.*

NAVIDALE is set in seven acres of woodland and garden that lead down to the sea. The hotel caters in particular for fishermen and outdoor enthusiasts. The owners and their professional team aim to ensure that your stay at Navidale is a memorable one. Also two luxury self-catering units available.

Sliced smoked duckling breast served on an orange and sweet pepper salad with a port and raspberry sauce. Helmsdale monkfish cooked in a tarragon, cream, garlic and white wine sauce. Home-baked choux pastry buns filled with caramel ice cream with a hot chocolate and Drambuie sauce.

STB ★★★ Hotel

◐ Open Feb to 1 Nov 🏨 Rooms: 15 en suite ⌑ DB&B £60–£80 B&B £35–£55 ▦ Special rates available ✗ Packed lunch available Lunch £ Dinner £££ Ⓥ Vegetarians welcome ⚹ Children welcome ⚭ Limited facilities for disabled visitors ⚞ No smoking in restaurant ▣ Credit cards: Mastercard/Eurocard, Visa, Switch ◪ Manager: S Fennell

Helmsdale Sutherland KW8 6JS Tel: 01431 821258 Fax: 01431 821531 ¾ mile north of Helmsdale on main A9 road overlooking the sea. [C3]

HOWGATE

Howgate Restaurant: Finalist The Macallan Taste of Scotland Awards 2000

- *"Delightful location – so handy for Edinburgh – delicious in every way."*
- *Modern Scottish cooking.*

THE à la carte style restaurant operates alongside a cosy intimate bistro with a welcoming open log fire in winter. Wide choice of less formal dishes offered on the Bistro menu. The cooking here is excellent, prepared and presented in innovative modern style, with countryside portions.

Smoked fishcakes with a coriander, wilted spinach and a creamy herb sauce. Minted leg of Borders lamb steak with wholegrain mustard mash and roasted root vegetables, topped with a redcurrant and red wine gravy. Home-made sticky toffee pudding with bonfire toffee sauce.

◐ Open all year except Christmas Day and New Year's Day ✘ Lunch ££ Dinner £££
Ⓥ Vegetarians welcome ✶ Children welcome ♿ Facilities for disabled visitors ⊞ Credit cards: Mastercard/Eurocard, American Express, Visa, Diners Club, Switch, Delta ⦿ General Manager: Peter Ridgway; Head Chef: Adrian Rowe

Howgate Nr Penicuik EH26 8PY
Tel: 01968 670000 Fax: 01968 670000
E-mail: nigel@howgate.f9.co
Web: www.howgate.f9.co.uk
Situated on B6094 about 1 mile north of Leadburn. [D6]

HOWWOOD

Bowfield Hotel & Country Club

- *"Warmth and hospitality for all ages in a relaxed atmosphere."*
- *Traditional food with Scottish influences.*

BOWFIELD HOTEL & Country Club is a refreshingly different country retreat close to town and city attractions. It enjoys many international visitors and is a popular retreat for weekend leisure breaks, combining a well-converted building with modern facilities – pool, spa and gym – and a relaxing dining experience. Imaginative menus using good quality produce cooked with skill and flair.

Smoked fish risotto topped with grilled red mullet and a Loch Fyne mussel and dill vinaigrette. Prime Scottish beef fillet on dauphinoise potato with wild mushrooms and red wine jus. Butterscotch flan with honey and Drambuie ice cream.

STB ★★★★ Hotel

◐ Open all year ⌂ Rooms: 23 en suite ⇔ B&B £37.50-£65 ⓢⓟ Special rates available ✘ Food available all day £ Lunch £ Dinner ££
Ⓥ Vegetarians welcome ✶ Children welcome ⊘ No smoking in restaurant ⊞ Credit cards: Mastercard/Eurocard, American Express, Visa, Diners Club, Switch, Delta ⦿ General Manager: Aileen Adams

Howwood Renfrewshire PA9 1DB
Tel: 01505 705225 Fax: 01505 705230
Web: www.bowfieldcountryclub.co.uk
From the M8 at Glasgow Airport take A737 (Irvine) for approx 6 miles. Exit left (Howwood) onto B787 then either take second right onto a single track shortcut or drive into Howwood and take right onto B776 for 1 mile to Bowfield at top of hill (large white gateposts). [C6]

INVERARNAN

The Stagger Inn

- *"Excellent choice of interesting dishes – you won't know what to choose."*
- *Skilled and imaginative Scottish cooking.*

AT THE Stagger Inn venison is a speciality as are hearty portions which are appreciated by all who visit here. All customers are assured of a quality meal cooked and presented in a professional and skilled way by head chef Rob Watkinson. Runner-up (Category 1) in The Taste of Scotland Scotch Lamb Challenge Competition 1999. Inspected under previous owners.

Black pudding and clapshot cake with an Arran mustard sauce. Rabbit loin with Dunsyre Blue cheese and bacon. Home-made steamed pudding, Drambuie mousse.

◑ Open 1 Apr to 30 Sept and weekends only in Oct ✘ Lunch except Tue Wed Thu ££ Dinner ££ Ⓥ Vegetarians welcome ⚹ Children welcome ♿ Facilities for disabled visitors ⚞ Smoking is permitted in the restaurant after last orders (9 pm) ▣ Credit cards: Mastercard, Visa, Switch

*Inverarnan Ardlui by Arrochar G83 7ZZ
Tel: 01301 704 274 Fax: 01567 820269
On the roadside at Inverarnan, 7 miles south of Crianlarich on the A82 to Glasgow. [C5]*

INVERKEILOR

Gordon's Restaurant

- *"In a class of its own!"*
- *Modern Scottish cooking.*

Gordon's Restaurant buys local fish, meats and fruits to produce imaginative, modern Scottish cooking. An à la carte menu changes regularly. Gordon's has 2 AA Rosettes. Winner (Category 2) and Overall Winner in The Taste of Scotland Scotch Lamb Challenge Competition 1999. Winner of The Macallan Taste Of Scotland Rural Restaurant Award 1999.

Pavé of smoked trout on chive blinis with crushed avocado and goats cheese. Fillet of pork with foie gras mousseline and slow-braised belly, vanilla figs, Sauterne jus. Lemon and ginger pudding with salpicon of exotic fruits, lemon balm sorbet.

STB ★★★★ Restaurant with Rooms

◑ Open all year except last 2 weeks Jan ▥ Rooms: 2 en suite ⚲ DB&B £62.50-£72.50 B&B £35-£45 ✘ Closed Mon – residents only Lunch except Mon Tue Sat – booking essential ££ Dinner except Mon – residents only £££ Ⓥ Vegetarians welcome ⚹ Children welcome ⚞ No smoking area in restaurant ✥ Member of the Scotch Beef Club ▣ Credit cards: Mastercard/Eurocard, Visa ⚐ Owners: Gordon & Maria Watson

*Main Street Inverkeilor by Arbroath
Angus DD11 5RN
Tel: 01241 830364 Fax: 01241 830364
A92 Arbroath to Montrose, turn off at sign for Inverkeilor. [D5]*

INVERNESS

Bunchrew House Hotel

- *"A peaceful haven offering skilled cooking on the outskirts of Inverness."*
- *Excellent Scottish cooking with an imaginative modern flair.*

BUNCHREW HOUSE HOTEL has a magnificent dining room which overlooks the sea. The style of cooking is a fusion of traditional and modern styles with attention to detail. The high standard of furnishing and fittings throughout combined with welcoming staff – makes Bunchrew a very special place indeed.

Warm seafood terrine wrapped in herb crêpes accompanied by a lime and dill sauce. Saddle of West Highland venison with pancetta mash on a pool of juniper and rosemary sauce. Spicy poached pear feuillete accompanied by ginger butterscotch sauce.

STB ★★★★ Small Hotel

◐ Open all year ⌂ Rooms: 11 en suite ⚑ DB&B £70–£115 B&B £50–£85 ⚑ Special rates available ✘ Food available all day £ Lunch ££ Dinner £££ Ⓥ Vegetarians welcome ✸ Children welcome ⚑ No smoking in restaurant ⚑ No dogs in public rooms ⚑ Member of the Scotch Beef Club ⚑ Credit cards: Mastercard/Eurocard, American Express, Visa, Switch, Delta, JCB ⚑ Owner: Graham Cross

Bunchrew Inverness IV3 8TA
Tel: 01463 234917 Fax: 01463 710620
E-mail: welcome@bunchrew-inverness.co.uk
Web: www.bunchrew-inverness.co.uk
On A862 Inverness to Beauly. 10 minutes from the centre of Inverness. [C4]

INVERNESS

Cafe 1

- *"A modern-style city centre restaurant offering good food."*
- *Modern Scottish cooking.*

CAFE 1 has a new owner and a complete change of staff. It now has a bistro-ambience which is enhanced by its friendly staff. It is a popular venue and used by locals. The chef uses high quality local produce, balancing the combination of textures and flavours.

Brochette of seafood simply grilled and seasoned with a timbale of lemon and Mascarpone risotto. Smoked haddock, bubble-and-squeak, soft poached egg, served with a wholegrain mustard sauce. Bread and butter pudding with crème anglaise.

◐ Open all year except Christmas Day, Boxing Day and New Year's Day Closed Sun ✘ Lunch except Sun £ Dinner except Sun ££-£££ Ⓥ Vegetarians welcome ✸ Children welcome ⚑ Credit cards: Mastercard/Eurocard, Visa, Switch, Delta ⚑ Owner: Norman MacDonald

75 Castle Street Inverness IV2 4EA
Tel: 01463 226 200 Fax: 01463 716 363
Centrally located on Castle Street near castle. [C4]

INVERNESS

Culloden House Hotel

- *"Culloden is an experience of fine dining, luxury and professional caring staff."*
- *Country house cooking.*

CULLODEN HOUSE HOTEL is an upmarket country house hotel in lovely grounds. There is a majestic splendour and romance about the place. The standard of cooking is high, prepared by a chef committed to high quality. It is an excellent place from which to explore the surrounding historical area, whilst enjoying luxurious surroundings and excellent hospitality. 2 AA Rosettes.

Warm asparagus with Parma ham, wrapped in filo and served with a lime salad. Loin of Scottish lamb with Lanark Blue, bacon, spinach on a minted bordelaise. Strawberry and vanilla parfait.

STB ★★★★ Hotel

◐ Open all year ♞ Rooms: 28 en suite ⛁ DB&B £190–£340 B&B £145–£270 ▦ Special rates available off season ✕ Food available all day ££££ Lunch ££ Dinner ££££ Ⅴ Vegetarians welcome ✽ Children welcome ✌ No smoking in dining room and lounge ☙ Member of the Scotch Beef Club ⊞ Credit cards: Mastercard/Eurocard, American Express, Visa, Diners Club, Switch, Delta, JCB ▮ General Manager/Director: Stephen Davies

Inverness IV2 7BZ
Tel: 01463 790461 Fax: 01463 792181
E-mail: info@cullodenhouse.co.uk
Web: www.cullodenhouse.co.uk
3 miles from the centre of Inverness, off the A96 Inverness to Aberdeen road. [C4]

INVERNESS

Culloden Moor Visitor Centre Restaurant
National Trust for Scotland

- *"A friendly welcome awaits you at this self-service restaurant which serves local produce."*
- *Traditional Scottish.*

CULLODEN MOOR VISITOR CENTRE offers a great insight into the history and events in the area and there is the opportunity to walk the famous historic battlefield yourself. The restaurant is well-thought out and offers good, honest Scottish food to suit all appetites and tastes with a strong emphasis on quality local produce.

Tattie drottle served with a freshly baked cheese and herb scone. Scottish beef and heather ale casserole with fresh local vegetables. Whisky marmalade bread and butter pudding home-made vanilla ice cream.

STB Commended

◐ Open 1 Feb to 31 Dec except 24, 25 and 26 Dec ✕ Food available all day £ Lunch £ Ⅴ Vegetarians welcome ✽ Children welcome ♿ Facilities for disabled visitors ✌ No smoking throughout ⊞ Credit cards: Mastercard, Visa, Switch, Delta ▮ Restaurant Manager: Mrs Daska MacKintosh

Culloden Moor Inverness IV2 5EU
Tel: 01463 790607 Fax: 01463 794294
E-mail: dmacintosh@nts.org.uk
Web: www.nts.org.uk
B9006, 5 miles east of Inverness on National Cycle Routes 1 and 7. [C4]

INVERNESS

Dunain Park Hotel

- *"A luxurious pampering stay with the best of food and quality service."*
- *First rate Scottish cooking, with assured French influences.*

ANN AND EDWARD Nicoll have won a high reputation – and several awards. Ann goes to great lengths to source top quality fresh local produce and her style of cooking brings out the flavour of such produce, and enhances it with wonderfully assured sauces. The large kitchen garden supplies herbs, vegetables and soft fruit.

Terrine of chicken and Guinea fowl layered with venison, pigeon and hare served with home-made chutney. Medallions of venison rolled in oatmeal and served with a mushroom potato cake and a claret and crème de cassis sauce. Chocolate truffle and Drambuie cake.

STB ★★★★ Hotel
Green Tourism Two Leaf Silver Award

◐ Open all year ⌂ Rooms: 13 en suite ⊟ DB&B £104–£124 B&B £79–£99 ℗ Special rates available in the low season ✗ Dinner £££ Ⓥ Vegetarians welcome ☆ Well-behaved children welcome ♿ Facilities for disabled visitors – residents only ⌇ No smoking in dining room ♨ Member of the Scotch Beef Club ▭ Credit cards: Mastercard/Eurocard, American Express, Visa, Switch, Delta ⌇ Owners: Ann & Edward Nicoll

Inverness IV3 8JN
Tel: 01463 230512 Fax: 01463 224532
E-mail: dunainparkhotel@btinternet.com
Web: dunainparkhotel.co.uk
On A82, on left hand side, 1 mile from the Inverness town boundary. [C4]

INVERNESS

Glendruidh House Hotel

- *"Michael will help you to plan your day, while Christine cooks a welcoming meal."*
- *Traditional Scottish cooking.*

THIS IS an unusual and attractive small country house set in three acres of woodland and lawns – smoking is prohibited even in the grounds. The elegant dining room (residents only) has an Italian marble fireplace and overlooks the extensive gardens. Christine Smith's well-balanced table d'hôte menus change daily and offer classic dishes employing the best of fresh local produce.

Smoked hill venison with salad and wild rowan jelly. Baked rainbow trout with North Atlantic prawns. Queen of Puddings.

STB ★★★★ Small Hotel

◐ Open all year except Christmas Day ⌂ Rooms: 5 en suite (and 3 en suite rooms in Garden Villa) ⊟ DB&B £53.50–£97 B&B £29.50–£67.50 ℗ Special rates available ✗ Lunch – residents only ££ Dinner – residents only ££-£££ Ⓥ Vegetarians welcome ☆ Children welcome ♿ Limited facilities for disabled visitors ⌇ No smoking throughout ▭ Credit cards: Mastercard/Eurocard, American Express, Visa, Diners Club, Switch, JCB ⌇ Proprietors: Michael & Christine Smith

by Castle Heather Old Edinburgh Road South Inverness IV2 6AR
Tel: 01463 226499 Fax: 01463 710745
E-mail: tos@cozzee-nessie-bed.co.uk
Web: www.cozzee-nessie-bed.co.uk/intro.html
Two miles from Inverness centre. ½ mile south off Sir Walter Scott Drive. At the 2nd roundabout turn left and take the first right at the 'Hotel 300 yards' sign. [C4]

INVERNESS

The Riverhouse Restaurant: Finalist The Macallan Taste of Scotland Awards 2000

- *"The Riverhouse offers outstanding meals on the banks of the River Ness."*
- *A blend of traditional and contemporary Scottish cooking.*

MARCUS BLACKWELL prepares meals in the open plan kitchen in full view of the guests leaving no doubts as to the skill and level of work in each dish. There is an interesting and appetising range of fish dishes; meat and game dishes are certainly worthy of a mention. Booking essential. 1 AA Rosette.

Salad of gravalax, crabmeat, quails eggs, season leaves and a herb dressing. Monkfish wrapped in air-dried ham served on a bed of spinach with a roast red pepper sauce. Amaretto bavarois with summer fruits.

◐ Open 1 Feb to 30 Dec except Christmas Day and Boxing Day Closed Sun Mon – 1 Oct to 1 June ✕ Dinner £££ Ⓥ Vegetarians welcome ✸ Children welcome ♿ Facilities for disabled visitors ✄ No smoking throughout 🖃 Credit cards: Mastercard/Eurocard, American Express, Visa, Switch, Delta ⌘ Owner: M Blackwell

1 Greig Street Inverness IV3 5PT
Tel: 01463 222033 Fax: 01463 220890
Situated on the corner of Greig Street and Huntly Street, on the west side of the River Ness close to Balnain House. [C4]

INVERNESS

The Taste of Moray

- *"A specialist steak and seafood restaurant to be enjoyed after shopping downstairs in the foodhall and cookshop."*
- *Scottish cooking.*

TASTE OF MORAY has a seafood and steak restaurant, food hall and cookshop. It is run by Robin and Celia Birkbeck and finished to an exceptionally high standard. The restaurant is open all day and offers everything from light refreshments to a full dinner menu all cooked using fresh local produce.

Char-grilled Aberdeen Angus sirloin steak garni. Diver harvested scallops, wrapped in Morayshire bacon, served with hollandaise sauce. Profiteroles with chocolate sauce.

◐ Open all year except 25, 26, 31 Dec and 1 Jan N.B. Jan to 1 Apr evening meals by booking only ♵ Licensed ✕ Food available all day £ Lunch £ Dinner ££ Ⓥ Vegetarians welcome ✸ Children welcome ♿ Limited facilities for disabled visitors 🖃 Credit cards: Mastercard/Eurocard, Visa, Switch, Delta ⌘ Proprietors: Robin & Celia Birkbeck

Gollanfield Inverness IV2 7QT
Tel: 01667 462340 Fax: 01667 461087
E-mail: info@tasteofmoray.co.uk
Web: www.tasteofmoray.co.uk
Between Inverness and Nairn on the main A96. Inverness 8 miles, Nairn 5 miles. [C4]

INVERNESS

Woodwards Restaurant

- *"A fine dining experience in the heart of Inverness."*
- *Modern Scottish cooking.*

WOODWARDS is a small tastefully refurbished 'Auld Hoose'. Local produce is very much in evidence and attention to detail prominent. A small corner bar and seating area provide space for waiting – or for after-dinner relaxation. Celtic music and good Scottish cooking set the scene for a thoroughly enjoyable dining experience.

Breast of Cawdor woodpigeon on a red onion marmalade, served with a black pudding on a balsamic jus. Lightly grilled halibut served with fresh egg pasta and a red wine and basil butter sauce. Caramelised fruit flan with soft poached berries.

◐ *Open all year* ✘ *Lunch ££ Dinner £££*
Ⓥ *Vegetarians welcome* ⚹ *Children welcome*
✘ *No smoking in restaurant* ⊞ *Credit cards: Mastercard/Eurocard, American Express, Visa, Diners Club International, Switch, Delta*
⚐ *Proprietor: Kay Frew*

99 Castle Street Inverness IV2 3EA
Tel: 01463 709809 Fax: 01463 790999
E-mail: woodwards@lineone.net
Looking onto historic Castle of Inverness, centre of town, turn right at Town House. Restaurant at the top of Castle Street, on the left. [C4]

INVERSHIN

Falls of Shin Visitor Centre

- *"Good food at a delightful location with an interesting selection of Scottish produce in the shop."*
- *Home cooking and baking.*

THE FALLS OF SHIN VISITOR CENTRE is dramatically positioned alongside the Shin Waterfall. It is well worth a visit for the breathtaking experience of the wild Atlantic salmon leap to survival. The self service, licensed restaurant has a commitment to the quality produce of the Highlands, from superb home-made beef burgers to salmon dishes.

Pickled herring, salad and oatcakes. Salmon steaks, mashed potatoes with fresh salad. Banoffee pie and locally made ice cream.

◐ *Open Feb to Dec* ✘ *Food available all day £ Lunch £ Dinner July and Aug only £*
Ⓥ *Vegetarians welcome* ⚹ *Children welcome*
♿ *Facilities for disabled visitors* ✘ *Smoking area in dining room* ⊞ *Credit cards: Mastercard/Eurocard, Visa, Switch, Delta* ⚐ *Owner: Peter Campbell*

Achany Glen Lairg Sutherland IV27 4EE
Tel: 01549 402231 Fax: 01863 766500
E-mail: info@fallsofshin.co.uk
Web: www.highlandescape.com/fallsofshin
Next to Shin Falls Waterfall on B837 Lairg to Bonar-Bridge. [C3]

INVERURIE

Pittodrie House Hotel

- *"Elegance, comfort, fine food and fine wine inside – and an impressive range of outdoor leisure pursuits outside."*
- *Well-cooked Scottish cuisine.*

PITTODRIE HOUSE originally belonged to a branch of the family of the Earls of Mar. In the dining room the robust table d'hôte menus are well-balanced and offer just the kind of dishes one would expect in a grand country house, accompanied by herbs and vegetables from the hotel's own garden and a delicious selection of desserts.

Ramekin of poached smoked haddock topped with a Gruyère and garlic crust. Roast monkfish wrapped in smoked bacon set on crisp vegetables, complemented by a fresh mussel sauce. Vanilla crème brûlée flavoured with stem ginger, accompanied by home-made shortbread fingers.

STB ★★★ Hotel

◑ Open all year 🛏 Rooms: 27 en suite ⛌ DB&B £65–80+ B&B £52.50–£65 💷 Special rates available ✖ Lunch £-££ Dinner £££ 🅥 Vegetarians welcome ⚹ Children welcome ⌁ No smoking in dining room 💳 Credit cards: Mastercard/Eurocard, American Express, Visa, Diners Club, Switch, Delta 🕴 General Manager: Nigel Guthrie

Chapel of Garioch Inverurie AB51 5HS
Tel: 01467 681444 Fax: 01467 681648
E-mail: info@pittodriehouse.com
Web: wwwpittodriehouse.com
Off A96 just north of Inverurie 21 miles north of Aberdeen, 17 miles north of airport. [D4]

INVERURIE

Thainstone House Hotel & Country Club

- *"A palladian mansion house offering good hospitality and a well equipped country club."*
- *Modern Scottish cuisine.*

AN AWARD-WINNING team offer an extensive table d'hôte menu in 'Simpsons' Restaurant. Portion sizes and the quality of the raw materials are influenced only by the rich farming country within which Thainstone stands. For more informal dining there is Cammie's Bar. 2 AA Rosettes.

Risotto of fine vegetables with goats cheese and fresh basil. Mille feuille of salmon and aubergine, served with a thyme jus. Poached pear with cinnamon ice cream and a warm claret syrup.

STB ★★★ Hotel

◑ Open all year 🛏 Rooms: 48 en suite ⛌ DB&B £66–£90 B&B £45–£80 💷 Special rates available ✖ Food available all day ££-£££ Lunch £££ Dinner ££££ 🅥 Vegetarians welcome ⚹ Children welcome ⌁ Facilities for disabled visitors ⌁ No smoking in restaurant 💳 Credit cards: Mastercard/Eurocard, American Express, Visa, Diners Club, Switch, Delta 🕴 General Manager: Sylvia Simpson

Inverurie Aberdeenshire AB51 5NT
Tel: 01467 621643 Fax: 01467 625084
E-mail: reservations@thainstone.macdonald-hotels.co.uk
Web: www.macdonaldhotels.co.uk
On A96 north of Aberdeen, 8 miles from airport turn left at first roundabout after Kintore. [D4]

IRVINE

Montgreenan Mansion House Hotel

- *"A wonderful hotel, professionally run, which is indeed a pleasure to visit."*
- *Modern Scottish.*

BUILT in 1817, and set in 50 acres of parklands and gardens, Montgreenan retains the impressive architecture and decorative features of the period. Accommodation has been refurbished to a very high standard. Public rooms are elegant and comfortable. The staff at Montgreenan are friendly, efficient and attentive. The hotel has 1 AA Rosette.

Strips of chicken marinated with Cajun spices in a summer leaf salad. Saddle of lamb topped with petit ratatouille and glazed with goats cheese. Home-made spicey apple, pear and cinnamon crumble served with pouring cream.

STB ★★★★ Hotel

☾ *Open all year* ⌂ *Rooms: 21 en suite* 🛏 *DB&B £65–£109.50 B&B £80–£175* 🆂 *Special rates available* ✗ *Food available all day ££ Lunch ££ Dinner £££* Ⓥ *Vegetarians welcome* ✱ *Children welcome* ⌔ *No smoking in restaurant* 💳 *Credit cards: Mastercard/Eurocard, American Express, Visa, Diners Club* ⓚ *Proprietors: James & Nicole Leckie*

Montgreenan Estate nr Kilwinning
Ayrshire KA13 7QZ
Tel: 01294 557733 Fax: 01294 850397
E-mail: info@montgreenanhotel.com
Web: www.montgreenanhotel.com
Just off the A736, 4 miles north of Irvine. 30 minutes from Glasgow, 20 minutes from Ayr.
[C6]

ISLE OF ARRAN

Apple Lodge

- *"An attractive Edwardian house in charming island village."*
- *High quality home cooking.*

APPLE LODGE is tranquilly located, set in its own appealing gardens. It has been furnished beautifully to a very high standard. Relax in the comfortable surroundings watching wild deer graze a few yards from the garden whilst Jeannie Boyd will be creating a deliciously mouth-watering dinner for all to enjoy.

Gâteau of locally smoked chicken and avocado, with a citrus dressing. Char-griddled fresh tuna steak with ginger, spring onions and summer leaves. Terrine of three crushed fruits with a kiwi sauce.

STB ★★★★ Guest House

☾ *Open all year except Christmas week* ⌂ *Rooms: 4 en suite* 🛏 *DB&B £47–£52 B&B £30–£35* 🆂 *Special rates available* Ⓤ *Unlicensed – guests welcome to take own wine* ✗ *Packed lunches £ Dinner ££ Residents only* Ⓥ *Vegetarians welcome* ✱ *Children over 12 years welcome* ⌔ *No smoking in dining room and bedrooms* 💳 *No credit cards* ⓚ *Proprietor/Chef: Jeannie Boyd*

Lochranza Isle of Arran KA27 8HJ
Tel: 01770 830229 Fax: 01770 830229
E-mail: applelodge@easicom.com
From Brodick, head north and follow the road to Lochranza (around 14 miles). As you enter the village pass the distillery and Apple Lodge is situated 300 yards on the left opposite golf course. [B6]

ISLE OF ARRAN

Argentine House Hotel

- *"Unusual international influences complement local produce."*
- *Scottish produce with a continental touch.*

ASSYA AND BRUNO Baumgärtner have refurbished this lovely villa to suit the local heritage, making a comfortable and relaxing home which is well cared for. Menus change daily, depending on produce available and guests' taste. Vegetarians are well-cared for and every taste is met. Food combinations are interesting, innovative and well-executed.

Skirlie of organic oatmeal, onions, bacon and herbs on crusty bread. Seared salmon on a vinaigrette of sun-dried tomatoes, Arran mustard and herbs from the garden served on a barley risotto with home-grown mange tout. Sorbet of Arran strawberries and home-made lemon yoghurt ice cream served on a coulis of brambles and kiwi.

STB ★★★ Small Hotel

◐ Open Mar to mid Jan ♣ Rooms: 5 en suite ⬛ DB&B from £42 B&B from £23 ▦ Special rates available ✘ Dinner ££-£££ Non-residents – by arrangement Ⓥ Vegetarians welcome ⌇ No smoking in dining room ▣ Credit cards: Mastercard/Eurocard, Visa, JCB ▨ Owners: Assya & Bruno Baumgärtner

*Whiting Bay Isle of Arran KA27 8PZ
Tel: 01770 700 662 Fax: 01770 700 693
E-mail: info@argentinearran.co.uk
Web: www.argentinearran.co.uk
8 miles south of ferry terminal. First hotel on seafront at village entrance. [B6]*

ISLE OF ARRAN

Auchrannie Country House Hotel

- *"A comfortable hotel with vibrant restaurant suitable for all age groups and excellent facilities for all its guests."*
- *Modern Scottish cooking.*

AUCHRANNIE is a delightful, comfortable hotel. Brambles Cafe Bar is the informal venue for snacks and meals, and the Garden Restaurant offers more formal dining with a well balanced table d'hôte menu offering a good range of local Scottish meat and fish dishes complemented by fresh vegetables and a daily vegetarian speciality. 2 AA Rosettes.

Terrine of vegetables set in a tomato coulis. Saddle of Arran lamb topped with a herb parfait fricassee of garden vegetables. Iced Drambuie and Heather Honey parfait.

STB ★★★★ Hotel
STB ★★★★★ Lodges

◐ Open all year ♣ Rooms: 28 en suite ⬛ DB&B £51.00-81.00 B&B £34–£61.00 ▦ Special rates available ✘ Food available all day £ Lunch £ Dinner £££ Ⓥ Vegetarians welcome ✻ Children welcome ♿ Facilities for disabled visitors ⌇ No smoking in Garden Restaurant Smoking area in Brambles Bistro ▣ Credit cards: Mastercard/ Eurocard, American Express, Visa, Switch ▨ Managing Director: Iain Johnston

*Brodick Isle of Arran KA27 8BZ
Tel: 01770 302234 Fax: 01770 302812
E-mail: info@auchrannie.co.uk
Web: www.auchrannie.co.uk
One mile north of Brodick Ferry Terminal and 400 yards from Brodick Golf Club. [B6]*

ISLE OF ARRAN

Brodick Castle Restaurant, National Trust for Scotland

- *"Wonderful home baking and lunch dishes served in the castle."*
- *Home cooking and baking.*

IN THE castle itself is the restaurant which offers tasty home-cooked meals and light snacks, all made from locally sourced ingredients. The wonderful home baking is hard to resist. On a sunny day visitors may also sit outside to eat on the terrace and enjoy the magnificent views and grounds.

Traditional or alternative soups served with cheese scones and Arran mustard or castle-baked bread. Arran lamb with raspberries and tarragon. Traditional puddings both hot and cold.

STB Highly Commended Visitor Attraction

◑ Open 1 Apr to 31 Oct and winter weekends until 31 Dec ♗ Licensed ✘ Food available all day £ Lunch £ Ⓥ Vegetarians welcome ☆ Children welcome ♿ Facilities for disabled visitors ⚭ No smoking throughout ▦ Credit cards: Mastercard/Eurocard, Visa ♞ Property Manager: Mr Ken Thorburn

Brodick Isle of Arran KA27 8HY
Tel: 01770 302202 Fax: 01770 302312
E-mail: mrkenthorburn@thenationaltrustfor Scotland.org.uk
Web: www.thenationaltrustforscotland.org.uk
2 miles north out of Brodick on the Lochranza Road. Follow signs for the castle. [B6]

ISLE OF ARRAN

The Distillery Restaurant

- *"An appealing restaurant within a superb visitor attraction to suit all ages and tastes."*
- *Fresh and innovative to suit all tastes.*

THE DISTILLERY RESTAURANT offers a fine quality of dining but with an informality – to appeal to all tastes and ages. Evening dinner is a candlelit affair with a more formal approach. In the kitchen, Head Chef Duncan McKay is skilfully creating some unique yet very appealing dishes alongside the more traditional.

Rare seared tuna loin flavoured with lime and coriander, served on a sesame biscuit and drizzled with an oyster dressing. Suprême of Guinea fowl, stuffed with a pigeon breast on a bed of beetroot and aubergine compote with a bitter sweet jus.

STB ★★★★ Visitor Attraction

◑ Open 7 days Apr to Oct (with reduced winter hours) Closed Mon evening ✘ Food available all day except Mon evening £ Lunch £ Dinner except Mon ££ Ⓥ Vegetarians welcome ☆ Children welcome ♿ Facilities for disabled visitors ⚭ Smoking area in restaurant ▦ Credit cards: Mastercard/Eurocard, Visa, Switch, Delta, JCB ♞ Head Chef: Duncan McKay

Isle of Arran Distillers Lochranza Isle of Arran KA27 8HJ
Tel: 01770 830264 Fax: 01770 830364
E-mail: visitorcentre@arranwhisky.com
Web: www.arranwhisky.com
From Brodick follow signs to Lochranza. The Distillery Restaurant is located on the upper floor of the visitor centre. [B6]

ISLE OF ARRAN

Kilmichael Country House Hotel

- *"Kilmichael is a real gem of a place – wonderful surroundings, excellent hospitality and exquisite cooking."*
- *Superb modern cooking.*

KILMICHAEL is an elegant and compact lodge, exquisitely furnished. The menus are very interesting and demonstrate French and Italian influences. Every dish has something unique and authentic about it, with piquant flavours and delicately spiced sauces. Winner of The Macallan Taste of Scotland Country House Hotel of the Year Award 1998.

A tart of 3 Italian cheeses with caramelised red onions and fresh sorrel sauce. Breast of Guinea fowl stuffed with home-smoked mussels, apples and sage with a vermouth cream sauce. Rhubarb and elderflower fool with home-made rhubarb ice cream and hazelnut shortbread.

STB ★★★★★ Small Hotel

Open from Apr-Oct ⬤ *Rooms: 8 en suite* ⬤ *DB&B £85.50–£100.50 B&B £60–£75* ⬤ *Special rates available* ✘ *Dinner £££ Dinner for non-residents – booking essential* ⬤ *Vegetarians welcome* ⬤ *Facilities for disabled visitors* ⬤ *No smoking in dining room and bedrooms* ⬤ *Credit cards: Mastercard/ Eurocard, Visa, Switch* ⬤ *Partners: Geoffrey Botterill & Antony Butterworth*

Glen Cloy, by Brodick Isle of Arran KA27 8BY Tel: 01770 302219 Fax: 01770 302068 From Brodick Pier take road north ½ mile, then turn left at golf course following signs about ¾ mile. [B6]

ISLE OF BENBECULA

Stepping Stone Restaurant

- *"Stunning food to come back to Benbecula for – time and time again."*
- *A blend of traditional and contemporary Scottish cooking.*

THE STEPPING STONE is an inspirational restaurant. Food is available all day from 10am-9pm including a mixture of sandwiches, rolls and home baking to more substantial meals. In the evening there is also a table d'hôte menu offering three, four or five course options including Scottish cheeses. Take away food is also available.

Pan-fried local cockles in oatmeal. Roast Uist venison with rowanberry jelly. Home-grown strawberries with whisky cream.

⬤ *Open all year – 7 days a week* ✘ *Food available all day £££ Lunch ££ Dinner £££* ⬤ *Vegetarians welcome* ⬤ *Children welcome* ⬤ *Facilities for disabled visitors* ⬤ *No smoking throughout* ⬤ *Credit cards: Mastercard/ Eurocard, Visa, Switch, Delta* ⬤ *Manager: Ewen MacLean*

Balivanich Benbecula Western Isles HS7 5DA Tel: 01870 602659 Fax: 01870 603121 Drive south from Lochmaddy – heading for Benbecula, take sign for Balivanich – after 2½ miles turn into restaurant, just of the main road. [A4]

ISLE OF BUTE

New Farm Bed & Breakfast & Restaurant

- *"A unique experience – living on an island farm with cooking that skilfully uses nature's larder."*
- *Enthusiastic, adventurous and talented cooking.*

NEW FARM is the home of Carole and Michael Howard. To stay here and sample Carole's creative cooking and wonderful baking is a joy. On arrival you are offered home-baked afternoon tea. Guests are invited to pick their own vegetables for dinner. Guests can choose to eat on their own but most people prefer to join the other guests.

Home-made broths served with home-baked bread. Honey glazed New Farm lamb casseroled on a bed of apricots and fresh tarragon. Bournville baked bananas served in a 'puddle' of cream.

STB ★★★★ B&B

◐ Open all year ⌂ Rooms: 7, 5 en suite ⚑ DB&B £39.50–£47 B&B £25–£32.50 ⌸ Unlicensed – guests welcome to take own wine ✘ Lunch – reservation essential £ Dinner – reservation essential ££ Ⓥ Vegetarians welcome ♿ Facilities for disabled visitors ⊞ No credit cards ⚐ Proprietor: Carole Howard

*New Farm Mount Stuart Isle of Bute PA20 9NA
Tel: 01700 831646 Fax: 01700 831646
E-mail: newfarm@isleofbute.freeserve.co.uk
Web: www.isle-of-bute.com/newfarm
Turn left on leaving Wemyss Bay to Isle of Bute ferry terminal. Drive 6 miles. Signposted on right 1½ miles past entrance to Mount Stuart House and Gardens. [B6]*

ISLE OF HARRIS

Allan Cottage Guest House

- *"Charming guest house, formal yet relaxed. Offering good food and a friendly base in Tarbert."*
- *Imaginative Scottish cooking.*

THIS ATTRACTIVE old building has been interestingly converted and furnished in cottage style. Bill and Evelyn Reed are wonderfully enthusiastic and look after guests with true island hospitality. The dinner menu is discussed with guests in the morning and the cooking is interesting and imaginative and of a very high standard.

Smoked sea trout with avocado and kiwi fruit salad and grapefruit dressing. Harris lamb with herb stuffing wrapped in filo pastry. Eighteenth century nutmeg cheesecake with brown bread ice cream.

STB ★★★★ Guest House

◐ Open 1 Apr to 30 Sep ⌂ Rooms: 3 (2 en suite, 1 private facilities) ⚑ DB&B £57–£62 B&B £30–£35 ⌸ Special rates available ✘ Residents only Dinner 4 course menu £££ ⌸ Unlicensed Ⓥ Vegetarians welcome – by prior arrangement ⚹ Children over 10 years welcome ⌇ No smoking in dining room and bedrooms ⊞ No credit cards ⚐ Proprietors: Bill & Evelyn Reed

*Tarbert Isle of Harris HS3 3DJ
Tel: 01859 502146 Fax: 01859 502146
Web: www.witb.co.uk/links/allancottage.htm
From ferry turn left, then hard first right on to the main village street. [A3]*

ISLE OF HARRIS

Ardvourlie Castle

- *"Ardvourlie has such a unique charm and excellent food you will wish to return again and again – and many do just that."*
- *Accomplished Scottish cooking.*

ARDVOURLIE CASTLE is set in a glorious location. It has elegant architecture and the dining room offers views over the wooded grounds to the mountains beyond. Derek and Pamela Martin are gracious hosts, providing all home comforts. Their fine cooking uses as much of the excellent local produce available on this remote island.

Segments of fresh grapefruit sugared and grilled. Half roast duckling basted and crisped with honey, served with baked creamed potatoes with crispy topping. Tipsy Laird.

STB ★★★★★ Guest House

◐ Open 1 Apr to 31 Oct 🏨 Rooms: 4 with private facilities (occasionally 4) 🍴 DB&B £90–£115 B&B £65–£90 🍷 Restricted licence ✗ Dinner 4 course menu £££ Residents only Ⓥ Vegetarians welcome – advance notice essential ♣ Children old enough to dine with their parents welcome ⚞ No smoking in dining room 💳 No credit cards 🧑 Owner: D G Martin

Isle of Harris HS3 3AB
Tel: 01859 50 2307 Fax: 01859 50 2348
¼ mile off A859. 24 miles from Stornoway, 12 miles from Tarbert. [A3]

ISLE OF HARRIS

Leachin House

- *"Leachin House is a charming home offering excellent food and hospitality in a superb location."*
- *Modern Scottish cooking.*

THE SKILL and care with which Linda cooks and presents the food is worth a journey to Harris just to eat at Leachin House! The wonderful produce of the islands feature regularly on the fixed menu and each course illustrates a well-judged mix of both simple and complex food preparation.

Flaky smoked salmon with an avocado salsa. Collops of Scotch beef with a Drambuie cream sauce. Edinburgh Fog.

STB ★★★★ Guest House

◐ Open all year except Christmas and New Year 🏨 Rooms: 3 (1 en suite, 1 with private facilities) 🍴 DB&B £75 B&B £45 💷 Special rates available 🚫 Unlicensed ✗ Dinner £££ Residents only ♣ Children over 10 years welcome ⚞ No smoking in dining room or bedrooms 💳 Credit cards: Mastercard/Eurocard, Visa, Delta 🧑 Owners: Linda & Diarmuid Evelyn Wood

Tarbert Isle of Harris Outer Hebrides HS3 3AH
Tel: 01859 502157 Fax: 01859 502157
E-mail: leachin.house@virgin.net
Web: www.leachin-house.com
1 mile from Tarbert on A859 to Stornoway, sign-posted at gate. [A3]

ISLE OF HARRIS

Scarista House

- *"The best local and organic produce is used to create wonderful food and is served to you in this romantic and tranquil setting."*
- *Creative cooking using the finest ingredients.*

NEW OWNERS Tim and Patricia Martin offer a truly welcoming stay at Scarista House. The cooking is adept and full of flavour and organic produce is used whenever possible. Superb fish and shellfish, fresh vegetables and herbs together with fresh eggs from the hotel's hens and the best of home-made bread.

Ravioli of Sound of Harris langoustines with squat lobster butter sauce. Roast rack of Island lamb with heather honey scented gravy, stovies and confit of carrots, parsnips and celery. Floating islands with crème anglaise and strawberry and green peppercorn coulis.

STB ★★★★ Guest House

◐ Open all year closed occasionally in winter
🛏 Rooms: 5 en suite ⚍ DB&B £90.50 B&B £61
🍷 Residents and table licence ✘ Dinner £££
Ⓥ Vegetarians welcome ✴ Children welcome
🚭 No smoking in dining room, bedrooms and drawing room Smoking permitted in the library
💳 Credit cards: Mastercard/Eurocard, Visa
👥 Owners: Tim & Patricia Martin

Isle of Harris HS3 3HX
Tel: 01859 550238 Fax: 01859 550277
E-mail: tnpmartin@ukgateway.net
Web: www.scaristahouse.com
On A859, 15 miles south-west of Tarbert (Western Isles). [A3]

ISLE OF ISLAY

The Croft Kitchen

- *"Sample the best of Islay produce and good home baking."*
- *Modern Scottish.*

THE CROFT KITCHEN offers a daytime menu of home baking, home-made soups, snacks and a good range of daily specials chosen from a blackboard at very reasonable prices. You will also find seafood freshly caught and simply, yet skilfully, prepared. There is a separate menu for dinner in the evening.

Fresh steamed local mussels with garlic mayonnaise. Lagavulin scallops cooked in butter and parsley. Raspberry and Bowmore malt whisky cranachan.

◐ Open mid Mar to mid Oct Note: Closed 2nd Thu in Aug (Islay Show Day) 🍷 Licensed ✘ Food available all day £ Lunch £ Dinner ££
Ⓥ Vegetarians welcome ✴ Children welcome
🚭 No smoking in restaurant 💳 Credit cards: Mastercard/Eurocard, Visa 👥 Joint Proprietors: Joy & Douglas Law

Port Charlotte Isle of Islay PA49 7UN
Tel: 01496 850 230 Fax: 01496 850 230
E-mail: douglas@croftkitchen.demon.co.uk
On the main road into Port Charlotte opposite the Museum of Islay Life. [A6]

ISLE OF ISLAY

Glenmachrie

- *"A gastronomic delight aimed to satisfy the largest appetites."*
- *The best of home cooking.*

RELAX in the atmosphere of this family-run working farmhouse. No effort is spared by proprietor, Rachel Whyte, to meet the slightest whim of the guests. Rachel and her family are most attentive hosts. Splendid home cooking is served here with menus including Islay beef and lamb and wonderful home baking.

Timbale of smoked salmon and prawns with an orange and tarragon dressing. Dunlossit pheasant on a bed of caramelised onions drizzled with a redcurrant sauce. Pear, chocolate and frangipane tart with a jug of double cream.

STB ★★★★ Guest House
Green Tourism Three Leaf Gold Award

◐ *Open all year* 🛏 *Rooms: 5 en suite (2 twin, 3 double)* 🍴 *DB&B from £50 B&B from £30* 🍷 *Unlicensed – guests welcome to take own wine* ✘ *Dinner ££ Residents only* ♣ *Children over five years welcome* ♿ *Facilities for disabled visitors (ground floor bedroom)* 🚭 *No smoking throughout* 💳 *No credit cards* 🔑 *Proprietor: Rachel Whyte*

Port Ellen Isle of Islay PA42 7AW
Tel: 01496 302560 Fax: 01496 302560
E-mail: glenmachrie@isle-of-islay.com
Web:
www.isle-of-islay.com/group/guest/glenmachrie
Midway on A846 between Port Ellen and Bowmore. [B6]

ISLE OF ISLAY

Kilmeny Country Guest House

- *"Fine island views and sensational food in this beautifully restored country home."*
- *Unpretentious top quality cuisine.*

MARGARET AND BLAIR Rozga enjoy a loyal following of guests from all over the world. Margaret is a highly accomplished cook and uses only the finest produce creating mouthwatering dishes. Her menus are well-planned and imaginative demanding skill and careful organisation – all of which she accomplishes single-handedly to great effect.

Grilled 'Loch Gruinart' oysters with a leek and Islay cheese topping. Loin of Colonsay lamb, roasted with rosemary, carved and served with a bramble and port sauce. Steamed marmalade pudding with a whisky and vanilla sauce.

STB ★★★★★ Guest House

◐ *Open all year except Christmas and New Year* 🛏 *Rooms: 3 en suite* 🍴 *DB&B £60 B&B £36* 📋 *Special rates available* 🍷 *Unlicensed – guests welcome to take own wine* ✘ *Dinner except Sun ££ Residents only* Ⓥ *Vegetarians welcome* 🚭 *No smoking throughout* 💳: *No credit cards* 🔑 *Proprietor: Mrs Margaret Rozga*

Ballygrant Isle of Islay PA45 7QW
Tel: 01496 840 668 Fax: 01496 840 668
E-mail: info@kilmeny.co.uk
Web: www.kilmeny.co.uk
½ mile south of Ballygrant village – look for sign at road end, then ¾ mile up private road. [B6]

ISLE OF LEWIS

Handa: Finalist The Macallan Taste of Scotland Awards 2000

- *"Breathtaking views from every window and the warmth of Christine's hospitality and home cooking make for a wonderful stay."*
- *Accomplished home cooking.*

HANDA sits on top of a hill overlooking a private loch. Owner, Christine Morrison, runs the guest house with genuine island hospitality. Alongside traditional recipes, she does all of her own baking and uses the best of local seafood and fresh produce from her garden. The Macallan Personality of the Year 1995.

Flambeed scallops. Tarragon chicken, served with baby courgettes in whisky mustard. Pavlova with a difference.

STB ★★★★ B&B

◐ Open 4 May to 5 Oct 🛏 Rooms: 3, 1 en suite 🍽 DB&B £35–£40 B&B £18–£23 🍷 Unlicensed – guests welcome to take own wine ✗ Dinner ££ Residents only ⌇ No smoking throughout 💳 No credit cards 👤 Owners: Murdo & Christine Morrison

18 Keose Glebe Lochs Isle of Lewis HS2 9JX
Tel: 01851 830 334 Fax:
E-mail: handakeose@supanet.com
1½ miles off A859, 12 miles south of Stornoway, 25 miles north of Tarbert, Harris: last house in village of Ceos among the lochs of eastern Lewis. [A3]

ISLE OF LEWIS

Park Guest House & Restaurant

- *"Roddy offers a wide choice of Hebridean produce cooked with flair and imagination, with careful attention to the combination of flavours."*
- *Modern Scottish cooking with a continental influence.*

RODDY AND CATHERINE Afrin are friendly hosts. Roddy was formerly head chef on an oil rig in the North Sea. His robust à la carte menus use fresh fish from Stornoway and the West Coast fishing boats, and local lamb and venison, all cooked to order and skilfully prepared and presented.

Millefeuille of Stornoway black pudding and sweet potato, balsamic dressing. Fillet of halibut with herb crust served on risotto bed. Apple ice cream on a choux pastry ring, butterscotch sauce.

STB ★★ Hotel

◐ Open all year except 24 Dec to 5 Jan Note: Restaurant closed Sun Mon 🛏 Rooms: 8, 3 en suite 🍽 DB&B £38.50–£54 B&B £24–£29 ✗ Packed lunches available £ Dinner – residents only ££-£££ Dinner (Restaurant) Tue to Sat £££ Ⓥ Vegetarians welcome ⁂ Children welcome ♿ Facilities for non-residential disabled visitors 💳 Credit cards: Mastercard/Eurocard, Visa, Delta 👤 Proprietor: Catherine Afrin Chef/Proprietor: Roddy Afrin

30 James Street Stornoway Isle of Lewis
HS1 2QN
Tel: 01851 70 2485 Fax: 01851 70 3482
500 yards from ferry terminal. At junction of Matheson Road, James Street and A866 to airport and Eye Peninsula. [B3]

ISLE OF MULL

Assapol House Hotel

- *"A gem of tranquility offering a warm welcome and very fine food."*
- *Stylish country cooking.*

THE VISITOR to Assapol is immediately impressed by the care and attention of the Robertson family. The dinner menu offers a choice of starters and puddings and a set main course. The food is locally sourced and features local delicacies; it is sensitively cooked and imaginatively presented; and is extremely good value. 1 AA Rosette.

Smoked trout and salmon terrine with a dill and mustard seed vinaigrette. Saddle of venison with rösti potatoes, roast leeks and a port and juniper jus. Blackcurrant, apple and Calvados crumble tart.

STB ★★★★ Small Hotel

◐ Open Apr to Oct ⌂ Rooms: 5, 4 en suite ⌘ DB&B £68–£73 ⓢ Special rates available ⚑ Restricted hotel licence ✕ Dinner ££ Residents only Ⓥ Vegetarians welcome – by prior arrangement ⚸ Children over 10 years welcome ⚭ No smoking throughout ⊞ Credit cards: Mastercard/Eurocard, Visa, Switch, Delta ⚐ Partners: Onny, Thomas & Alex Robertson

*Bunessan Isle of Mull Argyll PA67 6DW
Tel: 01681 700 258 Fax: 01681 700 445
E-mail: alex@assapol.com
Web: www.assapol.com
From Craignure – A849 towards Fionnphort. When approaching Bunessan, pass village school on the right, take first road on left signed Assapol House Hotel. [B5]*

ISLE OF MULL

Calgary Farmhouse Hotel

- *"Lovely food in a delightful location."*
- *Modern Scottish cooking.*

THE SENSITIVELY converted Calgary Farmhouse has a warm, cosy environment. The Dovecote Restaurant's à la carte menu changes four times a week according to seasonal produce available. The accent is on skilful home cooking in an informal atmosphere. There is also a tea-room. The Carthouse Gallery is open throughout the day for light lunches and home baking.

Salad of summer vegetables and goat's cheese with toasted pumpkin seed dressing. Scallops grilled with a roasted garlic and chilli crust, oriental sauce vierge. Banana butterscotch sponge with ice cream.

STB ★★★ Small Hotel

◐ Open Apr to Oct incl ⌂ Rooms: 9 en suite ⌘ DB&B £47.50–£51 B&B £31.50–£35 ✕ Lunch £ Dinner ££ Ⓥ Vegetarians welcome ⚸ Children welcome ⚭ Smoking discouraged whilst others are eating ⊞ Credit cards: Mastercard/Eurocard, Visa, Switch ⚐ Proprietors: Matthew & Julia Reade

*by Dervaig Isle of Mull PA75 6QW
Tel: 01688 400256 Fax: 01688 400256
E-mail: calgary.farmhouse@virgin.net
Web: www.calgary.co.uk
About 4½ miles from Dervaig on B8073, just up the hill from Calgary beach. [B5]*

ISLE OF MULL

Druimard Country House

- *"A delightful country house offering the best of Scottish fayre."*
- *Impressive and competent Scottish cuisine.*

DRUIMARD has been beautifully restored by Haydn and Wendy Hubbard. The table d'hôte menu is innovative offering a large choice of fish which is locally caught, and meat which is traditionally reared. The cooking is assured, fresh and imaginative with unusual sauces and everything is prepared to order. 2 AA Red Rosettes.

Wild venison fillet with Parmesan biscuits, poached leeks, salad leaves and balsamic syrup. Pan-seared turbot on caramelised onions, spinach and goats cheese, with a bouillabaisse sauce. Chocolate and orange torte with orange liqueur syrup.

STB ★★★★ Small Hotel

◐ Open end Mar to end Oct 🏨 Rooms: 7 en suite 🛏 DB&B £62.50–£77 🍷 Restaurant licence only ✘ Lunch – residents only £ Dinner – non-residents welcome £££ Ⓥ Vegetarians welcome ★ Children welcome ⚕ No smoking in restaurant 🖶 Credit cards: Mastercard/Eurocard, Visa ⓝ Partners: Mr & Mrs H R Hubbard

Dervaig Isle of Mull PA75 6QW
Tel: 01688 400345 Fax: 01688 400345
E-mail: druimard@hotels.activebooking.com
Web: www.druimard.co.uk
Situated adjacent to Mull Little Theatre, well signposted from Dervaig village. [B5]

ISLE OF MULL

Druimnacroish Hotel

- *"Friendly, comfortable hotel with a homely atmosphere."*
- *Good quality Scottish cuisine.*

A LAID-BACK, friendly atmosphere surrounds this small spacious hotel with unspoilt views across the glen. Margriet is a welcoming host and Neil's cooking is skilled and assured and something to look forward to after a day exploring Mull. Games and 'wellies' are provided for guests who wish to stroll through the delightful gardens.

Isle of Mull scallops sautéed with white wine and lemongrass. Roast pheasant on a bed of game haggis, served with garden leeks with a Sgriob Ruadh Cheddar sauce. Drambuie and orange parfait.

STB ★★★ Hotel

◐ Open all year 🏨 Rooms: 6 en suite 🛏 DB&B £49–£59 B&B £35–£42 Ⓢ Special rates available ✘ Lunch £ Dinner ££ Ⓥ Vegetarians welcome ⚕ No smoking in dining room 🐕 Dogs by arrangement 🖶 Credit cards: Mastercard/Eurocard, American Express, Visa, Delta ⓝ Owners: Neil Hutton & Margriet van de Pol

Dervaig Isle of Mull PA75 6QW
Tel: 01688 400274 Fax: 01688 400274
E-mail: taste@druimnacroish.co.uk
Web: www.druimnacroish.co.uk
2 miles south of Dervaig on the Salen-Dervaig road. [B5]

ISLE OF MULL

Highland Cottage

- *"A real home-from-home with wonderful food."*
- *Skilled use of modern culinary trends.*

HIGHLAND COTTAGE is a delightful small hotel. Josephine Currie is a talented cook, uses excellent produce and her presentation is very professional. Josephine's husband Dave makes his guests feel relaxed and completely at home. 1 AA Rosette.

House-smoked salmon with avocado and dill salsa. Braised leg of Scotch lamb with wild mushrooms and honeyed shallots. Raspberry compote with burnt honey ice cream and shortbread.

STB ★★★★ Hotel
Green Tourism One Leaf Bronze Award

◐ *Open all year* ⋒ *Rooms: 6 en suite* ⋈ *DB&B £55–£69.50 B&B £32.50–£59.50* ⊞ *Special rates available* ✗ *Food available all day (residents only) £££ Snack/Light Lunch (residents only) Dinner £££* Ⓥ *Vegetarians welcome* ⚹ *Children welcome* ♿ *Facilities for disabled visitors* ⚕ *No smoking in dining room* ⚐ *Dogs welcome* ☙ *Member of the Scotch Beef Club* ⊞ *Credit cards: Mastercard/Eurocard, Visa, Switch, Delta, JCB* ▮ *Chef/Owner: Josephine Currie*

Breadalbane Street Tobermory Isle of Mull PA75 6PD
Tel: 01688 302030 Fax: 01688 302727
E-mail: davidandjo@highlandcottage.co.uk
Web: www.highlandcottage.co.uk
On approaching Tobermory at the roundabout, carry on straight across narrow stone bridge and immediately turn right (signposted Tobermory-Breadalbane Street). Follow road round – Highland Cottage is opposite the Fire Station. [B5]

ISLE OF MULL

Killiechronan House

- *"This is a gem of a find, you'll want to return and return."*
- *Accomplished gourmet cooking.*

KILLIECHRONAN HOUSE has a happy and relaxed atmosphere, reflected by the staff under the professional eye of Donna Ingram. The food here is excellent and menus are made available early afternoon so that any dietary requirements can be met. Ideal for a relaxed holiday in a wonderful setting. 1 AA Rosette

Salad of smoked Argyll ham and beef with roasted onions and balsamic dressing. Grilled Mull salmon with fresh linguini, ruby grapefruit sauce and a stir-fry of broccoli and baby sweet corn. Dark chocolate Marquise with vanilla custard and fresh cherries.

STB ★★★★ Small Hotel

◐ *Open 4 Mar to 31 Oct* ⋒ *Rooms: 6 en suite* ⋈ *DB&B £59–£85* ⊞ *Special rates available* ⚐ *Residents licence* ✗ *Dinner £££* Ⓥ *Vegetarians welcome* ⚕ *No smoking in dining room and bedrooms* ⊞ *Credit cards: Mastercard/Eurocard, American Express, Visa, Switch, Delta* ▮ *Manageress: Donna Ingram*

Isle of Mull PA72 6JU
Tel: 01680 300403 Fax: 01680 300463
E-mail: me@managed-estates.co.uk
Web: www.highlandholidays.net
Leaving ferry turn right to Tobermory A849. At Salen turn left to B8035. After 2 miles turn right to Ulva ferry B8073. Killiechronan House on right after 300 metres. [B5]

ISLE OF MULL

The Old Byre Heritage Centre

- *"Home cooked traditional food in a relaxed setting."*
- *Home cooking and baking.*

THE LICENSED tea-room offers a range of light meals, home baking and daily specials, using fresh Mull produce. Vegetarians are well catered for, and meals can be organised for groups by prior arrangement. At the Old Byre orders are placed at the counter, but the food is served at the table for the customer.

Home-made crofter's soup. Tobermory trout with salad and warm roll. Clootie dumpling served warm with cream.

STB ★★★ Visitor Attraction

◐ *Open 8 Apr to 30 Oct* ✖ *Light meals served throughout day £* ♥ *Licensed* Ⓥ *Vegetarians welcome* ⚹ *Children welcome* 🃏: *No credit cards* ♖ *Joint Owners: Ursula & Michael Bradley*

The Old Byre Dervaig Isle of Mull PA75 6QR
Tel: 01688 400229
1½ miles from Dervaig. Take Calgary road for ¾ mile, turn left along Torloisk road for ¼ mile, then left down private road following signs.
[B5]

ISLE OF MULL

Tiroran House

- *"Comfort and excellent cooking await you at Tiroran."*
- *Modern Scottish.*

TIRORAN HOUSE is a charming country house owned and run by Colin and Jane Tindal. They are both welcoming hosts who make the stay at Tiroran a most pleasant and relaxing experience. Colin hosts front of house whilst Jane and a small team prepare excellent dishes using local and Scottish produce.

Pan-fried Mull scallops in lime juice with a red pepper coulis. Roast boned quail stuffed with pine nuts and celery, served with a port and orange sauce and home-made apple chutney. Squidgy chocolate roulade with rose water cream and strawberries in Drambuie.

◐ *Open 1 Apr to 28 Oct* 🛏 *Rooms: 6 en suite* ⚭ *DB&B £64–£74 B&B £39–£49* ⓢⓟ *Special rates available* ✖ *Dinner non-residents – by prior arrangement £££* Ⓥ *Vegetarians welcome* ⚞ *No smoking throughout* 🃏 *Credit cards: Mastercard/Eurocard, Visa* ♖ *Proprietors: Colin & Jane Tindal*

Tiroran Isle of Mull PA69 6ES
Tel: 01681 705232 Fax: 01681 705240
E-mail: colin@tiroran.freeserve.co.uk
Web: www.tiroran.com
Turn off A849 Craignure–Iona Ferry road at Kinloch signed 'scenic route to Salen'. Along the B8035 for 4 miles: Tiroran House sign at converted church – 1 mile along minor road.
[B5]

ISLE OF MULL

The Western Isles Hotel

- *"Lovely views and excellent service are enjoyed at this grand hotel."*
- *Scottish cooking with continental flair.*

THE WESTERN ISLES HOTEL occupies one of the finest positions set above the village of Tobermory. The bar lunch menu is extensive with a very wide choice. The dinner menu offers four courses on a table d'hôte menu of good, traditional Scottish cooking accompanied by a reasonably priced wine list.

Smoked Tobermory haddock in a puff pastry case, with a lemon and cashew nut sauce. Fine slices of local venison, with walnuts sautéed in hawthorn jelly. White chocolate cheesecake on a lake of rich chocolate sauce.

STB ★★★★ Hotel

◐ Open all year except 17 to 28 Dec ⌂ Rooms: 25 en suite ⌘ DB&B £55.50–£122.50 B&B £42–£98 ⊞ Special rates available ✘ Bar Lunch £ Dinner £££ Ⓥ Vegetarians welcome ✱ Children welcome ✙ No smoking in dining room ⊞ Credit cards Credit cards: Mastercard/ Eurocard, American Express, Visa, Switch ⓜ Proprietors: Sue & Michael Fink

Tobermory Isle of Mull PA75 6PR
Tel: 01688 302012 Fax: 01688 302297
E-mail: wihotel@aol.com
Web: www.wihotel.com
Leaving Tobermory seafront on the Dervaig Road take a sharp right and turn halfway up the hillside. [B5]

ISLE OF NORTH UIST

Langass Lodge

- *"All the best local produce is sourced for John's menus."*
- *Modern Scottish.*

LANGASS LODGE offers the old world comfort of a traditional shooting lodge with the added delights of a dedicated and skilled chef. Chef John Buchanan's daily changing menu features mainly fish dishes and the understated 'selection of seafood' is a memorable experience. The fishing in the area is renowned, naturalists can enjoy the wildlife.

Langass pâté served with salad, buttered toast, and sloe jelly. Uist prawns wrapped in cod fillet and grilled with a herb crust. Malt whisky cheesecake.

STB ★★★ Small Hotel

◐ Open all year except Christmas Day ⌂ Rooms: 6 en suite ⌘ DB&B £54–£70 B&B £36–£60 ✘ Food available all day ££ Lunch ££ Dinner £££ Ⓥ Vegetarians welcome ✱ Children welcome ♿ Facilities for disabled visitors ⌇ Dogs welcome ⊞ Credit cards: Mastercard/ Eurocard, Visa ⓜ Manager: Niall Leveson-Gower

Locheport Isle of North Uist The Western Isles HS6 5HA
Tel: 01876 580285 Fax: 01876 580385
E-mail: langass@aol.com
Web:
www.Western Isles Tourist.Board Web Site
Take the B867 south from Lochmaddy for 10 miles. The hotel is clearly signposted from the main road. [A3]

ISLES OF ORKNEY

Cleaton House Hotel

- *"A relaxed atmosphere and a fine dining experience, with Malcolm, in front of house, overseeing to your every need."*
- *Modern Scottish cuisine using high quality Orcadian produce.*

A REGULAR roll-on, roll-off ferry service connects Westray to Kirkwall, and Cleaton's owner, Malcolm Stout, is happy to meet you at the pier. Chef Lorna Reid marries her experience with outstanding local ingredients, producing quality cuisine, complemented by Malcolm's wine list. In season, herbs and vegetables come from the hotel's vegetable garden.

Terrine of rabbit and 'holmie' (a unique seaweed-eating lamb) fillet set on Cumberland sauce. Baked darne organic Westray salmon presented on clapshot and garnished with crispy kale and Orkney farm cheese. Chocolate and rum tart, decorated with a mint parfait.

STB ★★★★ Small Hotel

◐ Open all year except Christmas Day
🏠 Rooms: 6 en suite 🛏 DB&B £37–£61.50 B&B £32–£40 ⓢ Special rates available ✗ Lunch £ Dinner ££ Ⓥ Vegetarians welcome ☸ Children welcome ♿ Facilities for disabled visitors ⌁ No smoking in dining room ⊞ Credit cards: Mastercard/Eurocard, Visa, Switch, Delta, ⚒ Proprietor: Malcolm Stout

*Westray Orkney KW17 2DB
Tel: 01857 677508 Fax: 01857 677442
E-mail: cleaton@orkney.com
Web: www.orknet.co.uk/cleaton
Signposted 5 miles from Rapness (Westray)
Ferry terminal on road to Pierowall Village. [D1]*

ISLES OF ORKNEY

Creel Restaurant & Rooms

- *"A memorable dining experience is to be had at the Creel Restaurant."*
- *Innovative modern cooking with a hint of Orcadian influence.*

THIS SMALL, family-run restaurant has an international reputation. Menus change daily to suit the supply of fresh produce. Alan Craigie cooks with great skill and the Creel has rightly become a place of pilgrimage for gourmets, but its cheerful understated ambience remains unchanged. 2 AA Rosettes. Winner The Macallan Personality of the Year Award 1997.

Velvet crab bisque with chunks of fresh tusk. Pan-fried john dory accompanied with roasted hake served with butterbeans and wild sorrel sauce. Iced raspberry parfait with a little basket of fresh strawberries.

STB ★★★ Restaurant with Rooms

◐ Open weekends Oct to Mar except Jan: daily Apr to Sep – advisable to book, especially in low season Closed Christmas Day and Boxing Day, Jan, Feb and 3 weeks Oct 🏠 Rooms: 3 en suite 🛏 B&B £33–£35 ✗ Dinner £££ Ⓥ Vegetarians welcome ☸ Children 5 years and over welcome ⌁ No smoking in restaurant ☘ Member of the Scotch Beef Club ⊞ Credit cards: Mastercard/Eurocard, Visa, Switch, Delta ⚒ Owners: Joyce & Alan Craigie

*Front Road St Margaret's Hope Orkney KW17 2SL
Tel: 01856 831 311
E-mail: alan@thecreel.freeserve.co.uk
Web: www.thecreel.co.uk
Take A961 south across the Churchill Barriers into St Margaret's Hope. 14 miles from Kirkwall. [D2]*

ISLES OF ORKNEY

Foveran Hotel & Restaurant

- *"Foveran offers good hospitality with a view, in a relaxing atmosphere."*
- *Modern Scottish with Orcadian influence.*

ENJOY a real Orcadian experience in comfortable surroundings. The cooking here is skilled and makes the very best use of some of Orkney's exceptional quality produce all freshly prepared to order. The Foveran has been taken over by new owners, the Doull family, and was inspected under previous owners.

Local farmhouse cheese fritters with warm berry chutney. Prime Orkney fillet steak topped with sauteed onions, haggis, and a lattice of pastry, served with a creamy Highland Park whisky sauce. Orkney fudge-flavoured cheesecake accompanied with a raspberry coulis.

● Open all year ⌂ Rooms: 8 en suite ⛌ B&B £35–£45 ▣ Special rates available ✖ Food available all day on request only £ Lunch on request Dinner £££ Ⓥ Vegetarians welcome ✱ Children welcome ♿ Facilities for disabled visitors – ground floor restaurant ⚲ Smoking in lounge only ▣ Credit cards: Mastercard/Eurocard, Visa, Switch, Solo ▮ Owners: The Doull Family

St Ola Kirkwall Orkney KW15 1SF
Tel: 01856 87 2389 Fax: 01856 87 6430
E-mail: foveranhotel@aol.com
Web: www.foveranhotel.co.uk
From Kirkwall take the A964 Orphir Road, 2½ miles from Kirkwall on left, off the main road. [D2]

ISLES OF ORKNEY

Woodwick House

- *"Woodwick House offers good food and hospitality, set in tranquil surroundings."*
- *Orcadian produce imaginatively prepared.*

WOODWICK HOUSE is a welcoming country house set in 12 acres of bluebell woodland with a burn that cascades down to a secluded bay. Candlelit meals are prepared with care using prime quality local produce and seafoods. Situated on Orkney's West Mainland, Woodwick is an excellent place from which to explore these ancient islands.

Lightly seared local scallops with ginger and a white wine cream sauce. Roast leg of North Ronaldsay lamb with a juniper and rhubarb gravy. Chocolate roulade with Woodwick raspberries and cream, with a tayberry coulis.

STB ★★★ Hotel

● Open all year ⌂ Rooms: 7, 4 en suite ⛌ DB&B £40–£67 B&B £26–£44 ▣ Special rates available ✖ Lunch £ Dinner ££–£££ Ⓥ Vegetarians welcome ✱ Children welcome ♿ Facilities for disabled visitors ⚲ No smoking in dining room ▣ Credit cards: Mastercard/Eurocard, Visa, Delta ▮ Co-Proprietor: Ann Herdman

Evie Orkney KW17 2PQ
Tel: 01856 751 330 Fax: 01856 751 383
E-mail: woodwickhouse@appleonline.net
Web: www.orknet.co.uk/woodwick
From the A965 turn off to Evie. After 15 minutes, drive c. 7 miles turn right at sign to Woodwick House. Turn first left, pass by farm on left and continue to the burn and trees ahead. Go over small bridge. [D2]

ISLES OF SHETLAND

Almara

- *"Taste Shetland's produce served as hearty portions in a warm and welcoming atmosphere at Almara."*
- *Traditional home cooking.*

MARCIA's hospitality is a true reflection of her commitment to make every single guest's experience of Shetland a memorable one. The guest house is unlicensed, however guests are most welcome to take their own wine. Cooking here is accomplished yet kept simple, making the best of what is available locally. This is a little treasure.

Dressed Eshaness crab with Rebecca sauce. Scallop Arianne: scallop and monktail sauteed in sherry, topped with a delicious Parmesan sauce. Rachel's bombe.

STB ★★★★ B&B
Green Tourism Three Leaf Gold Award

◐ Open all year ⌂ Rooms: 3, 2 en suite ⌥ DB&B £32 B&B £20 ⓢ Special rates available ⓤ Unlicensed – guests welcome to take own wine ✘ Dinner ££ Residents only Ⓥ Vegetarians welcome ✱ Children welcome ✄ No smoking in bedrooms and sitting room ⓔ No credit cards ⓝ Proprietor: Marcia Williamson

Upper Urafirth Hillswick Shetland ZE2 9RH
Tel: 01806 503 261 Fax: 01806 503 261
E-mail: almara@zetnet.co.uk
Web: www.users.zetnet.co.uk/almara/
Follow the A970 north to Hillswick. 1½ miles before Hillswick follow signs to Upper Urafirth and Almara. [E2]

ISLES OF SHETLAND

Burrastow House

- *"A wonderful combination of fine cooking and hospitality to match."*
- *Fine cuisine with exceptional flavours.*

BURRASTOW will appeal to all ages and tastes. Bo Simmons is a wonderful cook and has published her cookery book which promotes the use of local produce. There is a meeting facility complete with demonstration kitchen.

Courgette, lemon and rocket carpacchio in a lemon and olive oil dressing. Poached fillet of turbot with a saffron and chive butter sauce. Dark chocolate mousse millefeuilles with blackcurrant sauce.

STB ★★★★ Hotel
Green Tourism Three Leaf Gold Award

◐ Open all year except Jan, Feb, Mar, Oct half-term, Christmas Day and New Year's Day Closed Sun night and Mon to non residents ⌂ Rooms: 5 en suite ⌥ DB&B £80–£85 B&B £58 ⓢ Special rates available off season ⓣ Table licence only ✘ Light lunch no booking, booking required 12 hours' in advance for 3 course lunch £-££ Dinner (except Mon to non residents) £££ Ⓥ Vegetarians welcome ✱ Children welcome ♿ Facilities for disabled visitors ✄ No smoking in dining room and bedrooms 🐕 Dogs on request only ⓔ Credit cards: Mastercard/Eurocard, American Express, Visa, Switch, Delta ⓝ Chef Proprietor: Bo Simmons

Walls Shetland ZE2 9PD
Tel: 01595 809 307 Fax: 01595 809 213
E-mail: burr.hs.hotel@zetnet.co.uk
Web: www.users.zetnet.co.uk/burrastow-house-hotel
Take A971 west to Walls and Sandness. Drive straight through Walls, over cattle grid, turn left at top of hill Burrastow – 2 miles. [E2]

ISLES OF SHETLAND

Monty's Bistro

- *"Monty's Bistro offers very good food and service in a relaxed atmosphere."*
- *Modern Scottish cooking.*

MONTY's is intimate with a wonderful atmosphere. The original stone walls and floor set the mood for a relaxed, informal eating experience. The menu and blackboard specialities are well-balanced and full of Shetland's finest ingredients. Guests at Monty's benefit from Raymond's in-depth knowledge of cooking and his accomplished, innovative style.

Crab mille feuille with citrus fruit dressing. Sea trout fillet pan-fried, on new potatoes, snap peas, saffron ginger sauce. Raspberry tart with lightly whipped vanilla cream.

◐ *Open all year except Christmas Day, Boxing Day, 1 Jan, last Wed in Feb, last week Oct and 1st week Nov Closed Sun Mon* ✕ *Lunch except Sun Mon £ Dinner except Sun Mon ££* Ⓥ *Vegetarians welcome* ★ *Children welcome* ⚠ *No smoking throughout* 💳 *Credit cards: Mastercard/Eurocard, Visa, Switch, Delta, JCB* ⚑ *Proprietor: Raymond Smith*

5 Mounthooly Street Lerwick Isles of Shetland ZE1 OBJ
Tel: 01595 696555 Fax: 01595 696955
Centre of Lerwick, behind Tourist Information Centre. Up Mounthooly Street, 20 yards on the left. [E2]

ISLE OF SKYE

Ardvasar Hotel

- *"Breathtaking scenery and a warm welcome awaits you at Ardvasar."*
- *Accomplished Scottish cuisine.*

MICHAEL AND CHRISTINE CASS are new owners to Ardvasar, and extend a warm welcome to everyone. The cooking is accomplished using the best of local produce. This is a hotel committed to good hospitality and quality eating. You may choose from relaxed eating in the lounge bar or a more formal dining room setting.

Spinach, Stilton and Brie roulade with spiced tomato sauce and crisp salad garnish. Seared venison fillet, finished in a red wine, juniper and strawberry jus. Dark chocolate tart with a duo of Tia Maria and chocolate sauces.

STB ★★★ Hotel

◐ *Open all year* 🛏 *Rooms: 9 en suite* 🛌 *DB&B £62.50–£72.50 B&B £40–£70* 🆂🅿 *Special rates available* ✕ *Food available all day ££-£££ Lunch £-£££ Dinner ££-£££* Ⓥ *Vegetarians welcome* ★ *Children welcome* ⚠ *No smoking in dining room* 🐕 *Dogs welcome* 💳 *Credit cards: Mastercard/Eurocard, Visa, Switch, Delta* ⚑ *Owner: Mrs Christine Cass*

Sleat Isle of Skye IV45 8RS
Tel: 01471 844223 Fax: 01471 844495
E-mail: christine@ardvasar-hotel.demon.co.uk
Short distance from Armadale Ferry close to Armadale Castle and Museum of the Isle. [B4]

ISLE OF SKYE

Atholl House Hotel

- *"A warm welcome and delicious food awaits you at this cosy hotel in the beautiful north west of Skye."*
- *Accomplished blend of traditional and contemporary Scottish cooking.*

SITUATED at the head of Loch Dunvegan, the Atholl House Hotel looks out on to the twin flat-topped mountains – the Macleod's Tables. The atmosphere here is friendly and the cooking highly accomplished, using much of the excellent local Skye produce.

Loch Dunvegan prawns with fanned avocado nestled on organically grown Glendale leaves. Fillet of Aberdeen Angus by a wholegrain mustard mash with a rich Drambuie sauce. Highland clootie dumpling smothered in a whisky cream sauce.

STB ★★★ Hotel

◐ Open all year ⌂ Rooms: 9, 8 en suite ⨝ DB&B £40–£56 B&B £24–£42 ▣ Special rates available ⚱ Full hotel licence ✗ Food available all day ££ Packed lunch available Lunch £ Dinner £££ Ⓥ Vegetarians welcome ⚸ Children welcome ⚿ Facilities for disabled visitors ⚞ No smoking in restaurant ▥ Credit cards: Mastercard/Eurocard, American Express, Visa, Switch ⚒ Owner: Joan M Macleod MHCIMA; Barbara

*Dunvegan Isle of Skye IV55 8WA
Tel: 01470 521219 Fax: 01470 521481
E-mail: reservations@athollhotel.demon.co.uk
Web: www.athollhotel.demon.co.uk
In the centre of the village of Dunvegan. From the bridge – follow A850 to Sligachan, turn left to Dunvegan – 22 miles. [B4]*

ISLE OF SKYE

Bosville Hotel

- *"Charming restaurant with excellent cuisine."*
- *French cuisine using the best of Scottish produce.*

THE BOSVILLE HOTEL commands fine views from its elevated position and the Chandlery Restaurant produces meals, reflecting the local produce, with some exceptional presentation. Table d'hôte lunch and dinner menus are presented, using local produce wherever possible and featuring a number of Scottish specialities. 1 AA Rosette.

Timbale of smoked wild sea trout with a mousse of squat lobster and smokie, with soft poached quails eggs. Pan-seared scallops on saffron mash with creamed kale, lemon and chervil nage. Roast banana in pastry, with a rum and butterscotch sauce, served with oatmeal ice cream.

STB ★★★★ Hotel

◐ Open all year ⌂ Rooms: 15 en suite ⨝ DB&B £44–£85 B&B £35–£60 ▣ Special rates available ✗ Food available all day £ Lunch £ Dinner ££ Ⓥ Vegetarians welcome ⚸ Children welcome ⚿ Facilities for disabled visitors ⚞ No smoking throughout ▥ Credit cards: Mastercard/Eurocard, American Express, Visa, Switch, Delta ⚒ Hotel Manager: Donald W MacLeod

*Bosville Terrace Portree Isle of Skye IV51 9DG
Tel: 01478 612846 Fax: 01478 613434
E-mail: bosville@macleodhotels.co.uk
Web: www.macleodhotels.co.uk/bosville/
Town centre, on terrace above Portree harbour. [B4]*

ISLE OF SKYE

Cuillin Hills Hotel

- *"Sensational views over the bay from this fine hotel. Delicious dining with great attention to customer care."*
- *French/Scottish traditional.*

THE HOTEl, which has been extensively refurbished, stands in 15 acres of mature, private grounds, overlooking Portree Bay. The bedrooms are comfortable and well appointed. Public rooms are decorated with quality furnishings. Chef Jeff Johnston's daily changing menu offers four courses, featuring fresh, local produce (incl beautiful Skye lamb) presented in an imaginative way.

Warm crab Niçoise salad served in fresh artichoke heart with a sauce vierge. Canon of Highland venison with pears poached in mulled wine with gin, redcurrant and juniper berry. Strawberry shortcake with an Atholl brose cream and fresh raspberry coulis.

STB ★★★★ Hotel

◐ Open all year ♠ Rooms: 30 en suite ⊨ DB&B £45–£101 B&B £40–£80 ☞ Special rates available ✘ Lunch £ Dinner £££ Ⓥ Vegetarians welcome ⚭ Children welcome ⚒ Facilities for disabled visitors ⚮ No smoking in restaurant ⊞ Credit cards: Mastercard/Eurocard, American Express, Visa, Switch, Delta ⚙ General Manager: Mr Murray McPhee

*Portree Isle of Skye IV51 9QU
Tel: 01478 612003 Fax: 01478 613092
E-mail: office@cuillinhills.demon.co.uk
Web: www.cuillinhills.demon.co.uk
Turn right ¼ mile north of Portree on A855 and follow hotel signs. [B4]*

ISLE OF SKYE

Dunorin House Hotel

- *"A relaxed family hotel offering panoramic views."*
- *Traditional, Scottish Island cooking.*

THE HOTEL enjoys panoramic views across Loch Roag to the Cuillin Hills. With many local recipes, the hotel's daily changing table d'hôte menu seeks to make the most of fresh local produce, such as scallops, venison, salmon, beef and lamb. The wine list is reasonably priced and varied.

Scallops in garlic butter. Fillet of West Coast lemon sole pan-fried in seasoned butter and lemon juice. Cloutie dumpling.

STB ★★★★ Small Hotel

◐ Open 1 Apr to 15 Nov except 2 weeks Oct ♠ Rooms: 10 en suite ⊨ DB&B £48–£60 B&B £30–£42 ☞ Special rates available ♀ Restricted hotel licence ✘ Dinner £££ Non-residents – bookings only Ⓥ Vegetarians welcome ⚭ Children welcome ⚒ Facilities for disabled visitors ⚮ No smoking in dining room ⊞ Credit cards: Mastercard/Eurocard, Visa ⚙ Partners: Alasdair & Joan MacLean

*Herebost Dunvegan Isle of Skye IV55 8GZ
Tel: 01470 521488 Fax: 01470 521488
E-mail: stay@dunorin.freeserve.co
Web: www.dunorin.com
From Skye Bridge A87 to Sligachan, then A863 to Dunvegan. 2 miles south of Dunvegan turn left at Roag/Orbost junction, 200m on right. [B4]*

ISLE OF SKYE

Flodigarry Country House Hotel & The Water Horse Restaurant

- *"Its lovely situation makes it ideal for exploring the northern coast of Skye."*
- *Scottish cuisine.*

IN THE Water Horse Restaurant, residents and non-residents can enjoy a daily changing table d'hôte menu, featuring traditional dishes, or choose from an à la carte menu. Bar meals are served in the conservatory and on the terrace. The Macallan Taste of Scotland Country House Hotel of the Year 1995.

Local lobster and langoustine. Medallions of prime Scottish beef set on a bed of haggis with a pink peppercorn and mushroom sauce. Janet's steamed Talisker and raisin sponge.

STB ★★★★ Hotel

● *Open all year* ✿ *Rooms: 19 en suite* ✉ *DB&B £74–£105 B&B £49–£80* ✱ *Special rates available* ✗ *Lunch Sun (Restaurant) ££ Dinner 4 course menu £££* Ⓥ *Vegetarians welcome* ✱ *Children welcome* ♿ *Facilities for disabled visitors* ✍ *No smoking in restaurant, conservatory or bedrooms* ▣ *Credit cards: Mastercard/Eurocard, Visa, Switch, Delta* ⚑ *Proprietors: Andrew & Pamela Butler*

*Staffin Isle of Skye IV51 9HZ
Tel: 01470 552203 Fax: 01470 552301
Web: www.flodigarry.co.uk
A855 north from Portree to Staffin, 4 miles from Staffin to Flodigarry. [B3]*

ISLE OF SKYE

Glenview Inn and Restaurant

- *"Family-run inn with robust Scottish cooking."*
- *Home-style cooking with fresh local produce.*

OWNER, Paul Booth uses local produce and eclectic techniques to produce well-priced and varied meals selected from an à la carte menu and blackboard featuring daily specials – from fresh local seafood and game to vegetarian and ethnic dishes. In the afternoon, home baking is a temptation to linger over.

Grilled brochette of creeled Staffin Bay prawns with whole fresh garlic roasted in olive oil. Shank of Scottish lamb braised with Heather Ale. White chocolate and hazelnut pudding.

STB ★★ Small Hotel

● *Open mid Mar to early Nov* ✿ *Rooms: 5 (4 en suite, 1 private facilities)* ✉ *DB&B £37.50–£47.50 B&B £25–£35* ✱ *Special rates available* ✗ *Lunch ££ Dinner £££* Ⓥ *Vegetarians welcome* ✱ *Children welcome* ✍ *Smoking restricted to certain areas* ▣ *Credit cards: Mastercard/Eurocard, Switch* ⚑ *Owners: Paul & Cathie Booth*

*Culnacnoc Staffin Isle of Skye IV51 9JH
Tel: 01470 562 248 Fax: 01470 562 211
E-mail: valtos@lineone.net
Web: www.smoothhound.co.uk/
12 miles from Portree on the Staffin road – signposted off the A855. [B4]*

ISLE OF SKYE

Hotel Eilean Iarmain

- *"An island haven for excellent food and Gaelic hospitality."*
- *Modern Scottish cooking.*

HOTEL EILEAN IARMAIN stands on the small rocky bay of Isle Ornsay and is owned by Sir Iain and Lady Noble. The award-winning restaurant serves an excellent four course table d'hôte menu using Skye local produce. The restaurant and lounge have been extended, decor by Lady Noble. 1 AA Rosette.

Pan-seared scallops in a corn tortilla basket with crème fraîche and salsa fresca. Roasted monkfish, crayfish, scallops and salmon scented with rosemary on a chive and garlic beurre blanc. Baileys and whisky crème brûlée.

STB ★★★ Hotel

Open all year Rooms: 16 (all en suite) incl 4 suites DB&B £91–£121 B&B £60–£90 Special rates available Lunch – booking essential ££ Dinner – advance reservation advisable £££ £ Vegetarians welcome Children welcome No smoking in restaurant Credit cards: Mastercard/ Eurocard, American Express, Visa, Switch, Delta, Solo Proprietors: Sir Iain & Lady Noble

Sleat Isle Ornsay, Isle of Skye Inverness-shire
IV43 8QR
Tel: 01471 833 332 Fax: 01471 833 275
e-mail: bookings@eilean-iarmain.co.uk
Web: www.eileaniarmain.co.uk
From Mallaig/Armadale ferry turn right on to A851 for 8 miles, then right at sign Isle Ornsay, hotel is down at waters edge. From Skye Bridge take road to Broadford and turn off at junction signed A851 to Armadale. [B4]

ISLE OF SKYE

Kinloch Lodge

- *"Relaxed and luxurious country home – delicious food in a spectacular setting."*
- *Outstanding traditional cooking with innovative influences.*

HOME of Lord Macdonald of Macdonald, Kinloch Lodge is full of portraits of ancestors, old furniture and family treasures. Lady Claire Macdonald, one of Scotland's best known cooks, presents a five-course table d'hôte menu each night using only fresh seasonal produce. 2 AA Red Rosettes. Winner of The Macallan Taste of Scotland Best Breakfast Award 1998.

Skye scallop terrine with locally-grown watercress and shallot sauce. Roast rack of black-face lamb with pinhead oatmeal and cracked black pepper crust, and minty hollandaise. Baked dark and white chocolate cheesecake with bitter orange sauce.

STB ★★★★ Hotel

Open all year except Christmas Rooms: 14 en suite DB&B £70-£130 B&B £45-£95 Special rates available Dinner 5 course menu ££££ Vegetarians welcome – prior notice required Children welcome by arrangement No smoking in dining room Member of the Scotch Beef Club Credit cards: Mastercard/Eurocard, American Express, Visa Proprietors: Lord & Lady Macdonald

Sleat Isle of Skye IV43 8QY
Tel: 01471 833214 Fax: 01471 833277
E-mail: kinloch@dial.pipex.com
Web: www.kinloch-lodge.co.uk
8 miles south of Broadford on A851. 10 miles north of Armadale on A851. 1 mile off A851. [B4]

ISLE OF SKYE

Rosedale Hotel

- *"Robust creative cooking, a warm welcome and fine views – what more could you want from a visit to Portree."*
- *Modern Scottish.*

THE ROSEDALE HOTEL has spread its wings and added a coffee shop and a wine bar overlooking the harbour. The first floor restaurant has splendid views out over the bay. Chef Kirk presents a daily changing table d'hôte dinner menu offering imaginative dishes, based on fresh local produce. 1 AA Rosette.

Local mussels steamed and then grilled with lime and tomato hollandaise. Boned pheasant with an apple, black pudding and skirlie stuffing on onion mash with wood berry sauce. White chocolate mousse with home-made shortbread.

STB ★★★★ Hotel

◐ *Apr to Nov* 🏨 *Rooms: 23 en suite* 🛏 *DB&B £56–£70 B&B £34-£49* 🆂🅿 *Special rates available* ✘ *Dinner £££* Ⓥ *Vegetarians welcome* ✱ *Children welcome* ⊬ *No smoking in restaurant and all bedrooms* 🐕 *Dogs welcome* 💳 *Credit cards: Mastercard/Eurocard, Visa, Switch, Delta* 🅼 *Owners: Paul & Allison Rouse*

Beaumont Crescent Portree Isle of Skye
IV51 9DB
Tel: 01478 613131 Fax: 01478 612531
Web: www.rosedalehotelskye.co.uk
Down in the harbour, 100 yards from village square. [B4]

ISLE OF SKYE

Roskhill House

- *"Situated in this lovely part of Skye offering a homely atmosphere and good food."*
- *Traditional Scottish cooking.*

ROSKHILL HOUSE is a traditional croft house which was built in 1890. Owner Gillian Griffith succeeds in offering a very high level of comfort; warm and sincere Scottish hospitality, coupled with excellent home cooking. Menus are well-thought out and use excellent locally-sourced produce which is then cooked in a sympathetic style.

Chicken breast stuffed with haggis, served with a cream sauce. Sticky date and ginger pudding with real custard.

STB ★★★★ Guest House

◐ *Open all year (Christmas and New Year half board only)* 🏨 *Rooms: 4 (3 en suite, 1 private facilities)* 🛏 *DB&B £41.50–£49.50 B&B £27–£35* 🆂🅿 *Special rates available* 🍷 *Restricted hotel licence* ✘ *Dinner ££ Non residents – prior booking essential* Ⓥ *Vegetarian and special diets catered for* ✱ *Children over 10 years welcome* ⊬ *No smoking throughout* 💳 *Credit cards: Mastercard/Eurocard, American Express, Visa, Switch, Delta, JCB, Solo* 🅼 *Proprietor: Gillian Griffith*

by Dunvegan Isle of Skye IV55 8ZD
Tel: 01470 521317 Fax: 01470 521761
E-mail: stay@roskhill.demon.co.uk
Web: www.roskhill.demon.co.uk
2 miles south of Dunvegan on A863, turn off road at River Rosgill. [B4]

ISLE OF SKYE

Rowan Cottage

- *"Warm, homely and welcoming with stunning views from every window – they even provided a full rainbow for my visit!"*
- *Good home cooking.*

ROWAN COTTAGE is home to Ruth Shead and is a delightful, traditional croft house. It is an excellent spot from which to enjoy this beautiful part of Skye and has panoramic views over Loch Slapin. Ruth is an accomplished and enthusiastic cook who serves good home cooking using best local produce.

Roasted red pepper and tomato soup. Dived Skye king scallops pan-fried and served in a creamy mushroom and white wine sauce, served with seasonal vegetables. Home-made sticky toffee pudding with toffee sauce.

STB ★★★★ B&B

● Open 23 Mar to 30 Nov 🛏 Rooms: 3, 1 en suite 🍴 DB&B £36.50–£46.50 B&B £20–£25 🍷 Unlicensed ✗ Residents only Dinner ££-£££ Ⓥ Vegetarians welcome ✂ No smoking throughout 🐕 Dogs welcome 💳: No credit cards 👤 Owner: Ruth Shead

*9 Glasnakille By Elgol Isle of Skye IV49 9BQ
Tel: 01471 866287 Fax: 01471 866287
E-mail: rowan@rowancott.demon.co.uk
Web: www.rowancott.demon.co.uk
From Broadford take the A8083 to Elgol, 15 miles down a single track road. From Elgol take turning to Glasnakille for 2 miles, turn left at the T-junction by phone box. Continue for 100m to the 1st house on the left. [B4]*

ISLE OF SKYE

Skeabost House Hotel

- *"A super spot for everyone, with delicious food and lovely surroundings."*
- *Skilled contemporary cooking.*

THIS FORMER hunting lodge has been run by the owners for over 30 years. A buffet menu is available during the day and in the more formal surroundings of the elegant dining room. Angus McNab presents daily changing table d'hôte menus which demonstrate considerable flair and skill, particularly with fish and game.

Fresh Skye prawns with olive oil herb mayonnaise and Glendale leaves. Loin of Black Isle lamb with a herb crust, parsnip purée and red wine sauce. Skeabost cloutie dumpling with Drambuie sauce and farm cream.

STB ★★★ Hotel

● Open Mar to Nov 🛏 Rooms: 26, 24 en suite 🍴 DB&B £59–£85 B&B £40–£62 Special rates available ✗ Lunch £ Dinner £££ Ⓥ Vegetarians welcome ✱ Children welcome ♿ Facilities for disabled visitors ✂ No smoking in dining room 🥩 Member of the Scotch Beef Club 💳 Credit cards: Mastercard/ Eurocard, Visa, Switch 👤 Proprietors: Stuart & McNab Families

*Skeabost Bridge Isle of Skye IV51 9NP
Tel: 01470 532 202 Fax: 01470 532 454
E-mail: skeabost@sol.co.uk.
Web: www.sol.co.uk/s/skeabost
4 miles north of Portree on Dunvegan road. [B4]*

ISLE OF SKYE

Talisker House: Finalist The Macallan Taste of Scotland Awards 2000

- *"Grace and elegance with fine hospitality in a glorious setting."*
- *Modern Scottish cooking.*

TALISKER HOUSE is a charming, elegant house, beautifully maintained as is the extensive garden which supplies the kitchen with vegetables and herbs. The cooking is accomplished, menus are interesting and make best use of the excellent home-grown and local produce. Jon and Ros Wathen's Australian influence is evident on the wine list.

Zucchini and smoked venison flan served with freshly picked rocket and watercress. Baked fillet of Isle of Skye salmon with balsamic honey sauce and salsa verde. Crisp honey fritters with vanilla pod ice cream made from Talisker free-range eggs.

STB ★★★★ Guest House

◐ Open Mar to Oct incl 🏠 Rooms: 4 en suite 🍴 DB&B £68 B&B £43 ✕ Packed lunch – by request Dinner ££ Residents only Ⓥ Vegetarians welcome ♿ Limited facilities for disabled visitors – please telephone ✄ No smoking throughout 💳 Credit cards: Mastercard/Eurocard, Visa, JCB 👤 Proprietors: Jon & Ros Wathen

Talisker Isle of Skye IV47 8SF
Tel: 01478 640 245 Fax: 01478 640 214
E-mail: jon_and_ros.wathen@virgin.net
Web: www.talisker.co.uk
Take the A863 from Sligachan. Turn left towards Carbost on the B8009. At top of Carbost village veer left and follow signs to Talisker. [A4]

ISLE OF SKYE

The Three Chimneys Restaurant And The House Over-By

- *"There are not enough superlatives to describe this magical place – wonderful food in a marvellous location."*
- *Natural skilled Scottish cooking.*

AT THREE CHIMNEYS fresh Skye seafood is a speciality but fish, lamb, beef, game and a vegetarian option are also on offer. The wine list is extensive and carefully compiled. Winner of The Macallan Taste of Scotland Restaurant With Rooms Award 1999, and The Macallan Taste of Scotland Overall Excellence Award 1999. 3 AA Rosettes

Seared scallops with crispy smoked ham, Glendale salad leaves, orange and hazelnut vinaigrette. Grilled loin of lamb, leek and wild mushroom pearl barley risotto, spinach and wild garlic gravy. Iced cranachan parfait with fresh Skye raspberries.

STB ★★★★★ Restaurant with Rooms

◐ Open virtually all year Closed Sun lunch and lunch in winter months 🏠 Rooms: 6 en suite ✕ Lunch except Sun ££-££££ Dinner 3 course menu £££-££££ Ⓥ Vegetarians welcome 🧒 Children welcome ♿ Disabled access ✄ No smoking in restaurant 🐄 Member of the Scotch Beef Club 💳 Credit cards: Mastercard/Eurocard, American Express, Visa, Switch 👤 Owners: Eddie & Shirley Spear

Colbost by Dunvegan Isle of Skye IV55 8ZT
Tel: 01470 511258 Fax: 01470 511358
E-mail: eatandstay@threechimneys.co.uk
Web: www.threechimneys.co.uk
4 miles west of Dunvegan on B884 road to Glendale. Look out for Glendale Visitor Route signs. [A4]

ISLE OF SKYE

Viewfield House

- *"Gracious dining in a historic family residence."*
- *Traditional Scottish with modern influences.*

VIEWFIELD has been a family home for over five generations and many original features remain. Your host is Hugh MacDonald who welcomes you into his home with real Highland hospitality. The cooking here is exceptional and highly skilled using only the best produce prepared and presented with an innovative twist and successfully executed.

Pan-fried scallops with tarragon butter. Saddle of venison with hawthorn sauce. Spiced apple and almond shortbread.

STB ★★★ Small Hotel

◐ *Open mid Apr to mid Oct* ♜ *Rooms: 12, 10 en suite* ⊨ *DB&B £55–£65 B&B £35–£47.50* ⓢⓟ *Special rates available* ✗ *Dinner ££* Ⓥ *Vegetarians welcome* ⚹ *Children welcome* ♿ *Facilities for disabled visitors* ⊬ *No smoking in dining room* ⚞ *Dogs welcome* ⊞ *Credit cards: Mastercard/Eurocard, Visa* ▨ *Chef/Proprietor: Mrs Linda MacDonald*

Portree Isle of Skye IV51 9EU
Tel: 01478 612217 Fax: 01478 613517
Web: www.skye.co.uk/viewfield
Viewfield House is located off the main road from Kyleakin to Portree, as you approach Portree. [B4]

ISLE OF SOUTH UIST

Orasay Inn

- *"Wide menu and generous portions, with the emphasis on fresh local fish."*
- *Scottish home cooking.*

ORASAY INN is a small house which has been extended to form a small country hotel. The dining room commands stunning views across the Minch and also to the mountains of South Uist. There is also a very comfortable lounge in which to relax and enjoy the comforts in front of the peat fire.

Smoked salmon duo: a mix of Herbridean hot-smoked and cold-smoked salmon, served with green salad. Medallions of venison with redcurrant and port sauce, garnished with chestnuts. Home-made apple crumble with caramel sauce.

STB ★★ Inn

◐ *Open all year except Christmas Day* ♜ *Rooms: 9 en suite* ⊨ *DB&B £34–£75 B&B £29–£65* ⓢⓟ *Special rates available* ✗ *Food available all day £-££ Lunch £ Dinner ££* Ⓥ *Vegetarians welcome* ⚹ *Children welcome* ♿ *Facilities for disabled visitors* ⊬ *No smoking in dining room* ⊞ *Credit cards: Mastercard/ Eurocard, American Express, Visa, Switch, Delta JCB* ▨ *Proprietors: Alan & Isobel Graham*

Lochcarnan Isle of South Uist Western Isles HS8 5PD
Tel: 01870 610298 Fax: 01870 610390
E-mail: orasayinn@btinternet.com
20 miles from Lochboisdale A865, 26 miles from Lochmaddy. [A4]

JEDBURGH

Jedforest Hotel

- *"Excellent cuisine and presentation – well worth a visit."*
- *Modern Scottish*

AN ELEGANT, small country house with excellent accommodation and beautifully refurbished, this is actually the first hotel in Scotland on the A68. A gastronomic experience awaits in Bardoulets Restaurant where the team of chefs create outstanding Scottish cuisine. The hotel is ideally suited for golfing and fishing on its own stretch of the River Jed.

Roulade of smoked fish with lime, coriander and yoghurt. Aberdeen Angus fillet with potato pancake, wild mushrooms, shallot's confit and port jus. Caramelised lemon torte with home-made vanilla ice cream.

STB ★★★★ Hotel

❍ Open all year ⌂ Rooms: 8 en suite ⛌ DB&B £62-£77 B&B £42.50-£57.50 ▣ Special rates available ✘ Lunch ££ Dinner £££ Ⓥ Vegetarians welcome ✁ Smoking restricted to residents lounge only ▣ Credit cards: Mastercard/ Eurocard, American Express, Visa, Diners Club, Switch, Delta ▪ Owners: Samuel & Patricia Ferguson

Nr Jedburgh Roxburghshire TD8 6PJ
Tel: 01835 840222 Fax: 01835 840226
E-mail: mail@jedforesthotel.freeserve.co.uk
Web: www.jedforesthotel.freeserve.co.uk
200 metres from A68, main tourist route from Newcastle to Edinburgh. 7 miles north of border and 3 miles south of Jedburgh. [D6]

KELSO

Cobbles Inn Restaurant

- *"Busy Borders town restaurant, popular with all ages, with relaxed and informal setting."*
- *Good home cooking.*

THIS BLACK and white Listed building has a traditional pub-style atmosphere – black beams in ceiling and leaded windows. This small and busy restaurant is popular with locals and visitors alike. The cooking is based on fresh Scottish produce with a wide range of dishes on a standard menu with daily specials on a blackboard.

Cobbles salmon parcel: smoked trout mousse enclosed in smoked salmon. Stilton and apple pork roulade on redcurrant and port wine sauce. Lemon ginger torte: lemon mousse with a ginger biscuit base.

❍ Open all year except 17 to 24 Jan, Christmas Day and New Year's Day ✘ Lunch £ Dinner ££ Ⓥ Vegetarians welcome ✲ Children welcome ♿ Facilities for disabled visitors ✁ No smoking area in restaurant ▣ Credit cards: Mastercard/ Eurocard, Visa, Switch, Delta ▪ Director: Joan Forrest; Manager: Colin Maxwell

7 Bowmont Street Kelso TD5 7JH
Tel: 01573 223 548
E-mail: david@cobblesinn.freeserve.co.uk
Web: www.cobblesinn.freeserve.co.uk
Just off the main square in Kelso. [D6]

KELSO

Ednam House Hotel

- *"A delightful establishment in a superb location."*
- *Traditional and modern Scottish cooking.*

PROPRIETOR/CHEF Ralph Brooks describes his cooking as 'straightforward, but along classical lines', creating original dishes using unusual ingredients such as Berwickshire ostrich and wood pigeon, fashioning his menus from the fresh ingredients he can obtain locally and seasonally. At this hotel the customer comes first. A massive refurbishment will take place during 2000/2001.

Loch Awe mussels steamed with Pernod and garlic. Braised shank of Tweed Valley lamb in its rich gravy. Drambuie mousse served with raspberry coulis.

STB ★★★ Hotel
Green Tourism One Leaf Bronze Award

◐ Open all year except Christmas and New Year ⌂ Rooms: 32 en suite ⇔ DB&B £58–£79 B&B £42–£59 ⊞ Special rates available ✗ Food available all day £–££ Lunch £ Dinner ££ Ⓥ Vegetarians welcome – prior notice required ✚ Children welcome ⊞ Credit cards: Mastercard/Eurocard, Visa, Switch Ⓜ Proprietors: R A & R W Brook

Bridge Street Kelso TD5 7HT
Tel: 01573 224168 Fax: 01573 226319
E-mail: ednamhouse@excite.co.uk
Web: www.ednamhouse.com
Situated on Bridge Street, halfway between town square and abbey. [D6]

KELSO

The Roxburghe Hotel and Golf Course

- *"Luxurious surroundings with the warmth of Scottish hospitality."*
- *Traditional Scottish, with grand hotel touches.*

STANDING on the banks of the River Teviot in 200 acres of park and woodland, the hotel has a championship golf course. Although it is an imposing mansion, the Roxburghe retains the common touch. Well-constructed and interesting menus for lunch and dinner offer both light and complex dishes. The Roxburghe Hotel has 2 AA Rosettes.

Globe artichoke heart filled with salmon, crayfish and spring onion crème fraîche. Oven-baked saddle of venison with boulangere potatoes and cracked black pepper. Banana shortcake served with caramelised bananas and toffee sauce.

STB ★★★★ Hotel

◐ Open all year ⌂ Rooms: 22 en suite ⇔ B&B £120–£255 ⊞ Special rates available ✗ Lunch ££ Dinner £££–££££ Ⓥ Vegetarians welcome ✚ Children welcome ⌦ No smoking in dining room ⚜ Member of the Scotch Beef Club ⊞ Credit cards: Mastercard/Eurocard, American Express, Visa, Diners Club, Switch Ⓜ General Manager: Stephen Browning

Kelso Roxburghshire TD5 8JZ
Tel: 01573 450331 Fax: 01573 450611
E-mail: hotel@roxburghe.net
Web: www.roxburghe.net
Situated at the village of Heiton, on the A698 Kelso-Hawick road. Signposted at western end of village. [D6]

KELTY BY DUNFERMLINE

The Butterchurn

- *"Informal restaurant offering high quality, freshly cooked meals all day – don't miss the excellent food and gift shop."*
- *Fresh home style cooking.*

THE BUTCHERCHURN restaurant serves delightful fresh food, and also houses 'The Scottish Food and Craft Centre'; with speciality Scottish foods, home baking, and food demonstration events. Light meals are available all day right through to dinner. This whitewashed steading is a welcome place for the weary traveller.

Smoked venison salad with orange. Breast of Barbary duck with tangy papaya salsa. Home-made lemon meringue pie.

STB ★★★★ Visitor Attraction

◐ *Open all year except 25, 26 Dec and 1, 2 Jan* ❦ *Licensed* ✘ *Food available all day £ Lunch ££ Dinner ££* Ⓥ *Vegetarians welcome* ☆ *Children welcome* ♿ *Facilities for disabled visitors* 💳 *Credit cards: Mastercard/Eurocard, Visa, Switch, Delta* ◈ *Proprietors: Mr & Mrs K Thomson*

*Cocklaw Mains Farm Kelty Fife KY4 0JR
Tel: 01383 830169 Fax: 01383 831614
Just off the M90 motorway at junction 4 on B914. 500 yards west of junction. [D5]*

KENTALLEN

Ardsheal House

- *"A wonderful country house with perfect ambience and delicious food – this is a place not to be missed."*
- *Innovative country house cooking.*

NEIL AND PHILIPPA Sutherland open their family home to guests whose comfort and enjoyment is their main concern. Philippa is an accomplished cook and her set, four course menus change daily, Neil is a most attentive host. Winner of The Macallan Taste of Scotland Country House Hotel of the Year Award 1996.

Fish cakes with sweetcorn broth. Duck breast with orange and bramble sauce. Mascarpone cream.

STB ★★★★ Small Hotel

◐ *Open all year except Dec to Feb – when open by prior arrangement only* 🛏 *Rooms: 6 en suite* 🍽 *DB&B from £70 B&B from £45* ❦ *Restricted Hotel licence* ✘ *Dinner £££* Ⓥ *Vegetarians welcome* ✚ *No smoking in dining room* 💳 *Credit cards: Mastercard/Eurocard, American Express, Visa* ◈ *Owners: Neil & Philippa Sutherland*

*Kentallen of Appin Argyll PA38 4BX
Tel: 01631 740227 Fax: 01631 740342
E-mail: info@ardsheal.co.uk
Web: www.ardsheal.co.uk
On A828 Oban road, 4 miles south of Ballachulish Bridge, 28 miles north of Oban. About 1 mile up private road, signposted at main road. [B5]*

KILCHRENAN

Ardanaiseig Hotel

- *"The 'Ardanaiseig experience' is a memorable one – excellent food and delightful staff."*
- *Very experienced and beautifully presented modern Scottish cooking.*

STYLE and opulence are key words to describe this secluded and grand hotel. In the dining room true Scottish hospitality is delivered by chef Gary Goldie who selects only the best local produce, presented with flair and sophistication. Everything about Ardanaiseig is exquisite from the gardens and nature reserve to the tiniest details.

Smoked haddock ravioli, meaux mustard sauce and crispy leek. Roast squab, braised cabbage, pomme fondant, confit garlic, thyme jus gras. Hot chocolate fondant with caramelised milk ice cream.

STB ★★★★ Hotel

◐ Open all year except 2 Jan to 14 Feb
🛏 Rooms: 16 en suite 🛌 DB&B from £95.50 B&B £57–£120 ✕ Food available all day from £ Lunch from £ Dinner ££££ 💳 Credit cards: Mastercard/Eurocard, American Express, Visa, Diners Club 👤 General Manager: Robert Francis

*Kilchrenan By Taynuilt Argyll PA35 1HE
Tel: 01866 833 333 Fax: 01866 833 222
E-mail: ardanaiseig@clara.net
Web: www.ardanaiseig-hotel.com
1 mile east of Taynuilt, turn sharp left. Follow B845 to Kilchrenan. At Kilchrenan Inn turn left – 3 miles on single track road to Ardanaiseig. [B5]*

KILCHRENAN

Taychreggan Hotel Ltd

- *"Enjoy the charm and location of this converted Drovers' Inn while experiencing modern culinary trends in a beautifully appointed dining room."*
- *Elegant modern British cuisine.*

TAYCHREGGAN retains a sense of peace and history. Visitors, even well-behaved canine ones, feel like house guests. An experienced brigade of chefs present imaginative fine cuisine in the hotel's dining room. More simple bar lunches are no less carefully prepared. All complemented with an excellent award winning wine list. 2 AA Rosettes.

Pan roasted noisette of Argyll lamb with potato galette and a truffle jus. Tournedo of salmon with smoked leeks. Cappuccino crème brûlée wrapped in an almond biscuit.

STB ★★★★ Hotel

◐ Open all year 🛏 Rooms: 19 en suite 🛌 DB&B £80–£125 B&B £52–£97 📅 Special rates available ✕ Lunch ££ Dinner 5 course menu £££ Ⓥ Vegetarians welcome 🚭 No smoking in dining room 🐄 Member of the Scotch Beef Club 💳 Credit cards: Mastercard/ Eurocard, American Express, Visa, Switch 👤 Proprietor: Annie Paul

*Kilchrenan Taynuilt Argyll PA35 1HQ
Tel: 01866 833 211/366 Fax: 01866 833 244
E-mail: taychreggan@btinternet.com
Web: www.taychregganhotel.co.uk
Leave A85 at Taynuilt on to B845 through village of Kilchrenan to the loch side. [B5]*

KILMARNOCK

The Gathering

- *"Centrally located modern Scottish restaurant offering contemporary cooking in convivial surroundings."*
- *Informal modern Scottish.*

A LIVELY bustling restaurant: sit at the bar and read the newspapers provided, or admire the symbols of Scottish history adorning the walls. This decidedly Scottish restaurant has cheerful friendly staff who find time for a chat as they serve you. Menus offer dishes with a good selection of locally sourced seafoods and meats.

Goats cheese coated in coconut, baked on a herb croûton and home-made pesto. Venison sausages served on a bed of poppy seed mash potatoes and a tomato and onion gravy. Apple and cinnamon crumble with honey crème fraîche.

◐ Open all year except Christmas Day ✕ Food available all day £ Lunch £ Dinner £
Ⓥ Vegetarians welcome ✷ Children welcome until 7 pm ♿ Facilities for disabled visitors
▣ Credit cards: Mastercard, Visa, Switch, Delta
◪ Owner: Nicky Connolly

4B John Finnie Street Kilmarnock KA1 1DD
Tel: 01563 529022 Fax: 01563 529022
E-mail: thegathering@fsbdial.co.uk
In centre of Kilmarnock next to the train station on the A77 Glasgow to Kilmarnock Road. [C6]

KINCRAIG

March House

- *"March House is in a secluded location giving peace and tranquility only 15 minutes from Aviemore."*
- *Simple home cooking.*

MARCH HOUSE has a spacious pine conservatory which provides an idyllic setting for dinner. It is owned and enthusiastically run by Caroline Hayes, whose cooking and baking matches the fresh atmosphere of house. She uses all fresh local produce and presents a very well-priced table d'hôte menu. Small lunch party bookings welcome.

Crêpes with creamy leek, boned ham and wild mushroom stuffing. Lamb cutlets with a raspberry and fresh mint sauce, served on a bed of sweet potatoes and parsnip purée, with French beans. Fresh fruit crème brûlée.

STB ★★★ Guest House

◐ Open all year except 26 Nov to 26 Dec
🏠 Rooms: 6, 5 en suite 🛏 DB&B £37–£42 B&B £20–£25 ⓢ Special rates available ⓤ Unlicensed – guests welcome to take own wine ✕ Lunch – pre-arranged parties ££ Dinner – reservations essential for non-residents ££ Ⓥ Vegetarians welcome ✷ Children welcome ✌ Smoking permitted in the woodshed ▣ Credit cards: Mastercard, Visa ◪ Proprietor: Caroline Hayes

Feshiebridge Inverness-shire PH21 1NG
Tel: 01540 651388 Fax: 01540 651388
E-mail: caroline@marchhse01.freeserve.co.uk
Web: www.kincraig.com/march.htm
From Kincraig follow B970 to Feshiebridge. Cross the bridge and climb until red telephone box on right. Turn right and follow no through road for ½ mile. Turn left down drive. [C4]

KINGUSSIE

Auld Alliance Restaurant

- *"The Auld Alliance Restaurant offers good food in a French atmosphere."*
- *French and Scottish dishes.*

LYDIE, Chef/Owner, is French and a fully trained Chef de Cuisine, and the cooking here reflects that. All produce is sourced locally for freshness and quality, and given a traditional French/Scottish twist. The restaurant has a cosy, personal atmosphere and in the evenings is candlelit, making it a good choice for a romantic dinner.

Chilled langoustines with ginger and lime sauce. Roast marinated fillet of lamb and confites shallots. Chocolate Delight with nectar coffee.

◐ Open all year except Christmas Day Closed Mon Tue ⌂ Rooms: 4 en suite ⊟ DB&B £45–£55 B&B £20–£30 ✖ Lunch – by prior arrangement £££ Dinner except Mon Tue £££ Ⓥ Vegetarians welcome ⚹ Children welcome ♿ Facilities for disabled visitors ⌖ No smoking in restaurant ⊞ Credit cards: Mastercard/Eurocard, Visa, Switch, Delta ⧫ Chef/Owner: Lydie Bocquillon

Viewmount Guest House East Terrace Kingussie PH21 1JS
Tel: 01540 661506 Fax: 01540 662401
E-mail: theauldalliance@netscapeonline.co.uk
Web: www.auldalliancespeyside.com
Turn off A9 at Kingussie, left into village. Turn right at traffic lights up Ardbroilach Road, then 1st right into East Terrace. Auld Alliance is 100m on left. [C4]

KINGUSSIE

The Cross: Finalist The Macallan Taste of Scotland Awards 2000

- *"Dinner at The Cross is of an exceptionally high standard and a memorable experience."*
- *Innovative Scottish cooking.*

RUTH HADLEY is a member of the Master Chefs of Great Britain and treats ingredients with a deft yet experimental energy. She often uses less common produce and grows her own herbs. Tony Hadley makes a nightly selection of wines from one of the best cellars in Scotland. The Cross has 3 AA Rosettes.

Marinated and roasted quail on pickled vegetables. Atlantic cod fillet with a roasted red pepper sauce. Chocolate and raspberry mousse cake, Blairgowrie raspberries and lemon curd ice cream.

◐ Open 1 Mar to 1 Dec Closed Tue ⌂ Rooms: 9 en suite ⊟ DB&B £95–£115 ✖ Dinner except Tue ££££ Ⓥ Vegetarians welcome – prior notice preferred ♿ Facilities for non-residential disabled visitors ⌖ No smoking in dining room and bedrooms ⚘ Member of the Scotch Beef Club ⊞ Credit cards: Mastercard/Eurocard, Visa, Switch, Delta ⧫ Partners/Proprietors: Tony & Ruth Hadley

Tweed Mill Brae Ardbroilach Road, Kingussie Inverness-shire PH21 1TC
Tel: 01540 661166 Fax: 01540 661080
E-mail: fabulousfood@thecross.co.uk
Web: www.thecross.co.uk
From traffic lights in centre of village, travel uphill along Ardbroilach Road for c. 300 yards, then turn left down private drive (Tweed Mill Brae). [C4]

KINGUSSIE

The Osprey Hotel

- *"A Highland hotel offering a high standard of hospitality with food to match."*
- *Traditional Scottish cooking with French influences.*

ATTENTION to detail, good food and a fine cellar are all features of the Osprey which bring so many guests back to the hotel time after time. Aileen Burrow always cooks to order with skill and imagination showing in dishes. The Burrows are friendly accomplished hosts. 1 AA Rosette.

Sole and smoked salmon spirals with vodka cream. Pan-cooked venison with a red wine and onion sauce. Baked orange tart served with Grand Marnier cream.

STB ★★★ Hotel

◐ *Open all year* ⌂ *Rooms: 8 en suite* ⇌ *DB&B £42–£56 B&B £24–£36* ⓢⓟ *Special rates available* ✗ *Dinner £££* Ⓥ *Vegetarians welcome* ⚸ *Children over 10 years welcome* ♿ *Facilities for disabled visitors* ⚹ *No smoking in dining room and most bedrooms* ⊞ *Credit cards: Mastercard/Eurocard, American Express, Visa, Diners Club* ⋈ *Proprietors: Robert & Aileen Burrow*

Ruthven Road Kingussie PH21 1EN
Tel: 01540 661510 Fax: 01540 661510
E-mail: aileen@ospreyhotel.co.uk
Web: www.ospreyhotel.co.uk
South end of Kingussie main street. [C4]

KINLOCH RANNOCH

Bunrannoch House

- *"The home cooking at Bunrannoch makes a stay here a delightful one."*
- *Creative Scottish cooking.*

BUNRANNOCH stands in the shadow of the 'sleeping giant' mountain, near Loch Rannoch. The cosy lounge, with log fires complements the delicious aromas from the kitchen. Jennifer Skeaping is the chef/proprietor and her good cooking and friendly manner assure you of an enjoyable stay. The menus change daily, fresh food is sourced locally and tastefully prepared.

Three cheese tartlets with smoked venison. Tender lamb fillets in Madeira sauce garnished with sautéed kidneys and mushrooms. Lacy oat biscuits topped with heather honey and whisky ice cream and strawberries.

STB ★★ Guest House

◐ *Open all year except Christmas and New Year* ⌂ *Rooms: 7, 5 en suite* ⇌ *DB&B £36–£40 B&B £22–£25* ⓢⓟ *Special rates available* ✗ *Dinner ££* Ⓥ *Vegetarians welcome – prior notice required* ⚹ *No smoking throughout* ⊞ *Credit cards: Mastercard/Eurocard, Visa* ⋈ *Proprietor: Jennifer Skeaping*

Kinloch Rannoch Perthshire PH16 5QB
Tel: 01882 632407 Fax: 01882 632407
E-mail: bun.house@tesco.net
Web: www. bunrannoch.co.uk
Turn right after 500 yards on Schiehallion road, just outside Kinloch Rannoch off B846. White 3-storey building on left-hand side. [C5]

KINROSS

Carlin Maggie's

- *"Friendly family-run restaurant offering imaginative and skilfully cooked dishes."*
- *Good cooking with international accent.*

CARLIN MAGGIE'S takes its name from a local legendary witch by the same name. The restaurant is owned by Roy and Carol Smith, Roy is chef and Carol front of house and they make a dedicated team. The cooking here is skilled using good locally sourced produce which is prepared with an international and innovative flavour.

South Uist hot smoked salmon ravioli drizzled with seafood butter sauce and lemon oil. Perthshire beef fillet steak with sauteed chicken livers and Arran mustard and beef essence. Roulade of almond meringue and ginger cream with quenelles of garden rhubarb.

◐ Open all year except 1, 2 Jan and 30 Oct to 7 Nov Closed Mon ✗ Lunch except Mon £ Dinner except Mon £££ Ⓥ Vegetarians welcome ⚹ Children welcome ♿ Facilities for disabled visitors ⊞ Credit cards: Mastercard/Eurocard Visa, Switch, Delta, Solo, Visa Electron ▮ Proprietors: Roy & Carol Smith

191 High Street Kinross Tayside KY13 8DB Tel: 01577 863652 Fax: 01577 863652 Exit M90 at Junction 6 into town centre. Turn right at mini roundabout on to B966. Restaurant ¼ mile on left. [D5]

KINROSS

Grouse & Claret Restaurant

- *"A popular country restaurant offering skilful cuisine and warm hospitality."*
- *Modern Scottish cooking with some oriental flavours.*

THE RESTAURANT offers modern Scottish cooking, beautifully presented, including traditional and speciality dishes, such as seasonal game and fresh shellfish, using local produce with a daily vegetarian choice. Tastes of the orient are available in a monthly banquet. The detached accommodation is comfortable and of a good standard, with some bedrooms overlooking the trout lochans.

Scottish smoked salmon, filled with smoked trout mousse on a bed of salad leaves and garden herbs with a lime and coriander dressing. Grilled breast of Gressingham duck served with oriental noodles, stir-fry vegetables and a black bean sauce. Strawberry shortcake with vanilla cream.

STB ★★★ Restaurant with Rooms

◐ Open all year except 2 weeks end Jan, Boxing Day and New Year's Day Note: Closed Sun night and all day Mon ⌂ Rooms: 3 en suite ⛉ DB&B £55–£65 B&B £32.50–£39 ⚑ Table licence ✗ Lunch except Mon ££ Dinner except Sun Mon ££-£££ Ⓥ Vegetarians welcome ⚹ Children welcome ♿ Facilities for disabled visitors ⌇ No smoking in restaurant ⊞ Credit cards: Mastercard, Visa ▮ Proprietor: Meriel Cairns; General Manager: Vicki Futong

Heatheryford Kinross KY13 0NQ Tel: 01577 864212 Fax: 01577 864920 Exit at Junction 6 M90 then 1st left on A977 (opposite service station). [D5]

KIRKCALDY

Dunnikier House Hotel

- *"Dunnikier is a well run hotel offering friendly service and good food."*
- *Elegant Scottish cuisine.*

DUNNIKIER is set in the grounds of Dunnikier Park and its proprietor, Barry Bridgens, is only too happy to help with the needs of guests. This personal attention which includes a warm welcome combined with delicious food makes for a very comfortable destination, particularly popular with business people. 1 AA Rosette.

Salad of goats cheese served on a mango salsa with opal basil dressing. Suprême of salmon with a pesto crust served with roasted cherry tomatoes and a green pepper sauce. Passion fruit cheesecake with a peach syrup.

STB ★★★ Hotel

◐ Open all year ✿ Rooms: 14 en suite ⇔ DB&B £62.50–£80 B&B £60 ▣ Special rates available ✗ Food available all day £ Lunch ££ Dinner £££ Ⓥ Vegetarians welcome ✶ Children welcome ⊁ No smoking in restaurant ▣ Credit cards: Mastercard/Eurocard, American Express, Visa, Diners Club, Switch, Delta ▨ Partner: Barry Bridgens

*Dunnikier Park Kirkcaldy KY1 3LP
Tel: 01592 268393 Fax: 01592 642340
E-mail: recp@dunnikier-house-hotel.co.uk
Web: http://www.dunnikier-house-hotel.co.uk
Situated to the north of Kirkcaldy town in the grounds of Dunnikier Park. From the A92, 2 miles from Kirkcaldy west exit. 1 mile from Kirkcaldy east exit. [D5]*

KIRKCUDBRIGHT

The Selkirk Arms Hotel

- *"A popular hotel with good quality food."*
- *Modern Scottish.*

THIS PLACE is a gem. The cuisine is excellent, innovative and inspired and the dishes presented are of superb quality, enhanced by professional and courteous service. This is a small town hotel with good facilities but with a restaurant which is worth going out of your way to enjoy. 2 AA Rosettes.

Pan-fried breast of pigeon on a bed of roast vegetables and a red wine jus. Seared local king scallops on a herb salad with a dill and elderflower cream. White chocolate cheesecake flavoured with Glayva set on a chocolate shortbread.

STB ★★★★ Hotel

◐ Open all year except Christmas night ✿ Rooms: 16 en suite ⇔ DB&B £60–£65 B&B £45–£62 ▣ Special rates available ✗ Lunch £ Dinner £££ Ⓥ Vegetarians welcome ✶ Children welcome ♿ Facilities for disabled visitors ⊁ No smoking in restaurant ▣ Credit cards: Mastercard/Eurocard, American Express, Visa, Diners Club, Switch, Delta, JCB ▨ Partners: John & Susan Morris

*High Street Kirkcudbright Dumfries & Galloway DG6 4JG
Tel: 01557 330402 Fax: 01557 331639
E-mail: reception@selkirkarmshotel.co.uk
Web: www.selkirkarmshotel.co.uk
At the east end of the High Street in the old part of the town. [C7]*

KISHORN

Shore House

- *"The serenity of Shore House mixed with the Grays' professional approach, leave you wishing for nothing more."*
- Fine dining in homely atmosphere.

THIS BEAUTIFUL house sits on the shore at Kishorn, where a quality of cuisine – seldom encountered in small guest houses – is available. The food is outstanding, carefully sourced and lovingly prepared by Douglas in the kitchen. Attention to detail is evident throughout Shore House. A place to relax, unwind and enjoy good food.

Isle of Skye smoked salmon, sole and scallop terrine with salad leaves tossed in dill and lime dressing. Ross-shire lamb noisettes with red onion and rosemary marmalade and redcurrant jus. Dark chocolate and Glayva mousse with crème fraîche.

STB ★★★★★ Guest House

◐ Open 9 Apr to 8 Oct 🏠 Rooms: 3 en suite 🍴 DB&B £50–£59 B&B £30–£35 ✘ Residents only 💰 Special rates available 🍷 Unlicensed Dinner £££ Ⓥ Vegetarians welcome ⚞ No smoking throughout 💳 Credit cards: Mastercard/Eurocard, Visa 👤 Chef/Proprietors: Maureen & Douglas Gray

Ardaroch Kishorn Strathcarron
Wester Ross IV54 8XA
Tel/Fax: 01520 733333
E-mail: information@shorehouse.co.uk
Web: www.shorehouse.co.uk
Kishorn is almost mid-way between Shieldaig and Lochcarron on the A896. From Shieldaig, 10 miles south to Kishorn, take right turning signposted Achintraid, Shore House approx ¼ mile along this road on the right. [B4]

KNOYDART

Doune

- *A magical spot with a very hospitable family who offer expert help with trips, walks and feed you very well."*
- Fine dining with skilled seafood cooking.

DOUNE is a group of stone lodges which are located right on the waterfront and from which you can listen to the Sound of Sleat lapping over the pebbles. The verandah leads to the dining room which doubles as the information office where you may enjoy good hospitality and cooking.

Nut pâté with mixed leaf and herb salad from the garden, served with freshly baked granary rolls. Locally dived scallops in a delicate wine sauce, with new potatoes and garden vegetables. A Scottish cheese board served with our own home-made oatcakes.

STB ★★★ Guest house

◐ Open 15 April to 30 Sept 🏠 Rooms: 3 with private facilities 🍴 DB&B £48–£55 (incl packed lunch) min 3 night stay ✘ Lunch by arrangement ££ Dinner ££ Ⓥ Vegetarians welcome ⚲ Children welcome 💳 No credit cards 👤 Partner: Liz Tibbetts

Doune Knoydart By Mallaig Inverness-shire
PH41 4PL
Tel: 01687 462 667 Fax: By arrangement
E-mail: liz@doune-marine.co.uk
Web: www.doune-marine.co.uk
At Mallaig go to the public steps at the small boat pier (not the Skye ferry pier) to meet Doune's boat at the time arranged when booking made. [B4]

KNOYDART

Pier House

- *"A most welcoming place run by enthusiastic, hospitable young hosts."*
- *Imaginative cooking.*

THE PIER HOUSE is a most welcoming guest house with its own licensed restaurant which has been well maintained and cared for by Gwen Barrell and Murray Carden, the proprietors. They are caring and thoughtful hosts and have a complete commitment to quality, using only the best local produce which they prepare and present with style and appeal.

Mini-platter of Loch Nevis langoustines with salad and home-made bread. Knoydart wild venison casseroled in red wine, with rosemary potatoes and roast vegetables. Home-made whisky crunch ice cream.

STB ★★ Guest House

☾ *Open all year – recommend booking ahead* ⌂ *Rooms: 4, 2 en suite* 🛏 *DB&B £35–£40 B&B £25–£30* ✕ *Food available all day ££ Lunch except Sun £ Dinner ££* Ⓥ *Vegetarians very welcome* ☩ *Children welcome* 💳 *Credit cards: No credit cards* 🍴 *Owners: Gwen Barrell & Murray Carden*

Inverie Knoydart by Mallaig Inverness-shire
PH41 4PL
Tel: 01687 462347 Fax: 01687 462347
E-mail: eatandstay@thepierhouse.co.uk
Web: www.thepierhouse.co.uk
Central to village of Inverie. Access by regular ferry from Mallaig, or 17 mile walk from Kinlochourn. Recommend telephoning for information. [B4]

KNOYDART

Skiary

- *"A truly magical place – the food here is wonderful."*
- *Assured home cooking.*

THIS MUST be the most remote cottage accommodation in Scotland, but the journey is worth it. Christina's cooking is miraculous – almost everything is either home-produced or sourced locally – and fresh home baking is a speciality. A fantastic experience in a 'world apart', with open fires, oil lamps and no electricity or TV! Not for the faint-hearted!

Traditional home-made soups. Braised venison with oranges and red wine. Salmon baked with soured cream and tomatoes. Old-fashioned puddings, chocolate Marquise, home-made ice creams and parfaits.

☾ *Open Apr to Oct* ⌂ *Rooms: 3* 🛏 *£425 per week Full Board DB&B and packed/light lunch £70 per night* 🅂 *Special rates available* ✕ *Residents only* Ⓤ *Unlicensed – guests welcome to take own wine* ♿ *Downstairs bedroom suitable for mildly disabled visitors No parking at establishment but parking at Kinlochourn* 💳 *Credit cards: No credit cards* 🍴 *Owners: John & Christina Everett*

Kinlochourn Invergarry Inverness-shire
PH35 4HD
Tel: 01809 511214
From Invergarry (on A82 Fort William–Inverness road) take A87 Invergarry–Kyle road. After 5 miles turn left to Kinlochourn. Proceed for 22 miles to end of single track road (allow 1 hour). Park beyond farm car park, on small parking area marked 'For Skiary only'. You will then be met by boat by arrangement. [B4]

KYLE OF LOCHALSH

Conchra

- *"A charming guest house offering kind Scottish hospitality."*
- *Good fresh food, plainly cooked.*

CONCHRA means 'haven' and the aim of Colin and Mary Deans, resident owners, is to provide just this for their guests, in which they succeed. The place is wonderfully peaceful; guests are made to feel very much at home; the food is simple but intelligently cooked and appetising. A gem of a place.

Cream of celery and cashew nut soup served with crusty bread. Monkfish tails served in a garlic butter sauce with new potatoes and fresh vegetables. Freshly baked nectarine cheesecake.

STB ★★★★ Guest House

◐ *Open all year except 24, 25, 31 Dec and 1, 2 Jan* ⌂ *Rooms: 6, (5 en suite, 1 with private facilities)* ⌦ *DB&B £37.50–£57.50 B&B £25–£40* ▣ *Special rates available Open to non-residents – by arrangement* ♀ *Restricted licence* ✘ *Lunch – by prior arrangement ££* Ⓥ *Vegetarians welcome* ✱ *Children welcome* ✍ *No smoking throughout* ▣ *Credit cards: Mastercard/Eurocard, American Express, Visa, Switch* ▧ *Proprietors: Colin & Mary Deans*

Ardelve Kyle of Lochalsh Ross-shire IV40 8DZ
Tel: 01599 555 233 Fax: 01599 555 433
E-mail: reservations@conchra.co.uk
Web: www.conchra.co.uk
From south continue westwards 1km on A87 past Dornie/Eilean Donan Castle. Follow hotel signposts turning right for ¾ mile (Sallachy/Killilan Road). 8 miles out of Kyle on A87. [B4]

KYLE OF LOCHALSH

The Seafood Restaurant

- *"This delightful little restaurant is right on the station platform and is well worth a visit – whatever the occasion."*
- *Freshly cooked, good quality food.*

THE MENU here consists mainly of fish and shellfish (Jann's husband landing his catch daily) there are also meat and vegetarian dishes and a daily blackboard special. In the peak season there is a breakfast and lunch menu. You are advised to check opening hours as they vary depending on the time of year.

Queen scallops in oatmeal: Lochcarron queenies rolled in oatmeal, deep-fried and served with lemon. Seafood kebabs: fresh monkfish, scallops and langoustines grilled and served with a dill and orange sauce. Home-made ice cream: Skye whisky and honey ice cream served with shortbread.

◐ *Open Easter to Oct* ♀ *Table licence* ✘ *Lunch £ Dinner ££* Ⓥ *Vegetarians welcome* ✱ *Children welcome* ♿ *Limited facilities for disabled visitors* ✍ *No smoking in restaurant* ▣ *Credit cards: Mastercard/Eurocard, Visa* ▧ *Owner: Jann Macrae*

Railway Buildings Kyle of Lochalsh Ross-shire IV40 8XX
Tel: 015995 34813 Fax: 015995 77230
E-mail: thescottishtouristboardwww.host.co.uk
At Kyle of Lochalsh railway station on platform 1. Parking on slipway to station. [B4]

KYLE OF LOCHALSH

Seagreen Restaurant & Bookshop

- *"A delightful little restaurant, ideal for vegetarians and fish lovers, as well as cream cake addicts."*
- Modern Scottish cooking, innovative and of good quality.

SEAGREEN offers very good wholefoods but the emphasis is increasingly on fish and shellfish. An all-day counter service offers delicious salads, soups, home baking. The style of the food is different from that served during the day with a more sophisticated continental/European influenced menu. Investor in People Award.

Local goats cheese soufflé, walnut dressed salad. Sole fillets filled with Lochalsh crabmeat, coriander, lime with foaming red pepper hollandaise. Cock o' the North liqueur ice cream with blaeberries.

◐ Open all year except 25, 26 Dec and 1 Jan and 6 Jan to Easter ✗ Lunch £ Dinner ££-£££ reservations preferred Ⓥ Vegetarians welcome ✼ Children welcome ♿ Facilities for disabled visitors ✄ No smoking in restaurant 💳 Credit cards: Mastercard/Eurocard, Visa, Switch ⓝ Chef/Proprietor: Fiona Begg

Plockton Road Kyle of Lochalsh IV40 8DA
Tel: 01599 534388 Fax: 01599 534040
Just immediately outside Kyle on the Duirinish to Plockton visitor route. [B4]

LAIDE

The Old Smiddy Guest House

- *"The Old Smiddy is bursting with genuine talent and should be an essential stopover on any trip to this beautiful area."*
- Imaginative, creative, Scottish home cooking.

THE OLD SMIDDY is a warm and friendly little cottage with a well-appointed restaurant with beautiful views over the hills. Proprietors, Kate and Steve Macdonald are very skilled breadmakers, and their home baking/cooking is excellent with great attention to flavours. Winner of The Macallan Taste of Scotland Small Residence Award 1999.

Grilled red pepper and saffron soup with chilli cream. Trio of monkfish, turbot and salmon with langoustine and fennel sauce, served with Parmesan and lovage potatoes and rocket and oakleaf salad leaves. Fresh garden strawberry ice cream and raspberry almond torte.

STB ★★★★ Guest House

◐ Open Apr until Nov 🛏 Rooms: 3 en suite 🍽 DB&B £56–£64 B&B £32–£38 🍷 Unlicensed – guests welcome to take own wine ✗ Dinner £££ Ⓥ Vegetarians welcome ✄ No smoking throughout 💳 Credit cards: Mastercard/Eurocard, Visa ⓝ Proprietors: Kate & Steve Macdonald

Laide Ross-shire IV22 2NB
Tel: 01445 731425 Fax: 01445 731696
E-mail: oldsmiddy@aol.com
Web: www.s-h-systems.co.uk/hotels/oldsmid.html
On the main road at Laide, on the A832 Gairloch – Braemore road. [B3]

LARGS

Brisbane House Hotel

- *"A well run hotel in this popular West Coast seaside town."*
- *Accomplished Scottish cooking.*

THE HOTEL is located on the seafront in Largs. It is comfortable and well appointed, and has an attractive conservatory, allowing visitors to enjoy the hotel's setting. Menus are varied with all produce carefully sourced making best use of fresh local ingredients, with prices to suite every occasion. 1 AA Rosette.

Open ravioli of Galloway lobster, duck parfait, wild chantrelles and truffle oil. Confit of sea trout with baby clam risotto, aubergine crisps and a red wine sauce. Lemon curd parfait with blood orange sorbet and caramelised pineapple syrup.

STB ★★★★ Hotel

◑ *Open all year* 🏨 *Rooms: 23 en suite* 🛏 *DB&B £50–£110 B&B £40–£90* 💰 *Special rates available* ✗ *Food available all day ££ Lunch £ Dinner £££* Ⓥ *Vegetarians welcome* ⚲ *Children welcome* ♿ *Facilities for disabled visitors* 🐕 *Small dogs welcome* 💳 *Credit cards: Mastercard/Eurocard, American Express, Visa, Diners Club, Switch, Delta* 🛎 *General Manager: Timothy Kelly*

14 Greenock Road Largs KA30 8NF
Tel: 01475 687200 Fax: 01475 676295
E-mail: enquiries@maksu-group.co.uk
Web: www.maksu-group.co.uk
Follow M8 to Greenock then join A78 to Largs. [C6]

LARGS

Priory House Hotel

- *"Priory House offers peace and tranquility plus excellent cuisine."*
- *Modern Scottish Cooking.*

LOCATED on Largs Promenade, Priory House Hotel consists of two 19th century buildings linked with a magnificent conservatory lounge. It has been refurbished to a high standard, making best use of original features. Staff are efficient and relaxed. The Four Seasons Restaurant offers a warm welcome and fine Scottish dishes.

Medallions of venison with red onion jam, carrot chips and bramble and redcurrant sauce. Warm carpaccio of Aberdeen Angus beef with wild mushrooms, Parmesan shavings and chilli and spring onion oil. Warm chocolate and lime potted cream with lemon sable.

STB ★★★★ Hotel

◑ *Open all year* 🏨 *Rooms: 21 en suite* 🛏 *DB&B £50–£110 B&B £40–£90* 💰 *Special rates available* ✗ *Food available all day £ Lunch £-££ Dinner £££* Ⓥ *Vegetarians welcome* ⚲ *Children welcome* ♿ *Facilities for disabled visitors* 🐕 *Small dogs welcome* 💳 *Credit cards: Mastercard/Eurocard, American Express, Visa, Diners Club, Switch, Delta* 🛎 *Operations Director: Richard Gibbon*

Broomfields Largs Ayrshire KA30 8DR
Tel: 01475 686460 Fax: 01475 689070
E-mail: enquiries@maksu-group.co.uk
Web: www.maksu-group.co.uk
Follow M8 to Greenock, then join A78 to Largs. [C6]

LAUDER

The Lodge at Carfraemill

- *"An excellent place to visit whilst enjoying the beauty of the Borders."*
- *Traditional Scottish home cooking with flair.*

SINCE CARFRAEMILL was taken over by its present owner in 1997, it has undergone extensive renovation and modernisation. Jo Sutherland makes sure this is a most welcoming place for visitors, diners, locals and travellers, with comfortable surroundings and good food. The menus, with a strong emphasis on local produce, change regularly and meals are presented with flair.

Marinated Scottish salmon and deep-fried oysters surrounded by a citrus butter sauce. Roast loin of roe deer on a bed of crispy vegetables served with a game and chocolate sauce. Squidgy meringue cake drizzled with a fresh strawberry and elderflower coulis.

STB ★★★★ Small Hotel

◐ Open all year ⌂ Rooms: 10 en suite ⇌ DB&B £50–£70 B&B £35–£55 ⓢⓟ Special rates available ✗ Food available all day £ Lunch £ Dinner ££ Ⓥ Vegetarians welcome ⚝ Children welcome ⚞ No smoking area in restaurant and no smoking in bedrooms ⊞ Credit cards: Mastercard/Eurocard, American Express, Visa, Diners Club, Switch, Delta ⓝ Owner: Jo Sutherland

Lauder Berwickshire TD2 6RA
Tel: 01578 750750 Fax: 01578 750751
E-mail: enquiries@carfraemill.co.uk
Web: www.carfraemill.co.uk
Situated at the junction of the A68/A697, just 21 miles south of Edinburgh, 80 miles north of Newcastle and 70 miles from Glasgow. [D6]

LETHAM NR CUPAR

Fernie Castle Hotel

- *"Castle hotel in superb setting with its interesting surrounds, offering a warm welcome and good Scottish cooking."*
- *Modern Scottish.*

FERNIE CASTLE is over 450 years old, has great character and has been refurbished to a very high standard throughout. The Auld Alliance room is the ideal setting for a formal dinner with it's Georgian chandelier and candles. Menus are traditional and uncomplicated but well executed using high quality produce. 1 AA Rosette.

Black pudding and clapshot cake with an Arran grain mustard sauce. Roast sea bass fillet with a pesto herb crust. Poached Prince Charlie pears in a sloe berry coulis with fresh mint ice cream.

STB ★★★★ Hotel

◐ Open all year ⌂ Rooms: 20 en suite ⇌ DB&B £62.50–£95 B&B £40–£75 ⓢⓟ Special rates available ✗ Lunch £ Dinner £££ Ⓥ Vegetarians welcome ⚝ Children welcome ⚞ No smoking in dining room ⌇ Dogs welcome ⊞ Credit cards: Mastercard/Eurocard, American Express, Visa, Switch, Delta ⓝ Neil and Mary Blackburn

Letham Nr Cupar Fife KY15 7RU
Tel: 01337 810381 Fax: 01337 810422
E-mail: mail@ferniecastle.demon.co.uk
Web: www.ferniecastle.demon.co.uk
From Edinburgh follow signs to Glenrothes, then take the Tay Bridge, onto the A92, then 1 mile past Letham. 'Fernie Castle' is on the right. [D5]

LINLITHGOW

Livingston's Restaurant: 2000 Winner – Out of Town Restaurant

- *"A most excellent small restaurant offering really good food and service in pleasant, informal surroundings."*
- *Modern Scottish cooking.*

EXPOSED stone walls and assorted tables and chairs provide a charm and warmth, enhanced by dark red candles, table mats and napkins. There is also a conservatory which overlooks a pleasant little attractive garden. Chef Julian Wright shows skill and imagination, providing interesting menus, using fresh Scottish produce. Suitable for almost any occasion. Livingston's has 2 AA Rosettes.

Wild mushroom gâteau with balsamic-infused shallots and truffle oil. Saddle of wild Highland venison with a mille feuille of black pudding and onion. Iced rice pudding parfait with Armagnac scented prunes.

◑ all year except 2 weeks Jan, 1 week Jun and 1 week Oct. Closed Sun Mon ✕ Lunch except Sun Mon £ Dinner except Sun Mon £££ Ⓥ Vegetarians welcome ⚹ Children over 8 years welcome – evenings ♿ Facilities for disabled visitors ✄ Smoking permitted in conservatory ☙ Member of the Scotch Beef Club ▣ Credit cards: Mastercard/Eurocard, Visa, Switch ▌Manager: Fiona Livingston

52 High Street Linlithgow EH49 7AE
Tel/Fax: 01506 846565
At eastern end of the High Street opposite the Post Office. [C5]

LOCH LOMOND

Cameron House Hotel and Country Estate

- *"Fine seafood – well prepared – served by friendly and attentive staff."*
- *Modern contemporary cooking.*

A LUXURY hotel on the shore of Loch Lomond. Executive Chef Peter Fleming presents a highly sophisticated, imaginative menu in the hotel's main restaurant, the elegant Georgian Room. Smolletts Restaurant offers a wide variety of dishes from an à la carte menu; bar snacks are available in the Breakers Restaurant at the Marina. 3 AA Rosettes.

Roast langoustine tails, beside a crab risotto surrounded by a shellfish cream. Roast saddle of Scottish lamb accompanied by a sweet potato galette on onion chutney and port essence. Hot passion fruit soufflé served with exotic fruit sorbet.

STB ★★★★ Hotel

◑ Open all year N.B. Georgian room closed all day Mon ⌂ Rooms: 96 en suite ⚏ DB&B £200–£265 B&B £180–£245 ✕ Food available all day £-££££ Lunch except Sat ££ Dinner ££££ Ⓥ Vegetarians welcome ⚹ Children welcome ♿ Facilities for disabled visitors ✄ Smoking in public areas only ☙ Member of the Scotch Beef Club ▣ Credit cards: Mastercard/Eurocard, American Express, Visa, Diners Club ▌Executive Chef: Peter Fleming

Loch Lomond Dunbartonshire G83 9QZ
Tel: 01389 755565 Fax: 01389 759522
E-mail: devere.cameron@airtime.co.uk
Web: www.cameronhouse.co.uk
On A82 near Balloch, on the banks of Loch Lomond. At Balloch roundabout follow signs for Luss. Approx 1 mile, first right. [C5]

LOCH LOMOND

Coach House Coffee Shop

- *"King-size scones, muffins and cakes all made daily."*
- *Home baking and light meals.*

A WARM welcome is extended by the kilted Mr Groves whilst his wife supervises the making of delicious hearty snacks, home-made soups, light meals and good home baking. Hand made soft bread rolls are filled with chunky ham, honey-roasted on the premises and eggs from their own free-range Black Rock hens.

Carrot and parsnip soup served with a hunk of bread. Leek and cheese quiche served with salad, coleslaw and fresh or garlic bread. Victoria sandwich. Caffe latte: single espresso with steamed milk and a little frothed milk.

◐ *Open all year except Christmas Day*
⛔ *Unlicensed* ✘ *Food available all day £ Lunch £* Ⓥ *Vegetarians welcome* ⚹ *Children welcome* ♿ *Facilities for disabled visitors* ⌇ *No smoking throughout* 🐕 *Dogs welcome* 💳 *Credit cards: Mastercard/Eurocard, Visa, Switch, Delta, Solo* ⚀ *Proprietors: Gary & Rowena Groves*

Luss Loch Lomond Argyll G83 8NN
Tel: 01436 860341/336 Fax: 01436 860336
E-mail:
coachhouse@lochlomondtrading.fsnet.co.uk
Web: www.lochlomondtrading.co.uk
Turn off A82 (Glasgow to Crianlarich) at signpost for Luss. Park in car park, walk into the village and look for the church. [C5]

LOCH LOMOND

Inverbeg Inn

- *"Warm and friendly roadside hotel with beautiful views of Loch Lomond."*
- *Adventurous use of Scottish produce.*

THE INVERBEG INN is an old coaching inn which boasts superb views of Loch Lomond. Menus all use Scottish produce and are supplemented with blackboard daily specials. The cooking here is traditional with innovative twists and guests may choose bar meals or more formal dining in the restaurant.

Smoked venison served on mixed lettuce leaves. Seared breast of corn-fed chicken, complemented with roast shallots and served with a chervil and port wine jus. Traditional Scottish Crannachan, served in a chocolate cup.

STB ★★★★ Small Hotel

◐ *Open all year except Christmas Day*
🛏 *Rooms: 20 en suite* 🛌 *B&B £40–£75*
ⓢⓟ *Special rates available* ✘ *Food available all day ££ Lunch ££ Dinner £££* Ⓥ *Vegetarians welcome* ⚹ *Children welcome* ♿ *Facilities for disabled visitors* ⌇ *No smoking in restaurant*
💳 *Credit cards: Mastercard, American Express, Visa, Diners Club, Switch, Delta* ⚀ *General Manager: Andrew D. Scott*

Luss Loch Lomond Dunbartonshire G83 8PD
Tel: 01436 860678 Fax: 01436 860686
Web: www.scottish-selection.co.uk
2 miles north of Luss on main A82. [C5]

LOCH LOMOND

Lodge on Loch Lomond Hotel and Restaurant

- *"Wonderful bedrooms with the sound of Loch Lomond lapping underneath your window."*
- *Modern Scottish cooking.*

THE LODGE ON LOCH LOMOND is set in a particularly stunning location beside the conservation village of Luss. The bar and restaurant overlook the loch and present menus which offer something to suit every taste. Cooking is skilled, presentation is attractive, and imaginative use is made of local produce. 1 AA Rosette.

Loin of rabbit, Dunkeld black pudding, lambs lettuce and beetroot chutney. Monkfish wrapped in crispy cabbage and smoked bacon, paprika-spiced whitebait. Apricot bread and butter pudding with orange-flavoured custard.

STB ★★★ Hotel

◐ Open all year ⌂ Rooms: 29 en suite ⇋ DB&B £55–£85 B&B £30–£63 ⓢⓟ Special rates available ✘ Food available all day ££ Lunch ££ Dinner ££ Ⓥ Vegetarians welcome ⚹ Children welcome ♿ Facilities for disabled visitors ⌦ No smoking in restaurant ⊞ Credit cards: Mastercard/Eurocard, American Express, Visa, Switch, Delta ⚑ Manager: Niall Colquhoun

Luss Argyll G83 8PA
Tel: 01436 860201 Fax: 01436 860203
E-mail: lusslomond@aol.com
Web: www.loch-lomond.co.uk
In the village of Luss on the A82 main route along Loch Lomond side. Well-sign posted. [C5]

LOCHCARRON

Rockvilla Hotel & Restaurant

- *"Relaxed atmosphere with good food and lovely views."*
- *Traditional Scottish cooking.*

GOOD FOOD and warm hospitality comes naturally to Ken and Lorna Wheelan, An à la carte dinner menu offers excellent value and good choices. Local specialities and traditional favourites also appear. After a hearty breakfast guests are well set up for a day's walking, fishing or exploring the dramatic West Highlands.

Cocktail of Loch Torridon langoustine and squat lobster. Roast saddle of Scottish lamb with a red wine, tomato and rosemary sauce, on a Cheddar and herb mash. Shortbread cranachan with mixed berries on a raspberry coulis.

STB ★★★ Small Hotel

◐ Open all year except Christmas Day and 1 Jan (Restaurant closed 30 Sept to Easter) ⌂ Rooms: 3 en suite ⇋ B&B £22–£30 ⓢⓟ Special rates available Lunch £ Dinner ££ Ⓥ Vegetarians welcome ⚹ Children welcome ⌦ No smoking in restaurant ⊞ Credit cards: Mastercard/Eurocard, American Express, Visa, Switch, Delta, JCB ⚑ Proprietors: Lorna & Kenneth Wheelan

Main Street Lochcarron IV54 8YB
Tel: 01520 722379 Fax: 01520 722844
E-mail: rockvillahotel@btinternet.com
Web: www.rockvilla-hotel.com
Situated in centre of village, c. 20 miles north of Kyle of Lochalsh. [B4]

LOCHGILPHEAD

Bridge House Hotel

- *"Guests return time after time to receive Watty and Michaela's warm hospitality and good food."*
- *Traditional Scottish with flair.*

WATTY AND MICHAELA Dewar are friendly, welcoming hosts, who go out of their way for their guests. There are six bedrooms that have been refurbished to a high standard. The food is extremely wholesome, created with imaginative flair. There is a traditional dining room, and also a relaxing beer garden overlooking Loch Fyne.

Warm game salad with crisp smoked bacon and a red wine dressing. Pan-fried Aberdeen Angus fillet steak and poached scallops served in their own lightly creamed cooking juices. Hazelnut meringue with local fresh fruits and berries.

STB ★★★ Small Hotel

◐ *Open all year* 🛏 *Rooms: 6 en suite* 🛌 *DB&B £55–£75 B&B £35–£55* 💷 *Special rates available* ✘ *Lunch ££ Dinner £££* Ⓥ *Vegetarians welcome* ✹ *Children welcome* ♿ *Facilities for disabled visitors* ✣ *No smoking in dining room* 🐕 *Dogs welcome* 💳 *Credit cards: Mastercard/ Eurocard, Visa, Switch, Delta, Solo* 🅗 *Owners: Watty & Michaela Dewar*

St Claire Road Ardrishaig By Lochgilphead
PA30 8EW
Tel: 01546 606379 Fax: 01546 606593
E-mail: bridge-house@lineone.net
Web: www.smoothhound.co.uk/
From Lochgilphead take A83 Campbeltown road for 2 miles, next to Ardrishaig Boat Basin and Crinan Canal. [B5]

LOCHGILPHEAD

Fascadale House

- *"Exceptionally high standards for food and luxury awaits the guests at Fascadale."*
- *Stylish imaginative food.*

SET ON the shores of picturesque Loch Fyne this magnificent Victorian country house with it's grand interior is elegant, homely and relaxing. The cuisine offered meets an excellent standard with locally sourced produce enhancing the stylish, well prepared and imaginative menus. Alternative cottage accommodation is available within the gardens.

Seared hand-dived Islay scallops served with a Prosciutto and mixed leaf salad with a balsamic vinegar dressing. Ormsary Farm Highland beef sirloin with pink peppercorn sauce and rösti. Heather honey and lemon parfait with raspberry coulis

STB ★★★★ B&B

◐ *Open all year* 🛏 *Rooms: 4, 2 en suite* 🛌 *DB&B £42–£60 B&B £25–£35* 💷 *Special rates available* 🍷 *Unlicensed – guests welcome to take own wine* ✘ *Dinner ££* Ⓥ *Vegetarians welcome* ✹ *Children welcome* ✣ *No smoking throughout* 🐕 *Dogs welcome by arrangement* 💳 *Credit cards: Mastercard/Eurocard, Visa, Delta* 🅗 *Owner: Kay Davies*

Tarbert Road Ardrishaig Lochgilphead
Argyll PA30 8EP
Tel: 01546 603845 Fax: 01546 602152
E-mail: kay@fascadale.com
Web: www.fascadale.com
From Lochgilphead take A83 south to Campbeltown, through Ardrishaig. Go over the Crinan canal swing bridge and Fascadale is 1 mile further, on the right-hand side. [B5]

LOCHINVER

The Albannach

- *"A trip to Lochinver would not be complete without experiencing the wonderful food and service at The Albannach."*
- *Contemporary Scottish cooking with French influences.*

THE ALBANNACH has been tastefully decorated with a Victorian feel and a cosy atmosphere. Drinks are available in the conservatory; dinner is served in the candlelit dining room. Lesley Crosfield uses the finest produce for a creative, set, five course dinner menu. Winner of The Macallan Taste of Scotland Award For Overall Excellence 1998 and Best Restaurant With Rooms 1998.

Mousseline of turbot and crayfish with sauce vierge. Roast fillet of free-range Highland beef on skirlie with locally grown organic carrots. Hot chocolate soufflé with caraway ice cream and berry fruits.

STB ★★★★ Small Hotel

◐ Open last 2 weeks Mar to 27 Dec 🛏 Rooms: 5 en suite 🍴 DB&B £72–£105 💷 Special rates available 🍷 Table licence ✗ Dinner 5 course menu £££ Non-residents welcome – booking essential Ⓥ Vegetarians welcome – by prior arrangement ⚸ Children over 12 years welcome ⊁ No smoking throughout 💳 Credit cards: Mastercard/Eurocard, Visa, Switch, Delta, JCB 🍳 Chef/Proprietors: Lesley Crosfield & Colin Craig

Lochinver Sutherland IV27 4LP
Tel: 01571 844 407 Fax: 01571 844 285
From Lochinver follow signs for Baddidarroch. After ½ mile, pass turning for Highland Stoneware, turn left for the Albannach. [B3]

LOCHINVER

Inver Lodge Hotel

- *"Pamper yourself in this luxurious hotel set on the hill above Lochinver."*
- *Modern Scottish cooking.*

AT INVER LODGE the staff are well-trained and courteous. The table d'hôte menu features Lochinver-landed fish and shellfish and Assynt venison. The cooking is innovative and of high quality. Great care and effort goes into every aspect of Inver Lodge's hospitality. 1 AA Rosette.

Grilled Scottish salmon on asparagus boullion with herb crème fraîche. Fillet of Aberdeen Angus beef with summer truffle mash, cep ravioli and braised fine beans. Trio of chocolate.

STB ★★★★ Hotel

◐ Open 10 Apr to 1 Nov 🛏 Rooms: 20 en suite 🍴 DB&B £80–£120 B&B £65–£110 💷 Special rates available ✗ Lunch £ Dinner £££ Ⓥ Vegetarians welcome ⊁ No smoking in dining room 🐄 Member of the Scotch Beef Club 💳 Credit cards: Mastercard/Eurocard, American Express, Visa, Diners Club, Switch, Delta, JCB 🍳 General Manager: Nicholas Gorton

Iolaire Road Lochinver Sutherland IV27 4LU
Tel: 01571 844496 Fax: 01571 844395
E-mail: stay@inverlodge.com
Web: www.inverlodge.com
A837 to Lochinver, first turn on left after village hall. ½ mile up private road to hotel. [B3]

LOCKERBIE

Dryfesdale Hotel

- *"Friendly, family-run hotel offering good quality food in welcoming surroundings."*
- *Modern Scottish cooking.*

DRYFESDALE is set in delightful grounds which afford superb views of the countryside. This is a well-run, elegant hotel which has the benefit of food in both the Kirkhill Restaurant and the Sun Lounge. The aim of the hotel is to provide a very high standard of experience for its guests. Inspected under previous owners, the Dunbobbin Family.

Galloway smoked salmon with king prawns in a tempura batter, with a dill and mustard vinaigrette. Chicken fillet steaks with haggis, glazed with hollandaise sauce. Dryfesdale summer pudding served with fresh berries and vanilla ice cream.

STB ★★★ Hotel

◐ *Open all year, except Christmas Day night and Boxing Day* ⌂ *Rooms: 15 en suite* ⇌ *DB&B £75–£85 B&B £55–£65* ✕ *Food available all day ££ Lunch ££ Dinner £££* Ⓥ *Vegetarians welcome* ☙ *Children welcome* ♿ *Facilities for disabled visitors* ✄ *No smoking in dining room* ☞ *Dogs welcome on ground floor only* 🆔 *Credit cards: Mastercard, American Express, Visa, Switch, Delta* ♞ *Owners: Clive & Heather Sturman*

Dryfebridge Lockerbie Dumfries DG11 2SF
Tel: 01576 202427 Fax: 01576 204187
E-mail: reception@dryfesdalehotel.co.uk
Web: www.dryfesdalehotel.co.uk
Junction 17 on M74. Head towards Lockerbie at first roundabout take first left. Hotel entrance is 100 yards on left. [D6]

LOCKERBIE

Scott's At The Crown

- *"Bright restaurant at back of hotel – bistro style good home cooking using local produce, offering a sound selection of wines, all at modest prices."*
- *Homely style Scottish cooking.*

SCOTT'S restaurant is centrally located and has been recently refurbished to give a relaxed and informal atmosphere with quiet and effectively simple decor. Chef/Proprietor Ralph Scott specialises in homely style cooking skilfully prepared using fresh produce. Specialities include an excellent selection of Solway seafood and Galloway and Border beef and lamb dishes.

Monkfish and smoked salmon terrine. Scott's medallions of beef: tender fillet steak sliced and pan-fried with onions, mushrooms and red wine, in a rich glaze. Home-made cranachan ice cream: Raspberries, honey, Drambuie and oatmeal, folded with home-made ice cream.

◐ *Open all year except Christmas Day and 1 Jan* ✕ *Lunch £ Dinner ££* Ⓥ *Vegetarians welcome* ☙ *Children welcome* ♿ *Facilities for disabled visitors* ✄ *No smoking in restaurant* 🆔 *Credit cards: Mastercard, Visa, Switch, Delta, Solo, JCB, Electron* ♞ *Chef/Owner: Mr Ralph MacDonald Scott*

95 High Street Lockerbie DG11 2JH
Tel: 01576 202948
High Street in Lockerbie, at back of Crown Hotel. [D6]

LOCKERBIE

Somerton House Hotel

- *"Friendly atmosphere, with fine home cooked food."*
- *Classic contemporary.*

AT SOMERTON HOUSE HOTEL, diners have the choice of eating in the extensive cosy lounge where a bar menu is available; the conservatory; and in the delightful dining room where a full à la carte is served. The food is hearty and the dishes familiar but served with some style in these pleasant surroundings.

Lowland Ham and Haddie: a local speciality of smoked haddock and ham in a cream sauce topped with croûtons, tomato and cheese. Fillet of ostrich with a creamy tarragon sauce. Meringue and mango roulade.

STB ★★★ Hotel

◑ Open all year ✿ Rooms: 11 en suite ⛌ B&B £26–£30 ✕ Lunch £ Dinner ££-£££ Ⓥ Vegetarians welcome ✻ Children welcome ⌁ No smoking in dining room ⊞ Credit cards: Mastercard/Eurocard, American Express, Visa, Diners Club ⛨ Proprietors: Alex & Jean Arthur

*35 Carlisle Road Lockerbie DG11 2DR
Tel: 01576 202583 Fax: 01576 204218
Follow High Street eastwards towards M74, 1 mile from town centre. [D6]*

MALLAIG

The Fish Market

- *"A popular restaurant which offers wonderful fresh fish – or pop in for home bakes!"*
- *Imaginative Scottish cooking.*

THE FISH MARKET is relatively young and everything is fresh and clean. Items from large white bowls of prawns to fresh haddock and fries are served, with home baking for teas and coffees. Sandra McLean makes the very best of the plentiful supplies of fresh produce to ensure diners enjoy her cooking at its best.

Hebridean shellfish broth (oatmeal and leek soup with whole prawns, mussels, scallops and oysters). Pan-fried scallops with saffron and dill, with whole lemon sole stuffed with fresh prawns. Sticky toffee pudding with fresh cream or Orkney ice cream.

◑ Open all year except Christmas Day, 31 Dec and New Year's Day ✕ Lunch £-££ Dinner £-££ Ⓥ Vegetarians welcome ✻ Children welcome ♿ Facilities for disabled visitors ⊞ Credit cards: Mastercard/Eurocard, Visa, Switch, Delta ⛨ Proprietor: Sandra McLean

*Station Road Mallaig PH41 4QS
Tel: 01687 462299 Fax: 01687 462623
In the centre of village overlooking the harbour. A 2 minute walk from railway station and 5 minutes from ferry terminal. [B4]*

MELROSE

Burts Hotel

- *"A superb family run hotel offering excellent cuisine and hospitality."*
- *Modern Scottish cooking.*

BURTS HOTEL is run by Graham, Anne, Nicholas and Trish Henderson, professional and friendly hosts. Their restaurant has an excellent local reputation. Daily changing lunch and dinner menus are innovative and prepared by a skilled chef who knows how to balance preparation and presentation whilst enhancing flavours. 2 AA Rosettes.

Galette of venison, aubergine and red peppers, served with a rhubarb and ginger chutney. Cannon of Border lamb, served with chorizo and okra gumbo glazed with a saffron and coriander sabayon. Warm Selkirk Bannock pudding smothered in butterscotch served with toffee and praline ice cream.

STB ★★★★ Small Hotel

◑ Open all year except Boxing Day ⊞ Rooms: 20 en suite ⊟ DB&B £60–£69 B&B £44–£50 ▦ Special rates available ✘ Lunch except Christmas Day and Boxing Day ££ Dinner except Christmas Day and Boxing Day £££ Ⓥ Vegetarians welcome ⚹ Children welcome ⚕ No smoking in restaurant ⚘ Member of the Scotch Beef Club ⊞ Credit cards: Mastercard/Eurocard, American Express, Visa, Diners Club, Switch, Delta, JCB ⛨ Owner: Nicholas Henderson

Market Square Melrose Scottish Borders TD6 9PL Tel: 01896 822285 Fax: 01896 822870 E-mail: burtshotel@aol.com Web: www.burtshotel.co.uk B6394, 2 miles from A68, 38 miles south of Edinburgh. [D6]

MELROSE

Dryburgh Abbey Hotel

- *"A beautiful spot from which to explore the Borders."*
- *International and modern Scottish.*

DRYBURGH ABBEY's conversion into a first class hotel includes an indoor heated swimming pool. In the spacious, elegant Tweed Restaurant, head chef Rory McCallum offers a table d'hôte menu (lunch and dinner) which changes daily, and uses only fresh local produce. During the day and evening, light meals are also available, served in the lounge or bar.

Pressed pheasant and Guinea fowl terrine topped with sweet potato crisps and enhanced by red berry compote and balsamic syrup. Seared halibut on a smoked salmon and broccoli rösti, with a white truffle sauce, crowned with fried leek. Cinnamon and apple soufflé with an orange and Glenkinchie whisky essence.

STB ★★★★ Hotel

◑ Open all year ⊞ Rooms: 37 en suite ⊟ DB&B £54–£98 B&B £40–£85 ▦ Special rates available ✘ Food available all day £ Lunch from £–££ Dinner from £££ Ⓥ Vegetarians welcome ⚹ Children welcome ♿ Facilities for disabled visitors ⚕ No smoking in restaurant ⊞ Credit cards: Mastercard/Eurocard, American Express, Visa, Switch, Delta, JCB ⛨ General Manager: Matthew Grose

St Boswells Melrose Scottish Borders TD6 ORQ Tel: 01835 822261 Fax: 01835 823945 E-mail: enquiries@dryburgh.co.uk Web: www.dryburgh.co.uk Off A68 at St Boswells onto B6404. 2 miles turn left onto B6356. Continue for 1½ miles, hotel signposted. [D6]

MELROSE

Hoebridge Inn Restaurant

- *"A memorable meal cooked and prepared with great care and attention, and refreshingly imaginative."*
- Modern Scottish cooking.

THE HOEBRIDGE has a friendly, relaxed atmosphere with simple, tasteful decor in keeping with the building's white walls, wooden beams and wooden tables. The food here is good quality Scottish fare, presented and cooked by Maureen Rennie in a modern style. Attention to detail is excellent, imaginative food combinations impressively executed.
1 AA Rosette.

Warm salad of Stichill cream cheese croutons with mixed salad leaves. Char-grilled saddle of roe deer with beetroot and red wine jus, stir-fried baby beets and bok choy. Lemon tart with lemon verbena ice cream.

◐ Open Mar to Jan except Boxing Day and New Year's Day Closed Mon Christmas Day lunch ✗ Dinner ££ Ⓥ Vegetarians welcome ⊞ Credit cards: Mastercard/Eurocard, Visa, Switch, Delta ▮ Proprietors: Tony & Maureen Rennie

Gattonside Melrose Roxburghshire TD6 9LZ
Tel: 01896 823082
E-mail: hoebridge@easynet.co.uk
From A68 take sign to Gattonside. First left on entering the village of Gattonside. [D6]

MOFFAT

Well View Hotel

- *"A delightful place to stay with exceptional cuisine."*
- Modern Scottish cooking.

AT WELL VIEW prior reservation is essential for lunch and dinner. The six course taster dinner menu demonstrates an inventive approach to more familiar dishes, accompanied by light fruity sauces and dressings. John Schuckardt has a good knowledge of wine and has over 100 Bins available. German and a little French spoken.
2 AA Rosettes.

Fillet of Galloway salmon with a horseradish crust and a dill and Chardonnay sauce. Fillet of Stobo beef on a bed of roasted root vegetables with a red wine jus. Selection of fine cheeses and desserts.

STB ★★★★ Hotel

◐ Open all year ⌂ Rooms: 6 en suite ⇌ DB&B £62–£90 B&B £34–£65 ⓢⓟ Special rates available ✗ Lunch except Sat ££ Dinner 6 course menu £££ Ⓥ Vegetarians welcome ✳ Children over 5 years welcome at dinner ⌦ No smoking throughout ⊞ Credit cards: Mastercard/Eurocard, American Express, Visa ▮ Owners: Janet & John Schuckardt

Ballplay Road Moffat DG10 9JU
Tel: 01683 220184 Fax: 01683 220088
E-mail: johnwellview@aol
Web: www.wellview.co.uk
Leaving Moffat take A708. At crossroads, left into Ballplay Road – hotel on right. [D6]

MUIR OF ORD

Ord House Hotel

- *"This is such a peaceful relaxing place – relax in front of a log fire and enjoy good hospitality."*
- *Good country cooking.*

ORD HOUSE offers its guests the unhurried peace of a bygone age. The dining room offers honest country cooking that uses fresh meat, game and fish and vegetables in season from the hotel's own garden. Service is attentive without being fussy. The wine list is sound and inexpensive. Fluent French is spoken.

Salad of smoked halibut and gravadlax with dill sauce. Roasted salmon fillet wrapped in prosciutto with herby lentils, spinach and yoghurt. Pavlova roulade with raspberries and crème pastissière.

STB ★★ Hotel

☽ *Open 1 May to 20 Oct* ♞ *Rooms: 10 en suite* ⛉ *DB&B £59–£71 B&B £38–£48* ✘ *Lunch £ Dinner 4 course menu £££* Ⓥ *Vegetarians welcome* ♣ *Children welcome* ✌ *No smoking in dining room* ⬚ *Credit cards: Mastercard/ Eurocard, American Express, Visa* ⓘ *Proprietors: John & Eliza Allen*

Muir of Ord Ross-shire IV6 7UH
Tel: 01463 870492 Fax: 01463 870492
E-mail: eliza@ord-house.com
Web: htpp://www.ord-house.com
On A832 Ullapool-Marybank, ½ mile west of Muir of Ord. [C4]

NAIRN

Boath House

- *"An absolute gem!"*
- *Innovative Scottish with European influences.*

BOATH HOUSE is the epitome of style and elegance, coupled with superb cuisine. Wendy and Don Matheson are delightful hosts with a lovingly restored home. The menus are original and well-balanced, and visually appealing. Chef Charles Lockley's dedication to freshness is clear, using innovative ingredients and home-grown produce, which combine to a truly memorable experience.

Seared fillet of sea bass on a citrus cous cous, tapenade and a basil-infused oil. Roasted saddle of venison with a sweet potato purée, sauted foie gras, potato crisps and a Madeira and thyme sauce. Nectarine crème brûlée served with strawberry sorbet-filled tuille basket.

STB ★★★★ Hotel

☽ *Open all year except Christmas Day and Boxing Day Closed to non residents Mon Tue* ♞ *Rooms: 7 en suite* ⛉ *DB&B £82.50–£112.50 B&B £55–£80* ⓢⓟ *Special rates available* ✘ *Lunch booking required ££ Dinner £££* Ⓥ *Vegetarians welcome* ♣ *Children welcome* ♿ *Facilities for disabled visitors* ✌ *No smoking in restaurant* 🐕 *Residents' dogs only by agreement* 🐄 *Member of the Scotch Beef Club* ⬚ *Credit cards: Mastercard/Eurocard, American Express, Visa, Switch, Delta* ⓘ *Proprietor: Wendy Matheson*

Auldearn Nairn IV12 5TE
Tel: 01667 454896 Fax: 01667 455469
E-mail: wendy@boath-house.com
Web: www.boath-house.demon.co.uk
On A96, 2 miles east of Nairn. [C3]

NAIRN

Cawdor Tavern

- *"A bustling little tavern with good food and friendly hospitality."*
- *The best of traditional Scottish fare.*

CAWDOR TAVERN is a traditional country pub in a building which was originally the old castle workshop. Open log fires and a wood burning stove give a warm welcome to complement some real quality bar meals. The restaurant offers modern Scottish cuisine using fresh, local produce. Popular with locals and visitors.

Warm crab tart on a pool of white wine and chive cream. Loin of Scottish lamb carved on a pillow of black pudding, with rhubarb chutney and lovage jus. Chilled lemon posset with home-made shortbread fingers.

◐ Open all year, except 25 and 26 Dec ✕ Lunch £ Dinner ££ Ⓥ Vegetarians welcome ✶ Children welcome ♿ Facilities for disabled visitors ⊁ No smoking area in restaurant 🆔 Credit cards: Mastercard/Eurocard, American Express, Visa, Diners Club, Switch ⓝ Proprietor: Norman Sinclair

Cawdor Nairn IV12 5XP
Tel: 01667 404 777 Fax: 01667 404 777
E-mail: cawdort@aol.com
Web: www.cawdortavern.com
Turn off A96 to Cawdor. Tavern is clearly signposted. [C3]

NAIRN

Golf View Hotel & Leisure Club

- *"A popular hotel extending a big welcome and excellent facilities."*
- *Modern Scottish cooking.*

THE GOLF VIEW is within an hour's drive of 25 golf courses. Its leisure club has a magnificent pool and Nautilus equipped gym. Fish and shellfish feature strongly on the restaurant's nightly-changing table d'hôte menu, as well as locally-sourced meat and game. Vegetarian dishes show great imagination and fresh bread is baked daily. The Conservatory serves food all day.

Cullen skink risotto with leeks, finished with a wild forest mushroom mayonnaise, and freshly shaved Parmesan. Medallions of Sutherland venison with juniper rested on a red cabbage marmalade with brambles. Mille Feuille of shortbread and cranachan on a raspberry sauce.

STB ★★★★ Hotel
Green Tourism Two Leaf Silver Award

◐ Open all year 🛏 Rooms: 48 en suite 🛌 DB&B £70-£86 B&B £50-£65 🅂 Special rates available ✕ Food available all day £-££ Lunch £-££ Dinner 4 course menu £££ Ⓥ Vegetarians welcome ✶ Children welcome ♿ Facilities for disabled visitors ⊁ No smoking in restaurant and conservatory 🆔 Credit cards: Mastercard/Eurocard, American Express, Visa, Diners Club, Switch ⓝ Operations Director: Greta Anderson

Seabank Road Nairn IV12 4HD
Tel: 01667 452301 Fax: 01667 455267
E-mail: rooms@morton-hotels.com
Web: www.morton-hotels.com
At west end of Nairn. Seaward side of A96. Turn off at large Parish Church. Hotel on right. [C3]

NAIRN

The Newton Hotel & Highland Conference Centre

- *"A comfortable country house hotel in a superb setting."*
- *Modern Scottish.*

THE NEWTON HOTEL is set in 21 acres of secluded grounds with magnificent views over the Moray Firth and the Ross-shire Hills beyond. The restaurant offers interesting menus focusing on best use of local produce, which are treated skilfully and imaginatively by the chef.

Isle of Skye scallop and langoustine spring roll, ribboned with a Thai dressing. Barbecued rump of lamb, carved over a parsnip and potato mash, with a red onion gravy. Raspberry 'cranachan' cheesecake with a honey cream.

STB ★★★★ Hotel
Green Tourism Two Leaf Silver Award

◐ *Open all year* 🏨 *Rooms: 57 en suite* 🛏 *DB&B £75–£95 B&B £55–£75* SP *Special rates available* ✗ *Food available all day £££ Lunch £ Dinner £££* V *Vegetarians welcome* ☀ *Children welcome* ♿ *Facilities for disabled visitors* 🚭 *No smoking in restaurant* 💳 *Credit cards: Mastercard/Eurocard, American Express, Visa, Diners Club, Switch* ⚑ *General Manager: Kevin Reid*

Inverness Road Nairn IV12 4RX
Tel: 01667 453144 Fax: 01667 454026
E-mail: info@morton-hotels.com
Web: www.morton-hotels.com
West of Nairn town centre on A96. [C3]

NAIRN

Sunny Brae Hotel

- *"No wonder guests constantly return."*
- *Scottish cooking with European flair.*

SUNNY BRAE HOTEL is a stylish and welcoming small hotel with stunning sea views over the Moray Firth. The bedrooms are attractively appointed with quality furniture and fittings. Sylvia who is German is the chef – the menus have a distinct European influence with a strong emphasis on quality local produce.

Sautéed king scallops served on bed of mixed salad leaves with lemon, basil and white wine dressing. Braised Nairnshire lamb shank with red wine and rowanberry sauce, infused with rosemary and served with aubergine risotto and ratatouille. Cranachan with Royal Brackla malt whisky and Scottish summer berries.

STB ★★★★ Small Hotel
Green Tourism Two Leaf Silver Award

◐ *Open Mar to Oct* 🏨 *Rooms: 9 en suite* 🛏 *DB&B £57.50–£66.50 B&B £35–44* SP *Special rates available* ✗ *Lunch residents only ££ Dinner non residents booking essential ££* V *Vegetarians welcome* ☀ *Children welcome* ♿ *Limited facilities for disabled visitors* 🚭 *Smoking in lounge only* 💳 *Credit cards: Mastercard/ Eurocard, Visa, Switch, Delta, JCB* ⚑ *Owners: Sylvia & Ian Bochel*

Marine Road Nairn IV12 4EA
Tel: 01667 452309 Fax: 01667 454860
E-mail: sunnybrae@easynet.co.uk
Web: www.vacations-scotland.co.uk/sunnybrae.htm
Follow A96 Aberdeen-Inverness road through Nairn, at roundabout carry straight onto Marine Road, hotel on left. [C3]

NEW LANARK

New Lanark Mill Hotel

- *"An exciting opportunity to experience a unique hotel set amongst Scotland's industrial heritage."*
- *Modern Scottish.*

NEW LANARK MILL HOTEL has a magnificent location and has been cleverly modernised combining original features with all the contemporary facilities required in a modern hotel. The kitchen prepare fresh Scottish produce, respectfully presented in modern style by Head Chef Stephen Nye and his team. An interesting and appealing place.

Warm tart of sweet red onions glazed with Swiss cheese on a hazelnut dressing. Roasted loin of pork with a lemon and sage stuffing, served with caramelised apples. Steamed gingerbread pudding with a wicked chocolate sauce.

STB ★★★★ Hotel

◐ Open all year ⌂ Rooms: 38 en suite ⌘ DB&B £37.50–49.50 B&B £30–£37.50 ⊞ Special rates available ✖ Food available all day £ Lunch ££ Dinner ££ Ⓥ Vegetarians welcome ✲ Children welcome ♿ Facilities for disabled visitors ⊁ No smoking in restaurant ⌇ Dogs welcome ⊟ Credit cards: Mastercard/Eurocard, American Express, Visa, Diners Club, Switch, Delta ⚑ General Manager: Stephen Owen

*Mill One New Lanark ML11 9DB
Tel: 01555 667200 Fax: 01555 667222
E-mail: hotel@newlanark.org
Web: www.newlanark.org
From the town of Lanark, follow signs for New Lanark south for ½ mile. Hotel is through the gates and 100 metres to the right. [C6]*

NEWBURGH

Udny Arms Hotel

- *"A friendly well run hotel serving quality food in comfortable surroundings."*
- *Creative Scottish cooking.*

DINING is in the split-level bistro where Chefs Vincent Pasquelin and Cyril Kyzoprach change the extensive à la carte menu every six weeks, and include a handful of 'specials' which change daily. There is a Café Bar where bar food is served at alternative prices. 1 AA Rosette. Member of the Certified Aberdeen Angus Scheme.

Monkfish and scallop terrine with an aged balsamic vinaigrette and basil dressing. Char-grilled scallops on wilted spinach, served with saffron butter sauce. Five little 'Udny' treats, or the original sticky toffee pudding.

STB ★★★ Hotel

◐ Open all year except Christmas Night and Boxing Night ⌂ Rooms: 26 en suite ⌘ DB&B £40–£55 B&B £45–£82 ⊞ Special rates available ✖ Lunch £ Dinner ££ Ⓥ Vegetarians welcome ✲ Children welcome ♿ Facilities for disabled visitors ⊟ Credit cards: Mastercard/ Eurocard, American Express, Visa, Diners Club, Switch, Delta, JCB ⚑ Sole Owners/Proprietors: Denis & Jennifer Craig

*Main Street Newburgh AB41 6BL
Tel: 01358 789444 Fax: 01358 789012
E-mail: enquiry@udny.demon.co.uk
Web: www.udny.co.uk
On A975, 2½ miles off A90 Aberdeen-Peterhead – 15 minutes from Aberdeen. [D4]*

NEWTON STEWART

Corsemalzie House Hotel

- *"A comfortable country house in a peaceful woodland setting offering fresh home cooking."*
- *Modern, Scottish cooking.*

CORSEMALZIE is a peaceful and quiet country mansion. A cosy bar serves lighter meals and lunches while the dining room is more formal and looks out onto the well-tended gardens. The hotel has a kitchen garden which offers fresh vegetables to complement all meals. Corsemalzie also has its own game, fishing and shooting.

Roulade of smoked chicken and smoked local pheasant, with fruits of the forest chutney. Grilled Luce Bay scallops, wrapped in smoked salmon, and served with a ginger and lime butter sauce. Warm pear, strawberry and almond crumble served with real strawberry ice cream.

STB ★★★★ Hotel

◐ Open 1 Mar to 20 Jan except Christmas Day and Boxing Day ♜ Rooms: 14 en suite ⛉ DB&B from £59.50 B&B £40–£49.50 ⓢⓟ Special rates available ✕ Lunch £-££ Dinner £££ Ⓥ Vegetarians welcome ☇ Children welcome ⚒ Facilities for disabled visitors – ground floor only ⌒ No smoking in dining room ▣ Credit cards: Mastercard/Eurocard, American Express, Visa, Switch, Delta ⋈ Proprietor: Peter McDougall

*Port William Newton Stewart DG8 9RL
Tel: 01988 860 254 Fax: 01988 860 213
E-mail: corsemalzie@ndirect.co.uk
Web: www.corsemalzie-house.ltd.uk
Halfway along B7005 Glenluce-Wigtown, off A714 Newton Stewart-Port William or A747 Glenluce-Port William. [C7]*

NEWTON STEWART

Creebridge House Hotel

- *"A choice of interesting dishes all skilfully prepared using quality local produce."*
- *Imaginative country house cooking.*

AT CREEBRIDGE there is a choice of eating during the day; the Bridges, a welcoming bar/brasserie, or the Garden Restaurant, which is more formal. Tea/coffee is available on the terrace. Chef/proprietor Chris Walker presents imaginative table d'hôte menus and outstanding à la carte bar menus.

Seared Kirkcudbright scallops with asparagus and saffron cream. Smoked chicken on haggis with Drambuie cream. Iced banana and caramel parfait.

STB ★★★ Hotel

◐ Open all year except 24 to 26 Dec ♜ Rooms: 19 en suite ⛉ DB&B £45–£60 B&B £30–£42 ⓢⓟ Special rates available ✕ Lunch £ Dinner ££ Ⓥ Vegetarians welcome ☇ Children welcome ⚒ Facilities for disabled visitors ⌒ No smoking in restaurant ☙ Member of the Scotch Beef Club ▣ Credit cards: Mastercard/Eurocard, American Express, Visa, Switch, Delta ⋈ Proprietor: Chris Walker

*Minnigaff Newton Stewart Wigtownshire DG8 6NP
Tel: 01671 402121 Fax: 01671 403258
E-mail: info@creebridge.co.uk
Web: www.creebridge.co.uk
From roundabout signposted Newton Stewart on A75, through the town, cross bridge over river to Minnigaff. 250 yards – hotel on left. [C7]*

NEWTON STEWART

Kirroughtree House

- *"Relax and be pampered in this charming house, while indulging in stunning food and magnificent views."*
- *Gourmet Scottish cooking.*

KIRROUGHTREE has two dining rooms reached from the panelled lounge. Head Chef, Ian Bennett, was trained by the celebrated Michel Roux, and his cooking is highly-accomplished. The menus are short, creative and well-balanced. Everything at Kirroughtree is done to the highest standards – polished and professional without being stuffy. 3 AA Rosettes.

Grilled Solway scallops with vegetable relish and beurre blanc. Orange and ginger marinated breast of Gressingham duck served with galette potato, tomato fondue, Savoy cabbage and baby turnips, surrounded by a rich port sauce. Pear tarte tatin drizzled with sauce legere.

STB ★★★ Small Hotel

◐ Open mid Feb to 3 Jan ⌂ Rooms: 17 en suite ⇌ DB&B £70–£100 B&B £60–£85 ▦ Special rates available ✗ Lunch – booking essential ££ Dinner 4 course menu £££ Ⓥ Vegetarians welcome – prior notice required ⚹ Children over 10 years welcome ⤬ No smoking in dining rooms ♨ Member of the Scotch Beef Club ▭ Credit cards: Mastercard/Eurocard, Visa, Switch ▮ Manager: James Stirling

Newton Stewart DG8 6AN
Tel: 01671 402141 Fax: 01671 402425
E-mail: info@kirroughtreehouse.co.uk
Web: www.mcmillanhotels.com
From A75 take A712 New Galloway road, hotel 300 yards on left. [C7]

OBAN

Ards House

- *"Victorian villa with superb views, very good example of Scottish hospitality and traditional Scottish cooking."*
- *Traditional Scottish cooking.*

THIS COMFORTABLE small hotel stands on loch shores, with stunning views. John Bowman is an innovative cook and uses only the best local produce. His wife Jean is an exceptionally warm and friendly hostess – both treat their guests like friends. The daily changing set menu is displayed in the afternoon.

Broccoli, aubergine and saffron custard with local smoked sea trout. Seared saddle of venison on a parsnip and potato pancake with blueberries and a red wine jus. Chocolate ganache slice with florentine crunch and toffee sauce.

STB ★★★ Small Hotel

◐ Open Feb to mid Nov ⌂ Rooms: 7 (6 en suite, 1 with private facilities) ⇌ DB&B £48–£64 B&B £35–£47 ▦ Special rates available ⚑ Restricted licence ✗ Dinner 4 course menu £££ Non-residents – by arrangement Ⓥ Vegetarians – by arrangement ⚹ Children over 14 years welcome ⤬ No smoking throughout ▭ Credit cards: Mastercard/Eurocard, Visa, Switch, Delta, JCB ▮ Proprietors: John & Jean Bowman

Connel, by Oban PA37 1PT
Tel: 01631 710255
E-mail: jb@ardshouse.demon.co.uk
Web: www.ardshouse.com
On main A85 Oban–Tyndrum, 4½ miles north of Oban. [B5]

OBAN

Dungallan House Hotel

- *"Great attention to quality and freshness is shown in Janice Stewart's culinary skills."*
- *Traditional fresh Scottish/home cooking.*

DUNGALLAN HOUSE is owned by George and Janice Stewart. Menus take full advantage of the range of fresh fish and shellfish available locally. Janice Stewart does the cooking. The well-balanced table d'hôte menu offers four/five choices for each course complemented by a very good wine list. 1 AA Rosette.

Gruyère soufflé with a mushroom cream sauce. Mille feuille of seafood. Apple and strawberry pie with home-made vanilla ice cream.

STB ★★★ Hotel

☻ Open all year except Nov Feb ⌂ Rooms: 13, 11 en suite ⇌ DB&B £65–£73 B&B £40–£48 ⓢⓟ Special rates available ✗ Lunch by arrangement £ Dinner £££ Ⓥ Vegetarians welcome ⁕ Children welcome ⚐ Limited facilities for disabled visitors ⌥ No smoking in dining room ☙ Member of the Scotch Beef Club ⊞ Credit cards: Mastercard/Eurocard, Visa ⓚ Directors: Janice & George Stewart

Gallanach Road Oban PA34 4PD
Tel: 01631 563799 Fax: 01631 566711
E-mail: welcome@dungallanhotel-oban.co.uk
Web: www.dungallanhotel-oban.co.uk
In Oban, at Argyll Square, follow signs for Gallanach. ½ mile from Square. [B5]

OBAN

The Gathering Restaurant and O'Donnells Irish Bar

- *"A great atmosphere and interesting food."*
- *Good, plain cooking with lots of imagination.*

FIRST OPENED in 1882 as a supper room for the famous annual Gathering Ball, the Gathering has a distinguished pedigree and is rightly popular with Oban's many tourists. First-class, straightforward dishes use local meat and seafood, as well as imaginative starters and popular 'lighter bites'. The wine list is well-chosen and fairly priced.

Warm scallop salad. Prime Scottish fillet steak flame-grilled, simple but perfect. Selection of fine Scottish cheeses.

☻ Open Easter to New Year except Christmas Day, New Year's Day and some Suns Closed Sun off-season – please telephone Note: closed to public last Thu in Aug ✗ Bar lunch £-££: Bar evening meals £ off-season by reservation Dinner (Restaurant) ££-£££ Ⓥ Vegetarians welcome ⁕ Children welcome ⚐ Facilities for disabled visitors ⌥ No smoking in restaurant ⊞ Credit cards: Mastercard/Eurocard, American Express, Visa, Switch, Delta, JCB ⓚ Owner/Chef: Elaine Cameron

Breadalbane Street Oban PA34 5NZ
Tel: 01631 565421/566159/564849
Fax: 01631 565421
Entering Oban from A85 (Glasgow) one-way system. Turn left at Deanery Brae into Breadalbane Street (signs for swimming pool etc.) then right at bottom of Deanery Brae. [B5]

OBAN

Isle of Eriska

- *"Idyllic setting, wonderful food, a very special place."*
- *Gourmet country house cuisine.*

THE BUCHANAN-SMITH family run this exceptional country house with the highest standard of professional service. Chef Robert MacPherson has a well-established cooking style, his enthusiasm and skill are evident in the menus and dishes presented. The hotel has a full leisure complex. 3 AA Rosettes. Winner The Macallan Taste of Scotland Hotel of the Year Award 1994.

Wild rabbit and courgette timbale with squab pigeon, morels and a Puy lentil velouté. Fresh langoustines set around an open ravioli of squat lobsters and seared scallops together with spring vegetables and a Champagne sauce. Agen prunes poached in red wine and served with a claret sauce.

STB ★★★★★ Hotel

❶ Open all year except Jan and Feb ⌂ Rooms: 17 en suite ⌯ B&B £210–£260 ✖ Lunch – residents only Dinner 7 course menu ££££ Open to non-residents for dinner only Ⓥ Vegetarians welcome ☆ Children over 10 years old welcome at dinner ♿ Facilities for disabled visitors ⌦ No smoking in dining room ☙ Member of the Scotch Beef Club ⊞ Credit cards: Mastercard/Eurocard, American Express, Visa, Switch ⋈ Partner: B Buchanan-Smith

Ledaig by Oban Argyll PA37 1SD
Tel: 01631 720 371 Fax: 01631 720 531
E-mail: office@eriska-hotel.co.uk
Web: www.eriska-hotel.co.uk
A85 north of Oban, at Connel Bridge take A828 for 4 miles. North of Benderloch [B5]

OBAN

Knipoch Hotel

- *"A lovely country house hotel in a peaceful lochside location."*
- *Modern Scottish.*

THIS LOVELY house is owned by the Craig family who offer a house of tranquillity, good dining and solace for the traveller. Recent additions include a smokehouse, with produce incorporated into their menus, and a mail order service. The wine list is extensive, as is the range of malts and Cognacs.

Knipoch-smoked salmon: salmon cured and marinated then smoked for three days. Fillet of Aberdeen Angus beef, roasted whole then served sliced with a béarnaise sauce. Whisky crêpes served with whisky caramel sauce and vanilla ice cream.

STB ★★★★ Hotel

❶ Open mid Feb to mid Dec ⌂ Rooms: 16 en suite ⌯ DB&B £66–£101.50 B&B £37–£72 SP Special rates available ✖ Lunch ££ Dinner £££ Ⓥ Vegetarians welcome ☆ Children welcome ⌦ No smoking in restaurant ⌬ Dogs welcome ⊞ Credit cards: Mastercard/Eurocard, American Express, Visa, Diners Club, Switch, Delta ⋈ Director/Owner: Mr Nicky Craig

Knipoch by Oban Argyll PA34 4QT
Tel: 01852 316251 Fax: 01852 316249
E-mail: reception@knipochhotel.co.uk
Web: www.knipochhotel.co.uk
On the A816 south of Oban. ½ mile along Loch Feochan (6 miles) on left-hand side. [B5]

OBAN

Loch Melfort Hotel and Restaurant

- *"A mesmerising spot where time slips by...."*
- *Fresh, imaginative Scottish cuisine.*

UNDER owners Philip and Rosalind Lewis, the hotel has been tastefully extended to take advantage of the magnificent land and seascape. The hotel offers the best of fresh local produce – particularly local fish and shellfish – all skilfully presented and cheerfully served. Loch Melfort has a well balanced wine list. 2 AA Rosettes.

Courgette and rosemary soup. Roast saddle of Morayshire lamb with garlic and a sage and Dubonnet sauce. Baked chocolate pudding.

STB ★★★★ Hotel

◐ *Open all year except mid Jan to mid Feb* ⌕ *Rooms: 26 en suite* ⌕ *DB&B £45–£85 B&B £35–£55* ⌕ *Special rates available* ✕ *Food available all day from £ Lunch (Skerry Bistro) £ Dinner £££* Ⓥ *Vegetarians welcome* ✱ *Children welcome* ⌕ *Some facilities for disabled visitors* ⌕ *No smoking in dining room* ⌕ *Credit cards: Mastercard/Eurocard, American Express, Visa, Switch* ⌕ *Proprietors: Rosalind & Philip Lewis*

Arduaine by Oban Argyll PA34 4XG
Tel: 01852 200 233 Fax: 01852 200 214
E-mail: lmhotel@aol.com
Web: www.loch-melfort.co.uk
On A816, 19 miles south of Oban. [B5]

OBAN

The Manor House

- *"Delightful hotel offering excellent hospitality and wonderful views across Oban Bay."*
- *Modern Scottish with French influences.*

MANOR HOUSE retains much of the charm and atmosphere of the past and is a charming well maintained hotel in a stunning location. It offers a five course table d'hôte dinner menu which changes daily, according to what is available and seasonal. The cooking is fresh and creative. 1 AA Rosette.

Squat lobsters in garlic butter served on a seasonal salad. Tournedos of beef with crushed black pepper, sauté potatoes and bacon-bean parcel. Chocolate chip Drambuie parfait.

STB ★★★★ Hotel

◐ *Open all year N.B. From Nov to end Feb closed Sun 3pm through to Tue 3pm* ⌕ *Rooms: 11 en suite* ⌕ *DB&B £50–£80 B&B £30–£60* ⌕ *Special rates available* ✕ *Lunch 3 course menu from £ Dinner 5 course menu £££* Ⓥ *Vegetarians welcome* ⌕ *No smoking in dining room and bedrooms* ⌕ *Credit cards: Mastercard/Eurocard, American Express, Visa, Switch* ⌕ *Manageress: Gabriel Wijker*

Gallanach Road Oban PA34 4LS
Tel: 01631 562087 Fax: 01631 563053
E-mail: me@managed-estates.co.uk
Web: www.highlandholidays.net
From Argyll Square, Oban, follow signs for Gallanach and the car ferry. Continue for approx ¼ mile. Hotel on right-hand side of road. [B5]

OBAN

The Waterfront Restaurant

- *"Distinctive and talented seafood treatment in casual environment."*
- *Bold and skilled seafood.*

THE MOTTO here is 'from the pier to the pan as fast as you can'! It is bright and airy and the theme is positively 'fish'. The chef is 'on view' preparing fresh seafood for lunch/dinner. All produce is carefully cooked to order and presented professionally in a relaxed atmosphere.

Marinated scallop and langoustine tail salad with confit tomatoes. Whole black bream with pak-choi. Whisky poached pears with Irn-bru ice cream and rhubarb coulis.

◐ Open Easter to Christmas ✘ Lunch – depending on choice £-££££ Dinner £-££££ Ⓥ Vegetarians welcome ✿ Children welcome ⚑ Guide dogs welcome ⊞ Credit cards: Mastercard/Eurocard, American Express, Visa, Switch ⓝ Head Chef/Manager: Alex Needham

No 1 The Pier Oban Argyll PA34 4LW
Tel: 01631 563110 Fax: 01631 563110
Approaching Oban from north or south. Look out for the clock tower – park wherever you can and head for railway and ferry pier. Restaurant is well-signposted from start of pier. [B5]

OBAN

Willowburn Hotel

- *"Comfortable relaxing surroundings enhanced by good cooking."*
- *Outstanding Scottish cooking.*

WILLOWBURN stands in 1½ acres down to Clachan Sound and offers spectacular views from all rooms. Guests are made very welcome by owners Jan Wolfe and Chris Mitchell. Menus change daily and offer a generous choice of local produce served with fresh garden vegetables. The hotel has 2 AA Rosettes.

Our own smoked salmon with citrus fruits and tomato. Medallions of roasted venison saddle served on potato scones, with a hazelnut stuffing, game chips and an orange and juniper sauce. Tuille baskets with warm strawberries in vanilla sauce.

STB ★★★★ Small Hotel

◐ Open 1 Mar to 2 Jan 🛏 Rooms: 7 en suite 🍴 DB&B £50–£60 🛎 Special rates available for longer stays ✘ Lunch – residents only £ Dinner £££ Ⓥ Vegetarians welcome ✿ Well-behaved children welcome ⚬ Smoking permitted in bar only ⊞ Credit cards: Mastercard/Eurocard, Visa, Switch, Delta, JCB ⓝ Proprietors: Jan Wolfe & Chris Mitchell

Clachan-Seil by Oban Argyll PA34 4TJ
Tel: 01852 300276 Fax: 01852 300597
E-mail: willowburn.hotel@virgin.net
Web: www.willowburn.co.uk
On the Island of Seil, near Oban, just a few 100 yards from 'The Bridge over the Atlantic'. [B5]

OBAN

Yacht Corryvreckan

- *"After a day's sailing, gather round the table for a glass of wine, a wonderful freshly cooked dinner and some good stories."*
- *Best fresh home cooking.*

DOUGLAS AND MARY Lindsay offer a really unique experience – they make a really tremendous team on this beautiful yacht. Not only does Mary provide a dinner to be proud of, but also home-made soups every lunchtime and freshly baked scones and chocolate cake for that afternoon refreshment on the ocean wave.

A salad of fresh and smoked salmon, with strawberries. Venison, peppered with crushed juniper, with a wild berry sauce. Zingy lime parfait.

● Open Apr to Oct 🏠 Cabins: 5 twin berth cabins, 3 heads with shower 🛏 DB&B £445–£495 per person for 1 week cruise – all incl 💲 Special rates available for whole boat charter 🍷 Unlicensed – wine available with dinner 🚭 No smoking below deck Parking available 💳: No credit cards 👤 Proprietors: Douglas & Mary Lindsay

*Dal an Eas Kilmore, Oban Argyll PA34 4XU
Tel: 01631 770246 Fax: 01631 770246
E-mail: yacht.corryvreckan@virgin.net
Web: www.corryvreckan.co.uk
[B5]*

OLD DEER

Saplinbrae House Hotel

- *"A favourite with the locals – good value for money."*
- *Modern Scottish cuisine.*

SAPLINBRAE HOUSE HOTEL is a wonderful building with beautifully-kept gardens. There are two dining areas here; the bar offering a more casual dining experience and the brasserie where one can relax in more formal surroundings. Menus are appealing and offer an interesting modern Scottish theme using best local produce.

Carrot and clam mousse set on watercress with an orange and ginger coulis. Pork fillet stuffed with Stilton and prunes, rolled in oatmeal, oven-baked with a Calvados jus. Saplinbrae clarty pudding with rich toffee sauce.

● Open all year except Christmas Day, Boxing Day and 1, 2 Jan 🏠 Rooms: 7 en suite 🛏 DB&B £50–£75 B&B £33–£55 💲 Special rates available ✖ Lunch £ Dinner ££ 🆅 Vegetarians welcome 👶 Children welcome 💳 Credit cards: Mastercard, Visa, Switch 👤 Owners: Julia & Andrew Brown

*Old Deer, nr Mintlaw Peterhead Aberdeenshire AB42 4LP
Tel: 01771 623515 Fax: 01771 624472
E-mail: enquiries@saplinbrae.co.uk
Web: www.saplinbrae.co.uk
12 miles west of Peterhead and 1 mile west of Mintlaw on A950 New Pitsligo Road. ¾ mile from Aden Country Park. [D4]*

OLDMELDRUM

Meldrum House

- *"Charming hosts offering excellent food in lovely surroundings."*
- *Creative Scottish cooking.*

RESIDENT proprietors Douglas and Eileen Pearson are attentive and courteous hosts who make you very welcome to their home. Residents and non-residents can enjoy an imaginative and well-constructed four course table d'hôte menu carefully overseen by enthusiastic Chef, Mark Will. To complement the meal there is a comprehensive, reasonable priced wine list.

Cod and rosemary fish cakes with saffron and lime sauce. Breast of duck with ginger and grapefruit sauce. White and dark chocolate mousse with caramelised sugar.

STB ★★★ Hotel

◐ Open all year 🏚 Rooms: 9 en suite 🛏 DB&B £114–£124 B&B £105–£115 🆂🅿 Special rates available ✕ Lunch ££ Dinner £££ Ⓥ Vegetarians welcome ⚘ Children welcome ♿ Facilities for disabled visitors ⊬ No smoking in restaurant 💳 Credit cards: Mastercard/Eurocard, Visa, Switch ⚐ Proprietors: Douglas & Eileen Pearson

Oldmeldrum Aberdeenshire AB51 OAE
Tel: 01651 872294 Fax: 01651 872464
E-mail: dpmeldrum@aol.com
Web: www.meldrumhouse.com
Main gates on A947 (Aberdeen to Banff road). 1 mile north of Old Meldrum. 13 miles north of Aberdeen airport. [D4]

ONICH BY FORT WILLIAM

Allt-nan-Ros Hotel

- *"A real Highland atmosphere with a pride taken in the presentation of good produce."*
- *Modern Scottish cooking.*

ALLT-NAN-ROS is an attractive 19th century shooting lodge personally run by James and Fiona Mcleod. Dinner is served in a delightful picture-windowed room overlooking the loch. Menus offer a range of familiar Scottish dishes, prepared from locally sourced ingredients cooked with French influences and presented in an imaginative and innovative style. 2 AA Rosettes.

Peppered home-smoked lamb, combined with basil leaves, rocket and Parmesan. Fillets of lemon sole, served with potato, tarragon and pear compote, cherry tomato confit, mint butter and woodland mushroom quenelles. Brioche pudding, chocolate ganache, lime marmalade and crème fraîche ice cream.

STB ★★★★ Hotel

◐ Open 1 Jan to 10 Nov 🏚 Rooms: 20 en suite 🛏 DB&B £60–£80 B&B £38–£55 🆂🅿 Special rates available ✕ Lunch from £ Dinner 5 course menu from £££ Ⓥ Vegetarians welcome ⊬ No smoking in dining room 💳 Credit cards: Mastercard/Eurocard, American Express, Visa, Diners Club, Switch, JCB ⚐ Proprietor: James & Fiona Macleod

Onich Fort William Inverness-shire PH33 6RY
Tel: 01855 821 210 Fax: 01855 821 462
E-mail: allt-nan-ros@zetnet.co.uk
Web: www.allt-nan-ros.co.uk
On A82, 10 miles south of Fort William. [B4]

ONICH BY FORT WILLIAM

Cuilcheanna House

- *"Assured, skilled cooking in a warm, welcoming and comfortable house."*
- *Creative Scottish fayre.*

This former farmhouse (17th Century origin), now a small hotel personally run by Linda and Russell Scott, overlooks Loch Linnhe with outstanding views towards Glencoe and the Isle of Mull. Linda makes good use of prime local produce and fresh herbs. The set four-course dinner is complemented by a hand-picked wine list and malt whisky selection. Excellent Scottish breakfasts.

Frittata of Feta, roasted red peppers and baby spinach, with a parsley and walnut dressing. Venison haunch steak with coriander and juniper crust and gin and lime sauce. Traditional Eyemouth tart with almond custard cream.

STB ★★★★ Small Hotel

◐ Open Easter to end Oct ⌂ Rooms: 7 en suite ⌘ DB&B £45–£48 B&B £29 ☞ Special rates available ✘ Dinner 4 course menu ££ Reservations essential for non-residents Ⓥ Vegetarians welcome ✄ No smoking throughout ▣ Credit cards: Mastercard/Eurocard, Visa, Switch, Delta ⚐ Proprietors: Linda & Russell Scott

Onich Fort William Inverness-shire PH33 6SD
Tel: 01855 821226
E-mail: relax@cuilcheanna.freeserve.co.uk
Signposted 300m off A82 in village of Onich – 9 miles south of Fort William. [B4]

ONICH BY FORT WILLIAM

Four Seasons Bistro & Bar

- *"A popular location with hill-walkers, with a welcoming fire, and where a tasty steak can be had."*
- *Modern home style Scottish cooking.*

FOUR SEASONS is a warm, welcoming haven with views of Loch Linnhe and Ardgour. It is a family business, with pleasant staff, exuding a happy atmosphere. The menus are interesting, with well-cooked food, and much evidence of fresh, locally caught seafood prepared and presented with care and attention to detail.

Salad of langoustine with hot garlic butter and lemon and parsley dressing. Rack of lamb with a honey, chilli and soy sauce glaze served with steamed rice and stir-fried vegetables. Caramelised banana tart with vanilla custard.

◐ Open Christmas and New Year period Winter limited opening until Easter Ⓥ Vegetarians welcome ✱ Children welcome ♿ Facilities for disabled visitors ✄ No smoking in eating areas ▣ Credit cards: Mastercard/Eurocard, American Express, Visa ⚐ Manageress: Susan Heron

Inchree Onich by Fort William PH33 6SE
Tel: 01855 821393 Fax: 01855 821287
E-mail: enquiry@restaurant-scotland.com
Web: www.restaurant-scotland.com
8 miles south of Fort William. Take Inchree turn-off, ¼ mile south of Corran Ferry, then 250 yards. [B4]

ONICH BY FORT WILLIAM

The Lodge On The Loch Hotel

- *"Elegant dining with a friendly atmosphere and flavoursome food."*
- *Stylish Scottish cooking.*

THIS IS a traditional, comfortable hotel with friendly, helpful staff and managed by professional husband and wife team Jamie and Jackie Burns. The decor reflects the beauty of the surrounding gardens and countryside. Bedrooms are comfortable and the dining room has delightful loch views. The table d'hôte menus feature several Scottish dishes.

Arbroath smokie potato cake, tomato and chilli salsa and balsamic syrup. Pan-seared Aberdeen Angus steak, rosemary mash, veal jus and pear and rosemary jelly. Lemon mousse with mango and raspberry sauces and, cookie spoons.

STB ★★★★ Hotel

◐ Apr to Oct also open Xmas and New Year 🏨 Rooms: 20, 18 en suite 🛏 DB&B from £69.50 ℗ Special rates available ✕ Light lunch £ Dinner 4 course menu £££ Ⓥ Vegetarians welcome ⚹ Children over 12 years welcome ♿ Facilities for disabled visitors ✔ No smoking in dining room 💳 Credit cards: Mastercard/Eurocard, Visa, Switch, Delta 🍴 Managers: Jamie & Jackie Burns

Onich nr Fort William The Scottish Highlands PH33 6RY
Tel: 01855 821237 Fax: 01855 821463
E-mail: reservations@freedomglen.co.uk
Web: www.freedomglen.co.uk
On A82, 1 mile north of the Ballachulish Bridge. [B4]

ONICH BY FORT WILLIAM

Onich Hotel

- *"Sit in comfort and enjoy the view and the friendly service."*
- *Blends of traditional and contemporary Scottish.*

THE ONICH HOTEL is ideally located on the shores of Loch Linnhe. The hotel is well maintained from the interior to the well tended gardens. Managing Director Stewart Leitch's commitment to all aspects of the hotel is evident – from the calibre of staff to the quality of produce and cooking from the kitchen.

Roasted Loch Linnhe langoustines with garlic and garden herb butter. Braised shank of Lochaber lamb with rosemary and red wine jus. Summer fruits set in Champagne jelly with apple sorbet.

STB ★★★★ Small Hotel

◐ Open all year 🏨 Rooms: 25 en suite 🛏 DB&B £54–£78 B&B £32–£52 ℗ Special rates available ✕ Bar meals available all day ££ Dinner £££ Ⓥ Vegetarians welcome ⚹ Children welcome ♿ Facilities for disabled visitors ✔ No smoking in restaurant 🐕 Dogs welcome 💳 Credit cards: Mastercard/Eurocard, American Express, Visa, Diners Club, Switch, Delta 🍴 Managing Director: Stewart Leitch

Onich by Fort William PH33 7RY
Tel: 01855 821214 Fax: 01855 821484
E-mail:reservations@onich-fortwilliam.co.uk
Web: www.onich-fortwilliam.co.uk
On A82 in the village of Onich on the shores of Loch Linnhe – 12 miles south of Fort William. [B4]

PAISLEY

Makerston House

- *"A spacious guest house full of character, offering a friendly Scottish welcome."*
- *Scottish home cooking.*

MARY McCUE was housekeeper at Makerston in the past and now welcomes guests in her amicable style making them feel part of the family. Food is prepared and presented in simple style with attention to flavour and quality of ingredients. There is also much home baking here to be enjoyed 'in the jewel in Paisley's crown'.

Red pepper soup. Roast leg of lamb and poached minted pear with gratin dauphinoise, courgette and carrot batons and rosemary and thyme. Pavlova.

◐ Open 3 Jan to 24 Dec ⌂ Rooms: 11, 8 en suite ⌻ DB&B £37.50–£55 B&B £25–£35 Special rates available Lunch – pre booking for private functions ££ Dinner – pre booking necessary Ⅴ Vegetarians welcome ⚹ Children welcome ⚐ No smoking in dining room ▦ Credit cards: Eurocard, Visa ⓚ Owner: Mrs Mary McCue

19 Park Road Paisley PA2 6JP
Tel: 0141 884 2520 Fax: 0141 884 2520
Less than 5 miles from Glasgow Airport. Follow signs to Paisley University then to shopping centre, turn right into Falside Road, continue uphill until Park Road and house is on right hand side. [C6]

PEAT INN

The Peat Inn

- *"A first-class dining experience is to be had at The Peat Inn."*
- *Unpretentious top quality modern cuisine.*

CHEF AND owner David Wilson has created a world-class restaurant whose name is synonymous with good food. All ingredients are of the utmost freshness, quality and, with tremendous flair, transformed into truly memorable dishes. His wine list is formidable but provides great choice and value for money. 3 AA Rosettes.

Roasted scallops on leek, potato and smoked bacon with pea purée. Peat Inn 'cassoulet' of lamb, pork and duck with flageolet beans. Caramelised banana on a banana cake with coconut ice cream.

STB ★★★★★ Restaurant with Rooms

◐ Open all year except Christmas Day and New Year's Day Closed Sun Mon ⌂ Suites: 8 en suite ⌻ DB&B £90–£98, £65–£95 ✕ Lunch except Sun Mon 3 course menu ££ Dinner except Sun Mon 3 course menu £££ Ⅴ Vegetarians welcome ⚹ Children welcome ♿ Facilities for disabled visitors ⚐ No smoking in dining rooms ☙ Member of the Scotch Beef Club ▦ Credit cards: Mastercard/Eurocard, American Express, Visa, Switch, ⓚ Partners: David & Patricia Wilson

Peat Inn by Cupar Fife KY15 5LH
Tel: 01334 840206 Fax: 01334 840530
E-mail: reception@thepeatinn.co.uk
Web: www.standrews.co.uk/hotelspeatinn.htp
At junction of B940/B941, 6 miles south west of St Andrews. [D5]

PEEBLES

Castle Venlaw Hotel

- *"A relaxing atmosphere with true Scottish hospitality."*
- *Modern Scottish.*

CASTLE VENLAW is owned and run by John and Shirley Sloggie, both experienced and professional hoteliers. It has been totally refurbished to a very high standard whilst retaining many original features. It offers a warm welcome, comfortable surroundings and good food prepared by Chef Alex Burns in a traditional style with contemporary undertones.

Stack of egg and char-grilled peppers splashed with pepper purée and coriander essence topped with fried vegetables. Pan-fried cannon of venison presented on mint mash, glazed vegetables and local ale jus. Chocolate croissant pudding served with marmalade syrup and vanilla cream.

STB ★★★★ Hotel

◐ Open all year ⌂ Rooms: 13 en suite ⛌ DB&B £49.50–£90 B&B £45–£77 ⓢⓟ Special rates available ✗ Lunch ££ Dinner £££ Non-Residents welcome Ⓥ Vegetarians welcome ⚸ Children welcome ⚹ No smoking in dining room ⚐ Dogs welcome ⊞ Credit cards: Mastercard/Eurocard, Visa, Switch, Delta ⚑ Proprietors: John & Shirley Sloggie

Edinburgh Road Peebles EH45 8QG
Tel: 01721 720384 Fax: 01721 724066
E-mail: enquiries@venlaw.co.uk
Web: www.venlaw.co.uk
From Peebles take the Edinburgh road A703, hotel is ¾ mile on the right. From Edinburgh follow A703 to Penicuik and Peebles, the hotel drive is on the left just after the 30 mph sign. [D6]

PEEBLES

Cringletie House Hotel

- *"An elegant comfortable hotel offering excellent cuisine in a relaxed atmosphere."*
- *Modern Scottish cooking.*

CRINGLETIE HOUSE has been carefully restored to retain its 19th century features, retaining family portraits in the main room. The atmosphere here is both relaxing and romantic with attention to detail in both service and carefully designed menus. The hotel now has an open air theatre for musical evenings.

Charlotte of oak smoked salmon with shellfish mousseline, diced cucumber and caviar sauce. Breast of Gressingham duck on a garden rhubarb and vanilla compote, edged with cinnamon juices. Tower of sweet meringue and shortbread, layered with lemon curd and bitter orange marmalade, served with a citrus sorbet.

STB ★★★★ Hotel

◐ Open all year ⌂ Rooms: 14 en suite ⛌ DB&B £200 per room B&B £150 per room ⓢⓟ Special rates available ✗ Lunch ££ Dinner ££££ Ⓥ Vegetarians welcome ⚸ Children welcome ⚹ No smoking in restaurant ⚘ Member of the Scotch Beef Club ⊞ Credit cards: Mastercard/Eurocard, American Express, Visa, Switch, Delta ⚑ General Manager: Charles Cormack

Peebles EH45 8PL Tel: 01721 730 233
Fax: 01721 730 244
E-mail: enquiries@cringletie.com
Web: www.cringletie.com
From Peebles take A703, hotel 2 miles on left. [D6]

PEEBLES

Peebles Hotel Hydro

- *"Offers excellent facilities for all ages, not to mention the wide variety of Scottish produce on offer."*
- *Modern Scottish cooking.*

PEEBLES HOTEL HYDRO was custom-built and opened in 1907 with gracious style and most features are retained today. The format for providing facilities and entertainment for the new born to great-grandparents has been fine tuned over the years to create a wonderful resort for all the family. There is also Lazels coffee shop.

Timbale of Achiltibuie smoked salmon with a mousse of broad beans on a strawberry vinaigrette. Loin of Stobo lamb baked in a spinach and raspberry farce, surrounded by a whisky cream. An individual Heather Honey bavarois on a Drambuie sabayon.

STB ★★★★ Hotel

◑ Open all year 🛏 Rooms: 133 en suite 🛌 DB&B £66–£99.25 B&B £52–£84 🆂 Special rates available ✗ Food available all day £ Lunch £ Dinner £££ Ⓥ Vegetarians welcome ✴ Children welcome ♿ Facilities for disabled visitors ✌ Smoking is permitted in the restaurant after 8.45 pm only 💳 Credit cards: Mastercard/Eurocard, American Express, Visa, Diners Club, Switch 🍴 General Manager: Gerard Bony

Innerleithen Road Peebles EH45 8LX
Tel: 01721 720602 Fax: 01721 722999
E-mail: reservation@peebleshotelhydro.co.uk
Web: www.peebleshotelhydro.co.uk
Within Peebles boundaries, hotel is signposted. [D6]

PEEBLES

Sunflower Restaurant

- *"Ideally suited for a light lunch, glass of wine or just good home baking."*
- *Modern-style cooking.*

THE SUNFLOWER RESTAURANT has yellow walls, polished floors, and wooden tables, giving a bright airy atmosphere. The interior has been decorated with a minimalist appearance. The restaurant is ideal for everything, from morning coffee, afternoon tea or a light lunch – ranging from soup and sandwiches to dish of the day.

Crab and red pepper cake with sauce verde and deep-fried rocket. Fillet of Scottish beef with peppered cheese pastry, served with a Merlot and blackberry jelly. Drambuie bread and butter pudding with whisky ice cream.

◑ Open all year except Christmas Day, Boxing Day and 1, 2 Jan Closed Sun between Jan to Apr ✗ Food available all day £ Lunch £ Dinner except Sun to Wed £££ Ⓥ Vegetarians welcome ✴ Children welcome ✌ No smoking in restaurant; smoking room available 💳 Credit cards: Mastercard/ Eurocard, American Express, Visa, Diners Club, Switch, Delta 🍴 Chef/Manager: Valerie Brunton

4 Bridgegate Peebles Peeblesshire EH45 8RZ
Tel: 01721 722420
E-mail: kenny@kmphoto.co.uk
Web: www.kmphoto.co.uk/sunflower.htm
From Peebles High Street, turn down the Northgate, take first left into the Bridgegate. The Sunflower Restaurant is situated on the right. [D6]

PERTH

Ballathie House Hotel

- *"Elegant Victorian ambience – a lovely setting on the River Tay."*
- *Award-winning modern and classic Scottish cooking.*

BALLATHIE presents exceptional lunches and dinners. Menus change daily, use local produce and offer subtle variations on classic Scottish dishes. Winner The Macallan Taste of Scotland Country House Hotel of the Year 1994, and Special Merit for Best Lunch 1997. Winner (Category 1) in The Taste of Scotland Scotch Lamb Challenge Competition 1999. 2 AA Rosettes.

Home-cured salmon in citrus and dill marinade. Roast rack of Perthshire lamb with rosemary and garlic served with a confit of shallots, smoked bacon and thyme. Warm poached pear with fudge sauce, brandy snap basket with toffee ice cream.

STB ★★★★ Hotel

● Open all year ⌂ Rooms: 43 en suite (inc. 16 new Riverside rooms & suites) ⇌ DB&B £95–£140 B&B £70–£120 ▦ Special rates available ✕ Food available all day ££ Lunch ££ Dinner ££££ Ⓥ Vegetarians welcome ⚹ Children welcome ⚿ Facilities for disabled visitors ⚹ No smoking in dining rooms ⚘ Member of the Scotch Beef Club ⊞ Credit cards: Mastercard/ Eurocard, American Express, Visa, Diners Club, Switch, Delta, JCB ⚒ Manager: Christopher J Longden

*Kinclaven by Stanley Perthshire PH1 4QN
Tel: 01250 883268 Fax: 01250 883396
E-mail: email@ballathiehousehotel.com
Web: www.ballathiehousehotel.com
Off A9, 2 miles north of Perth – turn off at Stanley and turn right at sign to Kinclaven. [D5]*

PERTH

Hoy Tapas

- *"Stylish restaurant offering gourmet Scottish dishes of exceptional standard."*
- *Skillful Scottish cooking with international influence.*

THERE IS a real buzz about the restaurant, and the modern menus offer excellent local produce. At time of going to press the name of this establishment was changed from Exceed, it is still run with the same commitment to Scottish produce, by Willie Little, in a Spanish style.

Duck and roast pine kernel sausage with wilted spinach and ginger-braised rhubarb. Loin of pork stuffed with mixed dried fruits and clove jus. Caramel and almond tart with a nut brittle ice cream.

● Open all year except Christmas Day and New Year's Day ⚱ Table licence ✕ Lunch ££ Dinner £££ Ⓥ Vegetarians welcome ⚹ Children welcome ⚿ Facilities for disabled visitors ⚹ Smoking areas in restaurant ⊞ Credit cards: Mastercard/Eurocard, American Express, Visa, Switch, Delta, Solo ⚒ Chef Proprietor: Willie Little

*65 South Methven Street Perth PH1 5NX
Tel: 01738 621189 Fax: 01738 445758
E-mail: exceed@bt.connect.com
Situated between South Street and High Street. [D5]*

PERTH

Huntingtower Hotel

- *"Comfortable hotel offering the best of Scottish cooking."*
- *Country house cuisine.*

HUNTINGTOWER is an Edwardian mansion standing in four acres of landscaped gardens, located in the country yet only ten minutes drive from Perth city centre. There is a choice of two restaurants – the Garden conservatory with a light informal menu; Chef David Murray displays his talents in the fine dining Oak Room. 1 AA Red Food Rosette.

Leek and mussel mousseline lined by a saffron and chive infusion. Tornado of beef, pomme rösti, spinach and mushroom fricassee and mustard seed café au lait. Trio of chocolate mousse, pear and cinnamon compote and creamy anglaise.

STB ★★★★ Hotel

◐ Open all year ⌂ Rooms: 34 en suite ⇔ B&B £45–£50 ⌘ Special rates available ✕ Lunch £ Dinner ££ Ⓥ Vegetarians welcome ⚹ Children welcome ♿ Facilities for disabled visitors ⊞ Credit cards: Mastercard, American Express, Visa, Diners Club, Switch ⚑ General Manager: Michael Lee

Crieff Road Perth PH1 3JT
Tel: 01738 583771 Fax: 01738 583777
E-mail: reception.huntingtower@talk21.com
Web: www.huntingtowerhotel.co.uk
Signposted off A85 (nr Perth Mart), 1 mile west of Perth, towards Crieff. [D5]

PERTH

The Lang Bar & Restaurant, Perth Theatre

- *"Freshly cooked home-made dishes offering very good value for money."*
- *Innovative/traditional Scottish cooking.*

THE BAR, restaurant and coffee bar benefit from their situation and the period reproduction feel. Menus change to suit the current production. The food is of a high standard, covering the range of Scottish meat, fish and game with continental touches. The creative touch in the more traditional dishes demonstrates new Chef Gavin Hood's culinary energy and innovation.

Pork and spinach terrine, served with a beetroot salad and warm toast fingers. Chicken pot-roasted with fennel and ham, served with grilled tomato, vegetables and potatoes. Cherry and raisin pie, with an almond pastry served with fresh cream.

◐ Open all year except Christmas Day and Public Holidays Closed Sun Note: Please telephone to ensure Restaurant is open in the evening ✕ Food available all day ££ Lunch except Sun £ Dinner except Sun – booking advised ££ Ⓥ Vegetarians welcome ⚹ Children welcome ♿ Facilities for disabled visitors ⚞ Smoking areas in restaurant and coffee bar ⊞ Credit cards: Mastercard/Eurocard, American Express, Visa, Diners Club, Switch, Delta ⚑ Front of House & Catering Manager: Peter Hood

185 High Street Perth PH1 5UW
Tel: 01738 472709 Fax: 01738 624576
E-mail: theatre@perth.org.uk
Web: www.perth.org.uk/perth/theatre
Perth city centre in pedestrian zone at middle section of High Street. [D5]

PERTH

Let's Eat

- *"A truly gastronomic experience!"*
- *Modern Scottish cooking innovation.*

LET'S EAT continues to enjoy success, and deservedly so. The food is bistro-style with classic influences. Consistent popularity and high standards are maintained. Let's Eat has 2 AA Rosettes. Winner of The Macallan Taste of Scotland Restaurant of the Year Award 1997 and Winner of The Macallan Taste of Scotland Restaurant of the Year (Joint Winners) Award 1998.

Seared Skye scallops on toasted salad leaves with a chilli dressing. Grilled herb crusted fillet of halibut, on beetroot and tomato risotto. Honey, whisky and oatmeal parfait with local raspberries.

☼ *Open all year except 2 weeks mid Jul Closed Sun Mon* ✗ *Lunch except Sun Mon ££ Dinner except Sun Mon ££* Ⓥ *Vegetarians welcome* ☆ *Children welcome* ♿ *Facilities for disabled visitors* ⚞ *No smoking in restaurant area* ☙ *Member of the Scotch Beef Club* ⊞ *Credit cards: Mastercard/Eurocard, American Express, Visa, Switch, Delta* ⊠ *Partners: Tony Heath & Shona Drysdale*

77 Kinnoull Street Perth PH1 5EZ
Tel: 01738 643377 Fax: 01738 621464
E-mail: shona@letseatperth.co.uk
Web: www.letseatperth.co.uk
Restaurant stands on corner of Kinnoull Street and Atholl Street, close to North Inch. 3 minutes walk from High Street. [D5]

PERTH

Let's Eat Again

- *"Shona and Tony have done it again! Superlative cooking in the fair city of Perth."*
- *Modern Scottish.*

THIS BISTRO-STYLE restaurant is in Perth's shopping area. Green and burnt orange decor creates a relaxed and cool atmosphere. Staff are trained by proprietors Tony Heath and Shona Drysdale, who own sister restaurant 'Let's Eat', also in Perth. Chef Neil Simpson prepares food in classic style. The great ambience and 'cool' food make this difficult to beat.

Caesar's style salad with Rannoch smoked duck. Monkfish, prawn and crab gumbo. Warmed melting chocolate pudding with whipped cream.

☼ *Open all year except Christmas Day and Boxing Day, 2 weeks Jan and 2 weeks Jul Closed Sun Mon* ✗ *Lunch except Sun Mon ££ Dinner except Sun Mon ££* Ⓥ *Vegetarians welcome* ☆ *Children welcome* ⚞ *No smoking in restaurant* ☙ *Member of the Scotch Beef Club* ⊞ *Credit cards: Mastercard/Eurocard, American Express, Visa, Switch, Delta* ⊠ *Partner: Shona Drysdale*

33 George Street Perth PH1 5LA
Tel: 01738 633771 Fax: 01738 621464
E-mail: shona@letseatperth.co.uk
Web: www.letseatperth.co.uk
Town centre – one-way traffic in George Street. Restaurant is halfway up on right-hand side. [D5]

PERTH

Murrayshall House Hotel

- *"A relaxing hotel offering excellent golf facilities and food."*
- *Elegant Scottish cooking.*

MURRAYSHALL has two 18-hole golf courses and a driving range. The elegant Old Masters Restaurant has 2 AA Rosettes, with menus based on the best of seasonally-available produce, accompanied by an extensive wine list. The country club serves informal meals and is ideal for families.

Seared dived Oban scallops with caper berries, lemon and herbs. Roast loin of venison and pigeon with wild mushroom spatzeli and a juniper jus. Summer pudding with home-made ice cream and raspberry sauce.

STB ★★★★ Hotel

◐ Open all year ⌂ Rooms: 41 en suite ⇌ DB&B £48–£70 B&B £35–£55 ☉ Special rates available ✘ Lunch (Clubhouse) £ Dinner (Old Masters) ££ Ⓥ Vegetarians welcome ✱ Children welcome ▣ Credit cards: Mastercard/Eurocard, American Express, Visa, Diners Club, Switch ⋈ Sales Development Manager: Lin Mitchell

Scone nr Perth PH32 7PH
Tel: 01738 551171 Fax: 01738 552595
E-mail: lin.murrayshall@virgin.net
4 miles out of Perth, 1 mile off A94. [D5]

PITLOCHRY

Acarsaid Hotel

- *"Acarsaid has a comfortable and relaxed atmosphere making it an ideal place from which to explore this beautiful part of the country."*
- *Traditional home cooking with imagination.*

ATTRACTIVELY furnished throughout, the hotel is traditional and comfortable, with care given to small details, Residents receive complementary afternoon tea upon arrival. Of the public rooms one is 'smoking' and one 'non'. Good visibility of Scottish produce on menus. Ina and Sandy MacArthur are attentive hosts who really care for their guests' comfort.

Sliced wild venison topped with snippets of crispy bacon enhanced by a Perthshire raspberry coulis. Oven baked fillet of North Sea cod resting on a bed of herb mash dressed with a tomato salsa. Lime and lemon zest crème brûlée.

STB ★★★ Hotel

◐ Open all year except 2 Jan to 12 Mar ⌂ Rooms: 19 en suite ⇌ DB&B £39–£57 B&B £25–£40 ☉ Special rates available ✘ Lunch – residents only £ Dinner – non-residents welcome ££ Ⓥ Vegetarians welcome ✱ Children over 10 years welcome ⌇ No smoking in dining room ▣ Credit cards: Mastercard/Eurocard, Visa, Switch, Delta ⋈ Partners: Sandy & Ina MacArthur

8 Atholl Road Pitlochry PH16 5BX
Tel: 01796 472389 Fax: 01796 473952
E-mail: acarsaid@msn.com
Web: www.hotelperthshire.co.uk
On main road at south end of Pitlochry. [C5]

PITLOCHRY

East Haugh Country House Hotel & Restaurant

- *"A popular hotel close to Pitlochry offering an excellent choice of Scottish produce cooked to a high standard."*
- *Elegant Scottish cuisine.*

EAST HAUGH is run by Neil and Lesley McGown. Lunch menus are comprehensive and varied whilst dinner in the restaurant is a more formal affair with a menu which changes every two days. Traditional Sunday roast, a speciality. Winner The Macallan Taste of Scotland Special Merit Award Best Informal Lunch 1996.

Seared West Coast scallops wrapped in bacon with garlic butter. Roast rack of Perthshire lamb on a potato and onion rösti with fresh rosemary and shallot sauce. Fresh lemon tart with lemon and ginger cream.

STB ★★★ Small Hotel

◐ Open all year except 20 to 26 Dec N.B. Closed Mon to Thu for lunch during Nov, Dec, Jan, Feb and Mar – unless by prior arrangement ⌂ Rooms: 13, (12 en suite and 2 family with shared bathroom) ⊨ DB&B £49–£79 B&B £25–£55 ⓢⓟ Special rates available ✕ Lunch ££ Dinner ££-£££ ✝ Children welcome ✄ No smoking in restaurant ▣ Credit cards: Mastercard/Eurocard, Visa ⓜ Proprietors: Neil & Lesley McGown

*Pitlochry Perthshire PH16 5JS
Tel: 01796 473121 Fax: 01796 472473
E-mail: easthaugh@aol.com
Web: www.easthaugh.co.uk
1½ miles south of Pitlochry on old A9 road. [C5]*

PITLOCHRY

The Green Park Hotel

- *"A traditional hotel offering classic cuisine with excellent service."*
- *Traditional/classical cooking.*

THE GREEN PARK HOTEL is delightful and overlooks Loch Faskally. Alistair and Diane McMenemie know their customers well and make every effort to ensure that their stay is a special one. The cooking is classical and the best use is made of local produce to ensure the flavours dominate. The dining room is tastefully decorated and overlooks the gardens.

Marinated fillet of red mullet with green olives and sesame croûtons. Suprême of Guinea fowl with blue cheese mousse and a port wine sauce. Dark and white chocolate terrine with a vanilla sauce and ice cream.

STB ★★★★ Hotel

◐ Open all year ⌂ Rooms: 39 en suite ⊨ DB&B £39–£64 B&B £25–£42 ⓢⓟ Special rates available ✕ Lunch £-££ Dinner £££ Ⓥ Vegetarians welcome ♿ Facilities for disabled visitors ✄ No smoking throughout ▣ Credit cards: Mastercard/Eurocard, Visa, Switch ⓜ Proprietors: The McMenemie Family

*Clunie Bridge Road Pitlochry PH16 5JY
Tel: 01796 473248 Fax: 01796 473520
E-mail: bookings@thegreenpark.co.uk
Web: www.thegreenpark.co.uk
Following Atholl Road through Pitlochry, the hotel is signposted to the left at the town limits. [C5]*

PITLOCHRY

The Killiecrankie Hotel

- *"This hotel continues to charm guests – with its excellent hospitality and welcoming hosts."*
- *Modern Scottish cooking with classic influences.*

KILLIECRANKIE's resident owners, Colin and Carole Anderson, have decorated and furnished the house very tastefully, and have provided a high standard of comfort. Head chef Mark Easton's cooking is highly professional and imaginative, and his table d'hôte menus (four starters, four main courses) are well-balanced and appetising. A most attractive and well-run establishment. 2 AA Rosettes.

Prawn and coriander risotto with herb oil and Parmesan cheese. Pan-fried loin of lamb served with potato rösti and mange tout, and redcurrant flavoured jus. Dark chocolate flan with fruit coulis and white chocolate sauce.

STB ★★★★ Small Hotel

◐ Open 2 Feb to 3 Jan 🏠 Rooms: 10 en suite 🛏 DB&B £92 💷 Special rates available ✗ Lunch ££ Dinner 5 course menu £££ Ⅴ Vegetarians welcome ✶ Children welcome ✌ No smoking in dining room and most bedrooms ☙ Member of the Scotch Beef Club 💳 Credit cards: Mastercard/Eurocard, Visa, Switch, Delta ⚑ Owner/Proprietors: Colin & Carole Anderson

Killiecrankie by Pitlochry PH16 5LG
Tel: 01796 473220 Fax: 01796 472451
E-mail: enquiries@killiecrankiehotel.co.uk
Web: www.killiecrankiehotel.co.uk
B8079 on old A9, 3 miles north of Pitlochry. [C5]

PITLOCHRY

Knockendarroch House Hotel

- *"Relaxing atmosphere in elegant surroundings combined with quality cooking and good hospitality."*
- *Excellent classic cooking.*

THIS ELEGANT mansion enjoys wonderful views up the Tummel Valley to the south, and of Ben Vrackie to the north. The cooking is excellent in a traditional style and your hosts, Tony and Jane Ross, make every effort to make you feel at home – and they succeed. 1 AA Rosette.

A roulade of home-smoked salmon and cream cheese. Roast breast of pheasant filled with a mousseline of spinach and lemon set on a cranberry and red wine jus. Ecclefechan butter tart with toffee cream.

STB ★★★★ Small Hotel

◐ Open 1 Mar to Oct inclusive 🏠 Rooms: 12 en suite 🛏 DB&B £45–£62 B&B £35–£44 💷 Special rates available ✗ Dinner £££ Non-residents – prior booking essential Ⅴ Vegetarians welcome ✶ Children over 10 years welcome ✌ No smoking throughout 💳 Credit cards: Mastercard/Eurocard, American Express, Visa, Switch, Delta ⚑ Owners: Tony & Jane Ross

Higher Oakfield Pitlochry PH16 5HT
Tel: 01796 473473 Fax: 01796 474068
E-mail: info@knockendarroch.co.uk
Web: www.knockendarroch.co.uk
In a commanding position, 3 minutes walk from the town centre. Take Bonnethill Road and then take first right turn, into Toberargan Road and on to Higher Oakfield. [C5]

PITLOCHRY

The Old Armoury

- *"An excellent and memorable experience to be found at the Old Armoury."*
- *Accomplished modern Scottish.*

THIS COMFORTABLE and attractive restaurant is run by Alison Rollo and her husband George, who spend six months each year in New Zealand – there are some welcome New Zealand influences particularly evident on the wine list! The cooking here is fresh, skilled and innovative with good food available throughout the day.

King prawns pan-fried in chilli and garlic with a hint of cream, served with a timbale of couscous and wilted spinach. Breast of Highland pheasant stuffed with Scottish white pudding wrapped in prosciutto, set on a compote of red cabbage, pinenuts and courgette. 'Champagne cocktail' parfait: duo of brandy and Champagne on meringue with a strawberry coulis.

◐ *Open Easter Friday to 6 Oct* ✗ *Food available all day £ Lunch ££ Dinner £££* Ⓥ *Vegetarians welcome* ⚹ *Children welcome during the daytime (no children under 5 years allowed in dining room after 7pm)* ♿ *Facilities for disabled visitors* ✗ *No smoking throughout* 🐕 *Dogs welcome in the tea garden* 💳 *Credit cards: Mastercard/Eurocard, Visa* 🍴 *Proprietors: Alison & George Rollo*

*Armoury Road Pitlochry Perthshire PH16 5AP
Tel: 01796 474281 Fax: 01796 474447
Situated on Armoury Road close to Loch Faskally on the way down to the Dam and Fishladder. Signposted on a brown tourist board sign at Northern end of main road through town. [C5]*

PITLOCHRY

The Pitlochry Festival Theatre Restaurant

- *"Wonderful elevated views onto the River Tummel – a great place for an informal pre-theatre meal."*
- *Modern Scottish cooking enlivened with imaginative touches.*

AT LUNCHTIME the Pitlochry Festival Theatre restaurant is buffet style with a choice of hot and cold dishes, including local fish from the 'Summer Festival Buffet'. In the evening a table d'hôte dinner is served at 6.30 pm for theatregoers. Inspected late in season owing to closure for major refurbishment.

Trio of local smoked meats on a bed of rocket. Cushion of cod fillet with tapenade and Parmesan in herb crust on a red pepper coulis. Home-made terrine of dark and white chocolate on a Cointreau and orange sauce.

◐ *Open 4 May* ✗ *Lunch £* Ⓥ *Vegetarians welcome* ⚹ *Children welcome* ♿ *Facilities for disabled visitors* ✗ *No smoking in restaurant Smoking area in Coffee Bar* 💳 *Credit cards: Mastercard/Eurocard, American Express, Visa* 🍴 *Catering Manager: John Anderson*

*Port-na-Craig Pitlochry PH16 5DR
Tel: 01796 484600 Fax: 01796 484616
E-mail: admin@pitlochry.org.uk
Web: www.pitlochry.org.uk
On south bank of the River Tummel, approx ¼ mile from centre of town. Clearly signposted. [C5]*

PITLOCHRY

The Poplars

- *"A comfortable, relaxing hotel with an informal and friendly atmosphere."*
- *Scottish cooking to order, promoting traditional flavours.*

POPLARS is a friendly and comfortable hotel with stunning panoramic vista from the hotel across the Tummel Valley. The accommodation is comfortable and pleasant. Kathleen and Ian are friendly and hospitable hosts. The hotel concentrates exclusively on the provision of a truly memorable experience to its resident guests. Service is good, courteous and attentive.

Seared mackerel fillet served with a home-made rhubarb and ginger chutney. Succulent pan-fried venison collops carved round a bed of braised red cabbage and thyme with a red wine and blackcurrant sauce. Poached pears in a coffee and cardamom syrup served with crème fraîche and toasted almonds.

STB ★★★ Small Hotel

Open all year Rooms: 11 DB&B £41–£55 B&B £26–£40 Special rates available Dinner ££ Vegetarians welcome Children welcome Facilities for disabled visitors No smoking in restaurant and bedrooms Dogs welcome Credit cards: Mastercard/Eurocard, Visa, Switch Owners: Kathleen & Ian

27 Lower Oakfield Pitlochry PH16 5DS
Tel: 01796 472129 Fax: 01796 472554
E-mail: enquiries@poplars-hotel.co.uk
Web: www.poplars-hotel.co.uk
Between Lower Oakfield and Higher Oakfield Roads. Follow sign at south end of the town. [C5]

PITLOCHRY

Portnacraig Inn and Restaurant

- *"Informal friendly atmosphere where diners can eat outside in the garden overlooking the river."*
- *Modern Scottish cooking.*

THIS DELIGHTFUL stone-built inn, dating back some 300 years, has a buzz about it and the sort of place you can dress up or down, depending on the occasion. Portnacraig is a bistro-style restaurant with modern Scottish cooking with dining available on the picturesque riverside patio. Cooking is excellent and presented with imagination and flair.

Pan-fried breast of pigeon, with Morayshire air-dried ham and Puy lentils. Roast fillet of hare with juniper infused cabbage and a red wine and elderberry jus. Malt whisky and raisin tart with a Drambuie anglaise.

STB ★★★ Inn

Open Feb to Dec (open all day in season) Private parties available Rooms: 2 en suite DB&B £43–£50 B&B £25–£30 Special rates available Food available all day ££ Lunch £ Dinner ££ Vegetarians welcome Children welcome Facilities for disabled visitors Credit cards: Mastercard/Eurocard, Visa, Switch, Delta Partners: Bill & Andrew Bryan

Portnacraig Pitlochry PH16 5ND
Tel: 01796 472777 Fax: 01796 472931
E-mail: portnacraig@talk21.com
Directly below the Pitlochry Festival Theatre on the banks of the River Tummel. [C5]

PITLOCHRY

Westlands of Pitlochry

- *"Good quality food freshly prepared."*
- *Imaginative traditional cooking.*

WESTLANDS is personally run by its resident partners – Andrew and Sue Mathieson, and Ian and Allison Robertson. There is an interesting table d'hôte menu and an à la carte menu both of which are reasonably priced. Meals are served in the Garden Room Restaurant. Bar meals are also available.

Croquette of local haggis with creamy grain mustard sauce, with salad leaves and prunes. Fresh salmon grilled with crème fraîche on a bed of grilled citrus fruit served with fresh vegetables and potatoes. Home-made mincemeat pancakes served with maple syrup and ice cream.

STB ★★★ Hotel

◐ *Open all year except 25 and 26 Dec* 🏨 *Rooms: 15 en suite* 🛏 *DB&B £55.50–£63.50 B&B £37–£45* 🆂🅿 *Special rates available* ✘ *Lunch £ Dinner ££* Ⓥ *Vegetarians welcome* ★ *Children welcome* ✔ *No smoking in restaurant* 💳 *Credit cards: Mastercard/Eurocard, Visa* 🅿 *Partners: Andrew & Sue Mathieson/Ian & Allison Robertson*

160 Atholl Road Pitlochry Perthshire PH16 5AR
Tel: 01796 472266 Fax: 01796 473994
E-mail: info@westlandshotel.co.uk
Web: www.westlandshotel.co.uk
A924 into Pitlochry, Westlands at north end of town on right-hand side. [C5]

PLOCKTON

The Haven Hotel

- *"Elegant, stylish bedrooms with plenty of character, charming staff, and Seafood fresh from the boats around Plockton."*
- *Stylish Scottish cooking.*

PLOCKTON is known as the 'jewel of the Highlands.' The Haven stands yards from the beach, looking out onto the sea. As always it continues to offer the same high standard of cuisine. Dinner menus are table d'hôte, and combine fresh local produce with interesting sauces, changing daily. 1 AA Rosette. Member Aberdeen Angus Scheme.

Chilled turbot and salmon mousse sitting in a crispy salad, accompanied by blue cheese and Greek yoghurt dressing. Roast rack of Highland lamb decorated with minted pear and glazed with a redcurrant jelly gravy. A choice of home-made sweets.

STB ★★★ Hotel

◐ *Open 1 Feb to 20 Dec incl* 🏨 *Rooms: 15, 12 en suite* 🛏 *DB&B £53–£63 B&B £35–£39* 🆂🅿 *Special rates available* 🍷 *Restricted licence* ✘ *Lunch – 24 hours notice required ££ Dinner 5 course menu £££* Ⓥ *Vegetarians welcome* ★ *Children over 7 years welcome* ♿ *Facilities for disabled visitors* ✔ *No smoking in restaurant* 💳 *Credit cards: Mastercard/Eurocard, Visa, Switch, Delta* 🅿 *Owners: Annan & Jill Dryburgh*

Plockton Ross-shire IV52 8TW
Tel: 01599 544223/334 Fax: 01599 544467
E-mail: plocktonbay@fsnt.co.uk
Web: www.smoothhound.co.uk/hotels/thehaven.html
In the village of Plockton. [B4]

PLOCKTON

The Plockton Hotel

- *"Bustling and newly extended family hotel with friendly atmosphere."*
- *Good quality bar food specialising in fish and shellfish.*

TOM AND DOROTHY PEARSON are charming hosts and the hotel seems to continuously bustle with folk wanting to sample some of the local dishes – and there is really something for everyone on the menu. A small garden on the shore makes this a very restful spot to reflect on your day.

Plockton smokies: layers of smoked mackerel and herbs, cream, tomatoes and cheese, which is all baked and topped with toasted breadcrumbs. Lochcarron salmon fillet poached in lime leaves and topped with local crème fraîche flavoured with zest of lime. Iced crannachan parfait Plockton's version of the traditional Highland sweet.

STB ★★★ Small Hotel

◐ Open all year except New Year's Day ⌂ Rooms: 10 en suite ⚏ B&B from £30-£35 ⓢ Special rates available ✗ Food available all day ££ Lunch £ Dinner 5 course menu ££ Ⓥ Vegetarians welcome ✻ Children welcome ♿ Facilities for disabled visitors ✘ No smoking in dining room ♞ Dogs by arrangement only ☙ Member of the Scotch Beef Club ⎔ Credit cards: Mastercard/Eurocard, American Express, Visa, Switch, Delta ⍟ Partners: Dorothy, Tom & Alan Pearson

*Harbour Street Plockton Ross-shire IV52 8TN
Tel: 01599 544274 Fax: 01599 544475
E-mail: sales@plocktonhotel.co.uk
Web: www.plocktonhotel.co.uk
In the centre of Harbour Street, Plockton. [B4]*

POOLEWE

Pool House Hotel

- *"This lavishly furnished hotel offers high quality cuisine and outstanding views – not to be missed on a trip to Poolewe."*
- *Award-winning Scottish cuisine.*

POOL HOUSE HOTEL has a friendly family-run atmosphere, richly furnished and sits on the waterfront overlooking Loch Ewe. Chef John Moir uses only the best fresh local seafood and produce – his speciality being Loch Ewe scallops and the fresh catch of the day is a daily feature on his menus.

Char-grilled fillet of salmon marinated in ginger, soy sauce, lemon grass and lime. Roast loin of rabbit on a black pudding mash with game jus. Fresh gooseberry and lemon tart served with lightly whipped cream and mango sauce.

STB ★★★★ Hotel
Green Tourism Three Leaf Gold Award

◐ Open 1 Mar to 31 Dec ⌂ Rooms: 10 en suite ⚏ DB&B £75–£160 B&B £45–£130 ⓢ Special rates available ✗ Lunch ££ Dinner £££ Ⓥ Vegetarians welcome ✘ No smoking in dining room ⎔ Credit cards: Mastercard/Eurocard, American Express, Visa, Switch, Delta, JCB ⍟ General Manager: Elizabeth Miles

*Poolewe by Achnasheen Wester Ross IV22 2LD
Tel: 01445 781272 Fax: 01445 781403
E-mail: poolhouse@inverewe.co.uk
Web: www.inverewe.co.uk
6 miles north of Gairloch on A832. The hotel is situated by the bridge, alongside the River Ewe where it meets the sea and overlooks Inverewe Gardens. [B3]*

PORT OF MENTEITH

The Lake Hotel

- *"Imaginative cooking served in calming surroundings."*
- *Modern Scottish.*

STANDING on the shore of Scotland's only lake, The Lake Hotel with it's Art Deco style interior, continues to offer a very fine experience to its visitors. Cooking here is skilled, by an enthusiastic chef who prepares best fresh local produce and presents it with flair and excellent presentation.

Steamed West Coast mussels in a white wine, chilli and lime sauce. Aberdeen Angus fillet on a potato rösti, confit of wild mushrooms and a red wine jus. Tarte Tatin of pineapple and vanilla served with a lavender ice cream.

STB ★★★ Hotel

◐ Open all year except Christmas Day, Boxing Day and first two weeks in Jan closed Mon Tue from 1 Nov until 31 Mar ⌂ Rooms: 16 en suite ⌂ DB&B £52–£96 £35–£75 ⓢⓟ Special rates available ✗ lunch from £ Dinner £££ Ⓥ Vegetarians welcome ⚹ Children over 8 welcome in the restaurant in the evening ⚹ Facilities for disabled visitors ⚹ No smoking in dining room ⚹ Dogs welcome ⚹ Credit cards: Mastercard, American Express, Visa, Switch, Delta ⚹ Owner: Graeme McConnachie

Port of Menteith Perthshire FK8 3RA
Tel: 01877 385258 Fax: 01877 385671
E-mail: enquiries@lake-of-menteith-hotel.com
Web: www.lake-of-menteith-hotel.com
Turn off at junction 10 from the M9 onto the A84, this takes you to the A873 signposted Aberfoyle. Continue on this road until you reach Port of Menteith. At Port of Menteith turn left down the B8034 and hotel is 250m on the right. [C5]

PORTPATRICK

Fernhill Hotel

- *"Warm and friendly Portpatrick hospitality."*
- *Modern Scottish cooking.*

THIS DELIGHTFULLY located and well-maintained terraced hotel has gardens which fall away below the hotel. The large and delightful conservatory, with the best sea views, makes a pleasant dining room. Don't miss out on the house speciality – locally-caught lobster – now available in season fresh from the hotel's sea water holding tank.

Gâteau of Marrbury smoked chicken with tomato and red onions, served with a chive vinaigrette dressing. Surf-on-the-turf: char grilled 8oz Scotch beef fillet steak with a grilled half of fresh Mull of Galloway lobster and hot garlic butter. Port and Plum cheesecake, with a tangy port syrup.

STB ★★★★ Hotel

◐ Open all year ⌂ Rooms: 23 en suite ⌂ DB&B £67.50–£80 B&B £47.50–£60 ⓢⓟ Special rates available ✗ Lunch ££ Dinner £££ Ⓥ Vegetarians welcome ⚹ Children welcome ⚹ Facilities for disabled visitors ⚹ There is a smoking dining room ⚹ Credit cards: Mastercard/Eurocard, Visa, Switch ⚹ Manageress: Nicola Murchie

Heugh Road Portpatrick DG9 8TD
Tel: 01776 810220 Fax: 01776 810596
E-mail: info@fernhillhotel.co.uk
Web: www.fernhillhotel.co.uk
On entering Portpatrick take first right – Heugh Road – and hotel is c. 300 yards on left. [B7]

PORTPATRICK

Knockinaam Lodge

- *"Stunning reception, food, atmosphere, views etc. A truly luxurious retreat."*
- *Best modern British cooking.*

HERE IN this luxurious country house the welcome is warm and personal, your every desire met and gourmet cravings satisfied. Knockinaam has a stunning cellar and vast selection of malts. Winner of The Macallan Taste of Scotland Country House Hotel of the Year Award 1997 and Excellence 1997. 3 AA Rosettes.

Terrine of summer ratatouille with an olive oil and sardine dressing. Roast Scottish lamb cutlet with basil mousse, pomme anna and a rosemary and shallot reduction. Hot raspberry ripple soufflé with double vanilla bean ice cream.

STB ★★★★ Hotel

◐ Open all year ⌂ Rooms: 10 en suite ⊨ DB&B from £85–£165 ▦ Special rates available ✗ Food available all day ££ Lunch £££ Dinner ££££ Ⓥ Vegetarians welcome ⚹ Children welcome ⚿ Facilities for disabled visitors – restaurant only ⌇ No smoking in dining room ♨ Member of the Scotch Beef Club ⊞ Credit cards: Mastercard/Eurocard, American Express, Visa, Diners Club, Switch, Delta ⚑ Proprietors: Michael Bricker & Pauline Ashworth

Portpatrick DG9 9AD
Tel: 01776 810471 Fax: 01776 810435
From the A77 or the A75, follow signs for Portpatrick. 2 miles west of Lochans, Knockinaam sign on right. Take first left turning, past smokehouse. Follow signs for 3 miles to lodge. [B7]

PRESTWICK

Parkstone Hotel

- *"A friendly hotel in a quiet residential situation, yet right on the seafront."*
- *Traditional Scottish cooking.*

PARKSTONE HOTEL is well run by Stewart Clarkson, Jean Taylor and Jane Clarkson who have an evident commitment to continuously upgrading and improving the hotel. The menus at Parkstone are traditional offering a good choice and all items prepared only using the best local produce carefully sourced, prepared and presented.

Salad of smoked duck breast with caramelised apples in a honey and grain mustard dressing. Seared loin of lamb, cooked pink with roasted vegetables and a red wine and juniper sauce. Double chocolate and heather cream parfait drizzled with redcurrant coulis.

STB ★★★ Hotel

◐ Open all year except New Year's Day ⌂ Rooms: 22 en suite ⊨ DB&B £48–£54 B&B £33–£36 ▦ Special rates available ✗ Lunch ££ Dinner £££ Ⓥ Vegetarians welcome ⚹ Children welcome ⌇ No smoking in dining room ⊞ Credit cards: Mastercard/Eurocard, American Express, Visa, Switch, Delta ⚑ Partners: Stewart Clarkson, Jean Taylor & Jane Clarkson

Central Esplanade Prestwick Ayrshire KA9 1QN
Tel: 01292 477286 Fax: 01292 477671
E-mail: info@parkstonehotel.co.uk
Web: www.parkstonehotel.co.uk
From Prestwick town centre A79, follow signs to seafront (400 yards). Hotel last turning on the left before promenade, on Ardayre Road. [C6]

ST ANDREWS

The Old Course Hotel Golf Resort & Spa

- *"Excellent food and service in a spectacular location."*
- *Modern Scottish.*

THE HOTEL is set in a spectacular location, overlooking the infamous 17th Road Hole and the historic Royal and Ancient Clubhouse. The Old Course Hotel offers its guests a unique choice of dining experiences – fine dining in the Road Hole Grill; Sands, a contemporary brasserie-style restaurant; and the Jigger Inn, a popular golfing pub.

Hot smoked wild salmon with crab maki-style rolls, wasabi aiolis and soy and lime oil. Roast chateaubriand of Buccleuch beef with baby vegetables and an oxtail jus. Warm chocolate mousse with strawberry and mint salsa.

STB ★★★★★ International Resort Hotel

◐ Open all year ⌂ Rooms: 146 en suite ⇌ DB&B from £233 B&B from £195 💷 Special golf and spa rates available ✗ Food served all day £-££ Lunch ££ Dinner ££££ Ⓥ Vegetarians welcome ⚹ Children welcome ⚹ Facilities for disabled visitors ⚹ Pipe and cigar smoking not permitted in restaurants ⚹ Member of the Scotch Beef Club 💳 Credit cards: Mastercard/Eurocard, American Express, Visa, Diners Club, Delta, JCB ⚹ General Manager: Andrew Phelan

Old Station Road St Andrews Fife KY16 9SP
Tel: 01334 474371 Fax: 01334 477668
E-mail: reservations@oldcoursehotel.co.uk
Web: www.oldcoursehotel.co.uk
A91 to St Andrews on outskirts of town. [D5]

ST ANDREWS

Rufflets Country House & Garden Restaurant

- *"The best of food, service and accommodation."*
- *Highly accomplished Scottish cooking.*

AT RUFFLETS, the attractive Garden Restaurant has deservedly 2 AA Rosettes, among other awards. The daily changing menus are table d'hôte and the cooking combines the fresh seafood available from the East Neuk and good local meats and vegetables with imaginative sauces and stuffings. Chef's signature dishes are highlighted on menu.

Smoked haddock and leek risotto topped with a poached egg and a garden chive cream. Pan-fried collop of Rannoch venison and seared duck liver with dauphinoise potatoes, fresh asparagus and raspberry tea syrup glaze. Iced lemon and lime soufflé with a kumquat marmalade.

STB ★★★★★ Hotel

◐ Open all year ⌂ Rooms: 22 en suite ⇌ DB&B from £105 B&B from £85 💷 Special rates available ✗ Lunch (Restaurant) Sun from ££ Dinner from ££££ Ⓥ Vegetarians welcome ⚹ Children welcome ⚹ Facilities for non-residential disabled visitors ⚹ Member of the Scotch Beef Club, 💳 Credit cards: Mastercard/Eurocard, American Express, Visa, Diners Club, Switch ⚹ Owner: Ann Russell; Manager: John Angus

Strathkinness Low Road St Andrews Fife KY16 9TX
Tel: 01334 472594 Fax: 01334 478703
E-mail: reservations@rufflets.co.uk
Web: www.rufflets.co.uk
On B939, 1½ miles west of St Andrews. [D5]

ST ANDREWS

St Andrews Links Clubhouse

- *"Wholesome freshly cooked food available all day long – a great rendezvous for visitors and hungry golfers."*
- *Informal creative cooking.*

THE LINKS CLUBHOUSE dining room has been tastefully decorated with modern quality furniture and fittings. A fixed price menu and a comprehensive wine list are available here. Breakfast and light meals can be obtained in the lounge which has a relaxing atmosphere, making it ideal for drinks.

Sauteed crab röstis set on a sweetcorn salsa. Pan-fried and roasted rack of Perthshire lamb set on colcannon potatoes, surrounded by a fresh thyme jus. Tarte chocolate served with a vanilla cream.

◐ *Open all year except Christmas Day* ✗ *Food available all day Lunch £ Dinner ££* Ⓥ *Vegetarians welcome* ⚘ *Children welcome* ♿ *Facilities for disabled visitors* ⊞ *Credit cards: Mastercard/Eurocard, Visa, Switch* ⚑ *Food & Beverage Manager: Sue Hutchison*

West Sands Road St Andrews Fife KY16 9XL
Tel: 01334 466666 Fax: 01334 466664
E-mail: linkstrust@standrews.org.uk
Web: www.standrews.org.uk
From M90 take A91 to St Andrews (25 miles). In St Andrews follow signs to West Sands and golf courses. At beginning of Golf Place proceed ½ mile along road, towards beach. Clubhouse is on left. [D5]

ST ANDREWS OUTSKIRTS

The Inn at Lathones

- *"Excellent food and friendly hospitality in traditional surroundings."*
- *Excellent Scottish cooking.*

THE INN AT LATHONES is run by Nick and Jocelyn White, who offer traditional coaching inn hospitality. Guests feel immediately at home and this comfort is matched by a very high standard of cooking offered in the elegant, yet informal, dining room. A very special place on the outskirts of St Andrews.

Thai fish cakes with chilli crisps. Grilled lamb cutlets with lamb kidney in a Madeira sauce. Crème Catalan with pistachio ice cream

STB ★★★★ Inn

◐ *Open all year except Christmas Day, Boxing Day and Jan* 🛏 *Rooms: 14 en suite* 🛌 *DB&B £49.50–£67.50 B&B £50–£70* 🏷 *Special rates available* ✗ *Food available all day Apr to Oct ££ Lunch £ Dinner ££* Ⓥ *Vegetarians welcome* ⚘ *Children welcome* 🚭 *No smoking in restaurant* 🐄 *Member of the Scotch Beef Club* ⊞ *Credit cards: Mastercard/Eurocard, American Express, Visa, Diners Club, Switch, Delta* ⚑ *Proprietor: Nick White*

by Largoward St Andrews Fife KY9 1JE
Tel: 01334 840494 Fax: 01334 840694
E-mail: lathones@theinn.co.uk
Web: www.theinn.co.uk
5 miles out of St Andrews on the A915 towards Leven. The inn is on the main road, 1 mile before Largoward. [D5]

ST ANDREWS OUTSKIRTS

Old Manor Hotel

- *"Ideally situated for the golfers, complete with friendly staff and good food."*
- *Contemporary Scottish cuisine.*

OWNED and run by the Clark family their Aithernie Restaurant serves both à la carte and table d'hôte dishes, imaginatively prepared and presented. The restaurant's success has been reflected by awards for chef Alan Brunt. 2 AA Rosettes. Runner-up (Category 2) The Taste of Scotland Scotch Lamb Challenge Competition 2000.

Fresh saffron tagliatelle, West Coast mussels and scallops, with a light Lagavulin cream topped with crispy carrots. Duo of Scotch lamb, sweet potato, chive mash and poppy seed biscuits, served with butternut squash soufflé, celeriac quiche, roasted parsnips, and a red wine gravy. Warm vanilla and blackberry pudding with lemon ice cream.

STB ★★★★ Hotel

◐ Open all year except Boxing Day and New Year's Day ⌂ Rooms: 23 en suite ⇌ DB&B £45.50–£105 B&B £30–£90 ⓢ Special rates available ✕ Food available all day ££ Lunch ££ Dinner £££ Ⓥ Vegetarians welcome ⚹ Children welcome ⚿ Facilities for disabled visitors ⚱ No smoking in restaurant ⚘ Member of the Scotch Beef Club ⊞ Credit cards: Mastercard/Eurocard, American Express, Visa, Diners Club, Switch, Delta, JCB ⚑ Owners: Clark Family

Lundin Links Fife KY8 6AJ
Tel: 01333 320368 Fax: 01333 320911
E-mail: enquiries@oldmanorhotel.co.uk
Web: www.oldmanorhotel.co.uk
On A915 Kirkcaldy–St Andrews, 1 mile east of Leven, on right overlooking Largo Bay. [D5]

ST ANDREWS OUTSKIRTS

The Sandford Country House Hotel

- *"Good food served by caring staff in quiet surroundings."*
- *Scottish modern.*

SANDFORD is run by Fergus Buchan, General Manager, and is undergoing many improvements and ongoing refurbishment. There is a a choice of dining options from informal bar meals to the more formal Garden Room restaurant. Cooking by Chef Allan Lorente is skilled using seasonal produce skilfully prepared and presented.

Sandford's own smoked Tay salmon, served in a filo basket with an Arran mustard dressing. Medallions of venison pan-fried and served with glazed carrots, scented pear and potato, and a rich port sauce. Sticky toffee pudding with a hot fudge sauce and organic vanilla ice cream.

STB ★★★ Hotel

◐ Open all year ⌂ Rooms: 16 en suite ⇌ DB&B £85–£150 B&B £65–£130 ⓢ Special rates available ✕ Food available all day ££ Lunch ££ Dinner £££ Ⓥ Vegetarians welcome ⚹ Children welcome ⚿ Facilities for disabled visitors ⚱ No smoking in dining room ⌇ Dogs welcome ⊞ Credit cards: Mastercard/Eurocard, American Express, Visa, Switch, Delta ⚑ General Manager: Fergus Buchan

Newton Hill Wormit Fife DD6 8RG
Tel: 01382 541802 Fax: 01382 542136
E-mail: sandford.hotel@btinternet.com
Web: www.sandfordhotelfife.com
4 miles south of Dundee on A92, (formerly A914) at junction of B946 signposted Wormit. [D5]

ST BOSWELLS

Clint Lodge

- *"High standards throughout, with use of home-grown produce."*
- *Traditional Scottish cooking.*

BILL AND HEATHER Walker have carefully restored Clint Lodge, paying great attention to the finest of detail. Furnishings are carefully selected to blend into the traditional atmosphere recreated here amongst a treasure trove of family heirlooms and selected antique furniture. A real get-away-haven with excellent hospitality and superb cooking.

Potato pancakes with smoked haddock and lovage sauce. Noisettes of Border lamb served on a golden mash, with port and redcurrant gravy, and served with fresh garden vegetables. Strawberry and Drambuie cream with home-made shortbread biscuits.

STB ★★★★ B&B

◐ Open all year except Christmas, New Year and Feb ⌂ Rooms: 5 (4 en suite, 1 private facilities) ⌬ DB&B £50–£60 B&B £30–£50 ⓤ Unlicensed – guests welcome to take own wine ✕ Residents only Dinner ££ Ⓥ Vegetarians welcome ⒸⒺ Credit cards: Mastercard, Visa ⍟ Proprietors: Bill & Heather Walker

St Boswells Melrose TD6 0DZ
Tel: 01835 822027 Fax: 01835 822656
E-mail: clintlodge@aol.com
At St Boswells take the B6404, continue for 2 miles across the Mertoun Bridge, turn left onto B6356 through Clint Mains village veering left. Follow this road to Clint Lodge, 1 mile on right. [D6]

ST FILLANS

The Four Seasons Hotel

- *"A comfortable hotel offering good food on the idyllic loch side."*
- *Innovative Scottish cooking.*

THE HUGE picture windows bring the view indoors and are second to none. Recent owners have been gradually renovating the hotel giving close attention to detail and guests' comfort. Dinner is relaxed, with emphasis on high quality, well produced food. In the Tarken Room food is of the same standard but served in a less formal style.

West Coast scallops on a chive mash with Lagavulin nage. Trio of Perthshire game: venison, woodpigeon and hare – Geneva gin, bitter chocolate and raspberry vinegar sauce. Chocolate and whisky truffle cake with clotted cream.

STB ★★★ Small Hotel

◐ Open Mar to 4 Jan N.B. Closed some weekdays in Nov Dec ⌂ Rooms: 18 en suite ⌬ DB&B £53–£85 B&B £32–£64 ⓢⓟ Special rates available ✕ Food available £££ Lunch ££ Dinner £££ Ⓥ Vegetarians welcome ✼ Children welcome ⌫ No smoking in restaurant ⌘ Dogs welcome ⒸⒺ Credit cards: Mastercard/Eurocard, Visa, Switch, Delta ⍟ Manager: Andrew Low

St Fillans Perthshire PH6 2NF
Tel: 01764 685 333 Fax: 01764 685 444
E-mail: info@thefourseasonshotel.co.uk
Web: www.thefourseasonshotel.co.uk
A85 – west end of village on Loch Earn. [C5]

ST MONANS

The Seafood Restaurant

- *"Relaxed atmosphere, with superb food and views."*
- *Contemporary Scottish seafood.*

AT THE Seafood Restaurant Head Chef Craig Millar has no problem sourcing the freshest of seafood and uses only the best to prepare fish (and other) dishes with a contemporary innovative twist. An exceptional restaurant in a stunning setting. 2 AA Rosettes. Winner (Category 2) in The Taste of Scotland Scotch Lamb Challenge Competition 2000.

Pan-seared, hand-dived scallops with a basil oil and an orange, vanilla and cardamom reduction. Grilled turbot fillet with local chanterelle mushrooms and a meaux mustard dressing. William pear poached in lime and saffron with coconut ice cream.

☾ Open 1 Feb to 30 Nov Closed Mon Oct to Apr ✕ Lunch ££ Dinner £££ Ⓥ Vegetarians welcome ♿ Facilities for disabled visitors ✀ No smoking in restaurant 💳 Credit cards: Mastercard/Eurocard, American Express, Visa, Switch, JCB ⓧ Partner: Tim Butler

16 West End St Monans Fife KY10 2BX
Tel: 01333 730 327 Fax: 01333 730 327
E-mail: theseafoodrestaurant@virginnet.co.uk
Web: www.theseafoodrestaurant.com
From St Andrews drive south to Anstruther (B9131) then turn west along the A917 through Pittenweem to St Monans. Go down to the harbour and turn right. [D5]

SELKIRK

Philipburn House Hotel

- *"Local produce served in innovative style in relaxed informal atmosphere."*
- *Modern Scottish.*

PHILIPBURN is a relaxed and informal hotel with choices of both formal and informal dining in its restaurant or bar/bistro. Menus successfully combine traditional and modern items cooked skilfully, using only the best produce. The hotel has been sensitively refurbished to a very high standard by owner Alan Deeson.

Fantail of Galia melon, presented with smoked goose breast and citrus fruits enhanced with an elderberry fruit coulis. Marinated escalope of Border venison seared in basil oil enhanced with a port wine barley risotto surrounded with a marmalade and cranberry sauce. Choux pastry ring centred with a crushed meringue and honeycomb syllabub cream drizzled with a warm toffee sauce.

STB ★★★★ Hotel

☾ Open all year except 3 to 17 Jan 🛏 Rooms: 14 en suite 🛌 DB&B £55–£90 B&B £25–£70 ⓢ Special rates available ✕ Lunch ££ Dinner £££ Ⓥ Vegetarians welcome ✿ Children welcome ♿ Facilities for disabled visitors ✀ No smoking in restaurant 🐕 Dogs welcome 💳 Credit cards: Mastercard/Eurocard, American Express, Visa, Switch, Delta. ⓧ Proprietor: Mr Allan Deeson

Selkirk TD7 5LS
Tel: 01750 20747 Fax: 01750 21690
E-mail: info@philipburnhousehotel.co.uk
Web: www.philipburnhousehotel.co.uk
1 mile from Selkirk town centre, follow signs for the A72/A707 for Peebles/Moffat. [D6]

SKELMORLIE BY LARGS

Redcliffe House Hotel

- *"A warm welcome and wide range of local seafood make this comfortable hotel well worth visiting."*
- *Modern and traditional cuisine.*

REDCLIFFE HOUSE is surrounded by attractive gardens to the front overlooking the water. There is an atmospheric dining room which has incorporated many original features. The bedrooms are modern and well equipped. Seafood dishes are a speciality here, with both a table d'hôte and a la carte menus offered.

Bradon rost served hot with white wine and parsley sauce. Seafood in puff pastry case filled with fresh fish and shellfish, cooked in lobster coulis with Cognac and cream. Pears poached in honey and saffron syrup.

STB ★★★ Hotel

◐ Open all year 🛏 Rooms: 10 en suite 🍴 DB&B £42.50–£47.50 B&B £35–£40 💷 Special rates available ✗ Lunch ££ Dinner £££ Ⓥ Vegetarians welcome ⚘ Children welcome ⦸ No smoking in dining room 🐕 Dogs welcome by prior arrangement 💳 Credit cards: Mastercard/Eurocard, American Express, Visa, Diners Club, Switch, Delta ◨ Proprietors: George & Elaine Maltby

25 Shore Road Skelmorlie Ayrshire PA17 5EH
Tel: 01475 521036 Fax: 01475 521894
Web: www.redcliffehotel.com
From Glasgow take M8, A8 to Greenock then A78. Skelmorlie is just south of Wemyss Bay. Hotel is on main road/seafront. [C6]

SPEAN BRIDGE

Corriegour Lodge Hotel

- *"Always a smile and friendly service added to assured cooking and mesmerising views."*
- *Excellent modern Scottish cooking.*

CORRIEGOUR is run by Christian Drew and her family and is well maintained and attractively appointed. The food here is very good, using local produce with menus which change often reflecting the availability of the produce. The hotel's wine list is extensive and reasonably priced. A friendly, comfortable hotel.

West Coast crab cakes with a langoustine vinaigrette and a scallop mousse. Roast rack of Highland lamb served on colcannon, with a thyme jus and roasted ratatouille. Iced cranachan parfait with brandy snap petals and a compote of warm summer fruits.

STB ★★★★ Hotel

◐ Open 1 Feb to 30 Nov (weekends only 1 Feb to 31 Mar) and special 3/6 day breaks at New Year 🛏 Rooms: 9 en suite 🍴 DB&B £53–£75 B&B £43–£55 💷 Special rates available ✗ Lunch – by arrangement Dinner £££ Non-residents – dinner only Ⓥ Vegetarians welcome with prior notice ⚘ Children over 8 years welcome ⦸ No smoking in restaurant 💳 Credit cards: Mastercard/Eurocard, American Express, Visa, Switch, Delta ◨ Owner: Christian Drew

Loch Lochy by Spean Bridge PH34 4EB
Tel: 01397 712685 Fax: 01397 712696
E-mail: info@corriegour-lodge-hotel.com
Web: www.corriegour-lodge-hotel.com
Follow A82, 17 miles north of Fort William; 47 miles south of Inverness – between Spean Bridge and Invergarry. [C4]

SPEAN BRIDGE

Mehalah

- *"A delightful home where the personality of your hostess is reflected in the pretty bedrooms and the delicious food."*
- Country house-style cooking.

MEHALAH sits on the riverside overlooking the Spean River, the Grey Corries, and Aonach Mor. Gillian has refurbished the interior of the house, with style and skill using her interest in interior design. Cooking here is talented – with the use of organic produce – and menus are interesting. Look out for the home baking!

Baked asparagus with ricotta and fresh basil dressing. Wild salmon with roasted organic carrots served with an orange and crème fraîche sauce. accompanied by a selection of fresh organic vegetables. Pavlova roulade with raspberries and Mascarpone cream.

- Open all year except Christmas Day
- Rooms: 2 en suite DB&B £46 B&B £22
- Unlicensed ✗ Residents only Dinner £££
- Vegetarians welcome – with prior notice
- No smoking throughout No credit cards
- Proprietor: Gillian Cameron

Riverside House Lower Tirnidrish Spean Bridge
PH34 4EU
Tel: 01397 712893 Fax: 01397 712893
E-mail: mehalahrh@gofornet.co.uk
At Spean Bridge take the A86 to Roybridge. 'Mehalah sign' is a few hundred yards on the right then go down a short track to house. [C4]

SPEAN BRIDGE

Old Pines Restaurant with Rooms

- *"The ultimate food experience in totally relaxed surroundings."*
- Outstanding and sophisticated cuisine.

OLD PINES is the family home of Bill and Sukie Barber. Sukie offers the finest of Scottish food, cooked superbly and skillfully. All ingredients are sourced locally, and Old Pines has its own smokehouse. An unusual, well researched wine list complements Sukie's cooking. The Macallan Taste of Scotland Award 1998.

Scallops, squat lobsters and mussels with spinach and a vermouth and orange sauce. Roast leg of Scotch lamb with kidney and fresh herbs and a leek, cep and barley risotto. Brown sugar meringue with gooseberries, elderflower ice cream, kiwi and elderflower sauce.

STB ★★★★ Restaurant with Rooms
Green Tourism Three Leaf Gold Award

- Open all year except 2 weeks winter
- Rooms: 8 en suite DB&B £60–£75
- Special rates available ✗ Food available all day ££ Dinner 5 course menu except Sun (supper to residents) £££ Vegetarians welcome – prior notice appreciated Children welcome
- Facilities for disabled visitors No smoking throughout Member of the Scotch Beef Club
- Credit cards: Mastercard/Eurocard, Visa, Switch, Delta Proprietors: Bill & Sukie Barber

Spean Bridge by Fort William PH34 4EG
Tel: 01397 712324 Fax: 01397 712433
E-mail: goodfood@oldpines.co.uk
Web: www.oldpines.co.uk
From Spean Bridge take A82 to Inverness. 1 mile north take B8004 next to Commando Memorial 300 yards on right. [C4]

STIRLING

Bannockburn Heritage Centre, National Trust for Scotland

- *"A recently refurbished restaurant offering good quality home cooking."*
- *Scottish home cooking.*

LOCATED on this historic site, Bannockburn offers the best of Scottish home cooking with everything from good home baking to traditional hot meals. It is a lovely, fresh and attractively furnished restaurant with well trained and enthusiastic staff and offers very good value for money. Enjoy Breakfast until 12 noon here (including porridge!). All day breakfast at weekends.

Cock-a-leekie soup. Selection of filled sandwiches. Lamb stovies with traditional bannocks. Clootie dumpling.

STB Commended

◐ *Open 1 Mar to 24 Dec* ⓢⓟ *Special rates available* ⓤ *Unlicensed* ✘ *Food available all day £ Lunch £ (Dinner – private parties/functions only)* Ⓥ *Vegetarians welcome* ⚝ *Children welcome* ♿ *Facilities for disabled visitors* ⚭ *No smoking throughout* ⓒ *Credit cards: Mastercard/Eurocard, Visa, Switch, Delta, JCB* Ⓜ *Cafe Manager: Mrs Sarah Muirhead*

*Glasgow Road Stirling FK7 0LJ
Tel: 01786 812664 Fax: 01786 810892
Off M80/M9 at junction 9, 2 miles south of Stirling on the A872. [C5]*

STIRLING

Olivia's Restaurant

- *"Fresh seasonal food carefully cooked."*
- *Modern Scottish.*

OLIVIA'S is an appealing restaurant located in a historic part of Stirling centre. Decor is modern and reflects the informal style of eating here. The menus are interesting, featuring good local produce cooked with flair and imagination. It is advisable to pre-book.

Seared scallops with an orange and cardamom dressing. Roast loin of venison wrapped in pancetta with fennel mash and a rosemary and port gravy. Chocolate cinnamon tuile with Baileys ice cream and a poached pear.

◐ *Open all year except Christmas Day, Boxing Day, 1 and 2 Jan Closed Sun* ✘ *Lunch except Sun £ Dinner except Sun ££* Ⓥ *Vegetarians welcome* ⚝ *Children welcome* ♿ *Facilities for disabled visitors* ⓒ *Credit cards: Mastercard/Eurocard, Visa, Switch, Delta* Ⓜ *Manageress: Becky Spaven*

*5 Baker Street Stirling FK8 1BJ
Tel: 01786 446277 Fax: 01786 446277
From Stirling town centre follow directions to Stirling Castle. Restaurant is approx 800 yards from castle on approach. [C5]*

STIRLING

Scholars Restaurant At Stirling Highland Hotel

- *"An attractive, very well presented city hotel with excellent facilities."*
- *Modern Scottish cooking.*

IN KEEPING with the rest of the hotel, Scholars Restaurant is named with its former use in mind – that of the old high school. A formal restaurant, its à la carte and table d'hôte menus feature fresh local produce used with imagination and flair. Staff are well-trained, professional and friendly. Scholars Restaurant has 2 AA Rosettes.

Confit of salmon on a bed of Puy lentil broth. Grilled supreme of Grampian chicken with champ potatoes, asparagus and an Arran mustard sauce. Terrine of caramelised banana with a toffee anglaise.

STB ★★★★ Hotel

◐ Open all year Closed Sat lunch ⌸ Rooms: 94 en suite ⌸ DB&B £102.50 B&B £55-£82.50 ⌸ Special rates available ✘ Food available all day Lunch except Sat £ Dinner ££ Ⓥ Vegetarians welcome ⚹ Children welcome ⚹ Facilities for disabled visitors ⚹ No smoking in restaurant ⌸ Credit cards: Mastercard/Eurocard, American Express, Visa, Diners Club, Switch, JCB ⌸ General Manager: Andrew G Swinton

Stirling Highland Hotel Spittal Street
Stirling FK8 1DU
Tel: 01786 272727 Fax: 01786 272829
E-mail: aswinton@paramount-hotels.co.uk
Web: www.paramount-hotels-co.uk
From Stirling town centre follow directions to Stirling Castle. Stirling Highland Hotel is on the hill approx 500 yards below the castle in Spittal Street which is a one way street. [C5]

STIRLING OUTSKIRTS

Glenskirlie House

- *"A lovely experience, lovely staff."*
- *Modern Scottish.*

GLENSKIRLIE HOUSE is owned by Linda and John Macaloney and run by their son Colin. It is a unique impressive place where everything is of the highest quality. Menus are a successful combination of traditional and contemporary – all prepared with skill both in preparation and presentation – and using the best fresh produce. A very impressive place.

Escabèche of red mullet served with lobster roulade and chive sauce. Canon of lamb cooked with a lavender crust and served with black pudding mash and braised leek. Chocolate brûlée with Champagne and passion fruit sorbet with sugar twists.

◐ Open all year except 26, 27 Dec and 1, 2 and 3 Jan Closed Mon night ⌸ Licensed ✘ Bar Lunch £ Lunch ££ Dinner except Mon £££ Ⓥ Vegetarians welcome ⚹ Children welcome ⚹ Facilities for disabled visitors ⌸ Credit cards: Mastercard/Eurocard, American Express, Visa, Diners Club, Switch, Delta ⌸ General Manager: Colin Macaloney

Kilsyth Road Banknock Stirlingshire FK4 1UF
Tel: 01324 840201 Fax: 01324 841054
Web: www.glenskirliehouse.com
From Glasgow take A80 towards Stirling, take Junction 4, on A803 Kilsyth/Bonnybridge cut off. At T-junction turn right, restaurant 1 mile on right-hand side. [C5]

STIRLING OUTSKIRTS

The Topps

- *"A comfortable and humorous stay."*
- *Excellent home cooking.*

THE POPULAR restaurant complements the guest house facilities. It has a small bar and comfortable dining room. Scottish owners Jennifer and Alistair Steel both cook. The menus are straightforward, usually offering a choice of four main courses. As much produce as possible comes from the farm itself.

Alistair's gravadlax – herb marinated salmon. Lamb fillet with port sauce, fresh raspberries and wild mushrooms. Lacy crêpes filled with chocolate and Greek yoghurt sauce.

STB ★★ Guest House

◐ *Open all year* 🏠 *Rooms: 8 en suite* 🛏 *B&B £20–£32* ✖ *Dinner ££* Ⓥ *Vegetarians welcome – prior notice required* ★ *Children welcome* ♿ *Facilities for disabled visitors* 🚭 *No smoking throughout* 💳 *Credit cards: Mastercard/Eurocard, Visa* 🍴 *Owners/Chefs: Jennifer & Alistair Steel*

Fintry Road Denny Stirlingshire FK6 5JF
Tel: 01324 822471 Fax: 01324 823099
E-mail: jennifer@thetopps.f9.co.uk
Web: www.thetopps.com
On B818 Denny – Fintry road, off M80. 4 miles from Denny. [C5]

STRATHAVEN

The Waterside Pub & Restaurant

- *"A vibrant, friendly and cosmopolitan restaurant and pub offering something to suit all tastes."*
- *Modern Scottish cooking.*

AT THE WATERSIDE Pub & Restaurant there is an extensive menu and the style of the establishment is such that there is something here to suit everyone. A popular place with a friendly and welcoming feel which is a testament to its regular customers. An excellent selection of quality wines, by the glass, are available.

Breaded mushrooms filled with haggis, deep-fried and smothered with garlic butter. Roast Scottish salmon with sweet scallop risotto, flavoured with dill, coriander and white wine. Drambuie raspberries with honey mascarpone and shortcake ice cream served in a brandy snap basket.

◐ *Open all year* ✖ *Food available all day £ Lunch £ Dinner ££* Ⓥ *Vegetarians welcome* ★ *Children welcome* ♿ *Facilities for disabled visitors* 💳 *Credit cards: Mastercard/Eurocard, American Express, Visa, Diners Club, Switch, Delta* 🍴 *Manager: Elaine Anderson*

31 Waterside Street Strathaven South Lanarkshire ML10 6AW
Tel: 01357 522588 Fax: 01357 529000
E-mail: info@morris-inns.com
Web: www.morris-inns.com
Situated in the conservation village of Strathaven overlooking Allison Green. [C6]

STRATHPEFFER

Coul House Hotel

- *"This charming country house hotel offers good food and hospitality."*
- *Country house cooking.*

HOME TO Martyn and Ann Hill since 1978, this elegant country house hotel commands fine views. The 'Kitchen Bar', which serves bar lunches, is popular with locals. Mackenzie's Taste of Scotland Restaurant offers table d'hôte and à la carte lunch and dinner menus focusing on Scottish specialities. There is also the Tartan Bistro. 1 AA Rosette.

Salmon tagliatelle: thin strips of salmon tossed with pasta in a cream sauce with dill. Medallions of Scottish beef served on a bed of stir-fried vegetables with a red wine reduction. Honey wafers filled with Drambuie mousse on a raspberry coulis.

STB ★★★★ Hotel

◐ Open all year ⌂ Rooms: 20 en suite 🛏 DB&B £53.50–£80 B&B £38–£55 🆂🅿 Special rates available ✖ Lunch £-££ (Restaurant – prior booking only) Dinner 5 course menu £££ Ⓥ Vegetarians welcome ⚘ Children welcome ♿ Facilities for disabled visitors ⊁ No smoking in restaurant ❦ Member of the Scotch Beef Club 💳 Credit cards: Mastercard/Eurocard, American Express, Visa, Diners Club, Switch, JCB ⚑ Proprietors: Martyn & Ann Hill

Contin by Strathpeffer Ross-shire IV14 9EY
Tel: 01997 421487 Fax: 01997 421945
Web: www.milford.co.uk/go/coulhouse.html
North of Inverness, take A9 over Moray Firth Bridge. After 5 miles take second left at roundabout to A835. Follow road for about 12 miles until you reach the village of Contin. Hotel is ½ mile up private drive to the right. [C3]

STRATHYRE

Creagan House Restaurant with Accommodation

- *"Hospitable and well-informed hosts, excellent cooking make this a very special place to visit."*
- *Innovative Scottish cooking.*

CREAGAN HOUSE has been sympathetically restored to provide a 'baronial' dining room and five bedrooms. The cooking style allows the flavour of fresh local ingredients to emerge using herbs from the garden, and locally sourced produce. Great care and attention is given to preparation, cooking and presentation. 2 AA Rosettes.

Seared scallops on saffron sauce with asparagus and served with a salad of garden leaves. Saddle of venison on a greiseagan tomato galette with a bramble, port wine and orange sauce. Chocolate, hazelnut mousse cake with a compote of local berries.

STB ★★★★ Restaurant with Rooms

◐ Open all year except 3 to 28 Feb and 1 week Oct ⌂ Rooms: 5 en suite 🛏 B&B £42.50 🆂🅿 Special rates available ✖ Lunch parties can be arranged Dinner ££-£££ Booking essential for all meals Ⓥ Vegetarians welcome – with prior notice Children over ten years welcome ⊁ No smoking in dining hall and bedrooms ❦ Member of the Scotch Beef Club 💳 Credit cards: Mastercard/Eurocard, American Express, Visa ⚑ Chef/Proprietor: Gordon Gunn; Co-Proprietor: Cherry Gunn

Strathyre, Callander Perthshire FK18 8ND
Tel: 01877 384638 Fax: 01877 384319
E-mail: mail@creaganhouse.fsnet.co.uk
Web: www.milford.co.uk/go/creaganhouse.html
On A84, ¼ mile north of Strathyre. [C5]

STRATHYRE

Rosebank House

- *"A family run establishment with a relaxed atmosphere."*
- *Modern Scottish cooking.*

ROSEBANK HOUSE is run by Jill and Pete Moor who offer comfortable and welcoming surroundings, good food and a place for guests to relax and enjoy the area. Jill's many talents also extend to the kitchen where she prepares fine dishes using fresh local produce. Homemade preserves are a speciality here.

Home-cured gravadlax with wholegrain mustard and dill sauce. Local trout with almond and mushroom stuffing, seasonal local vegetables and home-grown herbs. Whisky Mac bread and butter pudding.

STB ★★★★ Guest House

◐ *Open all year* ⌂ *Rooms: 4, 2 en suite* ⇌ *DB&B £35–£38 B&B £20–£23* ⓢⓡ *Special rates available* ⓤⓛ *Unlicensed – guests welcome to take own wine* ✗ *Packed lunch £ Lunch – by arrangement ££ Dinner ££ Booking essential for all meals* Ⓥ *Vegetarians welcome* ⚲ *Children welcome* ⌦ *No smoking throughout* ⌂ *Dogs welcome* ⊞ *Credit cards: Mastercard/Eurocard, Visa, Delta, Switch* Ⓜ *Co-Proprietors: Jill & Pete Moor*

Strathyre Perthshire FK18 8NA
Tel: 01877 384 208 Fax: 01877 384 201
E-mail: rosebank@tinyworld.co.uk
Web: smoothhound.co.uk/hotels/roseban1.html
On the east side of the main A84 in the village of Strathyre. [C5]

STRONTIAN

Kilcamb Lodge Hotel: Finalist The Macallan Taste of Scotland Awards 2000

- *"Great attention to quality and flavour of produce is evident at Kilcamb where warmth and friendliness await you."*
- *High quality Scottish cuisine.*

KILCAMB LODGE is family-owned and run by Anne and Peter Blakeway. The excellence of the food has been recognised by the award of 2 AA Rosettes. Neil Mellis cooks, presenting a highly professional table d'hôte menu which changes daily and uses the best of the produce available that day. Investor in People Award.

Pan-fried veal sweetbreads with olive cake and truffle essence. Loin of Argyll lamb with a soft herb crust, vegetable gâteau and a rosemary jus. Hot passion fruit soufflé with raspberry sorbet.

STB ★★★★ Hotel

◐ *Open all year except Jan Feb N.B. Open New Year* ⌂ *Rooms: 11 en suite* ⇌ *Room only £60–£130* ✗ *Light Lunch £ Dinner 2 course menu ££ 4 course menu £££* Ⓥ *Vegetarians welcome – prior notice required* ⚲ *Children welcome* ♿ *Facilities for non-residential disabled visitors* ⌦ *No smoking in restaurant* ⊞ *Credit cards: Mastercard/Eurocard, Visa, Switch, Delta* Ⓜ *Directors: Peter & Anne Blakeway*

Strontian Argyll PH36 4HY
Tel: 01967 402257 Fax: 01967 402041
E-mail: kilcamblodge@aol.com
Web: www.kilcamblodge.com
On A861, 13 miles from Corran Ferry (A82), 8 miles south of Fort William). [B5]

SWINTON

The Wheatsheaf Restaurant with Rooms

- *"An excellent example of Scottish cooking served and presented in innovative style."*
- *Modern Scottish cooking.*

THE WHEATSHEAF's character has been carefully preserved. Bedrooms are prettily furnished, with en suite bathrooms. The menu is extensive, reasonably priced and changes daily. Excellent local produce is given added flavour by the chef's individuality and flair. The Wheatsheaf has 2 AA Rosettes. Winner of The Macallan Taste of Scotland Hotel of the Year Award 1997.

Seared scallops and langoustines on a salad of home grown leaves. Two medallions of Scotch beef fillet with wild mushrooms in a malt whisky sauce. Iced cranachan parfait with raspberries and Drambuie with brandy snap biscuits.

STB ★★★★ Restaurant with Rooms
Green Tourism Award Pending

◐ Open all year except 1 to 14 Jan Closed Mon
🏠 Rooms: 6 en suite ⇌ B&B £40–£52
💰 Special rates available ✘ Lunch except Mon
££ Dinner £££ Ⓥ Vegetarians welcome
☂ Children welcome ⚕ No smoking in restaurant 💳 Credit cards: Mastercard/Eurocard, Visa, Switch ⚒ Proprietors: Alan & Julie Reid

Swinton Berwickshire TD11 3JJ
Tel: 01890 860 257 Fax: 01890 860 688
Web: www.scot-borders.co.uk"accom"-swinton
On B6461 Kelso-Berwick-upon-Tweed, 12 miles west of Berwick or a few miles east of A697. [D6]

SYMINGTON AYRSHIRE

Nether Underwood

- *"Quite one of our most delightful properties offering the ultimate in home comforts and stylish cooking."*
- *Delicious modern Scottish cooking.*

A LARGE 1930s style country house lovingly restored by the Thomsons, whose good taste is evident. Meals are candlelit, with the light sparkling in silver and glass, yet this is still a family home. Felicity is a talented cook and offers her guests only the very best food, surroundings and service.

Cullen skink served with home-made granary bread. Pan-fried fillet of pork with coriander pesto, butterbean mash and baked spinach. Lemon and lime tart served with lemon ice cream and home-grown raspberries.

STB ★★★★★ Guest House

◐ Open all year except 24 Dec to 2 Jan 🏠 Rooms: 3 en suite (4th sometimes available) ⇌ DB&B £65–£75 B&B £40–£50 ✘ Dinner £££
Ⓥ Vegetarians welcome ☂ Children over 16 years welcome ⚕ No smoking throughout
💳 Credit cards: Mastercard/Eurocard, Visa, Switch ⚒ Chef/Proprietor: Felicity Thomson

By Symington Kilmarnock KA1 5NG
Tel: 01563 830 666 Fax: 01563 830 777
E-mail: netherund@aol.com
Web: www.netherunderwood.co.uk
On A77 from Glasgow, past Hansel Village on left then turn left at signs to Ladykirk and Underwood. Turn left at 'T' junction, turn left at bottom of hill past Wardneuk Farm. Pass Underwood House and immediately turn left into lane marked Nether Underwood. The house is on left, painted pink, through black 5 bar gate. [C6]

TAIN

Mansfield House Hotel

- *"Warm hospitality and lovely food make this a Highland gem."*
- *Good Scottish cooking.*

MANSFIELD HOUSE has been lovingly maintained and offers every comfort for travellers. The kitchen prides itself in preparing well-chosen Scottish produce for a selection of familiar and popular dishes. There is a friendly and relaxed atmosphere and the Lauritsen family, highly skilled and experienced, are excellent hosts. Investor in People Award.

Smoked poultry confit with kumquat and chilli jam. Seafood sausages with wilted greens and scallop sauce. Citrus soufflé with a light chocolate sabayon.

STB ★★★★ Hotel
Green Tourism Three Leaf Gold Award

◐ Open all year ⌂ Rooms: 18 en suite ⌸ B&B £50–£75 ⓢⓟ Special rates available ✖ Food available all day £-£££ Lunch £ Dinner £-£££ Ⓥ Vegetarians welcome ✻ Children welcome ♿ Facilities for disabled visitors ⊁ No smoking in restaurants ☙ Member of the Scotch Beef Club 🎫 Credit cards: Mastercard/Eurocard, American Express, Visa, Switch ▌ Proprietors: Norman, Norma & David Lauritsen

*Scotsburn Road Tain Ross-shire IV19 1PR
Tel: 01862 892052 Fax: 01862 892260
E-mail: mansfield@cali.co.uk
Web: www.mansfield-house.co.uk
Approaching Tain from south, ignore first entrance and continue north on A9 to second turning, signposted to police station and Royal Academy. [C3]*

TAIN

Morangie House Hotel

- *"Popular traditional hotel offering a high standard of comfort and hospitality."*
- *Traditional Highland fayre.*

THIS FINE Victorian mansion has been tastefully renovated and lovingly extended by the Wynne family. In the dining room they serve good local dishes using some of the freshest ingredients from the Dornoch Firth, opposite the hotel. They also offer bar, table d'hôte and à la carte menus. Investor in People Award.

Local fresh local mussels cooked in a white wine and cream sauce. Sirloin Rabbie Burns: tender Ross-shire sirloin steak filled with award-winning haggis and smothered in a Glenmorangie whisky and mushroom cream sauce. Sticky toffee pudding.

STB ★★★★ Hotel

◐ Open all year ⌂ Rooms: 26 en suite ⌸ DB&B £55–£80 B&B £40–£60 ⓢⓟ Special rates available ✖ Food available all day £ Lunch £ Dinner ££ Ⓥ Vegetarians welcome ✻ Children welcome ♿ Facilities for disabled visitors ⊁ No smoking in dining room 🎫 Credit cards: Mastercard/Eurocard, American Express, Visa, Diners Club, Switch ▌ Proprietor: John Wynne

*Morangie Road Tain Ross-shire IV19 1PY
Tel: 01862 892281 Fax: 01862 892872
E-mail: wynne@morangiehotel.com
Just off the A9 Inverness-Wick road on northern outskirts of Tain. [C3]*

TALLADALE

The Old Mill Highland Lodge

- *"The style is informal, the welcome genuine and the cooking excellent."*
- *Skilled home cooking.*

THIS CHARMING and elegantly furnished house is where Joanna and Chris Powell look after their guests with genuine warmth and charm. Chris is an enthusiastic cook and produces imaginative, colourful dishes utilising much locally-sourced Highland produce. Joanna uses her experience in the wine trade to complement the mouth-watering dishes with just the right wine.

Wee filo pastry parcels of haggis with a leek purée. Roasted local cod fillets with a crusted Pecorino and pesto topping, with bacon and tomato concassé. Melting chocolate pudding with a raspberry coulis and home-made ice cream.

STB ★★★★ Hotel

◐ Open all year except 15 Oct to 15 Dec
🏠 Rooms: 6, 5 en suite DB&B £45–£65
Special rates available Restricted hotel licence ✘ Dinner £££ Residents only
Ⓥ Vegetarians welcome – by prior arrangement
No smoking throughout No credit cards
Owners: Chris & Joanna Powell

Talladale Loch Maree Ross-shire IV22 2HL
Tel: 01445 760271
On A832 at Talladale – 10 miles north of Kinlochewe and 10 miles south of Gairloch. The only establishment on the left along Loch Maree heading north. [B3]

TARBERT ARGYLL

The Columba Hotel

- *"Nestling in the quiet end of the Harbour – enjoy a broad choice of quality Scottish produce with an unusually informative wine list."*
- *Scottish modern cooking.*

THE COLUMBA HOTEL nestles at the quiet end of Tarbert Harbour. The bar is popular for its wholesomely different bar food. The restaurant has been elegantly restored and offers a relaxed atmosphere and a menu which makes imaginative use of the excellent local produce. The seafood on the menu is of exceptional quality.

Warm queen scallop, Tarbert smoked salmon and cucumber salad with a malt whiskey and sorrel sauce. Pan-fried Inveraray venison saddle on salardaise potatoes. Raspberry and grenadine sorbet with dark chocolate and cinnamon shortbread; white chocolate and Glayva sauce.

STB ★★★ Hotel
Green Tourism One Leaf Bronze Award

◐ Open all year except 25 and 26 Dec
🏠 Rooms: 10 en suite DB&B £39.95–£58
B&B £34.95–£43 Special rates available
Lunch £ Dinner ££ Ⓥ Vegetarians welcome
✱ Children welcome No smoking in restaurant Credit cards: Mastercard/Eurocard, American Express, Visa Partners: Bob & Gina Chicken

East Pier Road Tarbert Loch Fyne Argyll PA29 6UF
Tel: 01880 820808 Fax: 01880 820808
E-mail: columbahotel@fsbdial.co.uk
Web: www.columbahotel.com
On East Pier Road, ½ mile to the left around the harbour. Hotel on roadside. [B6]

TARBERT ARGYLL

Stonefield Castle Hotel

- *"The view while dining is a breathtaking experience."*
- *Modern/traditional Scottish cooking.*

STONEFIELD CASTLE is set in 60 acres of woodland gardens, and is located on Loch Fyne – enjoy the breathtaking views while dining. The cooking here offers good local produce – seafood is caught locally – presented in a traditional style with modern influences, and is served by well-trained and friendly staff.

Islay king scallops with smoked bacon and garlic and chive butter. Fillet of Buccleuch beef with Dunsyre rarebit and port jus. Warm Drambuie and raspberry soufflé.

STB ★★★★ Hotel

◐ *Open all year* ⌂ *Rooms: 33 (32 en suite, 1 with private facilities)* ⌇ *DB&B £65–£85* ⓢⓟ *Special rates available Lunch £ Dinner £££* Ⓥ *Vegetarians welcome* ♿ *Facilities for disabled visitors* ⌇ *No smoking in restaurant* ⎚ *Credit cards: Mastercard/Eurocard, American Express, Visa, Diners Club, Switch, Delta*

Tarbert Loch Fyne Argyll PA29 6YJ
Tel: 01880 820836 Fax: 01880 820929
3 miles north of Tarbert on A83 to Lochgilphead. [B6]

TARBERT, ARGYLL

Victoria Hotel

- *"Interesting use of quality Scottish produce is enjoyed at this bright and cheerful location."*
- *Modern Scottish cooking.*

THE VICTORIA HOTEL is as popular as ever. It has been under the same ownership and chef for the last ten years and has built an enviable reputation for informal bar meals. The conservatory offers more formal dining. Menus offer locally-sourced produce described and presented with skill and flair, with the eating experience matching the description on the menus.

Fresh asparagus with Argyll smoked venison and slithers of Parmesan cheese, drizzled with extra virgin olive oil. Loch Fyne scallops with a saffron and coriander butter sauce, garnished with a slice of locally made black pudding. Polenta, almond and lemon cake with Islay whisky liqueur Mascarpone.

STB ★★★ Inn

◐ *Open all year except Christmas Day* ⌂ *Rooms: 5 en suite* ⌇ *DB&B £46–£48 B&B £27–£29* ⓢⓟ *Special rates available* ✘ *Lunch £ Dinner ££* Ⓥ *Vegetarians welcome* ♣ *Children welcome* ♿ *Facilities for disabled visitors* ⌇ *No smoking in restaurant* ⎚ *Credit cards: Mastercard/Eurocard, Visa, Switch, Delta* ⚑ *General Manager: Padraig Ahern*

Barmore Road Tarbert Argyll PA29 6TW
Tel: 01880 820 236/431 Fax: 01880 820 638
E-mail: victoria.hotel@lineone.net
First hotel as you enter the village (on A83 from Lochgilphead) on your right-hand side. [B6]

TAYVALLICH

Tayvallich Inn

- *"Good selection of fresh and smoked local seafood – however the vegetarian and the Aberdeen Angus steak fan are not overlooked."*
- *Good Scottish cooking with some innovation.*

THE TAYVALLICH INN is beautifully situated with a spectacular outlook onto Tayvallich Bay. The decor is rustic with a nautical theme reflecting the many yachtsmen who frequent this area. Andrew and Jilly's sourcing of good local produce is evident on the menus. Dishes are well-presented and offer good value for money.

Pan-fried sound of Jura scallops with fresh brown bread. Tayvallich seafood platter (jumbo prawns, mussels, oyster, smoked salmon, hot-smoked salmon, pickled herring, and crab claws). Lemon posset, served with a shortcake biscuit.

◐ Open all year except Christmas Day and New Year's Day ✗ Lunch except Mon Nov to Mar £-££ Dinner except Sun-Thu Nov to Mar ££-£££ Bar suppers except Mon Nov to Mar Ⓥ Vegetarians welcome ☆ Children welcome ♿ Access only for disabled visitors 🖃 Credit cards: Mastercard/Eurocard, Visa, Switch, Delta, JCB 🍴 Proprietors: Andrew & Jilly Wilson

*Tayvallich by Lochgilphead Argyll PA31 8PL
Tel: 01546 870282 Fax: 01546 870333
E-mail: tayvallich.inn@virgin.net
2 hours from Glasgow via A82 to Tarbert. Then take A83 to Lochgilphead. Follow signs to Oban then take B841 at Cairnbaan. After 4 miles take B8052 to Tayvallich, 6 miles on single-track road. [B5]*

THORNHILL DUMFRIES

Trigony House Hotel

- *"Good food in a relaxed atmosphere – popular with locals and visitors."*
- *Simple, elegant Scottish cooking.*

TRIGONY, a small country house in its own gardens, became a hotel over 20 years ago. New owners Adam and Judith Moore (mother and son) have an innovative approach to menus and cooking and continue to provide homely comfort in public and private rooms which are bright, airy and have charming views over the surrounding country.

Fresh Solway scallops in a fennel, cucumber and white wine sauce. Fillet of black-faced lamb with a herb crust, black olive gravy and a wild rice timbale. Turkish apple cake soaked in white wine with meringue and apple custard.

STB ★★★★ Hotel

◐ Open all year 🛏 Rooms : 8 en suite 🛌 DB&B £52.50-£62.50 B&B £35-£45 SP Special rates available ✗ Lunch £ Dinner ££ Ⓥ Vegetarians welcome ☆ Children over 8 years welcome 🚭 No smoking in dining room 🐾 Pets welcome 🖃 Credit cards: Mastercard/Eurocard, Visa, Switch, Delta 🍴 Proprietors: Judith & Adam Moore

*By Thornhill Dumfriesshire DG3 5EZ
Tel: 01848 331211 Fax: 01848 331303
E-mail: info@trigonyhotel.co.uk
www.trigonyhotel.co.uk
Situated off A76, 13 miles north of Dumfries. 1 mile south of Thornhill on the Dumfries-Ayr trunk road. [C6]*

THURSO

Forss Country House Hotel

- *"A fine Scottish welcome at this lovely country house – and fine fishing too!"*
- *Traditional Scottish cooking.*

FORSS COUNTRY HOUSE HOTEL is run by the MacGregor family, with Jamie MacGregor acting as 'mein host'. Catriona McLean does most of the cooking under the watchful eye of Jackie MacGregor. Best use of local produce is made in particular, locally-caught fish. This is a place from which to enjoy the splendour of the Highlands.

Seared Scottish scallops served in a garlic and white wine sauce with Gruyère cheese topping and crisp salad garnish. Pan-fried medallions of Caithness venison in a redcurrant and port jus. Choice of home-made sweets or extensive cheeseboard selection.

STB ★★★★ Small Hotel

◑ *Open 5 Jan to 23 Dec* 🛏 *Rooms: 10 en suite* 🍽 *DB&B £67–£80 B&B £45–£57.50* 💷 *Special rates available* ✕ *Food available all day ££ Lunch – residents only £-££ Dinner ££* Ⓥ *Vegetarians welcome* ✴ *Children welcome* ♿ *Facilities for disabled visitors* ✄ *No smoking in dining room* 💳 *Credit cards: Mastercard/Eurocard, American Express, Visa* 🔑 *Proprietors: Jamie & Jackie MacGregor*

by Thurso Caithness KW14 7XY
Tel: 01847 861201 Fax: 01847 861301
E-mail: jamie@forsshouse.freeserve.co.uk
Web: www. forsscountryhouse.co.uk
4 miles from Thurso heading west on A836.
[C2]

TIGHNABRUAICH

Royal Hotel

- *"Enjoy elegant dining with good service and beautifully presented food."*
- *Skilled and stylish Scottish cooking.*

AT THE ROYAL there is a stylish modern restaurant and an informal friendly bar-brasserie where local seafood (served straight from the fishermen's nets) and game is served. The food here is very popular – it is advisable to arrive early for the brasserie and booking is essential for the restaurant. Investor in People Award.

Peppered venison fillet with a Dunsyre Blue cheese and red onion salad. King scallops hand-dived in Loch Fyne with wilted spinach and herb butter. Figs, roasted and presented on sugared parfait with a fruit coulis.

STB ★★★★ Hotel

◑ *Open all year* 🛏 *Rooms: 11 en suite* 🍽 *DB&B £50–£80 B&B £32–£62* 💷 *Special rates available* ✕ *Food available all day ££ Lunch £ Dinner ££-£££* Ⓥ *Vegetarians welcome* ✄ *No smoking in dining room* 💳 *Credit cards: Mastercard/Eurocard, Visa, Switch, Delta* 🔑 *Owners: Roger & Bea McKie*

Tighnabruaich Argyll PA21 2BE
Tel: 01700 811239 Fax: 01700 811300
E-mail: royalhotel@btinternet.com
Web: www.royalhotel.org.uk
Overlooking the Kyles of Bute at the end of the A8003 in Tighnabruaich. [B6]

TONGUE

Borgie Lodge Hotel

- *"What a find – well worth seeking out!"*
- *Modern Scottish cooking.*

BORGIE LODGE is home to Peter and Jacqui MacGregor. A self-taught cook, Jacqui makes excellent use of the Caithness beef and lamb available, and the daily changing choice dinner menu will often feature the salmon and brown trout caught by the guests! Borgie Lodge has fishing rights and boats available.

Trio of spicy haggis with a malt whisky sauce. Seared fillet of wild salmon with a confetti of vegetables and curry oil. Chocolate torte with chantilly cream and sauce anglaise.

STB ★★★★ Hotel

- Open all year except 24 Dec to 3 Jan
- Rooms: 7, 6 en suite (1 private suite)
- DB&B £62.50–£72.50 B&B £40–£50
- Lunch £ Dinner £££ Vegetarians welcome
- Children welcome No smoking in dining room and bedrooms Credit cards: Mastercard/Eurocard, Visa Proprietors: Peter & Jacqui MacGregor

Skerray Tongue Sutherland KW14 7TH
Tel: 01641 521 332 Fax: 01641 521 332
E-mail: info@borgielodgehotel.co.uk
Web: www.borgielodgehotel.co.uk
Take A836 for 7 miles from Tongue, turn left at the Torrisdale Road. Borgie Lodge is ½ mile along on the right. [C2]

TONGUE

Tongue Hotel

- *"Historic converted hunting lodge in a spectacular location."*
- *Modern Scottish.*

THE TONGUE HOTEL was built as a hunting lodge in the late 1800s by the Duke of Sutherland. Bedrooms are comfortable, with public rooms having character and charm. Staff are of smart appearance and provide excellent service. The surrounding area, dominated by Ben Loyal, is of great geological and ornithological interest.

Baked goats cheese on seasonal leaves and pine kernels accompanied by a beetroot chutney. Loin of Scottish lamb on a black pudding mash complemented by a garlic and rosemary jus. Iced raspberry and Drambuie parfait.

STB ★★★★ Small Hotel

- Apr to Oct incl Rooms: 16 DB&B £40–£75 B&B £25–£50 Special rates available Food available all day ££ Lunch £ Dinner (please phone ahead) £££
- Vegetarians welcome Children welcome No smoking during meal times Dogs welcome Credit cards: Mastercard, Visa, Switch General Manager: Ms Karen Stoltman

Tongue Sutherland IV27 4XD
Tel: 01847 611 206 Fax: 01847 611345
Web: www.scottish-selection.co.uk
On A383 as you enter Tongue on right-hand side overlooking the Kyle of Tongue. [C2]

TORRIDON

Loch Torridon Country House Hotel

- *"A high class retreat with the added touches of family warmth."*
- Fine Scottish cooking.

THIS IS a luxurious, lovingly restored Victorian shooting lodge with ornate ceilings, wood panelling and open log fires. It is set on the shore of Loch Torridon in 58 acres of parkland. The kitchen garden grows herbs and vegetables for the excellent daily changing menu. Investor in People Award. 2 AA Rosettes.

Tartare of Gairloch salmon with a vegetable vinaigrette and oyster beignet. Fillet of Scotch beef with braised oxtail, fine beans, confit of shallots and cepe oil. Parfait of strawberries with braised garden rhubarb and jus fraise.

STB ★★★★ Hotel
Green Tourism Two Leaf Silver Award

◐ Open all year ⊞ Rooms: 20 en suite ⇔ DB&B £70–£300 B&B £50–£260 (per room) ⊞ Special rates available ✕ Food available all day ££ Lunch ££ Dinner ££££ Ⓥ Vegetarians welcome ⚛ Children welcome ♿ Facilities for disabled visitors ✂ No smoking in dining room ⊞ Credit cards: Mastercard/Eurocard, American Express, Visa, Diners Club, Switch ◩ Proprietors: David & Geraldine Gregory; General Managers: Daniel & Rohaise Rose-Bristow

*Torridon By Achnasheen IV22 2EY
Tel: 01445 791242 Fax: 01445 791296
E-mail: enquiries@lochtorridonhotel.com
Web: www.lochtorridonhotel.com
Turn off the A832 at Kinlochewe and take the A896 to Torridon – do not turn off to Torridon village but carry on. Follow hotel sign – hotel is 1½ miles on right-hand side. [B4]*

TROON

Cellars Restaurant & Cocktail Bar

- *"A vibrant, contemporary restaurant with a fine Scottish menu."*
- Modern Scottish cooking.

CELLARS is steeped in local history of the 19th century. However, its theme throughout is impressive Art Deco, with burning candles creating a romantic and highly charged atmosphere. Dishes are conceived from locally-sourced seafoods and the best Scottish beef, fruits and vegetables. International touches are added by Robbie O'Keefe. Menu is changed monthly.

Marinated strips of sea bass, dill and onion crêpe. Layered tournedos of beef with lobster, potato gallette, spring onion soufflé and port wine sauce. Poached pear, apple and Armagnac tart, with fresh custard.

◐ Open all year Closed Tue ✕ Lunch except Tue £-££ Dinner except Tue ££ Ⓥ Vegetarians welcome ⚛ Children welcome ♿ Facilities for disabled visitors ✂ No smoking in restaurant Smoking permitted in cocktail bar ⊞ Credit cards: Mastercard/Eurocard, American Express, Visa, Switch ◩ Proprietors: Malcolm & Karen Ronney

*149 Templehill Troon KA10 6BQ
Tel: 01292 317448 Fax: 01292 318508
E-mail: anchor1812@aol.com
Web: www.theanchoragehotel.com
On arriving in Troon follow directions to Troon harbour which will lead you to Templehill. The Cellars is located half a kilometre along on the left-hand side. [C6]*

TROON

Piersland House Hotel

- *"A well-presented and popular hotel in the heart of golf country."*
- *International cuisine.*

PIERSLAND has some fine Jacobean-style features. It stands in beautifully landscaped grounds that include an oriental garden. The hotel has 13 fully equipped cottage suites for guests wanting that little bit extra. Piersland has an informal dining area – The Brasserie Restaurant which overlooks the magnificent gardens. 2 AA Red Food Rosettes.

Guinea fowl and tarragon sausage, colcannon and brown lentils. Medallions of Scotch beef fillet with a wild mushroom and spring onion duxelle, bacon crisp and marinated vine tomato. Light tangy lemon posset accompanied by petticoat tail shortbread.

STB ★★★★ Hotel

◐ Open all year ⌂ Rooms: 28 en suite ⇌ DB&B £75–£90 B&B £55–£70 ⓢ Special rates available ✘ Lunch ££ Dinner £££ Ⓥ Vegetarians welcome ⚹ Children welcome ♿ Facilities for disabled visitors and residents ⊞ Credit cards: Mastercard/Eurocard, American Express, Visa, Diners Club, Switch, JCB ⓜ General Manager: Karel Kuhler

15 Craigend Road Troon KA10 6HD
Tel: 01292 314747 Fax: 01292 315613
E-mail: reception.piersland@talk21.com
Web: www.piersland.co.uk
South corner of Troon, opposite Royal Troon Golf Club and within 3 miles of Glasgow Prestwick International Airport. Troon is the Scottish port for the Seacat crossing to Belfast. [C6]

TURNBERRY

Malin Court Hotel

- *"Good food, attentive staff and welcoming surroundings to be found here."*
- *Modern Scottish cooking.*

MALIN COURT is very professionally-run and each member of staff takes an obvious pride in their work. Chef Andrea Beach is a highly committed and competent young woman, who with her team has earned the hotel a second AA Rosette. Menus are imaginative and complemented by a short, well-priced wine list.

Deep-fried crab cakes resting on a nectarine and lime salsa. Fillet of Scottish beef served with a barley bree and potato cakes. Warm apple and sultana tart with Drambuie ice cream.

STB ★★★★ Hotel
Green Tourism Two Leaf Silver Award

◐ Open all year ⌂ Rooms: 18 en suite ⇌ DB&B £65–£95 B&B £52–£82 ⓢ Special rates available ✘ Food available all day ££ Lunch from £ Dinner from ££ Ⓥ Vegetarians welcome ⚹ Children welcome ♿ Facilities for disabled visitors ⛊ Member of the Scotch Beef Club ⊞ Credit cards: Mastercard/Eurocard, American Express, Visa, Diners Club, Switch, Delta ⓜ General Manager: W R Kerr

Turnberry Ayrshire KA26 9PB
Tel: 01655 331457 Fax: 01655 331072
E-mail: info@malincourt.co.uk
Web: www.malincourt.co.uk
On A719 Ayr-Girvan, south of Maidens, just off the A77 which leads to Turnberry then to Maidens and onwards to Culzean castle. [C6]

TURNBERRY

Turnberry Hotel, Golf Courses and Spa

- *"A firm favourite offering grand and sumptuous surroundings and Stewart Cameron's highly skilled cooking."*
- Grand hotel cooking; also spa and grill-room styles.

TURNBERRY retains many opulent Edwardian features. The main restaurant offers the best classical cooking. Chef Stewart Cameron, a member of the Academie Culinaire de France, was The Macallan Personality of the Year 1996. During the week lunch is served in the Terrace Brasserie. The Turnberry Clubhouse serves roasts, grills, fries and sandwiches. 2 AA Rosettes.

Oak smoked Scottish salmon with lemon and black pepper. Tournedos of Buccleuch beef with fondant potatoes herbed with wild mushrooms and truffled cognac sauce. Iced cranachan parfait with raspberry compote and sweet mandarin jus.

STB ★★★★★ International Resort Hotel

Open all year Rooms: 221 en suite DB&B £105-£195 B&B £65-£145 Special rates available Food available all day ££ Lunch £££ Dinner ££££ Vegetarians welcome Children welcome Facilities for disabled visitors Member of the Scotch Beef Club Credit cards: Mastercard/ Eurocard, American Express, Visa, Diners Club, Switch General Manager: J Stewart Selbie

*Turnberry Ayrshire KA26 9LT
Tel: 01655 331000 Fax: 01655 331706
E-mail: turnberry@westin.com
Web: www.turnberry.co.uk
A77 – 17 miles south of Ayr. 2 miles after Kirkoswald. [C6]*

TURRIFF

Fife Arms Hotel

- *"A friendly and homely atmosphere offering wholesome fare."*
- Freshly cooked local produce.

FIFE ARMS with its Poachers Restaurant offers a cosy, informal venue for travellers and locals alike. The restaurant menu is written on a blackboard, changing daily according to availability of local produce, particularly the seafood which comes from Macduff. The lounge bar is a relaxing place with an open fire, and friendly service.

Deep-fried langoustine tails in tempura-style batter, with tartar sauce. Sauteed medallions of venison in brandy and raspberry sauce with fresh seasonal vegetables. Home-made sticky toffee pudding with ice cream and cream.

STB ★★ Small Hotel

Open all year Rooms: 9 en suite Lunch from £ Dinner from £-££ Vegetarians welcome Children welcome No smoking in restaurant Credit cards: Mastercard/ Eurocard, Visa, Switch, Delta Manager: Sandra Corless

*The Square Turriff AB53 4AF
Tel: 01888 563468 Fax: 01888 563798
Situated in Turriff town square on A947. 10 miles from Banff, 17 miles from Oldmeldrum. [D3]*

TURRIFF

Fyvie Castle, National Trust for Scotland

- *"Build your appetite by walking the wonderful grounds, then visit the tearoom for a snack or light lunch."*
- *Scottish.*

FYVIE CASTLE is set amidst the most wonderful grounds and, as a National Trust property, everything is maintained and kept to the highest standard. It is a busy and popular property which offers good Scottish home baking – afternoon fresh cream teas with home-made scones – cooking and light refreshments. Daily specials available.

Home-made lentil soup with crusty roll. Local Strathdon Blue cheese with sliced apple in a brown or white baguette, served with side salad. Apple crumble with cream or ice cream.

STB Commended

◐ Open daily 21 Apr to 31 Aug and weekends in Oct ⓢ Special rates available ✗ Food available £ Lunch £ Ⓥ Vegetarians welcome ✱ Children welcome ⚒ Facilities for disabled visitors ⌦ No smoking throughout ⊞ Credit cards: Mastercard, Visa ⓝ Catering Manager: Yvonne Bell

Turriff Aberdeenshire AB5 8JS
Tel: 01651 891266 Fax: 01651 891107
Web: www.nts.org.uk
Off the A947, 8 miles south east of Turriff and 25 miles north-west of Aberdeen. [D3]

TYNDRUM

The Green Welly Stop (Formerly known as The Clifton Coffee House)

- *"Hearty portions of real home-made Scottish fayre served in a warm and friendly family-run restaurant."*
- *Home cooking.*

THE OWNERS here have just celebrated their 35th anniversary in the business! The simple self-service restaurant has become a tourist attraction in its own right with the restaurant the focal point. Good home baking and cooking along with a wide variety of traditional Scottish meals and snacks are on offer.

Soups: haggis and neep, Highland fish, cock-a-leekie. Vegetarian salads and main courses. Strathappin lamb casserole. Sticky toffee pudding, lemon cheesecake, and Atholl brose trifle.

◐ Open 8 Feb to 4 Jan except Christmas Day, Boxing Day and New Year's Day ✗ Food available 8.30 am – 5 pm £ Lunch £ Ⓥ Vegetarians welcome ✱ Children welcome ⚒ Facilities for disabled visitors ⌦ No smoking area in restaurant ⊞ Credit cards: Mastercard/ Eurocard, American Express, Visa, Diners Club, Switch, Delta ⓝ Partners: DD, LV & IL Wilkie/L P Gosden/F D Robertson & E S Robertson

Tyndrum Crianlarich Perthshire FK20 8RY
Tel: Tel: 01838 400271 Fax: 01838 400330
E-mail: clifton@tyndrum12.freeserve.co.uk
Web: www.thegreenwellystop.co.uk
On A85 to Oban and Fort William. 5 miles north of Crianlarich. [C5]

UPPER LARGO

Scotland's Larder

- *"Delightful Scottish food shop and restaurant."*
- *Modern/traditional Scottish food.*

SCOTLAND'S LARDER is a unique centre providing a range of Scottish quality food, be it in the restaurant, the shop or seasonal cookery demonstrations. A range of foods from morning coffee to meals are served all day. Diners choose from a set menu and 'specials board' consisting of local natural produce.

Organic salad of Grimbister cheese and local tomatoes. New season lamb cutlets with a tomato salsa. Double chocolate terrine with orange sauce.

◗ Open all year except 3 weeks from 5 Jan ✕ Food available all day £-££ Lunch £-££ Dinner ££ Ⓥ Vegetarians welcome ✱ Children welcome ♿ Facilities for disabled visitors ⚭ No smoking throughout 💳 Credit cards: Mastercard/Eurocard, Visa, Switch, Delta 🍴 Proprietor: Christopher Trotter; Manager: Anne Kinnes

Upper Largo by St Andrews KY8 6EA
Tel: 01333 360 414 Fax: 01333 360 427
E-mail: scotlandslarder@connectfree.co.uk
Web: www.scotlands-larder
Take East Neuk tourist route to Upper Largo, on A915. Scotland's Larder is at eastern edge of village. [D5]

WICK

The Portland Arms Hotel

- *"Informality combined with modern Scottish food and flair."*
- *Bistro style, modern Scottish.*

PORTLAND ARMS was originally built as a staging post in the 19th century and has been maintained and upgraded to a high standard. The menus are bistro-style offering local produce, imaginatively presented. The same menu is offered in the formal dining room or informal bar to suit customer preference.

Filo baskets of North Sea prawns, mussels and scallops in olive oil and white wine vinaigrette. Suprême of chicken filled with award-winning haggis, wrapped in locally-cured bacon, served with a whisky sauce. Portland assiette: home-made raspberry cranachan, chocolate mousse and a choux swan.

STB ★★★ Hotel

◗ Open all year 🛏 Rooms: 22 en suite 🛌 DB&B £45–£65 B&B £34–£55 💷 Special rates available ✕ Food available all day £ Lunch £ Dinner ££ Ⓥ Vegetarians welcome ✱ Children welcome ♿ Facilities for disabled visitors ⚭ No smoking in dining room and some bedrooms 💳 Credit cards: Mastercard/Eurocard, American Express, Visa, Diners Club, Switch, Delta 🍴 General Manager: Mark Stevens

Lybster Caithness KW3 6BS
Tel: 01593 721 721 Fax: 01593 721 722
E-mail: portland.arms@btconnect.com
Web: www.portlandarms.co.uk
On A9 at Latheron take A99 direction Wick, after 3 miles small town of Lybster, hotel on left-hand side. [D2]

association of
scottish visitor attractions

Argyll Lodging, Stirling

OVER FOUR HUNDRED of Scotland's visitor attractions are members of ASVA, the Association of Visitor Attractions. Each one is committed to making your experience more pleasurable and exciting.

ASVA attractions offer added value for money, always striving to be the best of their type. You can visit historic homes, castles and monuments; linger in some spacious and relaxing private and public gardens and parks; take the children to the exciting new science museums.

If you love art, why not visit our galleries and museums, and if you're a nature lover we have sites all over the country.

Enjoy whisky? Many of the most delicious brands are members, so go and sample the water of life. We also represent craft outlets, archeological and green conservation projects. Just look into our web-site www.asva.org.uk and see where quality is located.

A few of our members are displayed in this brochure, hoping to entice you to stay a little longer in some beautiful area of Scotland. The Scottish Tourist Board recognizes ASVA members' quality through its Quality Assurance Scheme and all members proudly display their stars.

The association seeks to promote best practice in the attraction sector and is committed to ensuring that the visitor will return to ASVA members and to Scotland.

For further information on ASVA, its members and activities, contact ASVA, Argyll's Lodging, Castle Wynd, Stirling FK8 1EG.

All of the visitor attractions listed in the geographical areas are ASVA members with the exception of those marked with*.

scottish
tourist board

A holiday destination with wide appeal and a long tradition of welcoming visitors

Loch Katrine, The Trossachs

SCOTLAND is what you want to make it. Near at hand, far from crowded, this is a holiday destination with wide appeal and a long tradition of welcoming visitors. It simply is a great place to relax. For such a small country, the sense of space is inspiring - with big skies, clear air and hills to make the heart ache.

It also has a long tradition of welcoming visitors. As a result, there is a very wide range of accommodation from budget to luxury. Get-away-from-it-all country house hotels or well-equipped hideaway cottages are two options if you want to explore the countryside. City-breaks in stylish modern hotels will put you in touch with the vibrancy of urban Scotland in Edinburgh, Glasgow and beyond. But whether your idea of relaxing is listening to the silence as the sun goes down on a horizon filled with islands, or agonising over the starter at dinner in a top city restaurant setting, then you can do both, equally well, in Scotland - and all on the same short break, with only a little planning.

Getting to Scotland is easy. Rail and air competition ensures that prices are keen. A choice of multi-journey, flexible rail tickets means you can see the best of Scotland very economically. Excellent air links, including some great offers from low cost carriers, further broadens the choice. Remember, too, that Scotland's roads are a lot less crowded. In short, Scotland has the transport network for the 21st century and is simply a whole lot nearer than you may think.

Finally, Scotland is a sociable place. People are friendly, the pubs have character. Mountain grandeur, unspoilt coastline, spectacular wildlife, cosy and characterful towns and villages, vibrant cities; a Scotland for romance, spectacle, culture, gourmet dining, getting fit or just getting in touch with yourself. No matter what you need from Scotland, you can be sure of a quality experience.

scottish tourist board
(STB) quality assurance

FOLLOW THE STARS and you won't be disappointed when you get to the inn. The new Scottish Tourist Board Star System is a world-first. Quality is what determines our star awards, not a check-list of facilities. We've made your priorities our priorities.

Quality makes or breaks a visit. It is only the quality of the welcome and service, the food, the hospitality, ambience and the comfort and condition of the property which earns Scottish Tourist Board Stars, not the size of the accommodation or the range of available facilities.

This easy-to-understand system tells you at a glance the quality standard of all types and sizes of accommodation from the smallest B&B and self-catering cottage to the largest countryside and city centre hotels.

★★★★★ Exceptional, world class
★★★★ Excellent
★★★ Very Good
★★ Good
★ Fair and acceptable

A trained Scottish Tourist Board quality advisor grades each property each year to give you the reassurance that you can choose accommodation of the quality standard you want.

To help you further in your choice the Scottish Tourist Board System also tells you the type of accommodation. All the latest Star ratings are listed at the end of each Taste of Scotland entry where applicable.

The range of accommodation types included in this guide are:
Guest House, B&B, Hotel, Small Hotel, International Resort Hotel, Inn, Restaurant with Rooms.

Area Tourist Offices

F OR SPECIFIC INFORMATION on a particular part of Scotland, contact the following:

Aberdeen and Grampian Tourist Board
Tel: 01224 632727 Fax: 01224 620415
Web: www.holiday.scotland.net

Angus and City of Dundee Tourist Board
Tel: 01382 527527 Fax: 01382 527550
Web: www.angusanddundee.co.uk

**Argyll, the Isles, Loch Lomond,
Stirling & Trossachs Tourist Board**
Tel: 01786 475019 Fax: 01786 471301
Web: www.holiday.scotland.net

Ayrshire and Arran Tourist Board
Tel: 01292 288688
Fax: 01292 288686
Web: www.ayrshire-arran.com

Dumfries and Galloway Tourist Board
Tel: 01387 253862 Fax: 01387 245555
Web: www.galloway.co.uk

Edinburgh and Lothians Tourist Board
Tel: 0131 473 3800 Fax: 0131 473 3881
Web: www.edinburgh.org

**Greater Glasgow and
Clyde Valley Tourist Board**
Tel: 0141 204 4400 Fax: 0141 204 4772
Web: www.holiday.scotland.net

The Highlands of Scotland Tourist Board
Tel: 01997 421160 Fax: 01997 421168
Web: www.host.co.uk

Kingdom of Fife Tourist Board
Tel: 01334 472021 Fax: 01334 478422
Web: www.standrews.co.uk

Orkney Tourist Board
Tel: 01856 872856 Fax: 01856 875056
Web: www.orkneyislands.com

Perthshire Tourist Board
Tel: 01738 627958 Fax: 01738 630416
Web: www.perthshire.co.uk

Scottish Borders Tourist Board
Tel: 01750 20054 Fax: 01750 21886
Web: www.holiday.scotland.net

Shetland Tourism
Tel: 01595 693434 Fax: 01595 695807
Web: www.shetland-tourism.co.uk

Western Isles Tourist Board
Tel: 01851 703088 Fax: 01851 705244
Web: www.witb.co.uk

For general enquiries, please contact
The Scottish Tourist Board
23 Ravelston Terrace, Edinburgh
Tel: 0131 332 2433
Fax: 0131 343 1513
Web: www.visitscotland.com

Tower Restaurant

Edinburgh & Lothians

EDINBURGH, Scotland's beautiful historic capital, gives a stunning first impression. Edinburgh Castle dominates the skyline views from Princes Street. From the castle, the Royal Mile sweeps down through the medieval Old Town, a warren of closes, lanes and historic buildings.

As well as hosting the largest arts festival in the world, Edinburgh offers a wide range of galleries, theatres and museums. The city boasts more restaurants per head of population than anywhere else in Scotland, as well as pubs, cafes and bistros.

THE LOTHIANS run in a wide arc around the city. Long beaches, golf courses and attractive little towns are a feature of East Lothian.

There are historic places to visit as well as country parks and well marked paths providing easy access to unspoiled countryside for walkers, cyclists and birdwatchers.

For details of accommodation, events and attractions, see area tourist offices on page 273

LOCAL PRODUCTS

BRODIES (TEA & COFFEE)

Since 1867, we have brought the best coffees and teas from all around the world, back to Edinburgh to be expertly blended and roasted. Espresso, cappuccino – a coffee to suit every palette . . . and every tea we blend has a quality that is Tea Council Approved.

Brodies Melrose Drysdale & Co Ltd. Tel 0131 554 6331

CLARK BROTHERS

Fourth generation fishmongers established in 1919. The finest quality smoked salmon is our speciality, cured to an old family recipe. Fresh fish from all over the world is sold daily from our premises by the attractive Fisherrow Harbour, Musselburgh – 5 miles east of Edinburgh.

Tel 0131 665 6181

CROMBIE'S BUTCHER

Emphasis on fresh home made produce with one of the largest ranges of real Scottish sausages. Old fashioned dry cure bacon from outdoor reared pork, Border lamb and haggis, selected Scotch beef with properly matured steaks, organically reared poultry, Highland venison and game. Mail order available.

97 Broughton Street, Edinburgh EH1 3RZ Tel 0131 556 7643

LUCA'S

Old and new have come together to create a stylish new ice cream parlour/chocolatier/café in Morningside, Edinburgh to add to our famous Musselburgh parlour. Fresh classic 3 flavours as well as a range of speciality flavours. Enjoy a sundae, home made snowball, quality chocolates and sweets plus affordable and tasty main meals.

32–38 High Street Musselburgh EH21 7AG Tel 0131 665 2237

A MCLELLAND & SONS LTD

A McLelland now produce the major selling cheddar cheeses in Scotland, namely Galloway, McLelland Mature and Seriously Strong as well as Galloway Butter. These products, as well as several own label cheeses for the supermarket chains, are all sold through A McLelland & Son Ltd.

New Cheese Market, Black Street, Townhead, Glasgow G4 0EF Tel 0141 552 2962

LA SOLOGNE

At La Sologne, we bake our own croissants, scones, giant cheese straws and our famous Double Baked Almond croissants. We have a selection of fresh bread from sourdough and sunflower to baguettes. We also produce a wide range of fresh homemade quiches, red/green pesto, hummus, pâtés and tapenades.

Tel 0131 622 7080

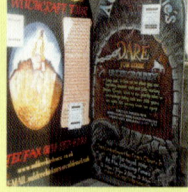

AULD REEKIE TOURS

Scotland's scariest tour company (as featured on television). Takes you on an underground journey into eerie caverns, working witches temples and a legendary haunted vault steeped in paranormal occurrences. All tours leave from the Tron Church on the Royal Mile.

Tel/Fax 0131 557 4700 Website www.auldreekietours.co.uk

CARBERRY CANDLE COTTAGE

Carberry Candles are made on site at our craft cottage where you can choose from a huge selection of perfumed candles. There is also a permanent Christmas Shoppe, a demonstration unit, a factory production video, a coffee shop and a bargain corner.

Musselburgh EH21 8PZ Tel 0131 665 5656

EDINBURGH CASTLE

The royal castle of Edinburgh is a most powerful symbol of Scotland which dominates the capital's skyline, offering stunning views of the city and countryside. The castle is home to the Scottish Crown Jewels, the Stone of Destiny, a magnificently restored royal apartment and the famous One O'Clock Gun.

EDINBURGH CRYSTAL VISITOR CENTRE

Superb craftsmanship, based on skills built up over generations, lies at the heart of every item produced by Edinburgh Crystal. Meticulous attention to detail is combined with real artistic flair to produce a world renowned portfolio of pieces large and small.

Eastfield Industrial Estate, Penicuik Tel 01968 675128

EDINBURGH ZOO

Scotland's largest and most popular wildlife attraction! Encounter over 1000 animals – furry, feathery and scaly – from all over the world. Discover the world's largest penguin enclosure, the African Plains Experience and the wonderful Magic Forest. It's wild!

Corstorphine Road, Edinburgh EH12 6TS Tel 0131 334 9171
Website www.edinburghzoo.org.uk

SCOTTISH SEABIRD CENTRE

Discover the fascinating world of seabirds using remote controlled cameras at the Scottish Seabird Centre, North Berwick Harbour. Observation deck with sweeping offshore views; visit our auditorium, shop and cafe. Fully licensed.

The Harbour, North Berwick EH39 4SS Tel 01620 890202
Website www.seabird.org

Loin of Lamb in a Herb Coat

Jeff Bland – Balmoral Hotel

INGREDIENTS

1 x eye of the loin (approx. 175g)
1 x large baking potato
50g baby spinach
16 x Scottish chanterelles
25g dice plum tomato
6 x Kalamatra olives
1 x baby leek
1 pint reduced lamb stock
1 glass red wine
3 slices of brioche
50g parsley and basil
Dijon mustard to brush on lamb
Garlic

METHOD

- Potato – Cut into 4mm thick round slices. Cook in boiling water for 2–3 minutes. Drain and dry. Brush with clarified butter and stack in to a pile. Bake in the oven for 10 minutes at 200°C until golden brown.
- Lamb – Season with salt and pepper. Sear in a hot pan. Roast for 3–4 minutes. Allow to rest before brushing with Dijon mustard and rolling in brioche crumbs. Slice into 6 pieces.
- Spinach – Sauté in a hot pan. Season and drain on a cloth.
- Chanterelles – Sauté gently in garlic and season.
- Sauce – Reduce lamb stock and wine together.
- Garnish – Blanch leek and cut into small pieces. De-stone olives and slice. Dice plum tomatoes and warm in a pan.

Serves 2

Wines – Fine red Bordeaux and Rioja Reserva are the classic accompaniment to lamb, but Cabernet Sauvignon and Cabernet/Merlot blends from Australia or New Zealand will make equally good partners, as will red Burgundy.

Stonehaven Harbour

Grampian Highlands, Aberdeen & the North East Coast

RICH IN HISTORIC CASTLES, royal connections and whisky distilleries this unique corner of Scotland has hills tumbling down to a dramatic coast with its fishing villages and beaches.

It has more than a hundred miles of unspoilt seacoast and more mountain tops over 4000 ft than anywhere else in Scotland. For those looking for a more action packed break, the north east offers everything from hillwalking to mountain biking and horse riding to mention a few. Added to this you can fly fish in some of the finest trout and salmon water anywhere in Scotland.

But don't think that this is some kind of rural backwater. Scotland's third city, Aberdeen offers the visitor a quality range of shopping, atmospheric restaurants, pubs and a wide range of cultural entertainment.

The buildings sparkle with silvery granite and the floral displays in the city's parks belies its northerly position.

For details of accommodation, events and attractions, see area tourist offices on page 273

LOCAL PRODUCTS

BAIN OF TARVES

One of the UK's leading suppliers of traditional quality game products. Recognised for our quality on a worldwide scale, our range includes venison, pheasant, certified Aberdeen Angus beef, poultry, home-cooked meats, savoury puddings, haggis and many more.

Braikley Park, Tarves AB41 7NJ Tel 01651 852000 Website www.bainoftarves.com

BRUCE OF THE BRECH

As a well-established family business, butchers Bruce of the Brech specialise in the classic cuts which make for the very best of Scottish cuisine.

Tel 01346 518606

THE ICE CREAM CABIN

Award-winning traditional quality Italo-Scottish Ice Cream – some even made with Malt Whisky from famous Speyside Distilleries. Available in 50 flavours, including our cup winning Strawberry – voted Best in Britain in a National Ice Cream Competition.

17 East Church Street, Buckie, Moray AB56 1EX Tel 01542 832140

A MCLELLAND & SONS LTD

Although cheese is no longer produced on a commercial scale in the region, Strathdon Blue (once made in Aberdeen) is now produced in Tain, Ross and Cromarty and is available in supermarkets and delicatessans throughout Scotland

New Cheese Market, Black Street, Townhead, Glasgow G4 0EF Tel 0141 552 2962

SUTHERLAND PORTSOY

Gourmet's Choice Scottish Smoked Salmon – the finest quality fresh fish, selected from the pure waters off the islands of Scotland. A family run business, steeped in the tradition of fish smoking since the turn of the century.

Harbourhead, Shore Street, Portsoy, Banff AB45 2RX Tel 01261 843255
www.gourmetschoice.net

WATMOUGH'S

Holders of 2 Royal Warrants, Watmough's carry a complete range of sea fish and shellfish and many exotic species, such as Red Snapper, Mullet Tuna and Sea Bass. Traditionally cured specialities include kippers, Finnans, smoked mackerel, smoked haddocks and smoked salmon.

29 Thistle Street, Aberdeen Tel 01224 640321

BALMORAL ESTATES

Balmoral Castle holds a unique place in history, many aspects of which – art, heraldry, fine arts, transport – feature in the exhibitions and displays in the Castle and around the estate. Gardens, walks, pony trekking complement the attractions for a great day out.

The Estates Office, Balmoral Estates, Ballater, Aberdeenshire AB35 5TB
Tel 013397 42334 Website www.balmoralcastle.com

BENROMACH DISTILLERY*

Benromach Distillery warmly welcomes visitors all year round. Located in Forres, this family owned and managed distillery has recently been revived. Tour the distillery and enjoy a dram in The Malt Whisky Centre – once the old drier house.

Invererne Road, Forres, Moray IV36 3EB Tel 01309 675968

DALLAS DHU HISTORIC DISTILLERY

Just South of Forres, this charming distillery is preserved as a Victorian time capsule. No production is carried out on site but there is a small quantity of whisky maturing which keeps the taste alive. Part of the Malt Whisky Trail, visitors can follow the old–style processes from start to finish.

GLENLIVET DISTILLERY

In this enchanted Speyside glen, the raw elements of life itself are transformed into the pure golden essence of The Glenlivet, the very heart and soul of Scotland's finest whisky region. Distillery located on B9008, 101 miles north of Tomintoul.

Tel 01542 783220 Website www.theglenlivet.com

JOHNSTONES OF ELGIN

Our mill is one of the most beautiful in the country and the only mill still to transform cashmere from fibre to garment. Visitors can take a guided tour of the mill and take the opportunity to browse through a wide range of products manufactured from the world's luxury fine fibres. Open all year – free admission

Newmill, Elgin, Morayshire IV30 4AF Tel 01343 554099

SPEYSIDE COOPERAGE VISITOR CENTRE

Speyside Cooperage, on the outskirts of Craigellachie village has excellent visitor facilities including a unique picnic area which has large wine casks fitted out with seating and tables. Open mid–January to mid–December, Monday to Friday, you can see the coopers repairing and raising–up casks for the whisky industry.

Dufftown Road, Craigellachie, Aberlour AB38 9RS Tel 01340 871108

Spicy Meat Loaf

David Wilson – Peat Inn

INGREDIENTS

1.125 kg Specially Selected Scotch Beef mince

1 tbsp olive oil for frying

1 finely chopped onion

2 cloves garlic, finely chopped

1 red pepper, halved, deseeded, skin removed then chopped

1 tsp cumin

1tsp mixed herbs

1/2 cup tomato sauce (good quality canned will do) or passatta (creamed tomato)

½ cup fresh breadcrumbs

½ cup beef stock

Salt and pepper to taste

METHOD

■ Put oil in pan and heat. Add onions, garlic and mixed herbs. Sweat over heat until onions are soft without browning. Transfer to large bowl and allow to cool.

■ Add tomato sauce, breadcrumbs and beef stock to the cooked mixture. Stir together. Break up the ground beef and add to mixture. Season to taste and mix together gently.

■ Pack this mixture into a 28 x 12 x 8 cm deep loaf tin and bake in a pre-heated oven (Gas Mark 4, 180°C, 350°F) for 50 to 60 minutes.

■ Remove carefully from oven, pour off any excess fat, let the loaf cool for about 10 minutes the slice and serve with crisp green salad, spicy tomato salsa and crusty bread. Can also be served cold.

Serves 8

Wines – Tangy, herby, medium–bodied reds should do well here, particularly those with a touch of rusticity. Wines from south–west France, such as Minervois or Corbières, are one option, with Chianti or the more savoury styles of red Burgundy – Mercurey, for example – providing an interesting alternative.

Glasgow & River Clyde

Greater Glasgow & the Clyde Valley

GLASGOW, Scotland's largest city, overflows with sheer personality and a sense of style. One of Europe's great cultural destinations, Glasgow has over twenty museums and galleries housing magnificent collections of arts and artefacts.

When it comes to shopping Glasgow is the UK's biggest retail centre outside London with top names in fashion and design as well as all the main High Street outlets.

Glasgow is a gourmet's paradise with the very best in just about any style of cuisine you can think of. You'll find something to suite every taste and budget.

Leaving behind the bustle of the city the Tourist Route winds through the Clyde Valley. With dramatic ruined castles, industrial heritage, country parks and historic towns and villages there are plenty of surprises to be found.

For details of accommodation, events and attractions, see area tourist offices on page 273

BRODIES (CHOCOLATES)

Renowned for our expertise in Teas & Coffees, we also produce a luxury range of handmade chocolates. Using only the finest natural ingredients, we create chocolates with distinction. Made by a dedicated team of chocolatiers, our range has won 'Scottish Food Awards' for taste, quality and innovation.

Tel 0131 554 6331

GARDINERS OF SCOTLAND

A family company manufacturing high quality, hand made confectionery ranging from speciality Malt Whisky fudges to assorted fudges in attractive tartan tins and cartons. Also a Millennium range featuring coffee, rum & raisin, chocolate, Malt Whisky vanilla and assorted fudges.

Turfholm, Lesmahagow ML11 0ED Tel 01555 894155

ANDREW GILLESPIE

Specialists for over 100 years supplying the finest quality fresh meat, award winning steak pies & sausages. A superb range of meats and pies cooked on the premises. A well known established family butcher, with a tradition for quality and service.

1601 Great Western Road, Glasgow G13 1LP Tel 0141 959 2105

MACCALLUMS OF TROON

Dedicated to supplying the serious cook with the best fresh produce available, we source from all corners of the world. With Scotland having one of the finest natural larders to be found in the world, it makes our job a little easier!

944 Argyle Street, Glasgow G3 8YJ Tel 0141 204 4456

MISS CRANSTON'S

Situated above a top quality bakers, confectioners & chocolate shop – an experience not to be missed. The traditions of Glasgow's past have been revived in a bright, modern, designer inspired setting. Open Monday to Saturday serving delicious cakes and scones from our own bakery – also lunch or afternoon tea.

33 Gordon Street, Glasgow Tel 0141 638 8000

P & C MORRIS

The finest handcrafted terrines and stocks, all produced in-house by our team of dedicated chefs. A range of fine Scottish foods sourced from individual small scale producers, mixed with a selection of speciality fish and dry goods.

M8 Foodpark, 1 Keppochill Place, Port Dundas, Glasgow Tel 0141 332 4474

VISITOR ATTRACTIONS

BOTHWELL CASTLE

In a beautiful setting overlooking the River Clyde, this fine 13th century castle was much fought over during the wars of Independence. In the most famous siege in 1301, 7000 English troops were deployed against this mighty castle. Remarkably, part of the original keep survives.

THE BURRELL COLLECTION*

Accumulated by wealthy Glasgow shipowner, Sir William Burrell, and gifted to the city in 1944, the Burrell Collection includes exceptional examples of medieval tapestries, stained glass, fine art and oriental artefacts. Open Monday-Thursday and Saturday 10am-5pm Friday and Sunday 11am-5pm.
2060 Pollokshaws Road, Glasgow G41 1AT Tel 0141 287 2550

CHATELHERAULT

Hunting Lodge designed by William Adam set in a country park with ten miles of woodland and river walks. Other attractions – Visitor centre, café, shop, adventure playground, garden centre, Cadzow Castle, ancient oaks and white Cadzow cattle. Open daily, admission free, car and coach parking, disabled access.

NATIONAL TRUST FOR SCOTLAND

Enjoy the variety of Glasgow's vibrant culture, from a typical tenement flat of 1892 to the stunning Edwardian interior of Pollok House in Pollok Country Park. A new exhibition at Hutchesons' Hall, in the city centre, celebrates the 'new' Glasgow style and examples by Alexander 'Greek' Thomson and Charles Rennie Mackintosh put it into context.

TALL SHIP AT GLASGOW HARBOUR

The Tall Ship at Glasgow Harbour is now open all year and offers the chance to explore one of the last remaining Clydebuilt tall ships, the s.v. Glenlee. Exhibitions, activities and events for children, a riverside cafe bar and nautical souvenir shop are on offer and Power Boat river trips are also available.
100 Stobcross Road, Glasgow G3 8QQ Tel 0141 339 0631

WILLOW TEAROOMS

The Willow Tea Rooms' unique ambience and elegance was created a century ago by Charles Rennie Mackintosh, arguably Scotland's greatest designer. Just as his genius has endured, that sense of style, quality and service is still celebrated here.
217 Sauchiehall Street, Glasgow G2 3EX Tel 0141 332 0521

Blairgowrie Raspberry Parfait, Eau de Vie Sabayon and Raspberry Tuilles
Ronnie Clydesdale – The Ubiquitous Chip

INGREDIENTS

Raspberry Purée
12oz fresh raspberries
6tbsp caster sugar
5oz water

Parfait 3 egg yolks
2oz caster sugar
¼ pint double cream lightly whipped
a little of the raspberry purée

Sabayon 2 egg yolks
1oz sugar
1oz of a raspberry flavoured eau de vie

Tuilles 1oz caster sugar
1oz unsalted butter, softened
1oz egg white
1 ½oz plain flour
1 tbsp raspberry purée

METHOD

■ Raspberry Tuille – Place all ingredients in a pot and heat until simmering. Remove from heat and purée. Pass through a sieve and allow to cool.
■ Parfait – Place eggs and sugar in bowl and whisk over boiling water until thick and pale in colour. Fold in the cream and flavour the mixture with purée – too much purée could turn your parfait icy. Spoon into 6 moulds and freeze.
■ Sabayon – Whisk eggs and sugar over boiling water until pale and thick. Add liqueur and whisk until well mixed. Spoon into plastic squeezy bottle.
■ Tuilles – Cream butter and sugar, slowly add egg white then flour and blend together. Add purée and refrigerate until firm.
■ Spread thinly on a silicone mat in 12 triangles. Bake at 190°C for 5 minutes. Remove and quickly drape 6 shapes over rolling pin to form curls.
■ Using squeezy bottle, decorate plate with sabayon. Lightly brown under grill. Place on moulded parfait in centre, garnished with raspberries and 2 tuilles.
Serves 6

Wines – Try a crisply fruity dessert wine such as Riesling from Germany or Canada, or a sweet Coteaux–du–layon or Vouvray from the Loire Valley.

Loch Bad a' Ghaill

Highlands & Skye

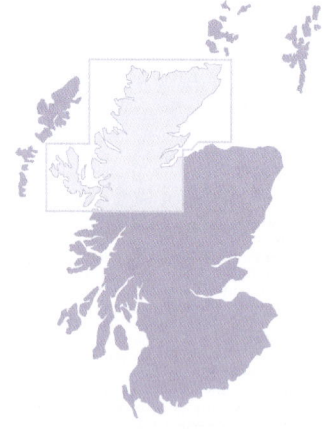

This is one of the last wildernesses in Europe. No single image can capture the scale and diversity of these northlands. This is an area which appeals directly to the heart.

Climbers and walkers, as well as touring visitors will all have their favourite area. Some favour the western peninsulas while other are drawn to the wide skies and long vistas of Caithness.

Yet others enjoy the forests of Speyside or the vertigo-inducing ridges of Glencoe. However the Highlands & Skye are not just about landscape. There are interesting towns and villages to discover as well as great beaches, golf courses and numerous walking trails amongst lots of other things to see and do.

It would be misleading however to suggest that the Highland and Skye are remote. The very best bit about the north is that you can encounter wild nature yet still indulge in a fine meal and a very comfortable hotel.

For details of accommodation, events and attractions, see area tourist offices on page 273

DUNDONNELL SMOKED SALMON

Premier quality smoked Scottish salmon sent First Class mail (almost next day) throughout the UK, Small Packet/Airmail to Europe under 2 kilos, over 2 kilos (34) via DHL. Our customers tell us 'it is the best!' and have been coming back for more – since 1983.

Sea View, Dundonnell IV23 2QZ Tel 01854 633317 www.smokedsalmon.uk.com

HIGHLAND FINE CHEESE

Highland Fine Cheese in Tain produce Caboc, Galic and Crowdie from recipes dating back to the 16th Century. In 2000, they are re-introducing a blue, cows' milk cheese, Strathdon Blue.

THE HIGHLAND TRUFFLE COMPANY

In the historic town of Elgin – the Malt Whisky Capital of the World – is a small workshop where sumptuous chocolates, truffles and petit fours are made by a small team of talented young confectioners. Indulge yourself, or choose a stylish gift from our exclusive range. Order online at www.highlandtruffles.com

16 Pinefield Parade, Pinefield Industrial Estate, Elgin IV30 6AG Tel 01343 552200

MACBETH'S BUTCHER

To castles or cottages, hotels and restaurants or to you in your own home, Macbeth's will supply the finest beef born and reared on our own farms, as well as local pork, lamb, poultry, venison and game Wholesale and mail order price list available with overnight delivery throughout mainland UK.

11 Tolbooth Street, Forres. Tel 01309 672254. www.scottish-beef.com

SCOTTISH QUALITY TROUT

Smoked Scottish Trout has become very popular in the last two years. Eat, just as you would smoked Scottish salmon but it has a finer texture and the flavour is perhaps just a little sweeter. 2 x 250 grams for £16.25 to your door from Dundonnell Smoked Salmon.

Sea View, Dundonnell IV23 2QZ Tel 01854 633317
Website www.smokedsalmon.uk.com

TODS OF ORKNEY

Manufacturers of the Stockan & Gardens brand of oatcakes, shortbread and biscuits – once tasted, never forgotten! Our oatcakes come in a range of shapes and flavours and, along with shortbread, are available in new gift boxes. We also operate a mail order service.

18 Bridge Street, Kirkwall, Orkney KW15 1HR Tel 01856 873165
Website www. stockan-and-gardens.co.uk

THE ACHILTIBUIE HYDROPONICUM

Take a guided tour of our extensively refurbished growing houses and step into a different world of lush, sub–tropical fruit trees, orchids, flowers and vegetables. Discover the secrets of growing without soil. Enjoy the relaxing atmosphere of the Lilypond Café, whilst indulging in fresh hydroponic produce.

Achiltibuie, Ullapool, Ross–shire IV26 2YG Tel 01854 622202

BALNAIN HOUSE

Built in 1726, Balnain House has established itself as an important focal point worldwide for performers, tutors, students and visitors alike. It is a unique and special place, dedicated to sustaining, promoting and developing Scotland's rich musical heritage – for everyone.

40 Huntly Street, Inverness IV3 5HR Tel 01463 715757 Website www.balnain.com

BAXTERS

After more than 130 years in business, Baxters of Speyside satisfy traditional and contemporary tastes with an extraordinary range of soups, jams and preserves. An unrivalled reputation for quality and flavour puts their products at the top of shopping lists around the world.

Fochabers, Moray Tel 01343 820393 Fax 01343 821696

BELLA JANE BOAT TRIPS

Taking you to Loch Coruisk and the seals in the heart of the Skye Cuillin mountains. Voted 'Most Enjoyable Visitor Attraction in Skye' and holds an STB 4–star grading. Also excursions to Isle of Rum. Telephone bookings essential between 7.30am–10.00am and 7.30pm–10.00pm.

Elgol, Isle of Skye IV49 9BJ Tel 0800 7313089 Website www.bellajane.co.uk

BEN NEVIS DISTILLERY VISITOR CENTRE*

Thousands of visitors have come to see our mythical giant, Hector McDram, on video telling his story of how our whisky came about. Recently we have introduced a pair of Highland cattle as added interest for the visitor. Come along and meet our cows, see Hector and taste our selection of exceptionally smooth whiskies.

Lochy Bridge, Fort William PH33 6TJ Tel 01397 702476

FORT GEORGE

Built following the Battle of Culloden, Fort George took 21 years to complete at a cost that today would be around £1 billion. It remains an active army barracks but has never seen a shot fired in anger. Reconstructed barrack rooms depict soldiers' lives in the 18th and 19th centuries.

Cranachan with Fresh Skye Raspberries and Three Chimneys Shortbread
Shirley Spear – The Three Chimneys

INGREDIENTS

Cranachan

500g fresh raspberries
½ pint of fresh double cream
1 tbsp of thick heather honey
1 generous tbsp of Talisker whisky
1 heaped tbsp of toasted oatmeal

Shortbread

375g plain flour
125g white rice flour
375g slightly salted Scottish butter
125g caster sugar

METHOD

■ Cranachan – Whisk the cream together with the honey and Talisker. Fold in the toasted oatmeal. Pile on top of fresh raspberries and serve.
■ Shortbread – Cream the butter and sugar together until pale and fluffy. Work the sifted flour and rice flour into the creamed mixture until it forms a firm paste. Knead it lightly on a well–floured board.
■ Roll it out until quite thin and cut biscuit shapes with the cutter of your choice. Using a palette knife, lift the biscuits onto a well-buttered baking sheet. ■ Bake on the centre shelf at Gas Mark 5, until pale golden in colour. Remove from the oven and sprinkle liberally with caster sugar while still warm. Lift on to a wire tray to cool and firm–up. Store in an airtight tin.

Wines – The combination of sweet, creamy, tangy flavours calls for a wine of similar style (sweet Riesling or Chenin Blanc) or possibly something a little more opulent such as a light Sauternes or any other Sémillon–based wine (Australia has some fine examples).

Old Man of Hoy

Outer Islands

THE OUTER ISLES appeal to visitors looking for the experience of somewhere different and especially to those who love the sea.

The Western Isles, lies at the very edge of Europe, where these peaceful islands have a natural, rugged beauty, with dazzling beaches, plentiful wildlife and a unique culture and tradition.

Shetland is special. Over 100 islands and skerries make up the archipelago of Shetland. Only 15 of the islands are continuously inhabited and most have excellent sea and air services.

On the vivid green islands of Orkney, standing stones and ancient mounds are an everyday part of the landscape – ever present reminders of these ancient northlands. However, Orkney is not entirely rural, Kirkwall its main town is busy with visitors and its main street offers an excellent choice of local craftware.

For details of accommodation, events and attractions, see area tourist offices on page 273

LOCAL PRODUCTS

THE ORKNEY CHEESE COMPANY

Producing Orkney Island Cheddar in Kirkwall. Medium, mature or vintage cheddar available at all major retail outlets or direct from the creamery. Loose or pre-packed and as 454g coloured, white and smoked rounds.

ORKNEY CREAMERY

Deliciously creamy ice cream that tastes the way ice cream used to. Made with naturally good milk and cream produced from Orkney's fabled pastures. Orkney Ice Cream is available in a wide range of tempting flavours and pack sizes to suit any occasion.

Crantit Farm, St Ola, Orkney KW15 1RZ Tel 01856 872542

ORKNEY HERRING

A delicious range of high quality sweet cured herring and salmon products. Available in retail and catering packs through wholesale distributors. Contact us for further information and recipe leaflets.

Garson Industrial Estate, Stromness, Orkney, KW16 3JU Tel 01856 850514

ORKNEY MEAT LTD

We have developed a superb quality product – 'Orkney Island Gold' beef and lamb, offering the most choice and light taste, guaranteed to satisfy even the most discerning palate. Strict selection system, coupled with traditional maturing and cutting.

Grainshore Road, Hatston, Kirkwall, Orkney KW15 1FL Tel 01856 874326

ORKNEY SALMON

Organically grown salmon, using a traditional style and low intensity methods which produce a firmly textured and subtly flavoured fish. Owned and managed by native Orcadians who have a deep regard for their environment. Whole salmon, fillets, steaks and portions as well as King Scallops.

Hatston, Kirkwall, KW15 1RG Tel 01856 876101 Website www.oscltd.demon.co.uk

TODS OF ORKNEY

Manufacturers of the Stockan & Gardens brand of oatcakes, shortbread and biscuits – once tasted, never forgotten! Our oatcakes come in a range of shapes and flavours and, along with shortbread, are available in new gift boxes. We also operate a mail order service.

18 Bridge Street, Kirkwall, Orkney KW15 1HR Tel 01856 873165
Website www.stockan-and-gardens.co.uk

VISITOR ATTRACTIONS

ASVA

Over four hundred of Scotland's visitor attractions are members of ASVA, the Association of Visitor Attractions. Each one is committed to making your experience more pleasurable and exciting. You can visit historic homes, castles and monuments, linger in some spacious and relaxing private and public gardens and parks or take the children to the exciting new science museums.

HEBRIDEAN FESTIVAL*

An annual four-day festival of music and culture featuring the best of Scottish traditional music, song and dance, incorporating performances by artistes from throughout the Celtic nations. Now firmly established as the largest festival of its kind in the North of Scotland – one of the major highlights of the Celtic Music year.

Tel 07001 878787 Website www.hebceltfest.com

SKAILL HOUSE

Orkney's finest 17th century mansion house, built in 1620 by Bishop George Graham. Open to the public from 1 April–30 September under a joint ticket with Skara Brae. In-house Gift Shop selling a wide range of quality local crafts and Scottish gifts. Self catering accommodation available in north wing.

Sandwick, Orkney Tel 01856 841501 Website www.skaillhouse.com

SKARA BRAE

In 1850, a storm uncovered the ruins of the best preserved prehistoric village in Europe. Skara Brae dates from around 3000BC, inhabited before the Egyptian pyramids were built. The surviving houses are remarkably complete, containing stone furniture and hearths, presenting a remarkable picture of life in Stone Age times.

UIST ANIMAL VISITOR CENTRE*

A unique opportunity to see some of Scotland's colourful wildlife – including the rarely-seen wildcat – makes a trip to Uist Animal Visitor Centre a memorable experience.

Tel 01876 510706

WILDABOUT ORKNEY TOURS*

Wildabout History Tours will take you on an imaginative journey into 500 years of the rich historic tapestry that awaits you here in Orkney. Walk through Neolithic, Pictish, Viking and Scottish history, taking time at each location. Walkabout is Fun, Flexible and Educational. It's an UNUSUAL TOUR!

5 Clouston Corner, Stenness, Orkney KW16 3LB Tel 01856 851011

Iced Clootie Dumpling Parfait

Alan Craigie – The Creel Inn & Restaurant

INGREDIENTS

Clootie Dumpling

6oz self raising flour

6oz brown breadcrumbs

6oz suet

4oz currants

6oz sultanas

6oz raisins

1tsp baking soda

4oz soft dark brown sugar

2tbsp syrup

1 cup of milk

Dash of ginger, nutmeg and cinnamon

Iced Parfait

4 egg yolks

½ pint double cream

2oz caster sugar

Few drops Vanilla essence

1 tbsp Macallan Single Malt

6oz white chocolate

METHOD

■ Clootie Dumpling – Mix all dry ingredients and blend with the milk and syrup. Boil cotton tea towel in large pot, remove and place dumping mixture in the centre and tie with string. Place the dumpling in pot of simmering water and poach for 2 ½ hours.

■ Iced Parfait – Whisk the egg yolks, sugar and vanilla together in a bowl until the sugar has dissolved. Bring the cream to a gentle simmer in a thick bottomed pan. Pour the cream over the egg and sugar mixture, whisking gently as you pour. return the mixture to a clean pan and cook slowly, stirring until the custard coats the back of a spoon. Remove from the heat. Blend the white chocolate until dissolved. Blend the Macallan Single Malt and chill mixture for 30 mins. Line a terrine dish or loaf tin with cling film. Chop the Clootie Dumpling into rough, large pieces and fold into the parfait mixture. Pour the mixture into a terrine dish, cover with cling film and freeze overnight.

Wines – Not the easiest dish to match with wine, and perhaps a dram might be the safest option. However, a light, Muscat–based sweet wine may *just* pull it off!

Blair Castle

Perthshire, Angus & Dundee and the Kingdom of Fife

THIS IS AN AREA of dramatic contrasts combining the rich farming patchwork of Fife with the high hills of Perthshire, the city bustle of Dundee with the peace of the Angus Glens.

Angus and Dundee makes an excellent touring base. Heathery hills and glens, castles, gardens and beaches are matched by a full range of accommodation, places to eat and shopping.

A relaxing atmosphere prevails throughout the ancient Kingdom of Fife with its wealth of castles, palaces, cathedrals and gardens just waiting to be discovered.

With delightful villages nestling amongst the natural harbours of the coastline to St Andrews, the home of golf, there is something for everyone.

In the heart of Scotland, on the edge of the Highlands, Perthshire makes the ideal holiday destination. Whether you want an active holiday in the great outdoors with hiking, golfing and fishing or a relaxing break enjoying theatres, museums and restaurants, Perthshire has it all.

For details of accommodation, events and attractions, see area tourist offices on page 273

LOCAL PRODUCTS

DUNKELD SMOKED SALMON

Specialist smokers of wild, farmed and angler's salmon. Springwell's is a traditional and artisan smokehouse in the ancient cathedral town of Dunkeld, on the River Tay, where salmon are filleted and cured, then slowly smoked over a mix of oak dust and whisky barrel chips.

Brae Street, Dunkeld, Perthshire PH8 0BA Tel 01350 727639

E & O FISH

A traditional wholesale and retail fresh fish merchant, specialising mainly in East Coast fish and shellfish seasonal products. Shop open 7 days – why not visit us on weekdays to see the process of making a famous Arbroath Smokie?

East Grimsby, Arbroath DD11 1NX Tel 01241 873574

LURGAN FARM

Quality, natural, local and organic produce. A hill farm producing Blackface Lamb, Aberdeen Angus and Highland Beef, we also sell game, free range and organic eggs, organic fruit and vegetables and a large range of organic dried food. The kitchen provides delicious meals, home baking and a large range of preserves.

Drumdewan, by Aberfeldy, Perthshire PH15 2JQ Tel 01887 829303

MACKAYS OF CARNOUSTIE

Award winning preserves and confectionery. Our preserves, marmalades and curds are all made in traditional open pans using 100% natural fruit. This combination creates that special home made flavour. Food From Scotland Excellence (Export) Award for our Luxury Preserves.

21 Thistle Street, Carnoustie, Angus DD7 7PR Tel 01241 853109

THE TARTAN BEAN

Using hand selected coffee beans, roasted in our premises under the watchful eye of our Mater Roaster, we are are able to offer the coffee lover a guaranteed cup of the finest coffee. This guarantee of quality is available to both the catering and retail markets.

Fife Food Base, Unit 2, Southfield Ind. Est., Glenrothes KY6 2RU Tel 01592 630150

WATSON OF LEVEN

We buy the finest Scotch beef direct from our farm in Fife. Members of the Quality Guild of Butchers and Guild of Master Craftsmen, we supply over 90 catering establishments throughout Tayside, Kinross Perth, Fife Edinburgh and the Lothians. Online ordering available.

Tel 01333 350351. www.scotch-beef.net

VISITOR ATTRACTIONS

BLAIR CASTLE

Fairytale-white Blair Castle is on the A9 close to Pitlochry. We have some 30 fully furnished rooms packed with beautiful furniture, fine paintings, arms, armour, china, lace, embroidery and other unique treasures. Something for everyone – allow half a day if you can!

Blair Atholl, Pitlochry, Perthshire PH18 5TL Tel 01796 481207
Website www.blair-castle.co.uk

DRUMMOND TROUT FARM & FISHERY

Feed the fish, see the salmon ladder and our underwater camera. Enjoy the views, spy on the wildlife or catch your tea! Young or old, the choice is yours at Drummond Trout Farm and Fishery. 1 mile west of Comrie – just off the A85.

Comrie, Perthshire PH6 2LD Tel 01764 670500

GLENTURRET DISTILLERY

Glenturret is set in one of the loveliest glens in Scotland. Try our delicious home made food prepared by our award winning chef and his team and enjoy a free taste of The Glenturret Single Highland Malt Whisky. You can also look for quality gift ideas in our shop.

Crieff, Perthshire Tel 01764 656565 Website www.glenturret.com

NATIONAL TRUST FOR SCOTLAND

A rich heritage reflects this area's important role in the country's past. Historic Killiecrankie was the scene of the first shots fired in the Jacobite cause and many of the buildings in the picturesque town of Dunkeld date from the Battle of Dunkeld in 1689. In Kirriemuir, visitors can even visit Never Never Land at the birthplace of Peter Pan author JM Barrie!

SCOTTISH CRANNOG CENTRE

Walk over water, back 2600 years at this award–winning heritage attraction featuring Scotland's only authentic recreation of an Iron Age loch–dwelling. Guided Crannog tours and ancient crafts bring the past to life. New Exhibition Centre features ancient artefacts, videos and range of displays, as well as a giftshop and refreshments.

Kenmore, Loch Tay, Perthshire PH15 2HW Tel 01887 830583

ST ANDREWS CASTLE

The castle of the Archbishops of St Andrews sits alongside what was once the largest cathedral in Scotland. Today, visitors can enter the mine and counter–mine built during the great siege of 1546–47 and look down into the bottle dungeon from which death was the only release.

Discovery Tart with a Marmalade Ice

Wendy Barrie

INGREDIENTS

Pastry (8" flan ring)

175g self raising flour

100g butter

1 egg yolk

25g caster sugar

1tbsp water (if necessary)

Sponge

75g self raising flour

25g ground almonds

100g softened butter

100g caster sugar

Pinch of grated nutmeg

75 sultanas

1tbsp Macallan

2 eggs

Ice Cream

4 egg yolks

50g caster sugar

300ml single cream

60ml double cream

1tbsp shredded marmalade

METHOD

▪ Pastry – Rub flour and sugar with butter in a bowl until it resembles breadcrumbs. With a knife, mix in egg yolk and cold water to make a soft pliable dough. Turn out onto floured surface and roll out to line greased flan ring. Fork and bake in pre–heated oven 180˚C (Gas Mark 5) for 8 mins.

▪ Sponge – Soak sultanas in Macallan for 1–2 hours to plump up fruit. Cream butter and sugar in a bowl until light and fluffy. Beat in the eggs and fold in the flour, nutmeg and almonds. Lastly, fold in fruit and spoon into par–baked pastry case. Bake for a further 25–30mins.

▪ Ice Cream – Heat cream to scalding hot. Whisk yolks and sugar until light, frothy and holding a trail. Pour hot cream over the mixture, whisking in bowl over a pan of hot water until custard thickens to a coating consistency. Stir in marmalade, allowing to melt. Pour mixture into a container and cool. Cover and freeze until firm (for 3+hrs) during which time, beat 3–4 times.

Serves 6

Wines – Rich, sweet fortified wines make good partners here. Choose from Malmsey Madeira, liqueur Muscat or top–notch PX sherry.

Isle of Arran

South of Scotland

THE SCOTTISH BORDERS – An area of tranquil villages, textile towns and varied scenery including a rugged coastline. Visitors can enjoy a wide range of attractions including working woollen mills, craft workshops and many magnificent historic houses and great Border abbeys. The Scottish Borders echoes the landscape theme of the whole area; green river valleys and low-ground woodlands, with soaring hills beyond.

AYRSHIRE & THE ISLE OF ARRAN – Ayrshire abounds with deep history and industrial heritage, from castles to historic buildings. The birthplace of Robert Burns, Scotland's most famous poet, Ayrshire boasts over 30 golf courses as well as a wide range of attractions and activities. Sometimes called 'Scotland in Miniature' the spectacular mountain profile of the Isle of Arran fills the horizon viewed from the Ayrshire coast. Playground for generations of outdoor enthusiasts, Arran is easily reached by ferry from Ardrossan.

DUMFRIES & GALLOWAY – Lonely hills rolling down to pasture and dark woods give way to rich farmlands and a sunny south facing coast. Scotland's southwest is blessed with a mild climate – the Atlantic waters of the Gulf Stream warm this coastline. There is plenty to entertain the visitor such as birdwatching, cycling and golf or touring photogenic villages and dramatic castles.

....
For details of accommodation, events and attractions, see area tourist offices on page 273

BURNSIDE FARM FOODS

We specialise in supplying fresh poultry, game and exotic products to hotels and restaurants. Game from our own and surrounding estates is processed on site, ensuring traceability. Imported and local poultry is available. We bone, stuff and vacpac products on site, depending on customers' requirements.

Rutherford Lodge, Kelso TD5 8WW Tel 01835 822418

CARSWELLS CHOCOLATES

Welcome chocolate lovers and chocoholics to delicious chocolates hand–made from the finest ingredients, brought to you from the artist colony town of Kirkcudbright by Carswells – The Scottish Chocolate Maker. Please feel free to order that unique, special chocolate gift foe every occasion.

10–12 St Cuthbert Street, Kirkcudbright DG6 4HZ Tel 01557 330664

COLFIN SMOKEHOUSE

Flavours that are subtle, sophisticated and always distinctive have earned Colfin Smokehouse its enviable reputation.

Tel 01776 820622

CREAM O' GALLOWAY

We have over 30 delicious ice creams made only with ingredients you'd be proud to use in your own kitchen, including favourites Sticky Toffee, Caramel Shortbread and Malt Whisky. There are also 4 organic ice creams and 4 organic frozen yogurt flavours including Elderflower and Honey & Ginger.

Rainton, Castle Douglas DG7 2DR Tel 01557 814040

ALEX DALGETTY & SON

First producer of the famous Selkirk Bannocks in Galashiels at the turn of the century and making bannocks to the original recipe here ever since – also Scotch Black Bun and Shortbread. Buy from our shops in Galashiels, Melrose and at outlets throughout Scotland and North of England. Mail order.

21 Island Street, Galashiels Tel 01896 752508 Website www.alex-dalgetty.co.uk

THE GALLOWAY CHEESE COMPANY

The Galloway Cheese Company in Stranraer is the most modern cheese making plant in Europe. There has been a creamery on site for over 100 years they produce Scotland's best selling cheddar cheeses – Galloway, McLelland Mature and Seriously Strong. Marketed by A McLelland & Sons Ltd. Glasgow..

AIKWOOD TOWER

A fine 16th Century Border Tower, restored as a family home by Lord and Lady Steel of Aikwood. The legendary home of Michael Scott, the Border Wizard. Historic home of a family of Border Reivers. Mediaeval style Garden. Permanent exhibition : James Hogg (The Ettrick Shepherd). Temporary exhibitions by contemporary artists.

Ettrick Valley, Selkirk TD7 5HJ Tel 01750 52253

THE BIG IDEA

Take a mind–blowing adventure through the history of inventions of mankind. Experience the 'pink–knuckle' ride through the history of explosions and interact with exhibits through our unique 'I Button' technology. Construct and keep your own inventions. A spine–tingling attraction for kids aged 5 to 95.

The Harbourside, Irvine KA12 8XX Tel 08708 404030 Website www.bigidea.org.uk

BURNS NATIONAL HERITAGE PARK

The Tam O'Shanter Experience Restaurant is set amidst beautiful landscaped gardens and is open daily throughout the year. The menu is extensive and offers everything from tea, coffee and delicious home baking to snacks and hot meals. It is also available for evening functions.

Murdoch's Lone, Alloway, Ayr KA7 4PQ Tel 01292 443700

DUNASKIN OPEN AIR MUSEUM

Dunaskin is unique. Europe's best preserved Victorian Ironworks situated in the heart of beautiful Ayrshire countryside on the A713, Dunaskin has been rated 4–star by the Scottish Tourist Board. Gift shop, restaurant, audio–visual presentations and guided tours.

Waterside, Patna, Ayrshire KA6 7JF Tel 01292 531144

MARYMASS FESTIVAL*

Irvine is rich with tradition but none is held more highly than the Marymass Festival. Every year for almost 1000 years, the festival has been celebrated on the third Saturday following the first Monday of August. The actual proceedings are worthy of note because of the survival of the ancient pageantry.

North Ayrshire Council, Cunninghame House, Irvine KA12 8EE Tel 01294 324482

MELROSE ABBEY

Once the richest abbey in Scotland, the ruins at Melrose retain a unique elegance with a fine collection of medieval carvings including gargoyles of demons, hobgoblins and even a pig playing the bagpipes. A medieval casket containing an embalmed heart – believed to be that of Robert the Bruce – is buried in the grounds.

Fresh Lobster with new Ayrshire potatoes and salad

Laurie Black – Fouters Bistro

METHOD

From June to September, Scotland is blessed with superb–tasting lobsters. Nowhere is this more so than on the West Coast where for many years, Fouters has been offering a renowned 'lobster lunch' – freshly cooked lobster, salad, mayonnaise and Ayrshire potatoes.

But what to do with lobster at home? Ideally, lobster should be purchased live and cooked at home. However, it is possible to buy cooked lobster from a good local fishmonger.

Beware of frozen, cooked lobster – you cannot know where they are from or how old they are! As with all foods, fresh is best.

■ Lobsters are dark blue when alive and turn orange once cooked. Lobsters can create a poison as soon as they die – which is why they must be cooked immediately. The kindest way to cook a lobster is to immerse it in warm salted water, bring to the boil and simmer for 2 minutes, then remove lobster and allow it to cool.

■ Place the cooked lobster on a firm chopping board and insert a large knife along the back of the body, splitting it in two. Remove the small sack just inside the head as this would be very dangerous if swallowed. Remove the tail piece in one and lift out, discarding the mud sack. Carefully slice the tail meat on the slant so creating large, thin slices of meat. Lift these in one and arrange on the back of the half lobster. Split the claws open with the back of a large knife, remove meat and arrange with shell. Add some fresh seasonal salad leaves, fresh mayonnaise and new potatoes.

Wines – Lobster requires a fine, full–bodied, not too oaky white, particularly (but not exclusively) from Chardonnay. Burgundy is the obvious choice, but mature white Graves from Bordeaux, or even Champagne, will make sterling partners.

Duart Castle

West Highlands & Islands, Loch Lomond, Stirling & Trossachs

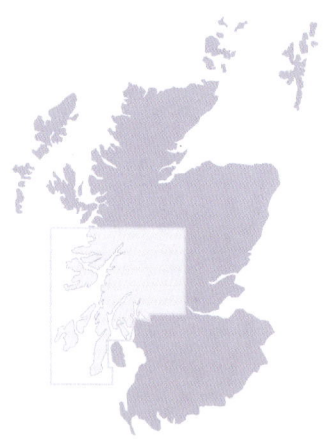

FROM THE ROMANTIC highland landscapes of Argyll to the gentler hills of the lowland edge, there is plenty to attract visitors. The islands add a special dimension to any visit here.

This beautiful area takes in Highland and Lowland, mainland and island, lochs both landlocked and salty. In fact it has just about everything!

However since Scotland is much more than petty landscape, the West Highlands and Islands, Loch Lomond, Stirling and Trossachs also offer a couple of centuries' worth of looking after visitors.

This means high standard of accommodation, an excellent range of visitor attractions, plus a grand choice of things to do.

For details of accommodation, events and attractions, see area tourist offices on page 273

GARDINERS OF SCOTLAND

A family company manufacturing high quality, hand made confectionery ranging from speciality Malt Whisky fudges to assorted fudges in attractive tartan tins and cartons. Also a Millennium range featuring coffee, rum & raisin, chocolate, Malt Whisky vanilla and assorted fudges.

Turfholm, Lesmahagow ML11 0ED Tel 01555 894155

INVERAWE SMOKEHOUSE

Continuing the traditional methods of smoking, so rarely found these days. Our delicious range of smoked fish, game. pates and meats is a must for all gourmets. Order direct from our mail order catalogue or our shop.

Taynuily, Argyll PA35 1HU Tel 01866 822446 Website www.smokedsalmon.co.uk

A MCLELLAND & SONS LTD

The creameries in Rothesay, Arran and Campbeltown produce high quality cheeses, which are available throughout Scotland or by mail order. Also in Campbeltown – specialist cheese 'Gigha Fruits' – flavoured cheese, shaped as fruits and waxed.

New Cheese Market, Black Street, Townhead, Glasgow G4 0EF Tel 0141 552 2962

MATHIESON FINE FOODS

One of Scotland's finest food producers, supplying a quality range of cakes, preserves and confectionery to the top gift, departmental and tourist outlets. Try our award winning Wallace and Tobermory Whisky cakes. Shops and restaurants throughout Central Scotland.

Williamson Street, Falkirk FK1 1PR Tel 01324 621276
Website www.mathiesons.co.uk

P & C MORRIS

The finest handcrafted terrines and stocks, all produced in-house by our team of dedicated chefs. A range of fine Scottish foods sourced from individual small scale producers, mixed with a selection of speciality fish and dry goods.

M8 Foodpark, 1 Keppochill Place, Port Dundas, Glasgow Tel 0141 332 4474

TASTE OF ARGYLL

Visit a traditional fishmonger and game dealer and see the range of fresh, locally caught fish and shellfish. Selection changes daily; smoked fish products, salmon, trout, kippers etc – all selected for their superb quality and value. Mail order available.

8 Stevenson Street, Oban DA34 5NA Tel 01631 562503

VISITOR ATTRACTIONS

CALLENDAR HOUSE

Callendar House sits in the middle of Falkirk. A unique and historic house, set in beautiful parkland, offers state of the art technology to discerning companies who wish to hold meetings conferences or corporate events, but still appreciate and enjoy Scotland's heritage.

Callendar Park, Falkirk FK1 1YR Tel 01324 503787
Website www.falkirkmuseums.demon.co.uk

DUART CASTLE

Duart Castle, home of the Chief of Clan Maclean. Built on a cliff, guarding the Sound of Mull, it is a 40-minute ferry ride from Oban and 3 miles from Craignure off the A849. The tearoom is in the old byre. We bake everything ourselves and serve soup at lunch time. Admission charge.

Isle of Mull, Argyll PA64 6AP Tel 01680 812309

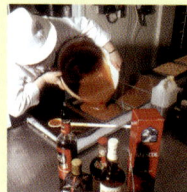

GREAT GLEN FINE FOODS*

We have the largest selection of Scottish speciality foods in the world. Visit our Confectionery Factory Visitor Centre and see our confectionery being made. Free admission and free tasting of tablet! Adjacent to Ballachulish bridge on A82.

Old Ferry Road, North Ballachulish, Ft William, Inverness-shire PH33 6RZ
Tel 01855 821277 Website www.robbins-associates.co.uk/greatglen

MOUNT STUART HOUSE & GARDENS

Magnificent Victorian gothic house set in 300 acres of glorious grounds on the Isle of Bute in the Firth of Clyde. Easily accessible by road, rail or ferry. Licensed restaurant and Courtyard Café – enjoy local seasonal produce freshly made in our kitchen.

Tel 01700 503877 Website www.mountstuart.com

NATIONAL TRUST FOR SCOTLAND

The stunning scenery and turbulent history of the Highlands and Islands is represented by The National Trust for Scotland through the properties in its care. Glorious gardens, historic houses, magnificent mountains, remote islands and the scene of the last major battle fought on mainland Britain reflect the cultural and natural heritage of the north of Scotland.

STIRLING CASTLE

The grandest of all Scotland's castles, Stirling overlooks two of the most famous battlefields in Scottish history – Stirling Bridge and Bannockburn. Inside, its architecture is outstanding with the recently restored Great Hall of James IV, the Renaissance Palace of James V and the Chapel Royal of James VI.

Hot Scottish Mature Cheese and Potato Terrine with Herb Oil and Mixed Leaves   Lochside Lodge and Roundhouse Restaurant

INGREDIENTS

4 large potatoes, peeled, sliced 2mm thick

250g Dunsyre blue cheese

250g Mull cheddar

250g Inverloch goats cheese

100ml olive oil (virgin)

25g pine nuts

1 tbsp balsamic vinegar

1 large handful of curly parsley, tarragon, chives

seasoning

mixed leaves & herbs for garnish

pinch of flour

50ml vegetable oil for cooking

METHOD

■ Blanch potatoes in boiling salted water for 4 or 5 mins. Line a 1lb loaf tin with cling film & line the base & sides with potatoes. Leaving some back for later. Place the olive oil into a liquidising jug with ¾ of the herbs & process. Pass through a fine sieve.

■ Grate all the cheeses & mix with the remaining herbs. Press mixture into the loaf tin pressing firmly layering with potatoes, then finish with a final layer of potatoes. Cover with cling film, then foil. Place in a deep tray with a little boiling water. Place in the oven & cook for 20-30 mins. until potatoes are cooked.

■ Leave to cool & place in a refrigerator to set. Remove from tin & slice 1½-2cm thick. Dust with flour & pan fry in a non-stick pan with a little vegetable oil or until golden brown on both sides. Serve in the middle of the plate with mixed leaves & herbs on top. Drizzle with herb oil, balsamic vinegar & toasted pine nuts.

Serves 6-8

Wines – Lightly–oaked Chardonnay or a rich, aromatic New World Sauvignon are two possibilities but any white of character will provide a tasty accompaniment.

a year in the life of taste of scotland

Facing page – Colin Clydesdale, Stravaigin
This page – Trout Kebab, Wendy Barrie
Photos courtesy of Graham Lees

THE TASTE OF SCOTLAND year begins as soon as this new 2001 Guide is published – almost before the ink is dry we start preparing for the coming year.

The team at Taste of Scotland is small but highly efficient and, above all, dedicated. Their efforts are augmented by the Inspectorate who make sure that the quality of Taste of Scotland members will meet the expectations of our readers.

Highly significant as they are, the Guide and our inspections are just two of our activities. Much of our time is taken up with a broad range of initiatives, all food-related and all with the ultimate goal of enhancing the quality of the food experience to be found in Scotland.

We work closely with our corporate partners and are always on the look-out for quality Scottish companies who we believe can help us achieve that ultimate goal. Here are just two examples of the many other projects to which we devote our time and resources in the course of the year.

THE NATURAL COOKING OF SCOTLAND

Caterers can really benefit by using more fresh local produce, simply prepared and presented, in their menus – and so, of course, do their customers. That's the message behind The Natural Cooking of Scotland initiative, of which Taste of Scotland has recently been appointed managing co-ordinator.

Links with The Scottish Executive tie the initiative directly to the Scottish Diet Action Plan to take the same message – local, fresh, quality – to our young people through schools and colleges. Catering industry suppliers are also being brought into the picture. The success of this initiative, combined with the work of Taste of Scotland member establishments, will see more catering outlets being able to offer a higher standard of quality food to their customers.

The Natural Cooking of Scotland initiative is funded by The Scottish Tourist Board, Highlands and Islands Enterprise and Scottish Enterprise.

Chefs and judges at work

QUALITY MEAT SCOTLAND

For many years now Taste of Scotland has worked with Quality Meat Scotland (formerly known as Scotch Quality Beef and Lamb Association) to encourage Taste of Scotland member chefs to make use of lamb in their recipes. We've done this by jointly running the Scotch Lamb Challenge Competition.

The overall winner of the 2000 Category 1 competition was Ross Bryan, the young 1st Commis Chef at The Balmoral Hotel, Edinburgh, with his *Lamb Loin with Minted Pea Mousse, Roast Salsafis and a Brioche and Pistachio Crust*.

If you would like a copy of Ross' recipe please contact Taste of Scotland and we will be happy to post/email this to you.

The other finalists were

- Greg Russell
  Cringletie House Hotel, Peebles
- Roger McKie
  Royal Hotel, Tighnabruaich
- James Scott
  Channings Brasserie, Edinburgh
- Robert Ramsay
  Altamount House, Blairgowrie
- David Caddick, Dormy Clubhouse, Gleneagles Hotel, Auchterarder
- Roberta Drummond
  Coachman's Bistro,
  Old Manor Hotel, Lundin Links
- Craig Millar (Category 2 Winner)
  The Seafood Restaurant, St Monans
- Scott Kirkham
  Howies, Edinburgh
- Pascal Theze
  The Columba Hotel, Tarbert
- Gavin Elden
  Cafe Hub, Edinburgh

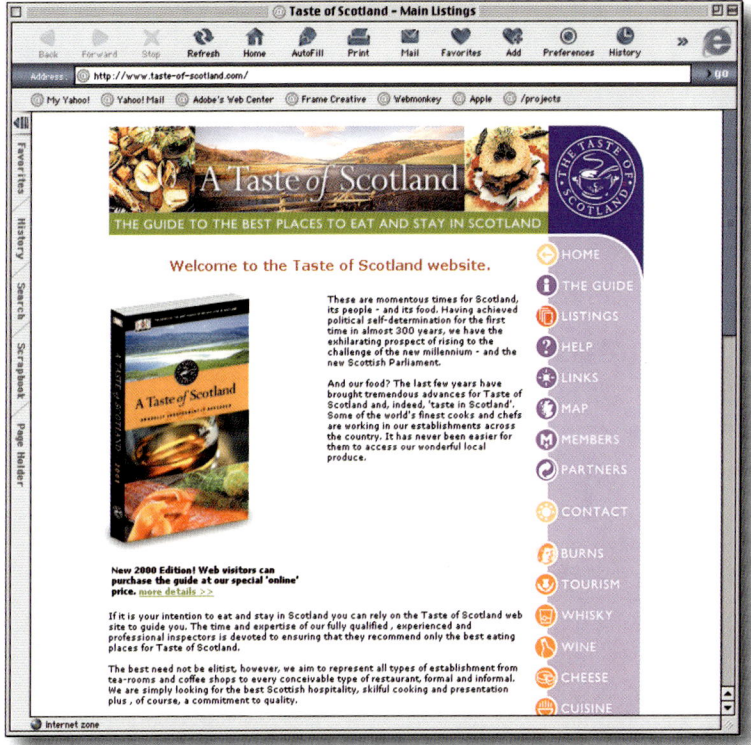

a taste of scotland
online

Wherever you are, you can always keep in touch with what's happening on the Scottish culinary scene by logging onto The Taste of Scotland website at:

www.taste-of-scotland.com

It includes details of all the hotels, restaurants, guest houses, bed& breakfasts and visitor attractions contained in the Guide.

And that's not all – you'll find articles and features on dining and drinking, as well as great ideas for recipes and relaxation.

Subscribe to our online newsletter and keep up to date with people, places and events in the news.

www.taste-of-scotland.com also provides links to a wide range of related sites reflecting the sights, tastes, flavours – and even the sounds of Scotland!

An inspector calls …
under cover, of course

Oh, wouldn't it be a great job to be a Taste of Scotland Inspector! If I had a penny for every time someone has said that to me I'd be a very wealthy woman. The reality, however, is not quite what you'd imagine.

Firstly, all of our Taste of Scotland Inspectors start with a professional qualification related to food and cooking. Unfortunately, there is no specific qualification (yet) for a food inspector and, until there is, we rely on experience of cooking with a formal college or university qualification.

You may ask why that's so important – the answer is simply that we demand the very highest standard of knowledge and expertise from our inspectors and cannot expect to get that if they do not have the right academic grounding.

Secondly, all of our inspectors have had experience in the catering industry. This can vary greatly from person to person but, again, we have found it essential that they understand the vagaries and operational challenges that our industry presents. This kind of background allows them to be sympathetic but retain a sense of realism and firmness at the same time. On top of all that, we then take them away for a residential course to ensure that all this knowledge is fine-tuned in such a way that you may benefit from their experience.

Thirdly, our inspectors must be able to travel alone – eat alone in a whole range of establishments – not disclose their identity to the establishment until the very last moment – and you may be assured that that can also present itself with quite a challenge especially in some small establishments who take a great pride in getting to know their guests. They have to have their cover story ready! We place great store on the incognito aspect of our inspections.

Our inspectors are, in effect, qualified customers – and they are our eyes and ears – they let us see what the customer will see and their reports to us allow us to ascertain the suitability of each and every establishment for Taste of Scotland.

Finally the inspectors must be diplomats, because once the inspection is complete they must announce themselves and give the chef/owner a full debrief of their findings – and all this before they write their report for the head office!

I can honestly say that we have a great team of inspectors, expertly led by our Chief Inspector Wendy Barrie. They are passionate, enthusiastic and hard working and they really believe in what they are doing. They make this Guide work for you. So spare a thought for the inspector – it is not always easy – but it is a most rewarding task.

Amanda J Clark
Chief Executive

TASTE OF SCOTLAND FEEDBACK

As visitors to Taste of Scotland member establishments, your views are vital in our continuing quest to present the very best of Scottish cuisine and hospitality.

Name ....

Address..

....

....

Tel No................................... Fax No ....

E-mail..

Comment on establishments visited

Date of visit .... Meal Taken ....

I would like to nominate the following establishments for a Macallan Taste of Scotland Award for exceeding my expectations:

....

....

....

Comments on this Guide:

....

....

....

Please put me on the mailing list for the 2002 Guide   Yes ❐   No ❐

Friends of Taste of Scotland will be launched in autumn 2000,
please send me information as it becomes available   Yes ❐   No ❐

TASTE OF SCOTLAND FEEDBACK

As visitors to Taste of Scotland member establishments, your views are vital in our continuing quest to present the very best of Scottish cuisine and hospitality.

Name ....

Address..

....

....

Tel No.. Fax No ....

E-mail..

Comment on establishments visited

Date of visit ....   Meal Taken ....

I would like to nominate the following establishments for a Macallan Taste of Scotland Award for exceeding my expectations:

....

....

....

Comments on this Guide:

....

....

....

Please put me on the mailing list for the 2002 Guide   Yes ☐   No ☐

Friends of Taste of Scotland will be launched in autumn 2000,
please send me information as it becomes available   Yes ☐   No ☐

Establishment Index

INDEX

** = New Member for 2001   NTS = National Trust for Scotland property

A

11 Park Avenue: Carnoustie **	92
36: Edinburgh	108
A Room In The Town: Edinburgh **	108
A Taste of Speyside Restaurant: Dufftown	103
Acarsaid Hotel: Pitlochry	236
Albannach, The: Lochinver	211
Allan Cottage Guest House, Tarbert: Isle of Harris	170
Allan Guest House, The: Aberdeen **	57
Allt-nan-Ros Hotel: Onich, by Fort William	227
Almara, Urafirth: Isles of Shetland	190
Altamount House: Blairgowrie	85
An Crann: Fort William	132
Anchorage Hotel & Restaurant, The: Dunoon	106
Apple Lodge, Lochranza: Isle of Arran	166
Ardanaiseig Hotel: Kilchrenan	195
Ardconnel House: Grantown-on-Spey	153
Ardoe House Hotel: Aberdeen	58
Ards House: Oban	221
Ardsheal House: Kentallen	194
Ardvasar Hotel, Sleat: Isle of Skye **	182
Ardvourlie Castle: Isle of Harris	171
Argentine House Hotel, Whiting Bay: Isle of Arran	167
Assapol House Hotel, Bunessan: Isle of Mull	175
Atholl Hotel: Aberdeen	58
Atholl House Hotel, Dunvegan: Isle of Skye	182
Atrium: Edinburgh	109
Auchendean Lodge Hotel: Dulnain Bridge	103
Auchrannie Country House Hotel, Brodick: Isle of Arran	167
Auchterarder House: Auchterarder	68
Auld Alliance Restaurant: Kingussie **	197

B

Babbity Bowster: Glasgow	137
Balbirnie House Hotel, Markinch Village: Glenrothes	152
Balcary Bay Hotel: Auchencairn	68
Balgonie Country House Hotel: Ballater, Royal Deeside	74
Balinakill Country House Hotel: Clachan, by Tarbert **	95
Ballathie House Hotel, Kinclaven: nr Perth	233
Balmoral Hotel, The: Edinburgh	109
Banff Springs Hotel: Banff	81
Bank Restaurant, The: Crieff	97
Bannockburn Heritage Centre (NTS): Stirling **	252
Beardmore Hotel, The, Clydebank: Glasgow (Outskirts)	147
blue bar cafe: Edinburgh	110
Boat Hotel: Boat of Garten	87
Boath House: Nairn	216
Borgie Lodge Hotel, Skerray: Tongue	263
Bosville Hotel, Portree: Isle of Skye	183
Bouzy Rouge: Airdrie	64
Bouzy Rouge: Edinburgh	110
Bouzy Rouge: Glasgow	137
Bowfield Hotel & Country Club: Howwood	158
Braidwoods: Dalry	99
Bridge House Hotel: Lochgilphead **	210
Bridge of Orchy Hotel: Bridge of Orchy	88
Brisbane House Hotel: Largs **	205
Brodick Castle Restaurant (NTS), Brodick: Isle of Arran	168
Brodie Castle (NTS): Forres **	131
Bunchrew House Hotel: Inverness	160
Bunrannoch House: Kinloch Rannoch	198
Burrastow House, Walls: Isles of Shetland	190
Burts Hotel: Melrose	214
Butterchurn, The: Kelty, by Dunfermline	194
Buttery, The: Glasgow	138

C

Cabin Restaurant, The: Glasgow	138
Caerketton Restaurant, Penicuik: Edinburgh (Outskirts) **	124
Cafe 1: Inverness	160
Café Gandolfi: Glasgow **	139
Cafe Hub: Edinburgh	111
Cairnbaan Hotel: Cairnbaan, by Lochgilphead **	90
Caledonian Hilton Hotel: Edinburgh	111
Calgary Farmhouse Hotel, Calgary: Isle of Mull	175
Cameron House Hotel and Country Estate: Loch Lomond	207
Cargills Restaurant & Bistro: Blairgowrie	86

Carlin Maggie's: Kinross	199
Carnoustie Hotel, Golf Resort & Spa: Carnoustie **	93
Carradale Hotel: Carradale	93
Castle Venlaw Hotel: Peebles **	231
Cawdor Tavern: Nairn	217
Cellars Restaurant & Cocktail Bar: Troon	264
Channings Restaurant: Edinburgh	112
Charleston House: Gairloch **	134
Chatters Restaurant: Dunoon	107
Chirnside Hall Country House Hotel: Chirnside **	95
City Merchant Restaurant: Glasgow	139
Cleaton House Hotel, Westray: Isle of Orkney	180
Clint Lodge: St Boswells	248
Coach House Coffee Shop: Loch Lomond	208
Cobbles Inn Restaurant: Kelso	192
Columba Hotel, The: Tarbert, Argyll	259
Conchra, nr Dornie: Kyle of Lochalsh	203
Cook's Room, The, Giffnock: Glasgow (Outskirts)	147
Corriegour Lodge Hotel, Loch Lochy: by Spean Bridge	250
Corrour House Hotel, Inverdruie: Aviemore	70
Corsemalzie House Hotel, Port William: Newton Stewart	220
Cosses Country House: Ballantrae	73
Coul House Hotel, Contin: by Strathpeffer	255
Craigadam: Castle Douglas	94
Craigellachie Hotel: Craigellachie	96
Craiglynn Hotel: Aberdeen	59
Crannog Seafood Restaurant: Fort William	133
Creag Mor Hotel: Gairloch **	135
Creagan House Restaurant with Accommodation: Strathyre	255
Creebridge House Hotel: Newton Stewart	220
Creel Restaurant & Rooms, St Margaret's Hope: Isle of Orkney	180
Crieff Hydro Hotel: Crieff	97
Crinan Hotel: Crinan	98
Cringletie House Hotel: Peebles	231
Croft Kitchen, The, Port Charlotte: Isle of Islay	172
Cromlix House, Kinbuck: by Dunblane	104
Cross, The: Kingussie	197
Cuilcheanna House: Onich, by Fort William	228
Cuillin Hills Hotel, Portree: Isle of Skye	183
Culdearn House Hotel: Grantown-on-Spey	154
Culloden House Hotel: Inverness	161
Culloden Moor Visitor Centre Restaurant (NTS): Inverness	161
Culzean Castle & Country Park Visitor Centre Restaurant (NTS): Ayr **	73

D

Dalhousie Castle, Bonnyrigg: Edinburgh (Outskirts)	125
Dalilea House: Acharacle **	63
Dalmunzie House Hotel: Glenshee	153
Daniel's Bistro: Edinburgh **	112
Darroch Learg Hotel: Ballater, Royal Deeside	74
Davaar House Hotel and Restaurant: Dunfermline	104
Daviot Mains Farm: Daviot, nr Inverness	100
Deeside Hotel: Ballater, Royal Deeside	75
Denfield House: Auchterarder **	69
Distillery Restaurant, The, Lochranza: Isle of Arran	168
Dormy Clubhouse, The: Auchterarder	69
Doune, Doune: Knoydart	201
Druimard Country House, Dervaig: Isle of Mull	176
Druimnacroish Hotel, Dervaig: Isle of Mull	176
Drum and Monkey: Glasgow	140
Dryburgh Abbey Hotel: Melrose	214
Dryfesdale Hotel: Lockerbie	212
Dubh Prais Restaurant: Edinburgh	113
Duck's at Le Marché Noir: Edinburgh	113
Dunain Park Hotel: Inverness	162
Dunans Castle: Glendaruel **	150
Dungallan House Hotel: Oban	222
Dunlaverock Country House: Coldingham Bay	96
Dunnikier House Hotel: Kirkcaldy	200
Dunorin House Hotel, Dunvegan: Isle of Skye	184

E

East Haugh Country House Hotel & Restaurant: Pitlochry	237
East Lochhead, Lochwinnoch: Glasgow (Outskirts)	148
Ednam House Hotel: Kelso	193

Eisenhower Apartment, The,
  Culzean Castle (NTS), Maybole: Ayr 72
Enmore Hotel: Dunoon 107

F

Falls of Shin Visitor Centre: Invershin 164
Farleyer House Hotel: Aberfeldy 62
Farriers Country Hotel: Alva 65
Fascadale House: Lochgilphead ** 210
Feorag House, Glenborrodale:
  Ardnamurchan 66
Fernhill Hotel: Portpatrick 243
Fernie Castle Hotel: Letham,
  nr Cupar ** 206
Fife Arms Hotel: Turriff 266
Fins Seafood Restaurant: Fairlie 127
Fish Market, The: Mallaig 213
Flodigarry Country House Hotel &
  The Water Horse Restaurant, Staffin:
  Isle of Skye 184
Forss Country House Hotel: Thurso 262
Four Seasons Bistro & Bar: Onich,
  by Fort William 228
Four Seasons Hotel, The: St Fillans ** 248
Fouters Bistro: Ayr 72
Foveran Hotel & Restaurant, Kirkwall:
  Isle of Orkney 181
Fyvie Castle (NTS): Turriff ** 267

G

Garvock House Hotel: Dunfermline 105
Gathering, The: Kilmarnock 196
Gathering Restaurant and O'Donnells
  Irish Bar, The: Oban 222
Gavins Mill Restaurant, Milngavie:
  Glasgow (Outskirts) ** 148
Glasgow Moat House: Glasgow 140
Gleddoch House Hotel & Country Estate,
  Langbank: Glasgow (Outskirts) 149
Glen Loy Lodge Hotel, Glen Loy: Banavie 79
Glen Lui Hotel: Ballater, Royal Deeside 75
Glendruidh House Hotel: Inverness 162
Glenfinnan Monument (NTS):
  Glenfinnan ** 151
Glenmachrie, Port Ellen: Isle of Islay 173
Glenmorangie House at Cadboll:
  Fearn by Tain 130
Glenskirlie House, Banknock: Stirling
  (Outskirts) ** 253
Glenturret Distillery: Crieff 98
Glenview Inn and Restaurant, Staffin:
  Isle of Skye 185

Golf View Hotel & Leisure Club: Nairn 217
Gordon's Restaurant: Inverkeilor 159
Grain Store Restaurant: Edinburgh 114
Grange Hotel, The: Edinburgh 114
Grange Manor Hotel, The,
  Grangemouth: Falkirk 127
Grape Vine Restaurant, The: Bothwell 87
Green Inn Restaurant With Rooms, The:
  Ballater, Royal Deeside 76
Green Park Hotel, The: Pitlochry 237
Green Welly Stop, The (Formerly known
  as The Clifton Coffee House): Tyndrum 267
Greywalls: Gullane 155
Grouse & Claret Restaurant: Kinross 199
Guinach House: Aberfeldy 63

H

Haddo House (NTS): Ellon ** 126
Haldanes Restaurant: Edinburgh 115
Handa, (Ceos) Lochs: Isle of Lewis 174
Hartree Country House: Biggar 83
Haven Hotel, The: Plockton 241
Henderson's Salad Table: Edinburgh 115
Highland Cottage, Tobermory:
  Isle of Mull 177
Hill House (NTS): Helensburgh ** 156
Hilton Craigendarroch Hotel & Country
  Club: Ballater, Royal Deeside 76
Hilton Glasgow (Camerons Restaurant):
  Glasgow 141
Hoebridge Inn Restaurant: Melrose 215
Holly Tree Hotel, The, Seafood & Game
  Restaurant, Kentallen: nr Glencoe 150
Horsemill Restaurant, Crathes Castle
  (NTS), The: Banchory ** 79
Hotel Eilean Iarmain, Sleat: Isle of Skye 185
House of Bruar, The: Blair Atholl 84
Houstoun House Hotel, Uphall:
  Edinburgh (Outskirts) 125
Howgate Restaurant: Howgate 158
Howies Restaurant: Edinburgh 116
Howies Stockbridge: Edinburgh 116
Hoy Tapas: Perth 233
Huntingtower Hotel: Perth 234

I

Igg's Restaurant: Edinburgh 117
Inchyra Grange Hotel, Polmont: Falkirk 128
Inn at Lathones, The, Lathones, by
  Largoward: St Andrews (Outskirts) 246
Inn On The Green, The: Glasgow ** 141
Inver Lodge Hotel: Lochinver 211

LIST OF ESTABLISHMENTS

Inverbeg Inn: Loch Lomond **	208
Isle of Eriska: Oban	223

J

Jackson's Restaurant: Edinburgh	117
Jedforest Hotel: Jedburgh	192

K

Keepers Restaurant: Edinburgh	118
Kilcamb Lodge Hotel: Strontian	256
Killiechronan House, Killiechronan: Isle of Mull	177
Killiecrankie Hotel, The: Pitlochry	238
Kilmeny Country Guest House, Ballygrant: Isle of Islay	173
Kilmichael Country House Hotel, by Brodick: Isle of Arran	169
Kind Kyttock's Kitchen: Falkland	129
Kinkell House, Easter Kinkell: Dingwall	100
Kinloch House Hotel: Blairgowrie	86
Kinloch Lodge, Sleat: Isle of Skye	186
Kirkton House, Cardross: Helensburgh	157
Kirroughtree House: Newton Stewart	221
Knipoch Hotel, Knipoch: by Oban	223
Knockendarroch House Hotel: Pitlochry	238
Knockinaam Lodge: Portpatrick	244
Knockomie Hotel: Forres	131

L

La Bonne Auberge Brasserie (Park Lodge Hotel): Falkirk **	128
La Bonne Auberge (Holiday Inn Hotel): Glasgow	142
Lairhillock Inn & Crynoch Restaurant at Lairhillock, Netherley: Aberdeen **	59
Lake Hotel, The: Port of Menteith **	243
Lang Bar & Restaurant, Perth Theatre, The: Perth	234
Langass Lodge, Locheport: Isle of North Uist	179
Le Café Saint-Honoré: Edinburgh	118
Leachin House, Tarbert: Isle of Harris	171
Let's Eat: Perth	235
Let's Eat Again: Perth	235
Little Lodge: Gairloch	135
Livingston's Restaurant: Linlithgow	207
Loch Fyne Oyster Bar: Cairndow	91
Loch Kinord Hotel: Ballater, Royal Deeside **	77
Loch Melfort Hotel and Restaurant, Arduaine: by Oban	224
Loch Torridon Country House Hotel: Torridon	264
Lochnagar, The: Bridge of Weir	88
Lodge at Carfraemill, The: Lauder	206
Lodge on Loch Lomond Hotel and Restaurant: Loch Lomond	209
Lodge On The Loch Hotel, The: Onich, by Fort William	229
Loft Restaurant, The: Blair Atholl	85
Lovat Arms Hotel: Beauly	82
Low Cattadale Farm: Campbeltown **	92
Lux: Glasgow	142
Lynwilg House: Aviemore	71

M

Mackeanston House: Doune, Perthshire	102
Made In Scotland: Beauly **	82
Makerston House: Paisley	230
Malin Court Hotel: Turnberry	265
Mallin House Hotel: Dornoch	101
Malt Barn Inn, Newton of Falkland: Falkland	130
Manor House, The: Oban	224
Mansfield House Hotel: Elgin	126
Mansfield House Hotel: Hawick	156
Mansfield House Hotel: Tain	258
March House, Feshiebridge: Kincraig	196
Marcliffe at Pitfodels, The: Aberdeen	60
Marque, The: Edinburgh	119
Mehalah: Spean Bridge **	251
Meldrum House: Oldmeldrum	227
Minmore House: Glenlivet	152
Monachyle Mhor: Balquhidder	78
Montgreenan Mansion House Hotel: Irvine	166
Monty's Bistro, Lerwick: Isles of Shetland	191
Moorings Hotel, The, Banavie: Fort William	133
Morangie House Hotel: Tain	258
Muckrach Lodge Hotel & Restaurant, Dulnain Bridge: Grantown-on-Spey	154
Murrayshall House Hotel: Perth **	236
Myrtle Bank Hotel: Gairloch	136

N

Nairns: Glasgow	143
Navidale House Hotel: Helmsdale	157
Nether Underwood: Symington, Ayrshire	257
New Farm Bed & Breakfast & Restaurant, Mount Stuart: Isle of Bute	170

New Lanark Mill Hotel: New Lanark	219
Newton Hotel & Highland Conference Centre, The: Nairn	218
No 3 Royal Terrace: Edinburgh **	120
No 4 Cameron Square: Fort William **	134
No 27 Charlotte Square (NTS): Edinburgh **	119
Nº Sixteen: Glasgow	143
Norwood Hall Hotel: Aberdeen	60

O

Old Armoury, The: Pitlochry	239
Old Bridge Inn, The: Aviemore	71
Old Byre Heritage Centre, The, Dervaig: Isle of Mull	178
Old Course Hotel Golf Resort & Spa, The: St Andrews	245
Old Inn, The: Gairloch **	136
Old Library Lodge & Restaurant: Arisaig	67
Old Manor Hotel, Lundin Links: St Andrews (Outskirts)	247
Old Mansion House: Auchterhouse, by Dundee **	70
Old Mill Highland Lodge, The: Talladale	259
Old Monastery Restaurant, The: Buckie	90
Old Pines Restaurant with Rooms: Spean Bridge	251
Old Smiddy Guest House, The: Laide	204
Old West Manse, The: Banchory	80
Olivia's Restaurant: Stirling	252
Onich Hotel: Onich, by Fort William	229
Open Arms Hotel, The: Dirleton	101
Orasay Inn, Lochcarnan: Isle of South Uist	191
Ord House Hotel: Muir of Ord, by Inverness	216
Osprey Hotel, The: Kingussie	198
Ostlers Close Restaurant: Cupar	99
'Oven Bistro, The', At Drumnacree House: Alyth	66

P

Park Guest House & Restaurant, Stornoway: Isle of Lewis	174
Parkstone Hotel: Prestwick **	244
Peat Inn, The: Peat Inn	230
Peebles Hotel Hydro: Peebles	232
Pend, The: Dunkeld	105
Perthshire Visitor Centre: Bankfoot	81
Philipburn House Hotel: Selkirk **	249
Pier House, Inverie: Knoydart **	202
Piersland House Hotel: Troon	265
Pines, The: Grantown-on-Spey	155
Pitlochry Festival Theatre Restaurant, The: Pitlochry	239
Pittodrie House Hotel, Chapel of Garioch: by Inverurie	165
Plockton Hotel, The: Plockton	242
Pollok House (NTS): Glasgow **	144
Pool House Hotel: Poolewe	242
Poplars, The: Pitlochry	240
Portland Arms Hotel, The: Wick **	268
Portnacraig Inn and Restaurant: Pitlochry	240
Potting Shed Restaurant at the Bruntsfield Hotel, The: Edinburgh	120
Priory House Hotel: Largs **	205
Puppet Theatre, The: Glasgow	144

Q

Quenelles Restaurant: Falkirk	129

R

Radisson SAS Airth Castle Hotel: Airth, by Falkirk **	65
Raemoir House Hotel: Banchory **	80
Ramnee Hotel: Forres	132
Ravenswood Hotel: Ballater, Royal Deeside	77
Redcliffe House Hotel: Skelmorlie, by Largs **	250
Reform Restaurant: Edinburgh	121
Restaurant At The Bonham: Edinburgh	121
Restaurant Rococo: Glasgow **	145
Riverhouse Restaurant, The: Inverness	163
Rock, The: Edinburgh	122
Rockvilla Hotel & Restaurant: Lochcarron	209
Roman Camp Country House Hotel: Callander	91
Rosebank House: Strathyre	256
Rosedale Hotel, Portree: Isle of Skye	186
Roskhill House, by Dunvegan: Isle of Skye	187
Rowan Cottage, By Elgol: Isle of Skye **	187
Roxburghe Hotel and Golf Course, The, Heiton: Kelso	193
Royal Dunkeld Hotel, The: Dunkeld **	106
Royal Golf Hotel, The: Dornoch	102
Royal Hotel: Tighnabruaich	262
Royal Marine Hotel: Brora	89
Rufflets Country House & Garden Restaurant: St Andrews	245

LIST OF ESTABLISHMENTS

S

St Andrews Links Clubhouse: St Andrews	246
Sandford Country House Hotel, The, Wormit: St Andrews (Outskirts) **	247
Saplinbrae House Hotel: Old Deer	226
Scarista House, Scarista: Isle of Harris	172
Scholars Restaurant At Stirling Highland Hotel: Stirling	253
Scotland's Larder: Upper Largo, nr St Andrews	268
Scott's At The Crown: Lockerbie **	212
Seafood Restaurant, The: Kyle of Lochalsh	203
Seafood Restaurant, The: St Monans	249
Seagreen Restaurant & Bookshop: Kyle of Lochalsh	204
Selkirk Arms Hotel, The: Kirkcudbright	200
Sheildaig Farm: Balloch **	78
Sheraton Grand Hotel: Edinburgh	122
Shieldhill: Biggar	83
Shore House: Kishorn **	201
Simpson's Hotel Bar/Brasserie: Aberdeen	61
Skeabost House Hotel, Skeabost: Isle of Skye	188
Skiary, Kinlochourn: Knoydart	202
Skirling House: Biggar	84
Somerton House Hotel: Lockerbie	213
South Kingennie House: Broughty Ferry	89
Stac Polly: Edinburgh	123
Stagger Inn, The: Inverarnan	159
Stepping Stone Restaurant, Balivanich: Isle of Benbecula	169
Stonefield Castle Hotel: Tarbert, Argyll	260
Stravaigin: Glasgow	145
Summer Isles Hotel: Achiltibuie	64
Sunflower Restaurant: Peebles **	232
Sunny Brae Hotel: Nairn	218

T

Talisker House, Talisker: Isle of Skye	188
Taste of Moray, The: Inverness **	163
Taychreggan Hotel Ltd: Kilchrenan	195
Tayvallich Inn: Tayvallich	261
Thainstone House Hotel & Country Club: Inverurie	165
Threave Garden (NTS): Castle Douglas **	94
Three Chimneys Restaurant and the House Over-By, The, Glendale: Isle of Skye	189
Tiroran House, Tiroran: Isle of Mull **	178
Tongue Hotel: Tongue **	263
Topps, The, Denny: Stirling (Outskirts)	254
Tormaukin Hotel: Glendevon, by Dollar **	151
Tower Restaurant: Edinburgh	123
Trigony House Hotel: Thornhill, Dumfries	261
Turnberry Hotel, Golf Courses and Spa: Turnberry	266

U

Ubiquitous Chip: Glasgow	146
Udny Arms Hotel: Newburgh	219
Uplawmoor Hotel, Uplawmoor: Glasgow (Outskirts)	149

V

Victoria Hotel: Tarbert, Argyll	260
Victoria Restaurant, The: Aberdeen	61
Viewfield House, Portree: Isle of Skye **	189

W

Water's Edge: Ardnamurchan **	67
Waterfront Restaurant, The: Oban	225
Waterside Pub & Restaurant, The: Strathaven **	254
Well View Hotel: Moffat	215
Western Isles Hotel, The, Tobermory: Isle of Mull	179
Westlands of Pitlochry: Pitlochry	241
Wheatsheaf Restaurant with Rooms, The: Swinton	257
Willowburn Hotel, Clachan-Seil: by Oban	225
Witchery by the Castle, The: Edinburgh	124
Woodside Hotel, The: Aberdour **	62
Woodwards Restaurant: Inverness **	164
Woodwick House, Evie: Isle of Orkney	181

Y

Yacht Corryvreckan: Oban	226
YES Restaurant, Bar & Café: Glasgow **	146

# EYEWITNESS TRAVEL GUIDES

COUNTRY GUIDES

AUSTRALIA • CANADA • FRANCE • GREAT BRITAIN
GREECE: ATHENS & THE MAINLAND • THE GREEK ISLANDS
IRELAND • ITALY • JAPAN • MEXICO • PORTUGAL • SCOTLAND
SINGAPORE • SOUTH AFRICA • SPAIN • THAILAND
GREAT PLACES TO STAY IN EUROPE • TASTE OF SCOTLAND

REGIONAL GUIDES

BARCELONA & CATALONIA • CALIFORNIA
FLORENCE & TUSCANY • FLORIDA • HAWAII
JERUSALEM & THE HOLY LAND • LOIRE VALLEY
MILAN & THE LAKES • NAPLES WITH POMPEII & THE
AMALFI COAST • PROVENCE & THE COTE D'AZUR • SARDINIA
SEVILLE & ANDALUSIA • SICILY • VENICE & THE VENETO

CITY GUIDES

AMSTERDAM • BERLIN • BRUSSELS • BUDAPEST • CRACOW
DELHI, AGRA & JAIPUR • DUBLIN • ISTANBUL • LISBON • LONDON
MADRID • MOSCOW • NEW YORK • PARIS • PRAGUE • ROME
SAN FRANCISCO • STOCKHOLM • ST PETERSBURG
SYDNEY • VIENNA • WARSAW • WASHINGTON, DC

NEW FOR SPRING 2001

BALI & LOMBOK • BOSTON • CHICAGO
CRUISE GUIDE TO EUROPE AND THE MEDITERRANEAN
GERMANY • NEW ENGLAND • NEW ZEALAND

FOR UPDATES TO OUR GUIDES, AND INFORMATION ON
DK TRAVEL MAPS & PHRASEBOOKS

VISIT US AT **eyewitnesstravel.dk.com**